Annals And Antiquities Of Lacock Abbey: In The County Of Wilts

William Lisle Bowles, John Gough Nichols

Nabu Public Domain Reprints:

You are holding a reproduction of an original work published before 1923 that is in the public domain in the United States of America, and possibly other countries. You may freely copy and distribute this work as no entity (individual or corporate) has a copyright on the body of the work. This book may contain prior copyright references, and library stamps (as most of these works were scanned from library copies). These have been scanned and retained as part of the historical artifact.

This book may have occasional imperfections such as missing or blurred pages, poor pictures, errant marks, etc. that were either part of the original artifact, or were introduced by the scanning process. We believe this work is culturally important, and despite the imperfections, have elected to bring it back into print as part of our continuing commitment to the preservation of printed works worldwide. We appreciate your understanding of the imperfections in the preservation process, and hope you enjoy this valuable book.

Drawn in 1834. G. Hollis sc

Annals and Antiquities

OF

LACOCK ABBEY,

IN THE COUNTY OF WILTS;

WITH

MEMORIALS OF THE FOUNDRESS
ELA COUNTESS OF SALISBURY,

AND OF

THE EARLS OF SALISBURY

OF THE

Houses of Sarisbury and Longespe;

INCLUDING NOTICES OF
THE MONASTERIES OF BRADENSTOKE, HINTON, AND FARLEY.

BY THE
REV. W. L. BOWLES, M.A. M.R.S.L.

AND

JOHN GOUGH NICHOLS.

E'en now, amid the wavering ivy-wreaths,
  While kindred thoughts the pensive sounds inspire,
Where the weak breeze in many a whisper breathes,
  I seem to listen to the chanting quire.
                    WARTON.

LONDON:
JOHN BOWYER NICHOLS AND SON,
25, PARLIAMENT STREET.

1835.

1462
.554
.204

14686
.554
.204

TO

CHARLTON BYAM WOLLASTON, Esq.

OF DORSETSHIRE,

ONE OF MY KINDEST AND OLDEST FRIENDS,

FROM SCHOOL-DAYS AT WINCHESTER,—

THIS HISTORY

IS AFFECTIONATELY DEDICATED,

BY

THE AUTHOR.

Salisbury, April 5, 1835.

PREFACE.

Having brought to a conclusion my meditated design, the thought of which was excited by an accidental and interesting circumstance, as related in the Introductory Chapter, I have only, in this place, to state the sources, and materials, of the present work, and to acknowledge the assistance which I have received in the course of my inquiries.

The Abbey of Lacock, like every other, had its Cartulary; and, like most of them, a chronicle, or something of the kind, peculiarly relating to its own history. The former is safely preserved at Lacock itself; the latter, there seems good reason to suppose, was destroyed at the fire which so seriously injured the Cottonian collection of Manuscripts in the year 1731.

It was quoted by Vincent and some others of the old Heralds as the Book of Lacock; being, when Vincent examined it, in the possession of Sir Robert Cotton, and previously, it seems, in the hands of John Stow. In the Report of a Committee of the House of Commons, which was made after the fire, no manuscript is mentioned under this name; but it may be well supposed to be the same as that which is thus described:

"*Epistolæ Beatricis, S. Mariæ et S. Benedicti de Lacoc Ministræ, continens Elogium fœminæ nobilissimæ et venerabilis Matris,* ELÆ, *quondam Abbatissæ, et Comitissæ de Warwike* [*Sarum*]."

This tract was the last of five which were bound up in the same volume, Tiberius B. XIII. and it is reported as " wholly destroyed." The middle of the volume, containing No. 2, with portions of Nos. 1 and 3, escaped, and now form the volume bearing the same number; but they have no relation to Lacock.

The fire was unkind to Lacock and to the memory of Ela: for there was another MS. containing matter relating to this House. This was Vitellius A. VIII. consisting of thirteen distinct treatises: of which No. 10 is entitled, "*Annales a Christo nato ad annum* 1448, *scripti a quodam monacho de Lacock;*" of which the portion rescued from the fire ends with the year 1120, that is, more than a century before Lacock was founded. No. 11 of the same volume, which was entitled, "*De Gulielmo Longspee, et filiis ejus,*" was wholly destroyed.

Thus, in the case of both volumes, the portions lost were those which related to the subject of our researches.

Vincent had transcribed from the Book of Lacock all that he deemed illustrative of the genealogy of the Foundress; a part only of which transcript, and that with an important omission, having been inserted by Dugdale in the Monasticon, the whole that is now known to exist of this curious and romantic history, has been printed at the close of the present volume.*

This singular monastic composition, full of romantic incidents, has led, in the present volume, to more extended researches into the lives and genealogy of the Earls of Salisbury,—a subject intimately connected with the history of a Monastery, which was founded by the heiress of that princely Earldom, and to which she herself retired to spend her latter days in peace and devotion.

With these accessories, our History has acquired a new character, no known fact having been omitted which could illustrate the Biography of the Earls of Salisbury, of the two first Houses, after the Conquest, bearing the names of SARISBURY and LONGESPÉ.

* Appendix, pp. i—v. and Addenda, p. 374.

The intricate mazes of Genealogy have been painfully, but I trust most successfully, traced by the indefatigable pains of a younger and far abler guide, Mr. J. G. NICHOLS; and I feel assured that no questions, relating to family history, have been more strictly investigated, than those of the connections of the noble Longespé, and the elder members of the House of Salisbury. My share of this most difficult portion of my work is concluded in the fourth chapter; and from the end of that chapter I had the advantage of the active co-operation of this intelligent and indefatigable investigator of family genealogy. In fact, having undertaken the task of relating the history of an establishment founded so long ago, devoted to piety, as piety was then understood, and connected with the history of monastic remains, consigned long since to destruction, I felt, when the storm seemed, not remotely, to lour over our own altars, that the time was comparatively mis-employed, in reverting to scenes, and institutions, and characters so long passed away, and was not unwilling to drop the record entirely, affected, if not awed, by the position of my own church and country.

Into the hands of Mr. J. G. Nichols, therefore, I delivered whatever papers and documents I had collected; and he did indeed more than, with any pains, I could have done, having a ready access to the great national repository of books and antiquarian documents in the British Museum.

To him, not myself only, but the literary world, is indebted for his scrupulous antiquarian researches, and for every thing more especially relating to ancient genealogy, contained in these pages. To him, therefore, I must express my first and chief obligations.

In the course of his inquiries he has received material assistance from THOMAS STAPLETON, jun. Esq. F.S.A. who has made very important collections respecting the Anglo-Norman families. He has also to express his obligations to Mr. COLE, the intelligent gentleman now in charge of the Augmentation Office, through whose obliging permission access was obtained to the monastic records of that depository, although, at the time, they had scarcely recovered from the confusion into which they were thrown by the late unfortunate Fire in the adjoining Parliamentary buildings.

These have been our latter coadjutors: but I must recur to those earlier friends, who, when I first undertook the work, encouraged and assisted me.

To the Rev. JOSEPH HUNTER, F.S.A. then resident at Bath, but now actively and most usefully employed in the metropolis, in the works of the Commission of Public Records, I was indebted for very valuable hints and communications; and to the venerated Father of Wiltshire Topography, Sir RICHARD COLT HOARE, of Stourhead, Bart. for various contributions, particularly for the drawings by the able antiquarian artist John Carter, from which some of the plates have been engraved.

To my friend ROBERT BENSON, Esq. Deputy Recorder of Salisbury, I have also to express my obligations for such papers as he had collected relative to the Longespé family; and I take this opportunity of saying that it was this gentleman who communicated to that most interesting and valuable work, the Excerpta Historica, the very curious poem relative to the Crusade of William Longespé, from which I have made some lengthened extracts.

To my friend C. W. LOSCOMBE, Esq. I have been indebted for the loan of some rare and valuable books on monachism, &c.; and to Mr. HATCHER, of Salisbury, for his contributions on the cathedral of Old Sarum, and the Gregorian liturgy.

The drawing in the Frontispiece was by the present accomplished and amiable Mistress of the Mansion, the lady of H. F. TALBOT, Esq. to whom I must add my acknowledgments for his courtesies and use of papers.

These are the names of those to whom I am most indebted, with the exception of an early and valued friend, whom, in questions of Heraldry, at the commencement of my history, I consulted, living in hopes to gratify him by the last production of studies akin, in many respects, to his own.

I allude to the late Rev. JAMES DALLAWAY, F.S.A. Secretary to the Earl Marshal, and Vicar of Letherhead, Surrey.* The reader will indulge me, as we are now about to part, perhaps for ever, if I should here speak more particularly of one of my oldest friends, the friend of my youth and my age.

Of his death I received the first intelligence amid the scenes of our youthful studies, at Oxford, and at the time of the festivities on account of the INSTALLATION OF THE DUKE OF WELLINGTON— when, after well nigh fifty years had passed away, I stood alone, in a corner of the grey quadrangle of New College. The morning sun was shining on the old dial, as in years past—I said to myself, " The friends of my youth, where are they?" Echo did not reply, " Where are they?" for one of them, the Senior Fellow of this college,† the " ripe

* Of whose garden-scenes, and interesting decorations, Mrs. Dallaway printed an elegant volume of etchings, for private distribution.

† Philip Duncan, Esq. I was not Fellow of New College myself; but, having been educated at Winchester, this college was always connected with congenial feelings and early friends. I had been senior of the School, and senior on the roll for succession to New College; but this year (1781) there was no vacancy.

scholar," and most estimable man, turned the corner near which I stood, thinking

> —— " of many friends, now scattered wide
> By many fates,"

and of more,

> ————"Now to dust
> Gone down,"

When he informed me, speaking in this place of "days departed," that Dallaway—whom I hoped to gratify by these pages—poor Dallaway, had just been added to the long list of those departed before us.

The clock struck eleven,—the well known sound of the organ was heard from within,—" Wickham's Peal was up," and I turned away—in tears!

I trust the reader will excuse this tribute to a deserving man, meriting well of letters; and with his name, in connection with the history of an ancient religious establishment in my own county and neighbourhood, I resign, possibly for ever, my historical and antiquarian pen, hoping what I have recorded of the Parish of Bremhill, and of Stanley, Bradenstoke, and Lacock abbeys, may be considered as the author's contributions to the more splendid HISTORY OF WILTSHIRE by my venerated friend Sir Richard Colt Hoare.

Bremhill, April, 1835.

CONTENTS.

	Page
PREFACE.—The Book of Lacock, p. v.	
INTRODUCTORY CHAPTER	1
Lines to Lady Valletort	12
William Longespé's Tomb in Salisbury Cathedral	14
Songs of Birds, the Wren, &c.	15
The ancient Hymn, " Gloria in Excelsis " (App. p. lv)	18
CHAPTER II. Ancestors and Family of Ela of Salisbury.—Walter le Ewrus—Edward of Domesday Book—Walter, the son of Edward—Last Visit of William the Conqueror to Salisbury—Patrick Earl of Salisbury—William his son and successor—Present state of Bradenstoke Priory	20
Rents of the Shrievalty of Wiltshire . . .	37
CHAPTER III. The lineage of Edward of Salisbury—Not connected with the Norman Comtes d'Evreux—The family of Rosmar or Roumare—The Battle of Brenmule—Family of Edward of Salisbury—Humphrey de Bohun, the Founder of Farley Priory—Old Sarum .	39
PEDIGREE I.—The House of Salisbury . . .	39
Sonnet—Cathedral at Old Sarum . . .	63
Lines on Children gathering flowers in the Cathedral Churchyard of New Sarum	64
PEDIGREE II.—The House of Romara, with illustrative Remarks	65
CHAPTER IV. Ela of Salisbury, the Foundress of Lacock Abbey—Coronation of Richard Cœur de Lion—	

		Page
Ela's concealment in Normandy—her discovery by a Troubadour Knight, and delivery to King Richard	.	80
The Lay of Talbot the Troubadour	.	89*
The Sisters, pretended and real, of Ela of Salisbury	.	96

CHAPTER V. Marriage of Ela of Salisbury to William Longespé—His mother Fair Rosamund—Particulars of his career as Earl of Salisbury—Fate of Arthur Duke of Britany—Salisbury's campaigns in Flanders—Wars of the Barons, and Ratification of Magna Charta—Death of King John 100

PEDIGREE III.—Descent of William Longespé, Earl of Salisbury, and of Ela his Countess, from William Longespé, Duke of Normandy 107

CHAPTER VI. Foundation of the Cathedral of New Sarum—The Earl's Campaign in Gascony—His last perilous Voyage—Hubert de Burgh's insult to Ela, the Earl's resentment, and his Death . . . 124

Dirge of William Longespé	142
Will of William Longespé, Earl of Salisbury . .	144
PEDIGREE IV.—The House of Longespé . . .	147
Descendants of the Countess Ela . . . 147—164
Roger de Meulan, Bishop of Coventry and Lichfield, mistaken for a Longespé	164
Miscellaneous records of the name of Longespé .	165

CHAPTER VII. The widowhood of the Countess Ela—The Earldom of Salisbury—Shrievalty of Wiltshire—Seal of the Countess Ela—Her Son's Marriage—Foundation of the Priory of Hinton Charterhouse and the Nunnery of Lacock—Descriptive notices of Hinton Priory 166

CHAPTER VIII. The transactions relative to the foundation of Lacock Nunnery, and notices of the first Charters—Constantia de Legh, assistant to the foun-

	Page
dation—Alicia de Garinges the first Canoness—The Augustine Rule	180
The Canonical Hours	198

CHAPTER IX. Contrast of the View at Old Sarum and the Forest of Chippenham—Ela retires to the society of the Nuns at Lacock—The reception of Novices, and Profession of a Nun 199

CHAPTER X. Ela is constituted Abbess of Lacock—The ceremonies of the Election and Consecration of Abbesses 214

CHAPTER XI. The career of the second William Longespé—His first Crusade, and Return—Claim to the Earldom of Salisbury—Interview with the Pope—His second Crusade, and quarrel with the Comte d'Artois . 221

Assumption of the Cross 235

CHAPTER XII. The assault of Mansoura, and Death of William Longespé—Vision of the Abbess Ela, in her stall at Lacock 237

Arabic Account of the Battle 259
Sir Robert de Vere, the Standard-bearer of William Longespé 260
Sir Alexander Giffard 263
André de Vitré 264

PEDIGREE V.—Family of Vitré, showing the maternal relations of Ela Foundress of Lacock, and their connections with the Dukes of Britany and Kings of England 265

CHAPTER XIII. Affairs of Lacock Abbey during Ela's abbacy—Early fate of William Longespé the Third—Tournament at Blyth—DEATH OF ELA—The Funeral of a Nun 268

CHAPTER XIV. Affairs of the Abbey after the death of the Foundress ELA — Succession of Abbesses—Pro-

CONTENTS.

	Page
perty of the Abbey in 1291—The hearts of Amicia Countess of Devon, and Bishop Nicholas Longespé—Ecclesiastical Survey of 1535	278
Pedigree of Temmes, the family of the last Abbess	291

CHAPTER XV. THE ESTATES OF THE ABBEY. Lacock—Notton—Hatherop—Woodmancote—Bishopstrow—Heddington—Shrewton—Chittern—Shorewell—Wiclescote—Albourn—Amesbury—Bristol—Bytton and Hanham—Calne—Chicklade—Chippenham—Cliff Pypard—Machinden—Slade—Trowbridge—Uffcote—Upham—Westbury 293

Pedigree of Sherington 297
Rectory of Lacock, 299. List of Vicars . . 301

CHAPTER XVI. Dissolution of Religious Houses in England—Dispersion of the Nuns of Lacock . . 335
Letter of the Abbess of Godstow 338
Letter of the Prior of Hinton 341

MODERN STATE OF LACOCK ABBEY 347
The Copy of Magna Charta at Lacock . . . 357
Visit of Queen Elizabeth to Lacock House . . 359
The surrender of Lacock House in 1645 . . *ib.*
The Nuns' Boiler 360
Last Visit to Old Sarum and concluding Reflections . 361
Final note on Stonehenge, &c. 366
Additions and Corrections 367. Lacock Cross . 373

APPENDIX.

The Book of Lacock	i
Foundation Charter of Hinton Priory	vi
Abstract of the Cartulary of Lacock	viii—li
Deed relating to the tolls at Lacock fair 1306	lii
The Gregorian Liturgy, in the Cathedral Library at Salisbury	liii

INTRODUCTORY CHAPTER
TO
ANNALS AND ANTIQUITIES
OF
LACOCK NUNNERY,
IN
WILTSHIRE.

NEARLY half-way between the towns of Chippenham and Melksham, in a spacious and level meadow, surrounded by elms, at the bottom of which winds, with many devious inflections, the river Avon—appear the walls, and tall spiral chimnies, and arches hung with ivy, of the ancient Nunnery of Lacock.*

Many circumstances in the history of this religious foundation are of peculiar interest, though it has not yet found a regular historian. The causes which have induced the present writer, at a late period of life, to take upon him that office, may be briefly related; but a few words will be necessary,

* The name is derived from Lea or Lay, a meadow, and Oche, water.

previously, to give a general idea of the features and character of the scene.

The Abbey is still in many parts entire, and stands conspicuously, in a spot formerly, it may be supposed, a solitary glade, between the ancient forests of Melksham and Chippenham, adjoining the vill or town of Lacock. This town, if it may be so called, was in the Saxon times of greater imimportance; for it is said in an ancient record, quoted by Leland, that " Dunwallo founded three cities with three castles, Malmesbury, Tetrouburg (supposed to be Trowbridge), and Lacock."* We need not remark that what might then have been called cities or castles, would not be much in accordance with our ideas of such places in the present age. On a hill, rising over the present town, some tower or walls of defence might have been raised, to resist the desultory incursions of the Danes, the memory of which, except in the uncertain records of the old chronicler, has perished.

The Nunnery of Ela is far more authentic and interesting than the Castle of Dunwallo. In the year 1232 Ela, only child of William Earl of Salisbury, and sole heiress of all her father's vast landed possessions in the county, laid the foundation of this religious house in her widowhood, in pious and affectionate remembrance of her husband William Longspee, in her right Earl of Sarum, who had then been dead six

* " Dunwallo tres civitates condidit cum tribus castellis, scilicet Malmesburg, Tetrouburg (nunc forsan Trouburgh in comit. Wiltshire), et Lacock." Collectanea, vol. I. p. 325.

years. This brave man was the eldest natural son of Henry the Second, by the lady whose transcendant beauty has become proverbial under the name of " Fair Rosamond." He laid the fourth stone of the beautiful Cathedral of New Sarum in the year 1220.* Six years afterwards, he was the first personage buried within those walls, where his tomb now remains. He died after a short illness, at the Castle of Old Sarum, in 1226, his death having been supposed to be by poison.

On the same day of the week, and at the same hour in the day, on which he had been received at the entrance of the new Cathedral, in jubilant procession, just eight weeks before,† namely, on Sunday morning at nine o'clock, his body was conveyed,‡ with chaunted Litanies, to his last repose, after a life of heroic enterprise and virtue. He § who led the funeral chant, meeting the procession of death at the great western porch, has left an affecting account of the ceremonials in manuscript. The remains were deposited in an oak tomb, on which some of the painting and gilding is yet visible, though six centuries have passed since the remains were thus deposited.

* The first stone was laid for Pope Honorius; the second, for the Archbishop of Canterbury; the third, by the Bishop of Salisbury; the fourth by Longspee; and the fifth by Ela, his Countess.

† January 13. ‡ March 9.

§ William de Wanda, the Precentor. The MS. is in the Bishop's muniment-room, with other valuable records.

The tomb has been removed from its original situation. It is surmounted by the Warrior's majestic figure, in armour, recumbent, with a border round the edge of the tomb of broken flowers.* His pointed shield, bearing six lioncels rampant, appears on his left side, with the LONG SWORD, extending to his spurs, from whence he was named, and which in youth was 'all his fortune.' His face is partly covered with a flat helmet; the chain-mail, under his chin, is continued to his feet, with a surcoat, which seems to have been azure; but there is neither name, title, or inscription. After the death and burial of her husband, Ela remained as custos of the Castle of Sarum, revering the memory of him on whom she had bestowed the amplest wealth—and having long meditated her pious design, the widowed mother of eight children, in this remote district of her hereditary domain, raised the walls which still remain to attest her affection and piety. She was probably led to select this spot, not only from a supposed revelation, but on account of its vicinity to the religious establishment of her ancestors at Bradenstoke, and that of Stanley, founded by her husband's father, in the parish of Bremhill, three miles distant. The first stone of the Nunnery of Lacock was laid in the year

---

* Perhaps in allusion to his untimely end, which suggested the quaint epitaph given by M. Paris,

Flos comitum Gulielmus obit, stirps regia! *Longus Ensis* vaginam cæpit habere *brevem*."

William, the *flower* of Earls, is gone, by death
Cut down! his *Long Sword* hath a *shorter* sheath.

1232, and that of the Priory of Hinton, near Bath (founded in pursuance of her husband's will), on the same day. Beneath the cloisters, which are still in the most perfect state of preservation, the stone that covers her remains, removed from the altar of the destroyed choir, is yet entire; and the following inscription, which I give correctly I believe for the first time, may be imperfectly traced in the Monkish verse of the times,—

> Infra sunt *defossa* Elæ venerabilis *ossa*,
> Quæ dedit has *sedes*, sacras monialibus *ædes*,
> Abbatissa *quidem*, quæ sancte vixit *ibidem*,
> Et comitissa *Sarum*, virtutum plena *bonarum*.

TRANSLATION.

> Beneath, the venerable Ela's bones
> Are buried; she, these scenes of sacred peace—
> Countess of Salisbury gave to the Nuns,
> Herself the Abbess here, and full of deeds
> Of Holy Charity.—

Who does not involuntary add?

> "Pray that she rest in peace!"

The situation and scene around naturally excite, unconnected with the religion she professed, such an inward prayer; and the river itself, in this spot, seems to steal by, lingeringly, in union with such associations, and as if it sought to wander, from the tumult of the world, in search of loneliness and silence; for, though its stealthy current—

> "Doth make no music with th' enamel'd stones"

yet, in the beautiful personification of the Poet of another Avon,

> " He gives a gentle kiss to every sedge
> He overtaketh in his pilgrimage,
> And so by many winding nooks he strays."

We may here pause a moment to remark, that the character of the scenery and situations of ancient abbeys, may be considered as representing, in a great degree, the character and feelings of their founders. Generally the most secluded spots were chosen, in unison with disappointed hopes, or passions thrown back on the heart, or bereaved earthly affections, settling from painful into pensive religious recollections.

Sometimes the most beautiful scenes of river and woodland were selected by those who sought religious peace, after a life of tumultuous contention— as at Tintern, &c.

> Sore beat with storms, in glory's arduous way,
> Here might Ambition muse, a Pilgrim sage,
> And raptur'd see religion's evening ray
> Gild the calm walks of his reposing age.
> WARTON.

Penitence and remorse have sought to shroud themselves in the rudest recesses of the most desolate rocks, as at the Chartreux—

> Per invias rupes, sonantes
> Inter aquas, nemorumque noctem.
> GRAY.

"Mid rocks, and sounding waters, and the night
Of woods."

Devoted to silence and abstraction, here the recluse, pressing to his heart the crucifix, day after day, might tell his beads, and by a life of privation thus hope to expiate offences not to be revealed.

Sometimes these sacred and secluded structures were VOTIVE, as when raised in consequence of *vows* for success in some perilous enterprise, or on account of escape from imminent danger, as shipwreck, &c. It is not improbable that Ela performed the *vows* of her husband, who, on his return to England from Gascony, about two months before his death, was (at the time it was thought) miraculously preserved in a storm.

Sometimes these abodes of religious peace were COMMEMORATIVE, as when affection sought a more intimate and spiritual communion with the departed,[*] and when daily religious rites seemed in a peculiar manner, from year to year, to hallow such undying and sacred remembrances.

And who shall say, that such ideas are contrary to the purest feelings of piety? when the solemn rites were performed as in the times of Ela, and the fumes of incense rose, and the harmony of

[*] No candid and well-informed Christian will, for a moment, imagine that I could be inclined to say a word in favour of that Pagan Purgatory, which was introduced by the Church of Rome, when a traffic was made of the purest and best feelings of the heart.

choirs was heard blending with the sad memory of hours, and days, and years, to return no more,—might not the spirits of those we loved, for ever removed from earth, amid such scenes and with such associations, be thought to be almost present, breathing a benediction unseen, and as life stole away, and the time of departure for the living was at hand, to whisper—

"Come, Sister, come?"—POPE.

Thus a widowed mourner like Ela, in a convent founded by herself, and consecrated to such pious meditations, in a far purer and more exalted sense than that of the Poet of the Paraclete, might be described—having lost the father of her children—

"In every hymn again his voice to hear."
ELOISA TO ABELARD.

We have spoken of the character of the slow and solitary Avon, winding through the seclusion of this scenery, at the bottom of a meadow, which is probably the very meadow, of 20 acres, spoken of in Domesday Book. In the course of fourteen or fifteen miles, not less than three religious houses, besides this of Lacock, rose on or near the borders of the same retired stream.

The traveller marks at a distance, over the woods, the high and lonely arch of Malmesbury Abbey, the august but melancholy mother, as she might be called, of these monastic seats on the retired margin of this river. The remains of Bradenstoke Abbey on the brow of the hill, overlooking the same river as it winds through the vale and pastures of Somerford and Christian Malford, may be distinguished, with its massy buttresses and battlements, far off in the sunshine. Of Stanley scarce a wreck is visible. Lacock is still inhabited, the most entire of all inhabited monastic establishments in England, with its cloisters as fresh as if from the architect's hand but yesterday. Two of these abbeys, those of Bradenstoke and Stanley, I have elsewhere* observed, were affiliated (if I might use the word) with the Nunnery of Lacock; the Abbey of Bradenstoke being the foundation of Ela's Norman ancestors, and Stanley the joint foundation of the Empress Matilda and her son Henry the Second, the father of Ela's honoured and heroic husband. In the History of Bremhill, I have spoken of the Abbey of Stanley, and its removal from Loxwell, and of its early name Drownfont, abbatia de Drogonis fonte.† Of this singular and romantic spring on the summit of a hill in Pewsham forest, and the origin of the first structure of Stanley Abbey, ascertained from various original and most curious documents never before published—I have there treated at large. The family connection between the founders of Bradenstoke

* History of Bremhill.
† The abbey of the fount of Drogo. Drogo was Matilda's Chamberlain. Henry's grant runs thus: "Quas ego et mater mea dedimus et concessimus Drogoni, matris meæ Camerario."

and Lacock, will form the subject of the next chapter, when we shall proceed to speak of Ela's Norman ancestors. In this introductory chapter I shall here only further remark, in reference to Ela, that when I last looked upon the dark marble stone under which her bones are deposited, it was on a moody day of the declining year 1831. As I stood over her grave, and thought of her youthful romantic history, and the revolutions of so many centuries, a gleam of pale sunshine stole out over the dark clusters of the ivy, and fell on the spot; while at the same moment a wintry bird, unseen in the umbrage, piped one small note, which was succeeded with stillness more profound, when the gleam departed, and no answering sound was heard distant or near. I remembered some exquisite lines of Archbishop Markham on the grave of William Longspee's unfortunate mother, Rosamond, in the Nunnery of Godstowe:

> Pallentes nocturna ciens campana sorores,
> Hinc matutinam sæpe monebat avem.

> —————————————————" The bell
> That, calling the pale sisters from their cell,
> O'er the deep woods, from the lone turret heard,
> Awoke, when all was dark, the morning bird."

This circumstance leads me now to mention the somewhat more singular yet pleasing associations which suggested the idea of writing the annals of those who have been, for six hundred years, removed from all the vicissitudes of earth.

It was in the gloomiest evening of dark October, when the papers of the day had brought the intelligence that the long debated Reform Bill had been rejected by a great majority of the Peers in Parliament; when the most awful anticipations of the result were foreboded; when all that was POSSIBLE, soon, in the shapings of the imagination, became PROBABLE; and all that seemed *probable*, in the mind's gloomy creations, as soon turned to *certainties*—it was *then*, the thought could not be suppressed, that, as at this very time the kingdom was the scene of frequent and mysterious incendiarism, all England might become another burning Bristol. The family was assembled in the long gallery leading to the room which is now the library, and which gallery, connecting the ancient apartments of the nuns, had lately been fitted up as a drawing-room. The winds of the night were heard *without; within*, all were listening to the music of the harp and the song. A young lady of the mansion, now Viscountess Valletort, with three other ladies, whose voices united in a singular harmony, one of them of of the church of Rome, and all of them highly cultivated in their delightful art, joined in singing the ancient sublime hymn, "Gloria in Excelsis!" I could not but recollect that such voices, entirely those of females, had often been heard chanting together those very words, nearly six hundred years ago; and these words were now most impressively sung in the nineteenth century, in a room over the grave of the Foundress of the very walls, forgotten in the cloisters below. The winds of winter were no longer heard: alarm as to the state of the political world was forgotten, while the sacred song from united female voices, in the very scenes where such voices, to the very same words of the same Latin hymn, were heard so many ages ago—came over the heart, like an instant spell of peace. The sacred music was a beautiful composition, by the young lady now Viscountess Valletort. And at the moment, the thought arose, which was afterwards expressed in the following lines, published in a periodical of the time, in consequence of some brilliant verses addressed to the same lady by one of the most popular living poets* of Great Britain, who had inadvertently omitted, in the enumeration of personal and mental qualities, all mention of music.

TO LADY VALLETORT,

After hearing her sing " Gloria in Excelsis," with three other young Ladies, at Lacock Abbey, Oct. 1831.

SENT ON HER MARRIAGE.

FAIR inmate of these ivied walls, beneath
Whose silent cloisters Ela sleeps in death—
Let loftier bards, in rich and glowing lays,
Thy gentleness, thy grace, thy virtues praise—

* Mr. Moore.

Be mine, to breathe one prayer—when all rejoice—
One parting prayer, still mindful of that voice,
And musing on the sacred song, which stole,
Sweet, as a spell of peace, upon the soul,
In those same scenes, where once the chapel dim,
Echoed the cloister'd sisters' vesper-hymn.

LIVE LONG! LIVE HAPPY! tranquil thro' the strife,
And the loud stir of this tumultuous life!

LIVE LONG! LIVE HAPPY! and when many a day
Has pass'd, in the heart's harmony, away;
When Eve's pale hand the gates of life shall close,
And hush the landscape to its last repose—
May sister-seraphs meet, with welcome song,
And gently say, " WHY HAVE YOU STAY'D SO LONG?"

To these lines, it was my intention to have added merely a note on the foundress of this Abbey; but, considering the numerous circumstances of historical and romantic interest in her life, I thought the events of that life, and the early history of the foundation, might be a work not unamusing to myself in the evening of my days, and perhaps not unacceptable to that part of the literary public which takes any interest in inquiries of this kind.

Such was the origin of the proposed ANNALS and ANTIQUITIES of Lacock Abbey, which will be pursued in the next Chapter.

NOTES AND ILLUSTRATIONS.

WILLIAM LONGSPEE'S TOMB IN SALISBURY CATHEDRAL.

For the following accurate and interesting remarks on the tomb of the illustrious personage first buried in the new Cathedral, I am indebted to Mr. Hatcher, of Salisbury, a gentleman well known for his general and extensive knowledge, and as the amanuensis and literary assistant of my predecessor, Archdeacon Coxe.

"I have examined the monument very closely. The shield in the heraldic phrase bears AZURE, 6 lioncels, 3, 2, and 1, OR. I observed the bright blue in several parts of it; the gilding of the animals is visible in every little indentation. To make this more indubitable, the arms are repeated on the surcoat, and the colours and gilding under the shield are as fresh as if laid on within a twelvemonth. The ground under the figure appears to have been very minutely diapered.

"The fleurs-de-lis round the edge of the stone, appear too regular and marked to have been a mere fancy ornament. They were originally gilt, and I think the extreme edges were bordered with blue. Whether the ground was a bluish green, like the diapering, or whether it was red, I cannot decide, for both colours can be traced in the indentations. I suspect, however, the red was used as a ground to give lustre to the gold."

There are two plates of this figure in Stothard's "Monumental Effigies;" it has also been engraved in Sandford's Genealogical History of the Kings of England, in Dodsworth's Salisbury Cathedral, and Britton's Salisbury Cathedral.

WINTRY BIRD IN THE CLOISTERS.—SONG OF THE WREN, &c.

The circumstance of a small and lonely bird, in the interior of the ivied cloisters, piping out one disconsolate note where the hymns of the choir were once heard, will be thought too poetical by a rigid antiquary, but it was a fact, and to my mind, at the time, impressive. I need not say this bird was the wren. In winter it is found generally among masses of ivy, and never heard to utter a note from its retreat, unless there is a momentary gleam of sunshine, when it pipes out, not cheerfully but plaintively, one single note, whilst in May it has five or six most cheerful and distinct notes; its notes indeed, in richness and variety, in May, are nearly allied to those of the canary bird.

The red-breast is seldom found in ivy in the winter, but often builds its nest there in the spring. Sunshine seems necessary as the exciting cause of melody to every bird of rural song.

I may here relate a little affecting incident, which occurred whilst I was writing this note. A child, about eight years old, was cautioning, with great earnestness, another girl of the same age, " NOT to tell!" She was so earnest in her entreaties, that Mrs. B., in her morning walk, overheard her, and asked " what was the secret to be concealed, for she ought not to conceal any thing?" The poor girl said, " Madam, there is a robin's nest just by, and so low among the ivy, close to the church-yard walk, that the boys can reach it! Last night one of the poor little birds fell out of its nest, so I told my mother, and she came and put it back, and I am afraid the boys should find the nest, and take away the little ones from poor robin; so I begged Sally not to tell them of it!"

If this interesting incident, occurring whilst I was writing, may be thought trifling, there are some readers who will pardon it. Whilst I am on the subject let me observe, that the winter and summer song of birds has been by no writer more faithfully described than by old Chaucer.

> The birdes that have left their song
> While they had suffered cold full strong,
> In weathers grylle,* and dark to sight,
> Ben in May, for the *sunne bright*,
> So glad, that they shewe in singing,
> That in their hearts is such liking,
> That they mote singe and ben light—
> Then dothe the nightingale her might—
> To *maken noise* and *syngen blythe*.

The tradition of the red-breast and the wren, that they are sacred, and that it is a sin to hurt them, is fast wearing out in country parishes. The feelings universally connected with this idea arose from the belief, affecting in itself, of their strewing leaves over dead bodies found in the woods.

> " Call for the robin red-brest and the wren,
>   Since o'er shady groves they hover,
>   And with leaves and flowers cover
> The friendless bodies of unburied men.
>   WEBSTER.

So poor Collins, over the grave of Fidele!—

> " The red-breast oft at evening hours,
>   Shall kindly lend his little aid,
>   With gathered moss and scattered flowers,
>   To deck the grave where thou art laid!"

I take the opportunity of adding a few more remarks on this not uninteresting rural subject. Of the character of the song of the nightingale, both Mr. Coleridge and Mr. Fox have spoken, as being lively and not melancholy. The passage from Chaucer is directly in point.

But neither Coleridge, nor any professed ornithologist, if I recollect, have remarked what I have no hesitation in saying

---

* " Grylle," is gloomy. Romance of the Rose, original by Abelard—so it appears by the most affecting letters of Eloise.

will be found a fact: the nightingale has *no notes of its own*, except its first short whistle, followed by—jug—jug—as if to prepare itself for its elaborate and rich song. It invariably opens, or, I should say, PRELUDES its varied song with these two, its only native notes. It then, distinctly and literally, as a MOCKING-BIRD, pours out, with richer, louder, and more mellow tones, the identical notes, in rapid succession, of other singing birds—from those of the thrush, the blackbird, the yellow-hammer, the lark, the red-breast, the wren, &c., until it is tired. I state this confidently, on the authority of those who can instantly pronounce, from the song which they hear, what bird sings, and that—from early habits—invariably. Additional beauty and propriety is given, from this circumstance, to the celebrated Eclogue of Strada, in his Prolusions, in which a nightingale is described as imitating a varied modulation of a harp, till she falls dead on the strings.

Another fact may be mentioned. The nightingale never sings without a twig, upon which it can rest its breast whilst it sings, as if to assist it in exerting all its powers; and for this reason it always lays a twig across its nest, for the purpose of teaching its young to resort to the same assistance in their future song, which is the origin of the idea of its singing only when lacerated by a thorn.

Whilst I am on the subject, I shall remark one more fact relative to singing birds. The bullfinch naturally has only *one* note, and that dull. To sing, it must have the regular instruction of art, and then it learns its varied song in cottagers' houses. It may be taught the perfect scale of eight notes, with the half and the whole notes, and modulate exactly any tunes, or *bits* of tunes, its rustic music-master teaches.

THE ANCIENT HYMN, "GLORIA IN EXCELSIS."

This Hymn of the Primitive Church is, as it ought to be, from its almost apostolical antiquity, simplicity, and sublimity, retained in our Prayer Book. It was generally and universally sung, in all religious houses, long before the days of Ela's Choir, as may be seen in a manuscript in the Cathedral in Salisbury, probably as old as the 9th century. In one of the copies of the Saxon Chronicle, in the Bodleian Library, it is said that the hymn "Gloria in Excelsis" was ordered to be sung *festis diebus*, by POPE* Telesphorus, anno 134.

* As an ingenious "Irish gentleman travelling in search of *a religion*," applies the word POPE to Clement, as if *Pope*-Clement and *Pope*-Hildebrand, or peradventure *Pope*-Joan, were the same kind of characters as the Fathers of the primitive church, I feel compelled to make one remark on these said "Travels," because I think the fact I am about to introduce will best show the difference between apostolic Popery, and the Popery of "infallible unwritten traditions."

When our Irish gentleman set out "*in search of a religion*," and had travelled as far as Germany, the country of Luther—it is a pity he had not gone to a celebrated city called Cologne on the Rhine! There he would have found an instance of the triumph of "unwritten traditions," which must completely have established his faith; or if he did not *quite* believe the tradition, it would have gone some way to make him Protestant again.

I will tell the story as briefly as I can :—About thirteen hundred years ago, as "*un*written tradition" truly attests, *a few young ladies*, from the county of Cornwall, in England, embarked with their governess in a ship, to cross the sea into Britanny, called Armorica, where there was a colony of expatriated British, who had fled from the yoke of the Saxons. These ladies were of the highest blood in the country, daughters of aristocrats,— not more than ELEVEN THOUSAND—with their governess, called St. Ursula! They were accompanied by some ladies' maids!— not more than SIXTY THOUSAND—all from Cornwall, a county at that time not so densely inhabited as it has been since. These ladies (on a fine morning we will suppose) went on board a ship to escape the terrible Saxons. We imagine a plaintive bard, or lyric Poet of the age, in love with them *all*, left on shore, sighing and singing—

"Oh! Ladies fair, where are you roaming?"

However, the anchor is up, the plaintive Bard is left behind, and the *eleven thousand noble virgins* and *sixty thousand virgin ladies' maids* are on the ocean!

Alas! they are driven out of their course. Where are they landed? On the shores of the Red Sea? No. Cast away, by St. Ursula, in the German Rhine! They were now in the same calamitous situation as the poor flying fishes—flying to avoid the dolphins, and becoming a prey to the starved kites! So these unfortunate ladies, as Lord Byron truly calls them, fled from the fierce Saxons to encounter the barbarous Huns! " *Unfortunate*," indeed! for how could *eleven thousand virgins* and *sixty thousand virgin ladies' maids*, with the *old* virgin, St. Ursula, at their head, defend themselves against the Huns? They were preserved only by a *miracle!* It is indeed impossible to entertain any doubt of this *miracle*, for their *bones* are shown this day, and all " Good Catholics" WORSHIP them!

If any obstinate heretic, notwithstanding, should have some misgivings respecting the truth of the story, the following fact cannot fail to convince him, for it is attested by " tradition *infallible*" as the " written word of God;" that after their poor bones had been buried in peace, for five or six hundred years, the bones of an infant, not born in wedlock, happened to be buried near them, and immediately such a clatter and noise every night was made, among the bones of the virgins, that prayers for their rest was offered up night and day! Still the same disturbance and clatter among the female bones was heard, till the offending cause was found out, when the bones of the intruding *baseborn* were expelled, since which all has been peaceable in the charnel-house of St. Ursula at Cologne.

When, many years ago, I visited this church, expressing some doubt as to the miracle, on looking up, I saw written in large characters on a board, an address to the Trinity, in these words:

" *Ut omnes* PERTINACES HERETICOS *longè arceatis*."

I need not say with what *haste* I left the Church of St. Ursula.

As to the beautiful ancient Catholic Hymn, it were well if all who call themselves Christians—Catholic or Protestant—Sub-Lapsarians or Supra-Lapsarians—Calvinists or Arminians—Moravians or Methodists—Sweet Singers of Israel, or those whom the spirit moves to *pray*, but never, by any accident, moved to *sing*, might join in the hymn of Pope Telesphorus, " GLORY BE TO GOD ON HIGH! AND ON EARTH PEACE! GOOD-WILL TOWARDS MEN." Amen.

CHAPTER II.

Ancestors and Family of Ela—Walter le Eurus—Edward of Domesday Book—Walter, the son of Edward—Last Visit of William the Conqueror to Salisbury—Reflections—Patrick Earl of Salisbury—William his son and successor—Present state of Bradenstoke Priory.

Before we listen to the orisons of the sequestered Sisters of Lacock, it will be proper to devote our attention to the ancestors of their Foundress—Edward of Domesday Book, and Walter his son, who founded that more ancient religious establishment of Bradenstoke, now called Broadstoke Abbey, in Wiltshire.

About seventy years after the melancholy curfew first, from the Abbey of Malmesbury,

"Toll'd the knell of parting day,"

this Priory was founded by Walter of Salisbury, the son of Edward the Sheriff of Wilts, who having married Sibilla de Cadurcis (or Chaworth), retired from the scenes of contention and licence, in the turbulent reign of Stephen, to the further and wildest district of his father's possessions, and raised that house of religious peace, where himself and his wife were buried, in one grave, and under one stone of black marble, without any memorial, leaving the completion of the endowment of the Priory, after his death, to his son, the grandfather of Ela.

The remains of the Norman Abbey of Bradenstoke yet appear conspicuous, as we have described, on the edge of the long sweep of hills which form the north-western bounds of the ancient forest of Braden, from whence the Danes descended, like a storm, to lay waste the country about Chippenham and Lacock.

For our knowledge of the ancestors of Ela, we are indebted to a singular work, called the Register of Lacock, preserved formerly at that Abbey, and now in the Cottonian collection of manuscripts. But to an historian the question arises, how far it is entitled to the claims of authentic veracity.

This book informs us, that among the illustrious Norman soldiers, who followed the standard of their Duke in his perilous expedition to England, "there was a noble warrior, named Walterus le Eurus, Count of Rosmar, to whom King William gave the entire domain of Sarisburia and Ambresburia, in consideration of HIS PROBITY." (Register of Lacock.)

Admitting the authority of the document, the reader will remark, that King William gave the entire domain of Salisbury and Amesbury to this Norman Lord, it is said, "propter probitatem." Dugdale translates the word *probitatem* " valour ;" it may be considered as " approved service ;" but I am inclined to think it meant the most honourable fidelity, as well as valour.

We are further told, that " BEFORE" Walterus le Eurus came to England, he had a son named Geraldus* le Gros, Count de Rosmar, who had a son called William, the second Count de Rosmar le Meschyn, whose son William, the third Count de Rosmar, died without issue. " AFTERWARDS" Walterus le Eurus had a son called Edward, " natione Anglus," who was Vice-comes, or Sheriff, of Wilts, and whose son, named Walterus de Sarisburia, was the founder of Bradenstoke Priory.

The first Walter, if we rely on this testimony, bore his banner at the eventful battle which placed his sovereign master on the throne. The successors of King William appear to have had the same reliance on the fidelity of his descendants. But now we advert to a singular fact. Only twenty years afterwards, the book of the great national survey, called Domesday Book, was completed; and in this book we find NOT the name of Walter, but of EDWARD, Vice-comes of Wilts, in possession of far greater wealth in the county than any other Baron. He appears in possession, not of THIRTY-THREE manors, as it is stated in Dugdale's Baronage, but of THIRTY-EIGHT, in Wiltshire,—for the number and

---

* Names given to the Normans, from particular circumstances; so Humfridus de Bohun, " cum barba;" William, " le meschyn," the avaricious; Geraldus, " le Gros," &c.

names may be ascertained from that most ancient and authentic document of the landed property of the kingdom, which remains a lasting monument of its sorrows and servitude. Nor is it in Wiltshire alone that the name of EDWARD OF SALISBURY occurs; he was also the lord of other manors in the counties of Somerset, Dorset, Hants, Berks, Surrey, Middlesex, Hertford, and Buckingham.

When Domesday Book was completed, we must consider old Walter dead, or returned to Normandy, leaving his land and honours to his son, who succeeded to his English possessions, and the castle on the imperial mound of Old Sarum. Admitting this statement, I shall first, as a matter of peculiar historical interest, connect this fact with the account in the Saxon Chronicle of the Conqueror's last visit to that city,* before he left his kingdom, never to return.

William, after many agitations under his feverish Crown, was now, for the last time, preparing to leave the land he had subdued—to return to his native country—to engage again in warfare, though the marks of age were gathering on his intrepid but thoughtful brow. He had completed the great national survey, and safely deposited this most important document at Winchester. He returned to Westminster; and from thence, before he embarked for the last time to Normandy, he came, Aug. 1, 1086, the year before his death, to " Seare-

* See Dr. Ingram's admirable translation of the Saxon Chronicle.

byrig," now Old Sarum, the seat and the citadel of "Edward the Sheriff."

Dwelling for a moment on a circumstance scarcely noticed by historians in general, let us think of the occasion, and the spot, where this proud assemblage were met — the castle,* the rising cathedral, the city on this aerial eminence — the Norman banner floating above the clouds from the citadel —the assembly of all the Barons, abbats, and prelates, with their crosses and crosiers, renewing here their oaths of allegiance. The portly Conqueror stands before us—his sword drawn, his helmet up, his eye vigilant and searching, his countenance commanding and stern, but worn by age and thought: and who is that, in the grace of early manhood, next to the mild and venerable Osmond, who had exchanged his sword for the crosier? —EDWARD OF SALISBURY, " born in England!" When we think we behold this concourse of the Norman chivalry—the Earls and Barons in arms— William standing thoughtful in front, while Humphridus de Bohun, " *cum barba*," † (to whom he had given Clarendon Forest, and whose son married Edward's daughter,) advances to swear allegiance on

* Seventeen castles are enumerated as built by the Conqueror; but nothing is said of the Castle at Salisbury. That it existed at the time there can be no doubt; for the Prebend of Stratford, more ancient than the Conquest, in the oldest deeds, is called " Stratford sub Castro."

† The first of the Bohuns had the name of Humphridus *cum Barba!* As it will be seen in the tapestry of Bayeux, the Normans generally were shaved, except on the upper lip.

his knees, &c.—the picture seems to rise in our view as august as interesting, and wants no colours of poetical imagination.

The plain 'Saxon Chronicle' shall speak for itself. On this day, on this lofty and castellated mound, "All the LANDSMEN, that were of ANY ACCOUNT, over ALL ENGLAND, became this man's vassals, and they all BOWED THEMSELVES before him, and became his men, and swore to him OATHS OF ALLEGIANCE that they would, against all other men, be FAITHFUL to him." (Saxon Chronicle.)

Increasing anxieties, as well as years, had now begun to bow the reluctant Conqueror. Harassed by enemies within and without his kingdom;—the great Thanes, the most powerful British subjects whom he sought to conciliate (Waltheolf and Edwyn), "flying out," as the Saxon Chronicle expresses their becoming voluntary outlaws;—the whole nation, as it were, under a cloud of the wrath of Heaven, and visited by famine, pestilence, and storm, from the year 1084 to 1086;—we need not wonder that the humble Chronicler should describe him at this time, as "very stern and also hot!" Fancy might think she recognised a gentler trait of nature in the harsh features of his stern and moody character; and in this light, the affecting circumstance to which I allude, would be worthy Shakspeare, for (continues the Saxon Chronicle) although "very stern and also hot," "he loved the tall deer, as if he were THEIR FATHER."

The plain Chronicler, whoever he was, distinctly informs us, " he often looked on him, and spent some time in his court;" and now, in his old age, encompassed by enemies—not knowing whom to trust, almost estranged from his kind—his wife, on whom all that was gentle in his nature, reposed, being dead—having no object of sympathy in the world, it is no wonder he loved the " tall deer" as a father.

The monk Matthew Paris sets his feelings, at this time, in a different point of view—" FERUS, FERAS amabat, quasi PATER FERARUM!" and complains that divine service was interrupted by the HARES! The same image is repeated by succeeding histories; but are hares or " tall deer" as ferocious as he is described?

Be the meaning as it may, it is interesting at this time to contemplate the great victor, again and for the last time, in his shortening days, exacting allegiance from his Barons, among whom stood the youthful ancestor of Ela—for who can doubt his being present at the chief city in the county of which he was Sheriff, and where his castle stood, when ALL the Barons " OF ANY ACCOUNT," were there? Before their liege Lord, all swore again to be " his men," while William vowed by his usual oath, " the resurrection and the throne of God,"*

---

* Rufus's usual oath was " the foot of St. Luke."

having thus secured all England, "to take vengeance on his insulting enemies beyond the sea."*

He died the next year in his native land—how miserably, let historians say—acknowledging with his last breath, the injustice of his claim to the throne he had filled, and penitent for the woes he had caused.

We pass to those who held wealth and state from his bounty. We have described Edward of Salisbury. His son, Walter, was married to Sibilla de Cadurcis; of whom was born Patricius, the first Earl of Salisbury.† This Walter, as we have said, founded the priory of Bradenstoke, and placed there Regular Canons "to serve God for ever!" as the Charter informs us. After the death of his wife, he took the tonsure and habit of the Canons; and "here their bodies were buried in the same grave near the chancel,‡ and whose souls rest in heaven,"§ quoth the

* The anecdote of the King of France is well known.

† He was created Earl of Salisbury by Matilda, in consequence of the part he took with her against Stephen.

‡ "Presbiterium" in the original; so called because the priests were alone allowed to enter, and secular persons forbidden,—

Cancello laicos prohibet scriptura sedere,
Ne sibi presumant Christi secreta videre.

The stone stalls for the priests remain on the south side of many ancient chancels.

§ Under the pavement in the Chapter House of Lanthony Abbey, near Gloucester, was found a stone with the name "Cadurcis;" and there the 3d, 4th, 5th, and 6th Humphrey

Register of Lacock. " Amen," quoth the Historian of Lacock Nunnery.

Patrick, the son of Walter, distinguished by hereditary fidelity, nobly supported Matilda against Stephen. The whole kingdom was at this time a prey to anarchy; and in 1142, his father, Walter the son of Edward, retired from the storm of the times—from scenes of rapine and violence—to the lonely woods of Bradenstoke, with feelings such as Cowper describes,

> " Oh! for a lodge in some vast wilderness,
> Some boundless contiguity of shade,
> Where rumour of oppression and deceit,
> Of unsuccessful or successful wars,
> Might never reach me more! My ear is pain'd,
> My heart is sick of every day's report
> Of outrage and of wrong."

With all his immense possessions, he lived after the death of her he loved, a melancholy monk, renouncing, according to the vows of his order, all individual property, though so rich in inheritances; and under such bereavement of mind, as from the circumstances recorded, we may imagine,—he chose this solitary retreat, in which to die in peace, far from the noise and strife of a savage and contentious age, nursing his devotional and doubtless his tenderest feelings, till buried in the same grave with

de Bohuns were buried, as may be seen in the Collectanea Topographica et Genealogica, p. 168.

her he loved and mourned. He married a lady of that family from which was descended the beautiful girl who awakened the first feelings of passion in the breast of the youthful Byron, called by him "The last scion of an ancient race," and of whom he has written in language of such pure affection. If Beauty be hereditary, (and who can say it is not ?) from all we know of the life of Walter, he might have been as impassioned and romantic as Byron, though without the faculties of a poet, to render his affections as deathless as his song. Walter of Sarum and Sibilla Chaworth were buried in one grave.

No inscription or memorial of any kind has been traced; but various unknown bodies, in unknown graves, have at different periods been discovered. The ashes of the son of Edward of Salisbury and of his wife, on whom so many possessions were bestowed, are scattered to the winds, and the remains of this monastic residence, overlooking the vale of Avon, only attest that "such things were!" Can we be insensible to the thought, that these great Lords of a conquered country, were actuated by a sense of lying under the judgment of God, when they raised in every part of the kingdom so many houses of religion, which they doubtless deemed expiatory?

Let the reader reflect on a few singular facts. The Conqueror himself died, forsaken of all whom he had enriched—his body, for a time, was denied a spot of rest—his eldest son went to the grave, sightless and broken-hearted. His second son, the heir to his throne, perished, untimely, by the glance of an arrow in the Forest, as in the same place, reserved for his animals of the chase, did another son.

The only son of Henry the First, and many of the youthful nobility of the realm, perished together, in the same disastrous shipwreck.

Henry the Second felt on his death-bed,

———— "How sharper than a serpent's tooth it is
To have a thankless child;"

having only his youngest natural son,* at that awful hour, to console him. His lawful son Richard, on his return from the Crusades, was for some time a captive in a foreign land, and died by an accidental wound. John laid his crown at the foot of a priest, was involved through life in hopeless contests, and died deserted.

Earl Patrick, the son and heir of Walter, was inhumanly murdered in a foreign land, when returning from a religious pilgrimage. He was Lieutenant for King Henry the Second in Guienne (or Acquitaine); and in 1167, when on his return from the shrine of St. James in Galitia, was slain by Guy de Lusignan. His body was interred in the church of St. Hilary in Poictou; and Queen Alianor (whose champion and defender he had been) procured, in consequence, from the King her husband, to join with her in bestowing upon that church, all their customs arising in Benai. King

* Brother of Longspé, by the same unfortunate mother.

Sigill: Eccl:e b:ate Marie de Gnadenostoka.

Henry afterwards drove Guy de Lusignan out of Poictou, and he took refuge in the army of the Crusaders.

Patrick, the faithful follower of the standard of Matilda, in her arduous struggles in favour of her youthful son for the crown of England, was twice married. By his last wife Ela, daughter of the Count de Ponthieu, and widow of Earl Warren, he had William Earl of Salisbury, father of Ela of Lacock, and three other sons, mentioned by their brother in his Confirmation-charter to Bradenstoke Priory. Patrick was at that time dead. The other brothers of Earl William were Walter and Philip. William married Alianor de Viteri, daughter of Tirrel de Mainers.* She died in 1194; and he followed to the tomb in 1196: both were buried at Bradenstoke, under a marble near the porch. They left one daughter, Ela, foundress of the nunnery of which we are now about to speak more particularly, almost a child.

We shall here recapitulate, that the more ancient Priory of Bradenstoke was founded, in 1142, for religious of the order of Augustine or Black Canons, in honour, as most houses of the kind were built, of the "Blessed Virgin," by Walter, son of Edward of Salisbury.

On the valuation taken of this Priory, shortly before its dissolution, its total income amounted to £270. 10s. 8d. and its net revenue, after deduc-

* The first name is mentioned in the Book of Lacock, and the second added in Dugdale's Baronage.

tions, to £212. 19*s.* 3*d.* It was granted in exchange to Richard Pexel 38 Henry VIII.*

From the heirs of Pexel, or Pecsall, it came by purchase into the possession of Methuens, of Corsham. In the History of Bremhill, I have noticed the singular circumstance of the preservation of a picture of the Virgin, uninjured, in the very place which has undergone, through so many years, so many eventful changes. My friend Paul Methuen, Esq. of Corsham House, in the neighbourhood, has placed this picture, in a PROTESTANT age and country, among his splendid collection of works of art, beyond the chance of injury, unless the despotism of democracy should sweep away pictures, title-deeds, houses, and lands together! Its preservation, through such various changes, might be marked as miraculous, by a " traveller in search of a religion!!" But alas! it could not protect the grave of the founder, or his possessions, from the ruthless hand of Henry.

* William Snow, first Dean of Bristol, was last Prior of this Convent; and, with thirteen monks, surrendered the same 8th January 1539, 30th Henry VIII., and had a pension of £60 per annum assigned him. Anno 1553, here remained in charge £2 in fees—£13. 6*s.* 8*d.* in annuities—and these pensions, to James Cove, canon, £6. 13*s.* 4*d.*; Edward Bruer, £5. 6*s.* 8*d.*; Richard Thompson, £5. 6*s.* 8*d.*; Ralf Styth, £5. 6*s.* 8*d.* (married); James Wykeman, £4. 13*s.* 4*d.* (married); Robert Ware, £4. 13*s.* 4*d.*; John Playsterer, £2 (married); John Hancocke, £2; and to Thomas Baker, £2 (married). (From Willis's Abbies.)

As Walter of Salisbury, and Sibilla de Cadurcis, were here buried in one grave, so here also, in one grave, were laid the bodies of William Earl of Salisbury and his Countess Alianor, father and mother of Ela, the foundress of Lacock nunnery. All the traces of a church or chapel at Bradenstoke have been long obliterated; but the site has been ascertained from Norman tiles and skeletons occasionally disinterred. Within these few years, on the removal of the ground, nearly twenty skeletons were found, two of which only were in stone coffins, and one appeared as if the corpse had been completely cased in leather.*

No other relic, however, has been discovered which might serve to identify the sepultures of the Founders or their immediate descendants, who were laid here, so long ago, in the presumed security of consecrated earth. The bones of Walter of Salisbury and his beloved wife, and those of the father and mother of Ela, have been mingled with the common dust; as have those of the youngest daughter of Ela, Petronilla, who was here buried; as here also, probably from feelings of peculiar devotional respect, was the *heart* of Ela's youngest son Stephen, by marriage Earl of Ulster, his body having been interred at Lacock.

We may conclude this account of the Priory of

* It is remarkable that the bones of fair Rosamond, mother of Longspé, at Godstow nunnery, near Oxford, were also found cased in leather.

Bradenstoke, by a more particular description of the building as it now appears, and a general sketch of the scenery from the spot.

The windows, buttresses, and lofty parapet, with one square turret on the north, appear far distant along almost the whole extent of the vale of the Avon. In front, and on either side, the horizon is bounded by the hazy appearance at times of the Cambrian hills beyond the Severn. Parts of Somerset, Berkshire, Gloucestershire, on to the woods of Lord Bathurst, lie beneath, as in a map.

The picturesque park of Draycot is distinguished by a rising knoll of woods in front; and immediately on the right, as a foreground to the landscape, another eminence hangs, dark with oak, almost under our feet; while the long course of the rural Avon is seen winding from village to village, far below, through its green and level pastures.

The front of the remaining building, which is used as a farm-house, is not materially altered. Semicircular arches, entirely relieved from the wall, connect the buttresses, and above them appear three narrow pointed windows. On the square northern turret grows an ancient thorn,* which I find represented in the view engraved by S. and N. Buck in 1732. Not far distant, on the level green, are two large fish-ponds; one, with the spring perpetually running, which I have no doubt from the transparent clearness, and from its always flowing in the dryest season, gave an idea of sacredness to the spot.

* It is called to this day, by the inhabitants, the *holy* thorn.

Not far distant, inclosed within the area of several earthern mounds, is a circular beacon hill, whose fires have often gleamed over a vast extent of country, from the time probably of the Danes, or earlier.

On entering the house, the visitor passes under a narrow groined vault, and, ascending a small stone staircase, enters a room which probably was that of the Prior. In this room is a chimney-piece of stone, richly carved and painted, with five plain shields in the centre of quatrefoils; the lower part being beautifully worked in lozenged panels, containing, raised on foliage, these four golden letters, " W. A. L. S." the import of which must be left to future explanation. This beautiful chimney-piece, which is crowned by an elegant cornice of leaves and a central bracket, is of the age of Henry VI.*

The principal apartment is a large and lofty room, retaining no other ancient features except the stone windows, and in the centre of the ceiling a single painted boss, containing a shield inscribed with the letter " S." perhaps the initial of Snow the last Prior, within a wreath of grapes and vine leaves.

In this room was preserved uninjured, through so many changes of owners and events, that paper-painting of the Virgin, to whom the Priory was dedicated, which has been before mentioned. †

---

* See the monument of Lady Tiptoft, in Gough's Sepulchral Monuments, vol. ii. pl. xlviii.

† History of Bremhill.

On returning from these silent and ancient halls to the light, the scene I have described seems more beautiful, sweeping far away, with masses of shade and sunshine, woods, and river, and the smoke of distant towns and villages. The most interesting object in sight, as far as human art is concerned, presenting itself, scarcely discerned, among the far-retiring trees, is Malmesbury Abbey, the majestic but mournful mother, as I have described, of the religious houses now desolate near the same stream.

Nothing can be conceived more wretched in appearance than the present village, which, as if in ludicrous contrast with these beauties of rural scenery, and these august remains, is called " Clack!" The ancient name of the manor was " Clake." It contains some straggling houses, and three forlorn-looking brick edifices, of the peculiar architecture of the Meeting-Houses for some religious denomination or other, which have succeeded the stately relics of elder piety.

About eight or nine years ago, in consequence of the discovery of the stone coffins of which we have spoken, I visited Bradenstoke, in company with the present possessor. The æra of the march of intellect and reform had not then commenced. Whether the storm,

" Hush'd in grim repose,"

may yet arise, to sweep to earth the majestic structures in which the services of the mild hierarchy of the scriptural Church of England are now performed, as it has long since left to devastation and silence the majestic monuments of a religion far less pure, will perhaps be determined when our grey heads are forgotten in the dust, perhaps before that time!

This account is concluded with every prayer for their preservation and inviolability. I shall only add, as somewhat remarkable facts, that the last Prior of Bradenstoke was the first DEAN of the new Protestant Cathedral of Bristol; and that Bishop Jewel, author of the celebrated " Apology for the Church of England," preached his last sermon at LACOCK,* near the grave of Ela, who had contributed to the foundation of that beautiful cathedral, over which that most distinguished Protestant Bishop presided, when its roofs resounded to purer services and more sublime and affecting music.

RENTS OF THE SHRIEVALTY OF WILTSHIRE.

We have already noticed in p. 22, the manors possessed by Edward of Salisbury, as recorded in Domesday Book; but as

* Having promised to preach at Lacock, in Wiltshire, a gentleman who met him observing him to be very ill, by his looks, advised him to return home, &c. but he would not be persuaded, but went thither and preached his LAST SERMON, out of the fifth of the Galatians, " *Watch in the spirit*, &c." when he did not finish without great labour and difficulty.—*Life of Bishop Jewel.*

the very curious enumeration of his official rents in kind, given in the same record, was not there noticed, I shall here extract it, having first prefixed the following illustrative remarks by my lamented friend the late Rev. James Dallaway:

"No COMES is mentioned in the Wiltshire Survey in Domesday, but there is EDWARDUS Sarisburiensis, who held the comitatus: he is there styled, by an insertion above his name, VICE-COMES, although he held the THIRD PENNY and the purveyance in FEE-FARM only. That he was merely the King's Tenant in Chief, is evident from the last line of the first paragraph in which the purveyance in kind is stated: " quando propositis FIRMA deficit, necesse est Edwardo restaurare de suo.'

"The King retained many of the counties (of which Wilts was one) in his own hands, and granted a Fee-farm to deputies, who were sometimes called Vice-comites, but not always."

Now for the yearly Rents of Edward as Vice-comes or Shire-Reeve. They were: "130 porkers and 32 bacon-hogs; 2 bushels and two pecks* of bread-corn *(frumentum)*, and the same of beer-corn *(brasium)*; 5 bushels and 1 peck of oats; 16 pottles of honey, or 16 shillings instead; 480 hens; 1600 eggs; 100 cheeses; 52 lambs; 140 fleeces; corn-rents *(blad. annonæ)* 162 acres, and also the value of 40*l.* within the Reeveland, and what he receives thence. When the farm fails with the bailiffs, then it is incumbent upon Edward to supply it from his own store."

This is important in one view, as illustrating the nature of Tithes taken in kind.

The pastor had—One egg, one hen, out of every ten; and it is remarkable, that in Ela's foundation charter, the rights to the Rector are preserved—but in all the subsequent institutions, Lacock is called a Vicarage.

* Eight sextarii. A sextarius is explained by Ducange as the 16th part of the modius or bushel; equal to the old English pottle, or two quarts.

CHAPTER III.

The lineage of Edward of Salisbury — Not connected with the Norman Comtes d'Evreux—The family of Rosmar or Romare—The Battle of Brennevill—Family of Edward of Salisbury—Humphrey de Bohun, the Founder of Farley Priory—Old Sarum.

HAVING spoken of Walter, Edward, Walter, Patrick, ancestors of William Earl of Salisbury, the father of Ela, I should wish, before we proceed further, to step back a little, in order to investigate the statements of the Book of Lacock, relative to the origin of this family; and also the further statements, which, though neither asserted by the Book of Lacock, nor countenanced by Dugdale, has been generally adopted by the writers who have mentioned the first Earls of Salisbury,—that their surname was Devereux, and that they were a branch of the Norman Counts of Evreux.

The person styled Walter le Ewrus, Earl of Rosmar, in the Book of Lacock, has been fixed upon by some of those writers as the ancestor of all the families of Devereux that have flourished in England, and he has been attached by them to the princely house of Evreux in Normandy, as the fourth and youngest son of Robert Comte d'Evreux, Archbishop of Rouen. By this assumption, an origin of the first rank was attained; for the Comtes d'Evreux were themselves a younger branch of the sovereign house of Normandy; the Archbishop being a younger brother of Duke Richard II. and great-uncle to King William the Conqueror.

The Archbishop, by his " wife, or rather concubine, Herleva," had three sons, whose identity is fully proved by records; namely, Richard Comte d'Evreux, his successor; Raoul, Lord of Gacé and Varenguebec, Constable of Normandy, and one of the guardians of the future Conqueror; and William, who married the widow of Robert Grandmesnil. " To these," says Pere Anselme, " some authors have added Walter de Rosmar, whom they make the ancestor of the Earls of Salisbury and Essex, in England;" but that eminent genealogist, whose researches were at once deep and comprehensive, had found nothing further to say of Walter than that he was so placed by "some" former writers, of whom he names only M. le Brasseur, the author of a History of the Comté d'Evreux, which had then been recently published.* Nor, on recurring to the volume of M. le Brasseur, do we find that he had any better authority; but he appears to have

* The words of Pere Anselme are " 4. Gautier de Rosmar est mis ici par quelques auteurs, (M. le Brasseur hist. du comté d'Evreux en 1722) qui le font le chef des seigneurs de Salisbury en Angleterre, depuis comtes d'Essex; mais ils descendent de Guillaume dit Longue épeé, batard du roi Henry II.; & les Comtes d'Essex de Guillaume dit d'Evreux, vivant en 1223." Histoire Genealogique et Chronol. des Pairs de France, fol 1726, vol. II. p 478.

readily taken the assertion upon trust,* from some unnamed English writer, for the sake of enlivening his work by the introduction of anecdotes of the English Earls of Essex, who flourished more than four centuries after!

Having thus consulted the best French peerage in vain, we are turned back to our English genealogists, and have first to inquire upon what authority they have asserted that Walter de Rosmar was a cadet of the Counts of Evreux. It is an ominous circumstance, at the commencement of the inquiry, that our standard English peerage, the Baronage of Dugdale, is not found among the supporters of this assertion. That judicious writer, who proceeded only upon evidence and not upon conjecture, has, under the title of Salisbury, merely transcribed the narrative of the Book of Lacock; and under the family of Devereux (Earl of Essex and Viscount Hereford), he claims for it no lineage from the Norman Counts of Evreux, but merely speaks of the *surname* as having been derived from that *town*, observing that "Of this family, which had their surname from Evreux a town of note in Normandy, there were divers generations here in England before they became Peers of the realm."† Nor, at this place, when he has arrived at the real Devereuxs, does Dugdale allude to any supposition that the early Earls of

* Hist. du Comté d'Evreux, pp. 81, 323.

† The earliest Devereux's mentioned by Dugdale, are *Reginald son of Robert de Ebrois*, who occurs in the Pipe Roll 31

Salisbury were of the same stock; nor to any family of Devereux having descended from the Earls of Salisbury.* But it has been in some more recent Peerage that the two accounts by Dugdale of the houses of Salisbury and Devereux have been first combined, and two distinct families thus confused together.† And how did this important error arise?

Hen. I. (quoted by Dugdale as the 5 Stephen); *William d'Evereux*, whose widow gave lands to Gloucester Abbey, in or before the reign of Henry II.; *Eustace* in 5 John; *Stephen* in 15 John. To these may be added *Rogerus de Ebrois*, a Domesday subtenant in Norfolk; and from Ordericus Vitalis, the name of *Ricardus Ebroicensis filius Fulconis Præpositi*, mentioned under the year 1119. On the first application of surnames, large towns gave a distinctive appellation to several persons wholly unconnected with one another in blood,—to any man, in short, who left one of them to reside elsewhere, not having otherwise acquired a personal surname; and it would be as reasonable to suppose that all persons bearing the names of English cities, have descended from the Earls of those cities (for which supposition there is not the slightest ground), as to conclude that the family of Devereux were necessarily descended from the Counts of Evreux. The genealogists of the house of Devereux may concede this fact to the force of historical truth, without detracting at all from the high antiquity, and scarcely from the high nobility, of a name which is certainly one of the proudest in the annals of England.

* The latter was the descent asserted in the Claim of James Edward Devereux, of Carigmenan, co. Wexford, Esq. to the service of bearing the Golden Rod and Dove at the Coronation of King George the Fourth.

† The statement does not occur in the earlier editions of Collins, in which Dugdale is strictly followed; but it seems to have been inserted in the edition of 1779, and adopted from a MS. Baronage by Sir Henry St. George.

As it seems, from the original alteration of only a single letter! In the Book of Lacock, as quoted by Vincent, by Brooke, and in the Monasticon, Walter de Rosmar is called "Walterus *le* Ewrus," which was the old orthography for *Heureux*, an epithet of a similar nature to that of his grandson, Gerold le Gros, and others noticed in a previous page.* But in the English version of the family history given in the Baronage,† this name was accidentally altered to Walter *de* Ewrus ‡; and from this clerical or typographical error some overzealous magnifier of the family of the Earls of Essex (now Viscounts Hereford), converted le Ewrus, or le Heureux, into Devereux. Such, after a long, careful, and scrupulous investigation, is proved to be the sole origin of the surname of Devereux having been bestowed upon the early Earls of Salisbury.

Their actual surname, which had been assumed by Edward the Sheriff, was de Sarisburie, or Salis-

* His son's name, Mantelec, was probably from his peculiar *mantelet*, or cloak; see Ducange, v. *Mantelletum*. King Henry I. as is well known, was designated Court-Mantel.

† It was not, however, an original error of Dugdale, for the Salisbury family are styled "de Eureux" in Camden's Britannia and Brooke's Catalogue of the Peers, 1619; yet neither does Brooke confound "de Eureux" with Devereux. Under the title of Essex he does not enter upon the early lineage of the Devereuxs. Brooke, Vincent, and Dugdale, in their extracts from the Book of Lacock, all have *le* Ewrus.

‡ In the same way, in the Earls of Chester, Ranulph le Meschyn, or Ralph junior, (for, though he was the first Earl of the name, his father's name was Ranulph,) has been transformed into a surname, *de* Meschines.

bury. Their ancestral name, which was retained by the elder branch of the family, was Rosmar, Rolmar, Roumare, or Romara. These Earls of Rosmar, as they are styled in the Book of Lacock, were evidently the same (though no writer has hitherto noticed that fact), as the family of which, in another part of his Baronage, Dugdale has given an account under the name of Romare; and whose name occurs in the Chronicle of Ordericus Vitalis, under the forms of de Rolmara and de Roumare. The earldom which this house possessed was not an obscure fief in Normandy, as the heralds, when translating the Book of Lacock, seem to have supposed; but the chronicler of Lacock gave them the title of Comes, because one of them was an English Earl, and that of no less an earldom than Lincolnshire, where he built the Castle of Bolingbroke, afterwards a residence of the royal house of Lancaster, and the birth-place of King Henry the Fourth.

The discovery of this latent identity of the Earls of Rosmar and the family of Romare, is the more valuable, in our present inquiry, from the additional credit which it confers upon the statements of the Book of Lacock. We will therefore here introduce, for examination, the genealogy translated *verbatim* from that authority.*

"There was a strenuous Norman soldier, Walter the Fortunate, Earl of Rosmar, to whom, on ac-

* "Erat quidam miles strenuus Normannus, Walterus le Ewrus, Comes de Rosemar; qui propter probitatem suam

count of his prowess, King William gave the whole demesne of Salisbury and Ambresbury. Before this Walter le Ewrus came into England he was the father of Gerold Earl of Rosmar, Mantelec; who was the father of William de Rosmar le Gros; who was father of William de Rosmar le Meschyn, the second; who was father of the third William de Rosmar, who died without children. After (he came into England) Walter le Ewrus had Edward, by nation English-born, who was subsequently sheriff of Wiltes." And then, having traced down the pedigree to Ela the heiress, " who was given to William Longspé, son of King Henry the Second," it is added, " to whom King Richard restored the Earldom of Rosmar, as the inheritance and hereditary right of him and Ela, which had devolved upon

Rex Guillelmus Conq. dedit sibi totum dominium de Saresburia et Ambresburia. Antequam iste Walterus le Ewrus in Angliam venit, genuit Geroldum Comitem de Rosmar Mantelec; qui genuit Guillelmum de Rosmar le Gros; qui genuit Gulielmum de Rosmar le Meschyn secundum; qui genuit Gulielmum tertium de Rosmar, qui obiit sine liberis. Postquam Walterus le Ewrus genuit Edwardum, natione Anglicum natum, postea Vicecomitem Wiltes," &c.—" Elam, quæ data est domino Gulielmo de Longspee filio regis Henrici Secundi, cui dominus Rex Ricardus reddidit comitatum de Rosmar, sicut hæreditatem et jus hæreditarium suum, id est ipsius Elæ, quod sibi accessit et accidit de jure hæreditario Edwardi de Saresburia filii Walteri le Ewrous." Vincent's Discovery of Errors in Brooke, fol. 1622. In the Monasticon the words " Mantelec; qui genuit Gulielmum de Rosmar " were omitted, by which a descent in the pedigree was lost.

her from the right of heirship of Edward of Salisbury, son of Walter the Fortunate."

This pedigree of Rosmar obviously alludes to the same parties whom Dugdale has noticed (somewhat incorrectly, as will be shown hereafter,) under the head of Romare, viz.—Gerold,—William Earl of Lincoln,—William, who died in his father's life, and was therefore called Meschyn, a word synonymous with *junior*,—and William "the third,"* who died without children. That the family had any other claim to the title of Earl† except as the first William was Earl of Lincoln, is not apparent; for his son died in his father's life-time, and the grandson, though he enjoyed much of the Lincolnshire estates, never had the dignity of Earl. It is probable, however, that part of the remaining possessions of Romara may have been granted by King Richard, as the Lacock chronicler says, to

* This was the designation by which the last William de Roumare was distinguished in charters and law proceedings; as we find from a plea-roll temp. John, respecting the advowson of Hareby, co. Lincoln, noticed in the Placitorum Abbreviatio, p. 75.

† If Rosmar or Roumare had been an earldom in Normandy, it would have occurred in the Norman historians, which it does not; and Ordericus Vitalis always speaks of William de Rolmar or Roumare without any title. It is true that, about a century after the Conquest, we find a Hawise Countess of Roumare; but this was evidently the surname, as in numberless other instances, and it is even doubtful whether that lady's name was not Redmer or Redvers, instead of Roumare (see hereafter, p. 75).

the Earl of Salisbury; for we find that the same Earl (but some years after King Richard's death), was joint Sheriff of Lincolnshire during the years 1217 to 1222, though Ranulph III. Earl of Chester was the Earl of that county during the same period.*

For the remaining history of the house of Romara, the reader may be referred to the *Sheet Pedigree*, and to the remarks, at the end of this Chapter. But the name of William de Romara, afterwards Earl of Lincoln, will presently again occur as the companion of his uncle Edward of Salisbury, upon one very remarkable occasion.

It should, however, be premised before we proceed to the next generation, that of Walter de Rosmar, le Ewrus, alleged by the Book of Lacock to have been the father of Gerold and of Edward of Salisbury, and to have been rewarded by the Conqueror as one of his most faithful followers, no mention has been found in any other authority; and what is still more remarkable is this, that in the only account of the companions of the Con-

* This is not the place to enter into a discussion respecting the Earldom of Lincoln; but it may be briefly remarked that John de Laci was Earl of Lincoln 1232—1240, in right of his wife Hawise, *niece to the Earl of Chester;* that Edmond his son was never Earl of Lincoln, though he enjoyed the Third Penny of the County; but that Henry de Laci, the grandson, having married Margaret de Longespé, *daughter of the Earl of Salisbury,* and thus, as we may suppose, *united the claims of the two houses,* was the acknowledged Earl from 1257 to 1312.

queror which can be depended upon, Wace's Roman de Rou*, we do not find any Walter de Rosmar (nor any Walter Devereux); but we do find, among that brief but authentic catalogue, the name of *William de Romare*.

Et dam Guill. de Romare.†

To give an explanation of this circumstance, which would admit of proof, would scarcely be possible. A variety of conjectural hypotheses might be formed; but, laying aside for the moment the discrepancy of the Christian name, may not so much at least as this be regarded as evident,—that, whether his name was Walter, or William like his successors, the *same* person, so highly distinguished by the Conqueror, *propter probitatem*, was intended by both writers?

---

* The corrupted and interpolated state of the lists going under the name of the Roll of Battle Abbey, is well known, and they were reprobated so long since as the days of Camden. Besides, was that Roll more trust-worthy, yet, as it does not give christian names, it could not identify individuals.

† So quoted by Sir Henry Ellis in his Introduction to Domesday Book, p. xii. from a manuscript of Wace's Poem in one of the Royal MSS. Brit. Mus. The name of Devereux in any guise does not occur in the Poem; but the historians of the Counts of Evreux say, that Richard, the Count at the invasion of England, and William his son and successor, both fought at Hastings.

In the list of the Norman invaders given by Holinshed from " the Chronicles of Normandie by one William Tailleur," we find also William, not Walter,—" Guillaume de Roumare, seig. de Lithare."

With Edward of Salisbury, from whom the Foundress of Lacock derived her lineal descent, our first indubitable evidence commences; and his name remains still inscribed, not only in the Book of Lacock, but also in various parts of the national records. The earliest documents in which it occurs, and that certainly some years anterior to Domesday Book, are the charters granted by the Conqueror to the Abbey of Selby and by the Conqueror's Queen to that of Malmesbury. In the former his name occupies a very conspicuous situation among the witnesses. Of the whole King's Court then present in London, he is named second; that is, next after Odo Bishop of Baieux, the half-brother of the Conqueror.* The date of this charter, however, it is not easy to determine. Selby Abbey is said to have been founded in 1069; but, as the document in question is a confirmation and not a foundation charter, the only guide given by that date is, that the deed must have been executed at some time subsequent to it. Bishop Remigius, another of the witnesses, was not consecrated to the see of

* " Data carta hæc et confirmata apud Lundonias, in præsencia istorum, scilicet, Odonis Baiocensis Episcopi, EDWARDI DE SALESBIRIA, Hugonis de Portu, Hugonis de Monteforti, Roberti de Olley, Ricardi filii comitis Gilberti, Baldwini fratris ejus, Remigii episcopi, Radulphi Talebois, Roberti de Tany, Gaufridi de la Wirchi, et totius curiæ Regis,"—Monasticon, 1655, vol. I. p. 371.

Dorchester (which he afterwards removed to Lincoln) until the year 1070; this (as far as our present information extends) is our earliest limit, and the latest is the year 1082, when Bishop Odo was disgraced.* If we approach this latest verge, which is nearly the same as that of the Malmesbury charter, which has a date, namely, 1081,—these documents (the latter of which is five years anterior to Domesday Book) appear to throw a degree of doubt upon the statement of the Lacock historian, that Edward was born after the Conquest, "natione Anglicus;" as, if so, he was placed as a witness to important charters before he was fifteen years old. However, it is clear that he must have been a youth, at most, at the Conquest, and but little advanced in manhood when he witnessed the Malmesbury charter; for we shall find him a valiant and active warrior at so late a period as 1120.

There can be no doubt that the "Signum Edwardi Vicecomitis," attached to the Malmesbury charter, was that of Edward of Salisbury. His name is here the last, but it is the last of a very illustrious list. †

* Vincent, however, on what grounds it does not appear, places the Selby charter in 21 Will. Conq. Second Discovery, p. 79.

† The King, Queen Matilda, Archbishop Lanfranc, Bishop Odo, Bishop Remigius, Osmund Bishop of Sarum, Godfrey Bishop of Constance, Walchelin Bishop of Winchester, Walter Abbat of Evesham, Robert the Earl, Baldwin the Sheriff, and EDWARD THE SHERIFF.

He was also a witness to a charter of the Conqueror to the Priory of Lewes, under the same title of " Edwardus Vicecomes." The date of this cannot be earlier than 1080, when William de Kairlipho became Bishop of Durham.*

The next document in which the name of Edward of Salisbury has been found, is the great national record called Domesday Book, in which he appears so largely endowed with lands and possessions that it is very evident that he (and probably with the Book of Lacock we may add his father, whether Walter or William,) was a person highly in favour with the Norman Conqueror.

At the same period the elder branch of the house of Romara was by no means so richly endowed with landed possessions in England. Yvo Tailbois, the first husband of the rich Saxon heiress Lucy, was living at the period of the Survey, and his name appears, though not as Earl of Lincoln (for there seems to have been no Earl at that time), yet as lord of Bolingbroke, and of a long list of manors.† Yvo died in 1104, and the Countess Lucia his

---

* Signatures: S. Willielmi regis. S. Will. fil. regis. S. Hamrici filii regis. S. Will. de Warenna. S. .... ingard nep. S. Osmundi ep. S. Wauchelini ep. S. Remigii ep. S. . . . . . . S. Willelmi ep. Dunelm. S. Hamrici. S. Michael de Tona. S. Walteri.... S. E. Vicecom. S. Milonis Crispini. S. . . . .

† Dugdale (Baronage, vol. i. p. 33,) styles Yvo Tailbois Count of Anjou, but see hereafter, p. 69.

widow was immediately re-married to Roger de Romara, the younger nephew of Edward of Salisbury. These events are thus recorded by Peter of Blois, the continuator of the history of Ingulphus of Croyland. " Yvo having died of paralysis, his wife, with moderate lamentations, but with the great joy of all the neighbourhood (for Yvo had been exceedingly oppressive to his vassals, and an especial enemy of the monks of Croyland), buried him in the Priory of Spalding. And when scarcely one month was elapsed after his death, being married to an illustrious youth, Roger de Romara, son of Gerold de Romara, and being much honoured by her husband's elder brother, William de Romara, Earl of Lincoln, she entirely forgot all remembrance of Yvo Tailbois. Their only daughter,* who had been nobly espoused, had indeed died before her father; for that evil shoots should not fix deep roots in the world, the accursed lineage of that wicked man perished by the axe of the Almighty, which cut off all his issue.†"

* It is remarkable that we find in the Register of Cockersand Abbey, an Ivo Tail*bot*, father of Elthredus, and ancestor of the family of Lancaster, Barons of Kendal (Monasticon, vol. II. p. 636); him Dugdale (Baronage, p. 421) identifies with Ivo Tail*boys*, who gave land to St. Mary's Abbey, York.

† The chronicler then pursues a bitter strain of invective which is too curious to be omitted, but would be spoiled by translation: " Quid ergo tibi jam prodest, in Christi servos et omnes tuos convicinos, O Yvo semper sævissime, sic contra

Of Roger de Romara we hear nothing further after his marriage. It seems probable that he died young, leaving his son William an infant, and the Countess Lucy was then married, for the third time, to the first Ralph Earl of Chester.

The years 1118 and 1119 are the first fixed periods at which we meet with William de Romara, evidently the uncle,* and at the same time with the last notice of EDWARD OF SALISBURY. King Henry had to contend, during those years, with an obstinate rebellion in Normandy, headed by Hugh de Gorney; in which William de Romara, then Governor of Newmarch, had at first been the sole upholder of the royal authority.† At length, in the year 1119, the King, in person, put an end to the rebellion at the decisive battle of Brennevill; in

Dominum surrexisse? In terram lapsus es connumeratus cum mortuis, in puncto ad inferos descendisti, successor, veteris Adæ, testa fragilis, glomum cineris, lutum fictile, pellis morticina, vas putredinis, fomes tinearum, cibus vermium, derisio superstitum, abjectio supernorum, servorum Dei sicut quondam publicus hostis, sic a cœtu sanctorum, sicut verisimiliter supponitur, exul et extorris, ac tenebris exterioribus tuis innumeris demeritis deputandus."—Rerum Anglicarum Scriptorum Veterum, fol. 1684, p. 125.

* The nephew could not then have been more than thirteen, and so could not possibly have been an active commander for the King, as Dugdale has made him. This alone would prove that there was such a person as William the uncle.

† "Solus Guillelmus de Rolmara Novimercati municeps, et commanipulares ejus illis obstabant." Ordericus Vitalis.

which Edward of Salisbury, though then undoubtedly advanced in age, was the royal standard-bearer, " a brave warrior (says the chronicler), whose valour was, from experience, well known, and his constancy of heart persevering to the last." *

This was therefore, in all probability, the final scene of Edward's active warfare. On his way home he evinced as remarkable a proof of prudence as he had lately shown of his valour. It was on the voyage back to England from this expedition that the King's two sons and Richard Earl of Chester, with a large number of courtiers, were lost by shipwreck. Edward of Salisbury and his nephew William de Rolmara were among those who had left the vessel before it sailed, " because they perceived it was filled with too great a multitude of wanton and arrogant youth.†"

Such are the last interesting notices of the life of Edward of Salisbury, the first English ancestor of the Foundress of Lacock. The date of his death is unknown. His wife was apparently a daughter of

* " Edwardus de Salisburia ibi portavit vexillum, fortis agonista, cujus robur erat probatione notissimum, et constantia perseverans, usque ad exitium." Ordericus Vitalis.

† " Duo siquidem monachi Tyronis et Stephanus Comes [the Earl of Morton, afterwards King Stephen] cum duobus militibus; Guillelmus quoque de Rolmara, et Rabellus camerarius, Eduardus de Salesburia, et alii plures inde exierunt, quia nimiam multitudinem lascivæ et pompaticæ juventutis inesse conspicati sunt." Ordericus Vitalis.

Roger de Reimes, or de Ramis,* who was a Domesday tenant in capite, in Essex, Middlesex, Norfolk, and Suffolk, and the head of whose barony was at the place now called Rayne, in the first named county. It would seem also, that Edward's widow was married to Payne, son of William de Hocton.† Matilda, one of Edward's daughters, was given in marriage, with several manors, to the second Humphrey de Bohun, surnamed the Great, steward of the household to King William Rufus, the son of Humphrey *cum Barba*, a kinsman of the Conqueror.‡ Another daughter, Leonia, was the wife

* " Uxor Roberti de Stuteville est de donatione Domini Regis, et de parentela Edwardi de Salisburia ex parte patris, et ex parte matris est de progenie Rogeri de Reimes." (Rotuli de Dominabus, &c. 31 Hen. II. 1185, edited by Stacey Grimaldi, F.S.A. 4to. 1830, p. 38.) In a charter of the Abbey of Welbeck (Monasticon, vol. II. p. 602.) Henry de Stuteville confirms a gift of his mother Leonia de Reynes.

† In the Pipe Roll, 31 Hen. I. (heretofore called 5 Steph.) in p. 81 of the edition printed by the Commissioners of Public Records, 8vo. 1833, are these two entries; first, William de Hoctona renders accompt of 200*l.* for the wife of Edward Sar'. with the land, to the benefit [opus] of Payne, his son; again, Paganus de Hoctona renders accompt of 200 marks of silver and 2 marks of gold for the wife of Edward Sar'.

‡ " Dominus Hunfredus de Bohun, *cum barba*, qui primò venit cum Willielmo Conquestore in Angliam de Normannia, cognatus dicti Conquestoris, genuit Dominum Hunfredum de Bohun secundum. Qui fuit vocatus Hunfredus Magnus; qui, per voluntatem et præceptum Willielmi Rous, filii dicti Con-

of Robert de Stutevill, and by him the mother of the wife of Robert de Bretteville.*

I may here remark that it was the same Humphrey de Bohun, styled the Great, and the husband

questoris, desponsavit Matildem filiam Edwardi de Salesbury; cum qua Matilda pater suus donavit dicto Hunfredo in liberum maritagium, omnia terras et tenementa sua quæ fuerunt ex perquisitione dicti Edwardi; viz. Weston juxta Salesbury, et Walton, Newenton, Piryton, Stauntone, Trobrege, et unum messuagium in Salesbury juxta portam orientalem, et advocationem ecclesiæ S. Crucis quæ est fundata supra portam antedictam, unà cum uno prato extra Salesbury. Et Weston prædicta postea fuit data in escambium pro Wynelesford et Manyngford; et omnia alia terræ et tenementa quæ fuerunt de hæreditate dicti Edwardi remanebant filio suo et hæredi, vocato Waltero Salesbury."—Ex Cronicis Abb. de Lanthoni, Dugdale's Monasticon, vol. II. p. 67.

* See the Rotulus de Dominabus, quoted in a preceding note; and the following entry from the Placitorum Abbreviatio, p. 41, " Rob'tus de Bretevill dicit q'd Edwardus de Salebir' qui *frater primogenit'* fuit ejusdem Graelent [Gradelent de Taneie], habuit filiam quandam Leoniam nomine quam Rob'tus de Stutevill desponsavit et implacitavit eundem Graelent in cur' D'ni Reg' Henr' et v'sus eum t'ram de Guneby recuperavit, et dedit eidem Rob'to medietatem t're illius pro servicio suo et medietatem in maritagium." The words " frater primogenitus" probably signify that Edward of Salisbury's *wife* Leonia was the *elder sister* of the *wife* of Gradelent de Tany. Alizia de Tany, said to be " de progenie Rogeri de Reimes," was living a widow in 1185, with five sons, of whom the heir was twenty years of age (that was to say, beyond his minority, and probably considerably more) and two daughters. (Rotuli de Dominabus, &c. p. 38).

of Matilda de Salisbury, who founded the priory of Farley in this county. This took place in the year 1125, according to the Register of Lewes Abbey. Dugdale, in his Baronage, though he was aware of that date, inadvertently ascribed the foundation to the third Humphrey de Bohun and Margaret his wife; but the authority in the Monasticon, from which he quoted, is not the foundation, but a confirmation, charter. The error was noticed, and corrected, by Tanner; who remarked that the third Humphrey "did not die until 1187, and was not likely to found this priory sixty-two years before." In corroboration of this corrected statement, I will notice another circumstance. "Matilda de Bohun," the wife of the second Humphrey, and the daughter of Edward of Salisbury, is mentioned in the same charter as having been a benefactress; which alone shows that the Priory was founded in *her* lifetime; and it is remarkable that, of the lands which she had brought her husband in dower, we find several named among the endowments of the monastery of Farley.*

* — "ecclesiam de Wivelisford .... decem solidos de ecclesia de Troubrig.... medietatem ecclesiæ de Waletona quæ ad nostrum feodum pertinet, et decimam dominii de Stanertona." See all these places mentioned in the note in the preceding page. " Et donamus eis similiter ecclesiam de Bissopestreu cum omnibus quæ ad ecclesiam pertinent, et unam hidam terræ in eadem villa *de dono Matildis de Bohun*, et pasturam

From an anxious consideration of all the circumstances of minute concurrent historical facts, we cannot but admit the general veracity of the Book of Lacock; and without having first endeavoured to throw all the light in our power on this material point, it would be useless to proceed, at least so far as Ela's early romantic history is concerned.

Having now said all which I have deemed it right to say on these obscure questions of genealogy,* I shall only detain the reader a few moments longer to mention one remarkable circumstance in addition to what has been already stated. It will be remembered that the first of this family who came with the invading army to Britain, bore the name of Walterus *le* Ewrus; and that his son Edward of Salisbury, when in early youth, was a witness to the Conqueror's charter to Selby Abbey.

---

ad centum oves et ad carucatam boum in eadem villa." Now " Biscopestreu" is described in Domesday Book among the lands of Edward of Salisbury, and the manor of Bishopstrow was one of those with which his descendant Ela endowed the nunnery of Lacock; but this hide of land, with the advowson of the church, had evidently been given by Edward to his daughter Matilda de Bohun, and she bestowed them upon the priory of Farley. They continued to belong to that house until the dissolution, at which period the annual rent of the land was 1*l.* 13*s.* 4*d.*; and the Prior down to the same period presented to the rectory. See Hoare's Hundred of Warminster.

* For the foregoing elaborate investigation I am indebted entirely to Mr. J. G. Nichols.

That abbey was founded when William, stung to madness by the massacre of his faithful Normans, made a vow to avenge their loss, and to leave the country, from the Ouse to the Tyne, from York to Durham, desolate. I will now request the reader's attention to a very singular circumstance. In the great cemetery of the abbey of Tynemouth, in which were interred the bodies of the most illustrious persons of the period of which we are treating, particularly of those slain in the fatal conflicts of that country, has been found a coffin with this remarkable inscription :

WALTERUS CELARIUS

which is of an exactly similar form to another coffin at Durham, which bears the name of GOSPATRICUS COMES,* of the same age. Thus, may we not, without any great stretch of fancy, suppose the former to be the tomb of one of William's most confidential warriors, who had fallen a sacrifice in that fatal insurrection which led to the votive foundation of Selby Abbey? The person commemorated surely could not be the obscure cellarer of a convent, so buried among the princes and kings

* I have been favoured with these inscriptions by my friend the Rev. John Skinner, F.S.A. of Camerton, Somerset, who first observed and took a drawing of the coffin, on which appeared nominis umbra (distinct to this day) WALTERUS CELARIUS.

of that royal cemetery, with a tomb exactly resembling the renowned Gospatrick's. Those who fell in this terrific and disastrous warfare, as Malcolm King of Scots and his son, slain 1071, were buried at Tynemouth. From his name, Walterus, he must have been a Norman—a most distinguished Norman; and probably, from the place of burial, among the illustrious slain. Might we not therefore be further allowed to suppose him the Cellarer of the King, if not *ipse Walterus strenuus*, surnamed *le* EWRUS? Butlerus is Norman latin for the *Butler*. Might not le Ewrus, or Cellarius, after all, denote a regal officer connected with the Ewrie or cellar? for the word Ewrus is invariably spelt with a w, not u.

It is true that this is all conjecture; but the circumstances are so remarkable, as connected with the Conqueror's revenge, and Edward of Salisbury's signature to the charter of Selby, in extreme youth, that I was unwilling that any circumstance, although of shadowy possibility, should be omitted, which might serve to illustrate the only record we possess of the history of the extraction, Norman parentage, and early years of the pious and celebrated foundress of Lacock Nunnery.

I shall now conclude the disquisition with a brief description of the scene and seat which the Conqueror bestowed upon his faithful follower at Sarisburie.

In looking at the now silent, sad, and vacant mound, on which stood a city once so distinguished, we might say, in the words of Ossian,

"Desolate is the dwelling of Edward!"

The vast mound, strewed with the relics of ancient years, rising over the wide extent of downs, which are seen spreading below as far as the eye can reach, was originally, like the knoll at Glastonbury, one of those elevated pyramidal hills peculiarly sacred to the Sun, in the Druidical worship.

This singular and solitary eminence I have suggested elsewhere * to have been the Hill of the *Sun*, connected with the "round temple," in which Diodorus Siculus, quoting Hecateus, says, "the praises of Apollo were sung night and day;" and I have presumed that Stonehenge, at least the inner circle of granite †, being the original temple,

---

* Hills of the shape of barrows, were sacred to Mercury, the Egyptian God of the Dead and the Resurrection. Hence the immense barrow at Avebury, "Mercurii tumulus." (Pliny.) See my History of Bremhill.

† The Monkish tradition is, that the stones at Stonehenge were brought from Africa to Kildare, in Ireland; from thence transported by the magic of Merlin. Might not this wizard of romance have been a traditionary personage derived from the Druidical Ma*rus*, who always accompanied the Phœnician ships? It is evident to me that the original temple consisted only of the smaller circles of *granite* (See Mr. Conybeare's Essay in the Gentleman's Magazine for November 1833, in corroboration of this previous remark of my own); the vast outward trigliphs, it has been suggested by my friend Warner,

this majestic mound, still preserving the traces of the early English name, "Solis," might be the Hill of the Bards, according to Diodorus.*

It was afterwards the chief military Roman post and seat of dominion in Western Britain; and from Cæsar it probably derived its subsequent name.†

were the work of the Belgic Britons, when they possessed this part of the country. They also worshipped the *Sun* and Fire, Solem et Vulcanum. The greater temple at Avebury I have considered the temple to the greater Celtic Deity Teut, from Thoth, the Mercury of the Latins and Hermes of the Greeks. Cæsar says, that "the Celts, as their chief Deity, worship Mercury, of whom there are many *simulacra*—structures of stone; and that *after* him, they worship Apollo." Hermes Britannicus.

* See Davies's Celtic Researches.

† Sarisburie and Sarum, from Cæsar and Cæsarum (Cæ-Saris, Cæ-Sarum), the first syllable being dropt, as Saragossa, Cæsaris-Augusta, &c. Salisbury may be from Solisbury; so Salisbury Crag, Edinburgh—Hills dedicated to the *Sun*—Salisbury Hill, Bath, from Aqua-Solis, called Aqua Sulis by the Romans, in compliment to the Britons. In some Latin verses on the death of Bishop Jewel, by George Coryat, the father of celebrated Thomas the Odcombian Traveller, I find precisely the same idea of the origin of Sarum, from Cæsarum; and indeed we know Fundus Cæsaris was an ancient name of this illustrious city,

> Julius Austriacus Cæsar cum vicerat Anglum,
>   Fertur ad occiduas castra locasse plagas,
> Et fundasse *suo de nomine Cæsaris urbem*
>   Sive Sarisburiam—*Cæsariam* ve voces.

That the idea was therefore formerly entertained there can be no doubt, and it seems to me most plausible, though it has been given up.

Masses of Roman masonry may still be visibly recognised amidst the scattered fragments; its original pyramidal point being in part levelled to form successively a seat of military command, or the basis of this singular city in the clouds.

About one hundred and forty years after the foundation of its new city, its last lingering inhabitants descended to the vale below, where the new cathedral rose in its beauty, to which the bones of its early prelates had been conveyed. The first of the *living*, buried in this new cathedral, was the heroic husband of the descendant of Edward of Sarisburie; and the tomb, as we have described it, yet appears of him who laid, at the foundation, the fourth stone. That the latter city and its *beautiful cathedral* may stand with better auspices than the former, ever will be our prayer, in casting a look on " the desolate dwelling of Edward."

This Chapter is concluded with the following lines, on this deserted seat of the first Earls of Salisbury, with its now perished cathedral; and on the living children gathering flowers in the churchyard of the new cathedral.

CATHEDRAL AT OLD SARUM.

Here stood the City of the Dead; look round,
  Dost thou not mark a visionary band,
  Druids and Bards, upon the summit stand
Of the majestic and time-hallow'd mound?

Hark! heard ye not, at times, the acclaiming sound
   Of harps, as when those Bards, in white array,
   Hail'd the ascending Lord of Light and Day?
No! all is hush'd in solitude profound!

Here, o'er the clouds the first Cathedral rose,
Whose Prelates now in yonder fane repose
   Among the mighty of years pass'd away—
For there her latest seat Religion chose;
   There, still to Heaven ascends the holy lay,
And never may those shrines in dust and silence close!

CHILDREN GATHERING FLOWERS IN THE CATHEDRAL CHURCHYARD OF NEW SARUM.

When summer comes, the little children play,
In the churchyard of our Cathedral gray,
Busy as morning bees, and gathering flowers,
In the brief sunshine. They, of coming hours
Reck not, intent upon their play, tho' TIME
Speeds, like a spectre, by them, and their prime
Bears on to sorrow.
          "ANGEL, CRY ALOUD!"
Tell them of life's long winter—of the shroud!—
No! let them play—for Age, alas! and Care,
Too soon will frown to teach them what they are.

Then, let them play; but COME, with aspect bland,
COME, CHARITY, and lead them by the hand;
Come, FAITH, and shew, amid life's saddest gloom,
A light from Heaven, that shines beyond the tomb.

When they look up, and, high in air, admire
The lessening shaft of that aërial spire,
So be their thoughts uplifted from the sod,
Where Time's brief flowers they gather—TO THEIR GOD.

April 1834.   W. L. B.

PEDIGREE II.

THE HOUSE OF ROMARA.

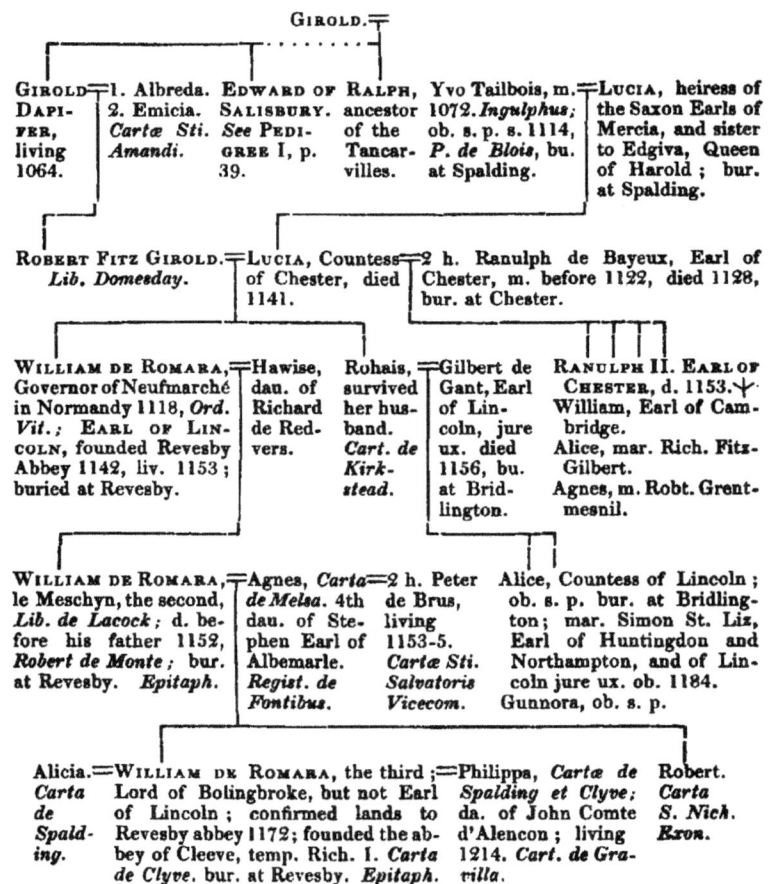

ILLUSTRATIONS OF THE PEDIGREE OF ROMARA.

SINCE the notices of the Family of Romara in the preceding Chapter were printed, we have been favoured with some very important communications by Thomas Stapleton, Esq. F.S.A. who has made the genealogies of Normandy his particular study: and the extracts he has obligingly supplied from authentic charters, will throw material light on this obscure subject, at the same time that they will show how little dependence can be placed on the accuracy of the monkish chronicles, from which our previous information has in great measure been derived.

The Chronicle of Ingulphus of Croyland, and his continuator Peter of Blois (from which the extract has been made in p. 52) is certainly in many parts apocryphal, a character which has been fully ascertained by Mr. Petrie, and Sir F. Palgrave. In the present case the monk makes Yvo de Tailboys die in 1114 (not 1104, as misprinted in p. 51) and to have been the first husband of Lucia, afterwards Countess of Chester; and yet there is contemporary evidence to show that William de Romara, her son by the person stated to have been her second husband, was of age in 1122; as he then claimed his inheritance. It appears probable (for reasons which will be stated hereafter) that the Countess Lucia was the daughter of Tailboys, instead of his wife; and that Roger son of Gerold, who is stated by Ordericus Vitalis to have been the first husband of Lucia, was the same person with the "Robertus filius Geroldi,"* the possessor of

---

* The difference is so small between Rotbertus and Rotgerus, that it cannot destroy the identity of persons, when supported by strong circumstantial evidence of tenure and descent. In the same manner Radulphus and Ranulphus were used indifferently, Osbernus and Osbertus, Edwardus and Evrardus.

Corfe Castle at the time of the Domesday survey. Above all, the story so circumstantially related, and so highly wrought by the eloquent Peter of Blois, proves to be wholly at variance with ascertained genealogical facts.

Again, there seems to be no foundation for the *Walter le Ewrus* of the Book of Lacock; the name has been fabricated from that of his grandson, Walter of Sarisbury.

Thirdly, the William de Romara of the poet Wace is also a fictitious personage, having a similar origin. Wace thought only of the heads of those Norman houses who were his own contemporaries, quite heedless of anachronism, and attentive only to his rhymes. Hence he set down the name of William in his couplet—

> E dam Guill. de Romare,
> E li sire de Litehare.

and these were two *distinct* personages—not one, as Holinshed made them, by dropping the conjunction " E ". The lord of Lithare was Eudo cum Capello, the Eudo Dapifer of Domesday.

As it is believed that the pedigree of Romara has always hitherto been stated both imperfectly and inaccurately, a few pages shall here be devoted to its illustration. In order to correct the previous accounts, it will first be necessary to quote the genealogy given in Dugdale's Baronage, which is as follows:—

Gerold de Romara.

Roger de Romara.=Lucia, dau. of Algar Earl of Chester, and widow of Yvo Tailboys.=Ranulph de Bricasard, Earl of Chester.

William de Romara, Earl of Lincoln.=Maud, dau. of Richard de Redvers.   Ranulph Earl of Chester.

William, ob. v. p. 1152.=Hawise, dau. of Stephen Earl of Albemarle.

William de Romara the third.

ILLUSTRATIONS OF THE PEDIGREE OF ROMARA.

It is remarkable that Milles, in his Catalogue of Honour, 1610, was correct in his statement of the wives of the two Williams, calling the first " Avis, daughter of Richard de Ripariis," and the second " the daughter of Stephen Earl of Albemarle."

But Brooke, adopting from Ordericus Vitalis the name of *Matilda* de Ripariis, unadvisedly transferred the name of Hawise to the daughter of the Earl of Albemarle (whose name happened to be vacant) ; having thus at once adopted one error, and perpetrated another, his next step was equally unfortunate ; for, still finding that the name of the Countess of Lincoln was certainly Hawise, he transferred the daughter of the Earl of Albemarle to that situation ; and then, losing sight of the statement of the Chronicler with which he started, that the husband of the supposed Matilda was the Countess Lucia's *son*, he bestowed " Maud de Rivers " upon her grandson, the second William, at the same time committing the further blunder of substituting the name of *Baldwin* Rivers as her father, instead of Richard.

Such is the extraordinary labyrinth of error in which Ralph Brooke involved this pedigree; and which neither Vincent nor Dugdale, nor any subsequent writer, has hitherto unravelled. It is a performance in which Vincent would have rejoiced to have found the arrogant " Master Yorke" entangled, and would, we may be sure, have submitted him without mercy to the torture ; but it is remarkable that this pedigree was passed entirely unnoticed by that acute and severe critic. Dugdale, partly perceiving Brooke's error, again transposed the ladies ; but this time the Christian names accompanied them, and consequently Dugdale has both names wrong, though he rectified the parentage.

Such being the state in which the pedigree has been handed down to us, it may not be unacceptable to detail the several evidences belonging to the family of Romara,—the kinsmen of the house of Sarisbury,—on which the pedigree here inserted has been formed.

ROUMARE, the place from which the name was derived, is a vill not far distant from Rouen, and gives name to the forest of Roumare. The church of this place was granted to the abbey of St. Amand in that city, by the same GEROLD who is mentioned in the Book of Lacock as the elder brother of Edward of Salisbury: but the title of "Comes," which is there ascribed to him, is entirely unsupported, and indeed disproved, by the evidence of his charters.

The following was copied by Mr. Stapleton from the original cartulary in the archives of Rouen. It has been printed, with some unimportant variations, in Pommeraye's Histoire de l'Abbaye de Saint Amand de Rouen, fol. 1662.

"In nomine, &c. Ego, *Geroudus*, miles Xp'i, omnibus notum facio quod concessione *Roberti filii mei et heredis mei* concessi et dedi pro salute anime mee et *Alberede uxoris mee*, quæ xii kl. Junii obiit, s'c'imonialibus s'c'i Amandi Roth'i, ecclesiam de *Romara*, &c. Inde sunt testes Maurilius archiep'us Rothom., Michael Abrincen. ep'us, Reinerius abbas s'c'e Trinitatis, *Radulphus frater Geroudi*, Hugo Broc, Osbertus de Novoforo,* Hugo filius Baudrici, Rogerus de Montegumerico, Robertus de Camera, et alii."

Another charter, to the same abbey, also conveying the church of Rolmare, &c. commences thus: "Ego Geroldus miles Christi, *in presentia Willielmi Regis Anglorum*, et eodem annuente, pro salute anime mee et Emiciæ uxoris mee," &c. (Dugdale's Monasticon, ii. 997). Dom Pommeraye gives the same, but without the mention of Emicia. To both these charters M. Pommeraye attributes the date 1067.

The Robert named in the first charter as the son and heir of Gerold, occurs in Domesday Book as a tenant in capite in the counties of Hants, Berks, Wilts, Dorset, and Somerset, by the name of ROBERTUS FILIUS GIROLDI. It is worthy of remark, that in Hampshire his name immediately follows that of Edward of Salisbury, and in Dorsetshire immediately precedes it.

* i. e. Neufmarché (see p. 69).

Robert Fitz Gerold is one of the witnesses to the Conqueror's charter to the church of Durham, dated at London in 1082.

There are strong grounds for supposing that RALPH, THE BROTHER OF GEROLD, one of the witnesses to the preceding charter of St. Amand, was the same as Ralph, the founder of the abbey of Bocherville, and ancestor of the Tancarvilles, Chamberlains of Normandy.* If such be the fact, then the name of Gerold de Romara's father was the same as his own; for Ralph names *Gerold* as his father in the Bocherville foundation charter. There seems, indeed, no sufficient reason for imagining that the " Walter le Ewrus, Comes de Rosmar," of the Book of Lacock, is any other than a fictitious personage.

Besides Roumare, Gerold was also lord of one-half of Neufmarché. Ordericus Vitalis, under the year 1064, gives an account of the circumstances under which Duke William disinherited Turketil, lord of Neufmarché, and gave it in moieties to Hugh de Grandmesnil, and GEROLD THE DAPIFER. In the charter granted by Duke William (and therefore before 1066) to the Abbey of Bocherville, occur the attestations of Geroldus Dapifer, and Robertus filius ejus—which Robert, by the St. Amand charter already cited, is proved to have been his heir.

William de Romara first appears in 1118 as the castellan of Neufmarché, "Novimercati municeps," and his services to King Henry at that time have been already noticed in p. 53. He evidently possessed this place † in right of his descent from Gerold, and consequently must have been heir to Robert. He was, in fact, the son of this Robert or Roger Fitzgerald, and of Lucia, who became by a second marriage Countess of Chester.

It will here be necessary to say a few words respecting this

---

* Dugdale, in his Baronage, vol. i. p. 411, has given an account of the family of Fitz Gerold, the successors, as he says, of Robert Fitz Gerold: but the descent is not made out; though there seems some apparent connection with the Tancarvilles, in the circumstance that Warine Fitz Gerold was *Chamberlain* and Treasurer to King Henry II.

† "Will'mus de Romara, 14 milites in Romeis apud Novum Mercatum, et si Dux mandaverit eum alibi, ibit cum tribus militibus, vel mil. 4." Liber Rub. Scacc. Hen. II.

70 ILLUSTRATIONS OF THE PEDIGREE OF ROMARA.

Lucia, and of Lucia the wife of Yvo Tailbois, with whom she has hitherto been identified.

The monkish historians* state that Lucia, the daughter of Algar, son of Leofric Earl of Leicester, and sister to the Earls Edwin and Morcar, as also to Edgiva the Queen of Harold, was married to Yvo Tailboys, whom, without just authority, they style Comte of Anjou. The fact of this marriage there seems no reason to doubt. "In the year 1085,"† says the cartulary of Spalding, "Ivo Tailboys gave to the church of St. Nicholas of Angers, the church in his town of Spalding, with a carucate of land, and the oxen, and all things appertaining to the church, for the rest of the souls of King William and Queen Matilda his wife, and for his own, and *his wife Lucy*, and of the ancestors of Torald, that is, those of his wife." This Torald, who had been the Saxon lord of Spalding, and sheriff of Lincolnshire, was brother to the Countess Godiva, wife of Earl Leofric, and consequently great-uncle to Lucia. The date of Yvo Tailboys' death is placed in the year 1114, by Peter de Blois, as already mentioned; which may be correct, if we conclude that Lucia Countess of Chester was his daughter, and not his wife.

And this it will not be difficult to show by a little comparison of dates and circumstances. Lucia, the daughter of Earl Algar, is stated by Ingulphus to have been married to Yvo Tailboys, so early as 1072; Yvo is stated by the same party (that is, by Peter de Blois, the continuator of the Croyland chronicle) to have lived until 1114, forty-two years after; and yet this same Lucy is made afterwards to marry, secondly, Roger de Romara, and not only to have a son by him (old enough, be it remarked, to assert his rights in 1122) but also to marry, thirdly, Ranulph Earl of Chester, and to have four more

---

* Ingulphus; Annales de Peterborough, Monasticon, vol. i. p. 306; Registrum de Spalding; and Genealogia Fundatorum de Coventry, ibid. p. 304.

† The Annals of Peterborough name the year 1074 as the date when Ivo de Tailboys made Spalding a cell to the Abbey of St. Nicholas at Angers.

children. This plain review of dates, chiefly taken from the Croyland chroniclers themselves, shows that this story of one Lucia and her three marriages, all fruitful, and the last the most so, at a time when she must have become advanced in years, is physically impossible.

There can therefore be little doubt that there were two Lucias, the second the daughter of the first; whilst the monk Peter's account of the brief widowhood of his single Lucy, and her "*moderate lamentations,*" which has been quoted in p. 52, must fall to the ground between the two, as historical, or rather poetical, embellishment; together with his statement that "she was much honoured by her husband's elder brother, William Earl of Lincoln," which is equally imaginary, as there was no such Earl until after her own death, twenty-seven years after the alleged period of her marriage. It is, however, remarkable that the same writer speaks of "an only daughter, nobly espoused," but whom he could not more particularly describe. That only daughter was evidently the Countess Lucia herself; and therefore it was that no other name had ever reached him.

This Lucia, "only daughter" of Yvo Tailboys and the Saxon heiress, was married, first to Robert Fitz Gerold de Roumare, already noticed, and by him had issue William de Romara, afterwards Earl of Lincoln. After Robert's death she was married, secondly, to Ranulph de Briquesard, also called le Meschin, Vicomte du Bessin, who in 1120 became Earl of Chester, and by him had issue, Ranulph II. Earl of Chester, surnamed Gernons[*]; another son, William, who is said to have been created Earl of Cambridge in 1153; and two daughters, Alice, married to Richard Fitz Gilbert, ancestor of the Earls of Clare; and Agnes, married to Robert de Greatmesnil, son of Hugh de Grentemesnil[†], sheriff of Leicestershire. Earl Ranulph, the husband of Lucia, died in 1128, and was buried at Chester; Lucia survived, and in the Pipe Roll of 31 Henry I. her name occurs as owing 100 marks of silver to the King, that

---

[*] From his moustaches; not, as some say, from the castle of his nativity.
[†] Ordericus Vitalis, lib. viii.

she should not take a husband within five years.* She confirmed the manor of Spalding to the monks; and is said to have been buried in the church of that priory,† unless we should rather ascribe that circumstance to the former Lucy, whose husband, Yvo Tailboys, had been previously interred at Spalding. The death of the Countess of Chester is placed in 1148.

We shall now proceed to trace the history of WILLIAM DE ROMARA, EARL OF LINCOLN. It was not long after the period when he had rendered such efficient services to King Henry I., in the suppression of the Norman rebellion, that he was himself instigated, by a sense of injustice, to throw off his allegiance. After the death of Richard the youthful Earl of Chester, who was lost with the King's sons in the fatal shipwreck in 1120, already alluded to in p. 54, that Earldom was granted to Ranulph de Bayeux, the nephew of the preceding Earl, Hugh, and the step-father of William de Romara. In exchange for the Earldom, if we may credit Ordericus Vitalis, Ranulph surrendered to the King a considerable part of the inheritance of his wife Lucy; thus sacrificing to his own aggrandizement the interests of the young heir of Romara: whereupon, says Orderic, "William de Romara demanded of the King the return of his mother's land, and also of another possession in England called Corfe; ‡ but the King did not

---

* "Ne capiat virum infra v. annos." She also accounted for £266. 13s. 4d. for *her father's land*; and for 45 marks to be given to whom the King pleased, of which the Queen had 20; and she owed 100 marks that she might have the privilege of administering justice in her court among her vassals.—Pipe Roll, 31 Hen. I. 8vo. 1833, p. 110.

† Genealogy of the Saxon Earls in Mon. Ang. i. 504.

‡ "Cormam" in the printed copies of Ordericus Vitalis; but it is "Corviam" in the original MS. preserved in the library of Alençon. The amended reading (for which also we are indebted to Mr. Stapleton) furnishes at once a corroboration of the descent of William de Romara from Robert Fitz Girold, and a correction of considerable importance to the history of Dorsetshire. At the Domesday survey Robert Fitz Girold held "CORF." Hutchins, the historian of the county, supposed

comply with his demand, and besides answered him with reproaches." On this the youth, much enraged, went immediately over to Normandy, and placing himself in the castle of Neufmarché, where he had previously so successfully maintained the King's interests, he eagerly renewed the flame of rebellion on behalf of the King's nephew William, son of Duke Robert Curthose. Nor were his military operations less successful than before; for he continued his hostilities for two years, "nor ceased until the King had given him competent satisfaction,* and restored to him a great portion of the right which he had demanded." Such is the account given by Orderic when first mentioning the subject; and, on recurring to it, he particularly mentions the event of "William de Romara being honourably reconciled to the King, and thenceforth becoming his familiar messmate and friend." It is then that Orderic mentions that the King gave him for a wife *Matilda*, the daughter of Richard de Redvers†—the

that "this must relate to Corfe Mullen, for Corfe Castle was then in the Crown (though not mentioned in Domesday Book) and not granted away till several ages after." (Hist. of Dorset, i. 276, iii. 38.) It certainly seems extraordinary that Hutchins should have adopted this notion, involving the two improbable circumstances, that so important a place as Corfe Castle should not be noticed in Domesday Book, and that Corfe Mullen, which never became a parish, and is an insignificant hamlet of Stourminster Marshal, should have consisted of *ten carucates, and have been of the yearly value of* 15*l*. There can now be no further question that the castle of Corfe, and its surrounding demesnes, had been granted out previously to the Norman survey to Robert Fitz Girold, and resumed prior to any other record except that so unexpectedly furnished by Ordericus Vitalis.

* It is probable that Henry did not restore him Corfe, &c., but compensated him with a grant of other lands; perhaps, inter alia, Cleeve.

† " quæ" he adds, " filium ei speciosum nomine Guillelmum Heliam peperit." Such a compound name would be very extraordinary; but it has evidently been an error of the copyist, and Mr. Stapleton has suggested, not improbably, that it should be " Willielmam et filium [*sc.* Rohesiam] peperit." In a previous passage of Ordericus, is a similar confusion of two brothers (where the children of the Earl of Chester are mentioned): "Guillelmum [et] Rannulfum." Here Ranulph should come first.

error of a name which, as already noticed, has contributed so much to confuse this pedigree; after which the Monk proceeds to remark, that "the said Knight was in his youth unsteady, and too much addicted to pleasure; but, being stricken from heaven with a very grievous sickness, and having conversed with Geoffrey the Archbishop (of Rouen, from 1111 to 1128), he vowed to God to amend his life. And then on retiring to Neufmarché, after his recovery, he placed seven monks in the church of St. Peter, instead of the four canons previously serving, considerably enlarged their endowment, and rebuilt the church and monastic houses."

It has been stated, that the death of the Countess Lucy has been assigned to the year 1141; and Brooke asserts that William de Romara "was created Earl of Lincolne in the sixth yeare of King Stephen," which dates agree. Though Brooke cites no authority for his statement, and though it was not adopted by Dugdale, there seems reason to suppose that he was Earl at that time if not before; and it may be imagined that the seizure of the castle of Lincoln, with which the rebellion of 1140 was commenced, was connected with his assertion of those rights which he deemed to have devolved upon him upon his mother's death. The account of this event which is given by Ordericus Vitalis deserves our attention from its immediate reference to his personal history, and from the circumstance of himself and wife being styled *Comes* and *Comitissa*, though without the title of Lincoln being directly mentioned.

"The castle of Lincoln," says Ordericus, "was in Stephen's own possession, when Ranulph Earl of Chester and William de Romara his uterine brother, seized upon it by stratagem. Craftily finding a time when the servants of the fortress were scattered abroad, they sent before them their wives into the tower as if for the sake of pleasure. And so, whilst *the two Countesses* continued their visit, playing and conversing with the wife of the Knight who was in charge, the Earl of Chester came unarmed, and without his coat of mail, as if to bring his wife away, followed by three Knights, no one suspecting any harm.

Thus having effected an entrance, they suddenly seized the crowbars and arms that lay near, and violently ejected the King's guards. Then WILLIAM, and armed Knights with him, arrived as had been before arranged. And so the two brothers subdued the castle, with the whole city, to themselves."

This occurrence took place shortly before Christmas in the year 1140; soon after which Stephen arrived, and invested the city. At this time, "*the two Earls*, with their wives and familiar friends, were within the castle;" but after a time, the Earl of Chester, who "was the younger, and more ready, and exceedingly bold,"* came out by night, and set out to his own vassals in the county of Chester. There he lost no time in assembling an army, which, with the aid of his father-in-law Robert Earl of Gloucester, he brought to Lincoln in time to relieve his besieged brother, and gave the King battle on Sexagesima Sunday, Feb. 2, 1114. In this conflict Stephen was taken prisoner. Among his companions in misfortune was a youthful Baron, named Gilbert de Gant, a great-grandson of Baldwin Count of Flanders, the brother-in-law of the Conqueror. The victorious Earl of Chester took advantage of the opportunity to form a favourable alliance for the daughter of William de Romara. It is stated by John of Hexham that Earl Ranulph "*compelled*" this illustrious youth to marry his niece. The injury inflicted was not upon the house of Gant, but upon that of Romara; for, in consequence of this alliance, Gilbert de Gant shortly afterwards obtained the Earldom of Lincoln, and, although the race of Romara continued, it did not return to them.

The next circumstance to be noticed in the life of William de Romara is his foundation of the abbey of Revesby in the county of Lincoln; which was about the year 1143.† His wife and son united with him in the foundation charter, under the style of "Willielmus de Romara, Comes de Lincolnia, et Willielmus filius ejus, et Hawdewisa Comitissa uxor ejus."

William the son died before his father. His decease is re-

* —"junior erat et facilior, et audacissimus."
† The Annals of Peterborough say 1142, those of Lowth Park 1143, and the MS. Cotton. Tiberius E. VIII. (belonging to Cleeve Abbey) the eighth year of King Stephen

corded under the year 1152, by the Norman historian Robert de Monte, who adds that he left two sons (the name of the second was Robert*) by a daughter of the Earl of Albemarle.

The register of Fountains Abbey states that the fourth daughter of Stephen Earl of Albemarle was married first to William de Romara, and afterwards to Peter de Brus. The lady's Christian name is still deficient; but it may be supplied with that of Agnes.†

In 1153, the year after his son's death, we find a charter of "William de Romara, Earl of Lincoln," dated at Rouen, by which he remitted to the Abbey of St. Ouen in that city the

* "Carta Will. de Rumare de Clive: test. Roberto fratre meo," to Exeter priory. Collectanea Top. et Geneal. vol. i. p. 186.

† This is the lady, to whom, as before noticed, Brooke transferred the name of Hawise, which was continued by Dugdale; but the latter, in his account of the family of Brus, (Baronage, vol. i. p. 449,) gives to Peter de Brus, who died 1211, besides Joan, the mother of his family, as "his *other* wife," "*Agnes*, widow of William de Romara, *Earl of Lincoln*." His only authority for this is "Mon. Ang. i. 797, n. 60," that is, the Register of Fountains, which, however, furnishes *no* Christian name, and does not give William de Romara any title of Earl. It is possible that the real source of Dugdale's information was this passage in the Historia de Melsa, caput 11,—"carucatam in Erghes inter North Dalton et Wartre, ubi grangiam Blanchmarl, Latinè Albamarla, confirmavit Will'mus de Rowmar, Comes Lincoln, et Agnes de Albemarlia uxor ejus." Although the title of "Comes Lincoln" is incorrect, there can be no doubt that the writer had seen the charter by which the grange of Blanchmarl had been conveyed to the monastery, and had thence taken the name of Agnes. It may therefore be considered as originally derived from an authentic source; but it was applied by Dugdale in a manner very wide of the truth: this Peter de Brus died in 1211, and even his *grandfather* in 1161, nine years after the death of William de Romara the younger. By the kindness of Mr. Stapleton, I am again furnished with a most important correction to Dugdale; showing that the second husband of Agnes was a collateral Peter, remaining at Bruis, now Brix (the cradle of the royal house of Scotland, near Valognes, in the diocese of Coutance), and who was living at the very time required. From a cartulary (now in the possession of Monsieur C. de Gerville, of Valognes), of St. Sauveur-le-Vicomte, an abbey not far from Brix, Mr. Stapleton has extracted two charters, dated 1153 and 1155, recording that Peter de Bruis, the son of William, gave to that

hawk which was yearly due to him, and the *pint of wine* * and *two loaves* which were due to him daily as often as he stayed in Rouen. †

With the highly excited feelings of religious contrition, of which so many examples are found among the headstrong chieftains of that violent age, Earl William appears to have evinced many tokens of zealous devotion in his latter years.

The event of his making a pilgrimage to the shrine of St. James in Galicia, is recorded by a deed of gift from his brother the Earl of Chester, being dated " in the *year* of his return."‡

The religious fervency of his deathbed was demonstrated by his being made a monk when *in extremis*,—a custom, indeed, then usual, and also performed, about the same time, in the case of his cousin Walter of Salisbury, the founder of Bradenstoke. The date of the Earl of Lincoln's decease is not known, but it probably ensued shortly after 1153; and he was buried in his abbey of Revesby, § as his son had been before

abbey, inter alia, the church of Bruis, " precepto et voluntate Adam de Bruis sui d'ni et cognati." The following table will show his relationship, in the *fifth* degree only, to Dugdale's Peter:

Robert de Brus, d. 1141.	William de Brus.		
Adam de Brus, d. 1161.	Peter de Brus, living 1153.	=Agnes of Albemarle.	=William de Romara, d. 1152.
Adam de Brus, d. 1185.			
Peter de Brus, d. 1211.			

* " Dimidium sextarii."
† Histoire de l'Abbaye de St. Ouen, par Pommeraye, p. 428.
‡ Ormerod's Cheshire, i. 25. The Countess Hawise is witness.
§ "—in extremis factus monachus, jacet apud Revesby." Genealogy of the Saxon Earls, before quoted, in the Monasticon, i. 304. The remainder of the same account, relating to the genealogy of the family of Romara, is far from being correct: " Post cujus obitum Willielmus de Romara filius [*lege* nepos] Luciæ Comitissæ ex Rogero, de Rogero de Romara (*ita*) obtinuit a Rege Henrico Secundo omnes terras quondam Willielmi de Romara patrui [*lege* avi] sui, et fundavit

him, and his grandson was at a subsequent period. A monastic pedigree, of no very remote antiquity,* has preserved their epitaphs. The Earl's tomb was before the high altar, and inscribed with "these verses:"

"Hic jacet in tumba Willielmus de Romare, Comes Lincolniæ, fundator istius monasterii sancti Laurencii de Rewisby."

The son's tomb was on the north side of his father's:

"Hic jacet in tumba Willielmus de Romare filius Willielmi Comitis Lincolniæ, qui ante patrem obiit sicut Deus voluit."

On the south side of the first was a third, inscribed:

"Hic jacet in tumba Willielmus de Romare, *filius Luciæ Comitissæ Lincolniæ,* † fundator monasterii beatæ Mariæ de Clyve."

A few words may now be said of the Countess Hawise, the wife of Earl William de Romara, whose marriage has been noticed from Ordericus Vitalis, under the erroneous name of Matilda. In a monastic pedigree of the founders of Christchurch Twynham, she is duly mentioned among the children of Richard de Redvers, Lord of Tiverton and Christchurch, and Adeliza his wife, as "Hadwysam de Romara Comitissam Lincolniæ." ‡ Besides the mention of her name in the founda-

---

monasterium de Cliva, et moriens sine sobole jacet apud Revesby; Ranulphusque Comes Cestriæ frater ejus obtinuit a Rege Johanne omnes terras suas." In the last clause the word "frater" is so far wrong as applied to the Ranulph Earl of Chester living in the reign of King John, who it is true became Earl of Lincoln in 1216, that he was *grandson* of that Earl Ranulph, who was half-brother to the founder of Cleeve's grandfather; so that in fact they were second cousins instead of brothers.

* Dugdale's Monasticon, i. 530, from MS. Cotton. Tiberius, E. VIII. f. 208 a. There are now no remains of the abbey church of Revesby; but the site has in modern times become " classic ground " as the residence of the late Sir Joseph Banks, Pres. R.S.

† These words must have been interpolated, either by the writer in his manuscript, or by the monks, through ignorance, on the stone.

‡ Monasticon Anglicanum, vol. ii. p. 179. Her father is there incorrectly styled Earl of Devon, which he never was; his

tion charter of Revesby already noticed, it occurs also as the first witness to a charter of the Earl to the abbey of Newhouse; and, by the title of "Hawysia Comitissa de Romare," she gave the advowson of Feltham in Middlesex to the hospital of St. Giles's in the Fields.*

There is ample evidence that Gilbert de Gant became the next Earl of Lincoln, though the date of his accession is unknown. There appears to be some reason to suspect that William de Romara was deprived of his Earldom by Stephen when he regained his ascendancy, and that Gilbert de Gant, who was a steady adherent of the King, was rewarded with it. The Priory of Rufford was founded by the latter either in 1146 or 1148; in his foundation charter he styles himself Earl of Lincoln.

In the chronicle of Vaudey, Gilbert Earl of Lincoln is stated to have made a grant at the request of Eugenius "the Roman Bishop" (1145–1153) and Bernard Abbat of Clairvaux.† In the cartulary of Kirkstead is a charter of "*Roheis* the wife of Gilbert Earl of Lincoln," done in the presence of Robert Bishop of Lincoln, after her husband's death. At the same time her daughter Alicia was the wife of Simon Earl of Northampton. ‡

Among the charters of Bridlington priory is a curious cove-

---

son Baldwin was not yet an Earl in 1138 (see Ordericus Vitalis). This is another instance of the caution required in following monkish genealogies. The surname of Redvers, it may be here remarked, was derived from the castle of Reviers near Bayeux.

* Her brother Earl Baldwin de Redvers gave land at Feltham to the same foundation, and Pope Alexander confirmed the two gifts together in the following words: "eccl'iam de Feltham, et t'ram qua' h'ent in eadem villa de donacione Comitis Baldewini de Redmero et Comitissæ Hawysiæ." (Parton's History of St. Giles's, p. 8, note.)

† G. Hollis's collections, vol. v, p. 526, MS. Lansd. 207 E.

‡ See three charters, evidently executed at the same time. 1. of Roheis wife of Gilbert Earl of Lincoln; 2. of Simon Earl of Northampton; 3. of Alicia Countess of Northampton; in the Kirkstead cartulary, MS. Cotton. Vesp. F. xiii, f. 99b, et seq.

nant of Earl Gilbert, binding himself to be buried at that monastery, *where he was born and brought up*. His daughter the Countess Alicia was also buried there.

There is also a charter of the first Gilbert Earl of Lincoln to the Priory of Bridlington, which is witnessed by his brother Robert, who became the successor to his barony, though not to the Earldom; and there is a confirmation charter from King Stephen, to the Priory of Rufford, granted in the lifetime of his son Eustace, who died in 1152. Stephen died in 1154, and Earl Gilbert himself in 1157. (Robert de Monte.)

We have seen that Earl William de Romara was alive at Rouen in 1153. It is probable that he took refuge in Normandy with the other adherents of the House of Anjou; and, though he might not live to feel the effects of Henry's gratitude, yet we shall see hereafter that his grandson was brought up by that monarch.

This is one view of the circumstances which introduced Gilbert de Gant to the acquisition of the Earldom of Lincoln. But if it was on the *death* of his father-in-law that he attained to that dignity, we must attribute his accession to the previous decease of his brother-in-law the second William de Romara, and the infant years of the grandson and heir male, who, as a child, could not be girded with the sword of the County.

In either case, the third William de Romara was never restored to his ancestral dignity. The next person recorded to have borne the title of Earl of Lincoln was a second Gilbert de Gant, the nephew of the former; but so far was he from having "succeeded" his uncle, as stated in some works on the peerage, that it was after an interview of sixty years; and he held the title for a period still shorter than the former. If the first was introduced by the sovereign will of Stephen, overruling the ordinary laws of inheritance, the second was obtruded by a still less competent authority,—the invader Louis of France. This was in the last year of the reign of John: and in the next year, 1216, he was taken prisoner at the battle then fought at Lincoln, and his brief career as an Earl was thereupon closed; the dignity being transferred to Ranulph Earl of Chester the great-grandson and representative of the first Ranulph and the Countess Lucia, who was evidently then considered to have been the heiress of the dignity, and to have transmitted it to her posterity.

That William de Romara "the third"* was really the grandson of the Earl of Lincoln, and that he inherited a considerable landed estate, is proved by the confirmation charter which he gave to the abbey of Revesby, in which he styled himself "nepos Willielmi Comitis, et hæres ejus." This is dated in the year 1172. "Nepos," in this document, cannot be translated *nephew*, as it is accompanied by "avus," which always signifies *grandfather*.

Still more complete is the view of the family which is given by one of his charters to Spalding, in which, styling himself "the grandson and heir of William Earl of Romara" he confirms for the souls of himself and *Philippa* his wife, the gifts of Lucia Countess of Chester, the mother of William Earl of Romara his grandfather, mentioning at the same time the successive lords of Spalding, Ivo Tailboys, Roger Fitz-Gerold, and Earl Ranulph. This charter was witnessed by Hugh Abbat of Revesby.† From a second charter to the same monastery, we find he had another wife named Alicia. ‡

It is stated by Brooke in his Catalogue, but without assigning any authority, that William de Romare the third died without issue in 1175; but it will be seen that that date is more than twenty years too early.

He is mentioned by the continuator of the Annals of Croyland, under the year 1191, as the familiar and sworn friend of Earl John§ (or, as we should now style him, Prince John) after-

---

* Placitorum Abbreviatio, p. 75.
† Cartulary formerly belonging to Beaupré Bell, esq. f. 136; transcript in Cole's collections, vol. xliii. (MS. Add. Brit. Mus. 5844) p. 148.
‡ Ibid. f. 331 a; p. 377.
§ "Comiti Johanni valde familiaris et jam juratus."

wards King. The Abbat of Croyland was a brother of William de Longchamp the Bishop of Ely and Lord Chancellor, whom King Richard, on leaving England for the crusade, had left Justice of the Kingdom. As John Earl of Morton headed a party opposed to the Chancellor, so William de Romare took the same occasion to prosecute an old dispute which had subsisted between the abbeys of Croyland and Spalding (of which latter he was the hereditary founder), relative to their rights of property in Croyland marsh. The monastic historian gives a graphic description of the scene which took place at the trial in London on Ascension day 1192, when Earl John, and his courtiers, as well as William de Romare, were present. The latter asserted that the Abbey of Croyland was in his fee; although, says the monk, "it was founded and made a royal abbey *before any of his race was known* *." Earl John denied the authority of a charter of his brother King Richard; because he declared that the Abbat had procured it from his brother the Chancellor, through private favour; but when John had heard read another charter of his father King Henry, then, says the chronicler, he was abashed.

Dugdale has noticed, from the Pipe Roll of 9 Rich. I. that William de Romara was then with the King in Normandy; and the same year, which was 1197-8, has been assigned to his foundation of the Abbey of Cleeve, in Somersetshire,† though there seems reason to date it seven or eight years earlier.‡ It was

---

* "Iste et W. cum aliquando super hoc a Comite J. deprecaretur, respondisse fertur, Domine dilecte Will. centum librarum in justitiam facerem et pro amore tuo." The construction is obscure; but the meaning seems to be that Earl John was ready to be fined 100*l*. from his regard to his friend William.

† MS. Cotton. Tiberius, E VIII. fol. 208 a.

‡ There are (in the Monasticon) two foundation charters of Cleeve granted by William de Romara; to the first of which Reinald Bishop of Bath is a witness, who died before the end of 1191; and the latter is addressed to King Richard, whose accession was in 1189. In the Annals of Waverly it is recorded under the year 1188, that Waleran Abbat of Cleeve then resigned his abbacy, and Alan of Bordesley succeeded him; if so, the foundation must have been prior to that year: Hugh,

founded, says his charter, "for the health and the soul of his lord Richard King of England, for the soul of King Henry his father, my lord who brought me up (*qui me nutrivit*), for those of all the King's ancestors and heirs, for his own soul, that of his wife Philippa, and the souls of all their ancestors, heirs, and successors." His wife Philippa is stated in the Monasticon,* to have been one of the daughters of Hubert de Burgh, Earl of Kent; but such statement is clearly unfounded. She was the daughter of John Comte d'Alençon, by Beatrix daughter of Elias d'Anjou Comte de Maine, and *Philippa* de Perche; which latter Philippa was a daughter of Rotrou first Comte de Perche, and his first wife Matilda, natural daughter of Henry I. King of England. This is shown by a charter of the priory of Graville, to which she gave in August 1214 the chapel of St. Mary la Salle in the parish of Montaigu near Valognes, in the diocese of Coutances.†

After the death of the last William, without issue, his inheritance appears to have devolved on the Earl of Chester, whose son afterwards obtained the Earldom of Lincoln, having defeated in 1216, as already stated, the second Earl Gilbert de Gant, a rebel to the King, but perhaps more unequivocally a rival to himself. J. G. N.

---

the Abbat of Revesby, by whom it was constructed, held that dignity in 1172, as appears by a charter of that date in the Monasticon.

* Vol. i. p. 531.

† "Henricus Constantiensis Antistes ann. 1214 confirmavit donationem præfatæ Heroinæ Philippæ de Romara." Neustria Pia, p. 864, where for "Henricus" read *Hugo*; but the same passage has led to a much more extraordinary error in the Gallia Christiana, vol. xi. p. 878, the ornamental epithet *Heroina* being there converted into a Christian name for the Countess of Alençon her mother!

It may be mentioned that in the same cartulary of St. Sauveur-le-Vicomte (quoted in 76), is a charter of Adelicia, sister of Agnes, and wife first of Robert Bertrand, Baron of Briquebec, a neighbouring castle to Brix, and secondly of Engelger de Bohun, one of the heads of the party of Geoffrey Count of Anjou in the Cotentin, in the struggle with Stephen.

CHAPTER IV.

Ela of Salisbury, the Foundress of Lacock Abbey—Coronations of Richard Cœur de Lion—Ela's concealment in Normandy—her discovery by a Troubadour Knight, and delivery to King Richard.

ENOUGH of the stern Conqueror and his fierce and iron-mailed Barons: enough of the intricate mazes of their early genealogy: of Walter le Ewrus, and Humphridus cum Barba! Farewell to the Earls of Salisbury of the first House! Our attention must now be directed to their orphan heiress, deprived of her father at eight years of age, and carried away a captive exile to a foreign land.

She was born at Amesbury, about seven miles from Old Sarum,* in 1188. Her father died in 1196; and, until that fatal event, Ela was doubtless reared, not only with care, but in princely state, within her native county of Wilts. Earl William, her father, was one of the most dis-

* Amesbury was distinguished by its nunnery, remarkable for its succession of Royal nuns, among whom were Isabella of Lancaster, prioress in 1202, and Mary daughter of King Edward I. Part of the parish, however, was retained by the Earls of Salisbury, as we find two manors, Amesbury Priorisse, and Amesbury Comitis; for the latter of which, Earl William Longespé obtained the grant of a weekly market in 1219. (Clause Rolls.) As Oxford castle had its *bower* at Woodstock, so the *ladies, bower* of Salisbury castle may have been at Amesbury.

tinguished subjects of the chivalric Richard; and evidently possessed a high place in the royal favour. He took a prominent part at both the Coronations of the Lion-hearted King. At the first, which was solemnized with great state at Westminster, Sept. 3, 1189, when each of the great Earls of the Kingdom occupied some prominent post in the ceremony, the Earl of Salisbury carried the Verge or Rod, having a dove upon its summit. At the second, which took place at Winchester, April 18, 1194, after Richard's return from his captivity in Germany, he was one of the four Earls who bore the canopy, namely, the Earls of Norfolk, the Isle of Wight (another style for the Earl of Devonshire), Salisbury, and Ferrers.*

In the same year, the Earl of Salisbury was also constituted keeper of the king's charter, or grant, for licensing Tournaments throughout the country, and was thus placed in a situation of the greatest responsibility in that age of chivalry. One of the five " steads," or fields then appointed for the exercise of tournaments in England, was situated between Salisbury and Wilton; and on that spot, when a child, the future Abbess of Lacock may

* Roger de Hoveden. Though frequently called a coronation by historians, the solemnity at Winchester was not attended by the ceremonies usually practised at the primary coronations of English sovereigns; which accounts for the Earl of Salisbury not being required to perform the same service as before, or one of similar prominence.

have first witnessed the perilous gaieties of knightly enterprise, and those proud exhibitions of personal courage and external splendour and gallantry.

Perhaps in all England could not have been found a spot more appropriate for the purpose of these " high heroic" games. The situation is well known, on the downs in front of the castle: the description of it, recently written by Mr. Hatcher, may here be introduced, on account of its accuracy and animation.

" Two vallies obliquely intersecting the tongue of land between the Bath and Devizes roads, offered situations for the purpose, as if formed by art, where ample space was afforded for the lists, and where thousands of spectators might have been accommodated without difficulty or danger. Those who have been transported back in idea, to the period of which we treat, by the vivid description of the tournaments in the Romance of Ivanhoe, can scarcely survey this ground without picturing to themselves the impressive effect of an assemblage, so varied, interesting, and magnificent, on the elevated down, in full view of the majestic fortress of Old Sarum on one hand, of Wilton and its venerable abbey on the other, and overlooking the rich and smiling bourns of the Avon and the Nadder *."

Such was the scene on which Ela in her childhood might have gazed, when animated with arms, and banners, and all the concourse of chivalry; and we

* Hatcher's Account of Salisbury, 1834, p. 29.

may imagine that a monarch like Richard would have rejoiced thus to celebrate her nuptials with his noble brother, had he lived to return to England after having bestowed her hand on William of the Long Sword. But, whilst still a child, on losing the protection of her father, this richly portioned heiress was suddenly snatched from the scenes familiar to her infancy, and subjected to a jealous seclusion in a foreign country.

All that is said in the Book of Lacock respecting this captivity of the maid of Salisbury, is this: "When Ela was now deprived of both her father and mother, she was secretly taken into Normandy by her relations, and there brought up in close and secret custody." [*] Who those relations were we are left to conjecture. It proves, however, to be a mistake that Ela's mother died before the Earl, for she was living eighteen years after;[†] and it is therefore probable that they were her mother and her mother's family, whose estates were either in Normandy or Champaign, and who could readily have found thereon a place of concealment for the heiress. This discovery seems to me unexpectedly to throw a most interesting light on her confinement. Let it be remembered that Ela had three uncles, the

[*] "Ela, patre et matre orbata, clam per cognatos et notos adducta fuit in Normanniam, et ibidem sub tuta et arcta custodia nutrita."

[†] See the record quoted in the Appendix to this chapter, p. 99; where will be found further particulars respecting her.

eldest of whom must have been interested—deeply interested—as the presumed heir of his brother Earl William, to his immense possessions, and high hereditary rank and honours, had not one infant daughter stood in his way. Where was He? In some accounts of the family it is stated that two of the brothers, Philip and Patrick, were monks in the abbey founded by their grandfather and father at Bradenstoke. This circumstance cannot now be traced to any ancient record, but is so stated in the old Peerage by Brooke.*

But in the document we have before spoken of,† it is stated not only that Ela's uncles Patrick and Philip were bred as monks at Bradenstoke; but that they exchanged the frock for the cuirass; that

---

* In Vincent's pedigree (B. 2, Coll. Arm.) the two brothers who were Canons of Bradenstoke are named Walter and William, and placed in the *preceding* generation. It is worthy of remark that in Watson's " Memoirs of the Earls of Warren and Surrey," we find *another* fate ascribed to Philip, *but equally without perceptible authority.* Among the Countess Alianor's children are named—" Patrick and Philip, both monks in the priory of Bradenstoke," and in a note it is added, " These monks are said to have been *slain at this priory!*" (p. 137.) In a charter of their half-sister Isabella Countess of Warren (witnesses Earl Hameline, R. Archdeacon of Surrey, and P. the Dean,) she directs the Canons of Southwark to pray for the souls of William, Patrick, and Philip her brothers. (Ibid. p. 164.) Her brother Walter therefore was probably living at the period of this charter, and Philip dead. (J. G. N.)

† Pedigree of Devereux, of Carigmenan; see before, p. 42.

Patrick was slain in Aquitaine, before the death of his brother the Earl; but that Philip, having seen the estates of his family go out of his house, went in 1203 to seek other fortunes in Ireland, where it is stated that he settled in the county of Wexford, and founded the family now bearing the surname of Devereux.

It is true that Earl William had two brothers, named Patrick and Philip, *besides another named Walter;* and it is also clear that Patrick died before him, as there is a charter of the Earl, directing the monks of Bradenstoke to pray for Patrick's soul, which is witnessed by Philip and Walter. But there is no positive evidence, beyond the unauthenticated statement of Brooke, that any of the brothers were monks of Bradenstoke Priory.

Nor is there any record of Patrick having been slain in Aquitaine; though we know from history that Earl *Patrick his grandfather* was actually slain in Aquitaine!

We presume we have shown, in a former chapter, that the name of Devereux, as applied to the house of Salisbury, had no contemporary existence, but is a visionary phantom, and a mere *nominis umbra*—still, whether there may be complete evidence or not, that Ela's uncles, Philip and Patrick, were in truth monks of Bradenstoke, certainly no one can produce, on the contrary, proof of either having had a wife, or any family, (nor, indeed, we must grant, of scarcely any other junior brother in the Peerage of such very early times,) but when Brooke, in

1619, stated both were monks, can we imagine that he knowingly and deliberately stated a falsehood, which could answer no purpose, and for which he had no authority at all?—he stated what he had some grounds for believing. I conclude, therefore, that being younger brothers, without property, wife, or family, they might have sought, in the inglorious age of John, the congenial habitation of a cloister founded by their father and grandfather, and that Brooke must have had some authority for the assertion.

With respect to the family of Devereux in Ireland, truth has compelled us to show, by documents which cannot be shaken, that this name could not have appertained to any of the family of Salisbury.

Of the descent of this family from Philip the monk of Bradenstoke, we must leave the document as it stands; only saying, that what is stated in it, and from tradition, that Philip on the death of his elder brother threw off the cowl, is not inconsistent with human nature, with his rank in society, and above all with Ela's history.

Granting the passions, avarice, or ambition, to be awakened, let us think of the prize before him!—let us think how often, pacing the solitary cloisters of Bradenstoke, he may have scowled on his books and beads when he thought, that but for his vows, and if this child were removed, he might be no longer a poor and obscure monk, but one of the most distinguished nobles in the land, with possessions equal to his dignity!

This is not inconsistent with nature; and, if true, would account for her daughter's confinement by an anxious and affectionate mother, that she might be placed out of reach of those who perhaps might have meditated worse than confinement; though it is true that the point of the story in the Book of Lacock is that she was removed from the *legal wardship* of the King her Sovereign, and from his prerogative of bestowing her in marriage.

The same fidelity to truth, which induced me to show that the Salisbury family did not bear the name of Devereux, has caused me to state the history of this family; to which is added this tradition, that Philip of Bradenstoke was absolved by the Pope from his vows of poverty, when he first drew the sword, and stood forward the claimant of the honours and wealth of the House of Salisbury.

Having felt it a duty to say thus much, and leaving the whole to the reader's consideration, begging him to remember that these circumstances are stated in the document of the family of Devereux, *eo nomine*, and of the same ancient religion in Ireland, presented to the King at the coronation of George the Fourth; and that it is also stated that Philip went to Ireland in 1203. It is remarkable that Ela would be just sixteen years of age at that time, and marriageable, and in this year, it may be presumed, she actually was married; when every hope of Philip must have been by that event completely destroyed, if credence be given to the account.

To return to the captivity of the youthful Ela, as related by our only authority, the Book of Lacock. It informs us that she was concealed by her "relations," who were, it is most probable, her mother's family. Immediately upon the inquisition held after her father's death, Ela's lands would in due course be taken into the possession of the King, as she had become a royal ward. But the abstraction of her person might probably throw some difficulty in the way of the inquisition, or the consequent legal proceedings. The sequel of events, which arises from these circumstances, is highly characteristic of the manners of that court, where the minstrel monarch, the lion-hearted Richard, presided over his train of gallant and chivalric Troubadours. An English knight, named William Talbot, undertook to discover the place of the youthful heiress's concealment; the idea having been suggested, if the fact be admitted, by King Richard's own discovery, a few years before, by the minstrel Blondel.

Assuming the garb of a pilgrim, the gallant Talbot " passed over into Normandy, and there continued his search, wandering to and fro, for the space of two years.* When, at length, he had found the Lady Ela of Salisbury, he exchanged his pilgrim's dress for that of a Harper or travelling Troubadour, and in that guise entered the Court† in which the maid was detained. As he sustained to perfection his

---

* Dugdale, in his Baronage, incorrectly says "months," instead of "years."

† "Curiam."

character of a gleeman*, and was excellently versed in the gests, or historical lays, recounting the deeds of former times, the stranger was kindly received, and soon treated as one of the household. At last, his

* " Homo jocosus." Talbot seems to have been one of the jongleurs of Richard's social board. These are the affectionate terms in which the joyous King speaks of two of his minstrels— " Chail and Pensavin, my minstrels and my friends—you, whom I have loved, and whom I shall ever love! by your songs," &c. Amid the stern and bloody scenes of the crusades, the Troubadours seem to have interposed their music, like the songs of the dove and nightingale, the most common similitudes of their tender or gallant strains. How exquisite an incense is contained in the few words of William Cabestaing. Speaking of his lady he says, " Would you know her name? it is written in the fairest characters, on the wing of every dove!" What is there in Ovid so tender, so fanciful, as the following kind of apologue to his mistress of Peter d'Auvergne?

" ' Go, sweet nightingale, go to the beauty I adore; tell her my feelings, and acquaint thyself with hers; let her charge thee to tell me, she forgets me not. Do not stay; fly fast back, and bring me word what thou hast heard; for I have neither parent nor friend in the world, from whom I so much wish to receive intelligence.' The pretty bird departs; he flies gaily along, inquiring every where, till he finds my fair one. On the view of her he begins those melting sounds, which he warbles forth on beholding the star of the evening. On a sudden he becomes silent, and reflects in what manner he should obtain her notice; then perching near her, he speaks thus:—' Your loyal friend has dispatched me to you, to pour forth those notes that may please and delight you. What shall I tell him, when he comes breathless to meet me at my return? If he receives a favourable answer, you ought to feel an equal joy, since he loves you more than ever;—but you are silent. I perceive that my message is ill received. Your friend, I protest to you, places all his happi-

chivalric undertaking was fully accomplished; when, having found a convenient opportunity for returning

ness in your love! Why do you pause? Embrace love while it is offered; seize the happy moment; it is a flower that swiftly fades away!'

"The lady thus replied:—' Your pretty bird came directly to me; your message I received with joy; he will assure you, my kind friend, that your absence afflicts me much; for no one interests me like yourself: but you quitted me too soon; and had I foreseen your absence, you would not have received such proofs of my regard. I now regret my past tenderness. My heart is so penetrated with love, that I am always melancholy, always sighing for the object of my affection. When with him I live in joy! I would not change him for aught the world can bestow. I wait with impatience to behold him. True love, like gold, continues always refining; mine for you is always increasing. Gentle bird, depart; tell him how much I love him! tell it him in thy softest tone. Fly; make haste.—What! art thou not yet gone?'"

This is what Mrs. Dobson, the translator, calls the *simple style!* The various feats expected from these Jongleurs—*homines jocosi*—are related by the Troubadour Girard Calanson:—

"' Learn to do well, speak well, and rhime well, and to contrive amusing games. Learn to play on the tabor, and the cymbals, and make symphony resound. Learn to throw and catch little apples on the points of knives; to imitate the songs of birds, attacks on castles, to jump through four hoops, to play on the cittall and the mandore, to perform on the clavicorde and the guitar, for they are delightful to all; to string the viol with *seventeen cords*, sound the bells, to play on the harp, and to compose a jig, that shall enliven the sound of the psaltery. Jongleur, thou shalt prepare nine instruments, of ten chords; if thou learnest to play well on them, they will furnish thee with ample melody.'"

From Monsieur de Saint-Palaye's great work on the History of Troubadours, Dobson's translation.

to England, he carried with him the heiress, and presented her to King Richard."

Such are the facts of this singular history, precisely as related in the Book of Lacock;* and the reader, I am sure, will excuse me, if, with such materials, an Old Poet should attempt to recite them with rather less brevity, in the more appropriate language of the romantic lay.†

THE LAY OF TALBOT THE TROUBADOUR.

PART THE FIRST.

At Rouen RICHARD kept his state,
  Released from captive-thrall;
And, girt with many a warrior-guest,
  He feasted in the Hall.

The rich metheglin mantled high,
  The wine was berry-red,
When tidings came that Salisbury,
  His early friend, was dead;

And that his sole surviving child,
  The heiress of his wealth,
By crafty kinsmen and allies
  Was borne away by stealth—

---

* The original Latin will be found in the Appendix to this volume.

† I have deviated from the Book of Lacock in placing King Richard in Normandy, because I believe that he never visited England during the two last years of his reign.

Was borne away to Normandy,
 Where, secretly confin'd,
She heard no voice of those she lov'd,
 But sigh'd to the north wind.

Haply, from some lone castle's tow'r,
 Or solitary strand,
E'en now she gazes o'er the deep,
 That laves her Father's land!

King Richard cried, " My minstrel-knights,
 Who will the task atchieve,
To seek, through France and Normandy,
 The orphan, the left to grieve?"

Young William Talbot then did speak,
 " Betide me weal or woe,
From Michael's Castle,* thro' the land,
 A Pilgrim I will go."

He clad him in his pilgrim's weeds,
 With trusty staff in hand,
And scallop-shell, and took his way
 A wanderer through the land.

For two long years, he journeyed on,
 A pilgrim, day by day,
Through many a forest, dark and drear,
 By many a castle grey.

At length, when one clear morn of frost
 Was shining on the main,

---

* Mount St. Michael, in periculo maris, answering to St. Michael's Mount, in Cornwall.

Forth issuing from a castle-gate,
   He saw a female train.

With lightsome step, and waving hair,
   Before them ran a child,
And gathering from the sands a shell
   Ran back to them, and smil'd.

Himself unseen, among the rocks,
   He saw her point her hand,
And cry, "I would go home,—go home,
   To my poor Father's land." *

The bell toll'd from the turret grey,
   Cold fell the freezing dew,
To the portcullis hast'ning back
   The female train withdrew.

Those turrets and the battlements
   Time and the storm had beat,
And sullenly the ocean-tide
   Came rolling at their feet.

Young Talbot cast away his staff,
   The harp is in his hand,
A minstrel at the castle-gate
   The porter saw him stand.

---

* An affecting story has been told of a poor savage youth from Africa, (I forget where I have seen it,) who was brought to England; and who after he had been taught the language, depressed with the thoughts of his far-distant home, was constantly and mournfully heard to iterate to himself, as he was often seen, alone, gazing on the Thames, "*Home—go*, Saldanna! *Home—go*, Saldanna!"

"And who art thou?" the Porter cried,
  "Young Troubadour, now say?
For welcome in the castle-hall
  Will be, to night, thy lay;

"For this the birthday is of one,
  Whose father now is cold,
An English maiden, rich in fee,
  And this year twelve years old.

"I love myself, now growing old,
  To hear the wild harp's sound.
But whence, young Harper, dost thou come,
  And whither art thou bound?"

"Though I am young," the Harper said,
  "From Syria's sands I come,
A minstrel-warrior of the Cross,
  Now poor and wandering home.

"And I can tell of mighty deeds,
  By bold King Richard done,
King Richard of the Lion's Heart,
  Foes quail to look upon.

"Then lead me to the castle-hall,
  And let the fire be bright,
For never hall or bower hath heard
  A lay like mine to-night."

The windows gleam within the hall,
  The fire is blazing bright,
And the young Harper's hair and harp
  Are shining in the light.

Fair dames, and warriors clad in steel,
   Now gather round to hear,
And oft that little Maiden's eyes
   Are glistening with a tear.

For when the Minstrel sung of wars
   At times, with softer sound,
He touch'd the strings as mourning those
   Now laid in the cold ground.

He sung how brave King Richard pined,
   In a dark tower immured,
And of the long and weary nights,
   A captive, he endur'd;

'Till faithful Blondel to his harp
   One song began to sing;
It ceas'd,—the King takes up the strain!
   IT IS HIS LORD AND KING!

Of Sarum then, and Sarum's plain,
   That poor child heard him speak,
When the first tear-drop in her eye
   Fell silent to her cheek.

For, as the Minstrel told his tale,
   The breathless orphan maid
Thought of the land where in the grave
   Her Father's bones were laid.

Hush! Hush! the winds are piping loud,
   The midnight hour is sped,
The hours of morn are stealing fast;
   Harper, to bed, to bed!

PART THE SECOND.

The two long years had pass'd away,
    When Castle Galliard rose,
As built, at once, by elfin hands,
    And scorning time or foes.*

It might be thought that Merlin's imps
    Were task'd to raise the wall,
That unheard axes fell'd the woods,
    While unseen hammers fall.

As hung, by magic, on a rock,
    The Castle-keep look'd down,
O'er rocks and rivers, and the smoke
    Of many a far-off town.

---

* "This magnificent ruin of the favourite Castle of Richard the First is on the banks of the Seine, near Les Andelys, the birth-place of Poussin and the retreat of Thomas Corneille. A single year sufficed to form its immense fosses, and to raise those walls which might seem to be the structure of a life-time. When Cœur de Lion saw it finished, he is said to have exclaimed, with exultation, ' How beautiful she is, this daughter of a year!' It was the last hold of the English in Normandy; and, under the command of Roger de Lacy, long mocked the efforts of Philip-Augustus, who came in person to invest it, in August 1203. The siege was memorable for its length, the incredible exertions of de Lacy, and the sufferings which the besieged endured until its capture in the following March. It was afterwards dismantled by one of the Louis, lest it should become the hold of any of the feudal Barons whom he dreaded. Since, or at

And now young knights and minstrels gay
  Obey'd their Master's call,
And, loud-rejoicing, held the feast
  In the new-rafter'd Hall.

His Minstrels, and his mailed Peers,
  Were seated at the board,
And, at his side, the highest sat,
  WILLIAM, OF THE LONG-SWORD.

the time of the Revolution, it was offered for sale by the French Government; but, as its walls offer too firm a resistance to those who might wish to destroy it, it is happily left to stand for the admiration of other centuries.

" Time has dealt hardly with thy state,
  Darling of England! yet Renown
Is grown thy vassal, nor can Fate
  Yet rob thee of that ancient frown
Which made thee fearful; on thy brow
  Sits Pride, while Freedom loves to say,
Of all her Norman holds the last
  Wert thou to own th' invader's sway.

Born in one year; in scorn baptized
  Of Peril; proof to all attacks
Save cold neglects,—thy strength disguised,
  Yet mocks the Goth's dismantling axe.
'Tis well! where Cœur de Lion dwell'd,
  And brave de Lacy fought, each stone,
Spared by the piety of eld,
  Should be preserved as Glory's own!"

Wiffen's Memoirs of the House of Russell, vol. i. p. 548.

In the splendid work by Mr. Cotman, of the Architectural Antiquities of Normandy, the ruins of this castle are given, from which the beauty of the scenery, and the position, may be judged.

This youthful knight, of princely birth,
   Was dazzling to behold,
For his chain mail, from head to foot,
   Was gilded o'er with gold.

His surcoat, dyed with azure blue,
   In graceful foldings hung,
And there the golden lions ramp'd,
   With bloody claws and tongue.

With crimson belt around his waist,
   His sword was girded on,
The hilt, a Cross, to kiss in death,
   Radiant with jewels shone.

The names and banners of each knight,
   It were too long to tell—
Here sat the brave Montgomery,
   There, Bertrand and Rozell.

Of Richard's unresisted sword
   A noble minstrel sung,
While to a hundred answering harps
   The blazing gallery rung.

So, all within was merriment,
   When suddenly a shout,
As for some unexpected guest,
   Burst from the crowd without.

Now, not a sound—and scarce a breath
   Through the long Hall is heard,
When, with a young Maid by his side,
   A vizor'd Knight appear'd.

Up the long Hall they held their way,
   On to the Royal Seat;
Then, both together, hand in hand,
   Knelt at King Richard's feet.

The Knight now raised his vizor up,
   And raising it he smiled,
Crying, "My honoured Leige, behold
   Earl William's orphan Child!"

"TALBOT! A TALBOT!" rung the Hall,
   With gratulation wild,
"LONG LIVE BRAVE TALBOT,* AND LONG LIVE
   EARL WILLIAM'S NEW-FOUND CHILD!"

Amidst a scene so new and strange,
   This poor Maid could not speak,
King Richard took her by the hand,
   And gently kiss'd her cheek.

Then placed her smiling through a tear
   By his brave Brother's side,
"Long live brave Longespé!" rung the Hall,
   Long live his future Bride!"

To noble Richard, this fair child,
   His ward, was thus restor'd, †
Destined to be the future Bride
   OF HIM OF THE LONG-SWORD.

---

* It is a singular circumstance that the present possessor of the ancient domain of Lacock should be a Talbot.

† She must have been presented to him the year in which Richard was killed, if Talbot was two years before he discovered her, for her father died in 1197.

APPENDIX TO CHAPTER IV.

PRETENDED SISTERS OF ELA OF SALISBURY.

ALTHOUGH no sufficient reasons have been found to discredit the statement of the Book of Lacock, that Ela was the sole daughter and heiress of her father, yet, as some authors of high reputation have been induced to suppose that she had sisters, it seems necessary to give their conjectures a due examination and discussion. The two sisters which have been given her are brought forward distinctly by different authors, and have never, it is believed, been placed together; and it will therefore be proper to examine their claims separately.

1. *Mabella, wife of Nigel Mowbray.*

This was a name put forth by the old herald Ralph Brooke, in his " Catalogue of Honour," and in his controversy with Camden. Mabel was the daughter of a William Patricius or Patry, a person whom Brooke chose to identify with William son of Patrick Earl of Salisbury. Camden replied that the said William could not be William Earl of Salisbury, because the latter for many years outlived Nigel Mowbray. However, Brooke persisted in his opinion, and his version of the story has been adopted by the modern historians of Surrey, in the following passage:

" We have seen that this manor (Banstead) belonged to the Bishop of Baieux, and was held of him by Richard de Tonebrige at the time of the Domesday Survey. The next possessor that we find was Tirel de Maniers, (ancestor of the present Duke of Rutland), who in the time of Henry I. gave the church of Benestede to the priory of St. Mary Overee. From him the manor descended in marriage, with Eleanor his daughter, to William Fitz-Patric Earl of Salisbury, who gave it to Nigel de Mowbray, with his daughter Mabel. Nigel was in possession in 16 Henry II. 1170, (Rot. Pip.) and confirmed the grant of the church made by Tirel his grandfather; at his death, about 3 Richard I. 1192, he gave to the same priory the church of Berges (Borough) belonging to that of Benestede." *

On this statement the following remarks may be made:

(1) For the assertion that Tirel de Maniers was an ancestor of the Duke of Rutland, there does not appear to be the least authority.

(2) The name of "Eleanor" is taken from the pedigree of the Earls of Salisbury; but the wife of William Earl of Salisbury was Alianor *de Viteri* (Monasticon, ii. 341, e Registro de Lacock). Dugdale (Baronage, i. 175,) has added to the name of Eleanor de Viteri, in a parenthesis, " (daughter of Tirrel de Mainers)"; but, as he quotes no authority, it is clear he had not examined that statement, and that it was only a memorandum of Brooke's account.

(3) The wife of Nigel de Mowbray was a Mabel; but the daughter, says a monastic pedigree of the Mowbrays, (Monasticon, vol. ii. 193, from MS. Cotton. Cleopatra, E. III.) of Edmund Earl of Clare. As no Earl of Clare named Edmund is known, Dugdale, in his account of the Mowbrays, (Baronage, vol. i. p. 124,) says "daughter of *the* Earl of Clare." That Mabel *was* of the family of the English Earls of Clare is supported by the circumstance that Bensted had been held by Richard de Tonebrigge, their ancestor.

(4) The words " Tirel his grandfather." are not to be found in the confirmation charter of Nigel de Mowbray; so that, in fact, even the assumed descent from Maniers to Mowbray does not hang together.

* History of Surrey, by Manning and Bray, vol. ii. p. 582. The same statement is partly repeated in pp. 460, 588, 591, and vol. iii. p. 564.

The charter of Tirel de Maniers is printed by Dugdale Monasticon, vol. ii. p. 85; with a second of Nigel de Mowbray, confirming the church and the manor of Benestede, which he had received in marriage with his wife, witnesses Hamelin de Warren and Roger de Mowbray; and a third of Mabel, wife of Nigel, granting a virgate of land to the Canons. In the *title* to the last she is called "the daughter of William Patrio." Brooke says (Discovery, p. 91) that there was also in the cartulary a "charta Patricii Comitis," but the "*Comitis*" may justly be doubted. Patricius was, in fact, the Latin form of the Norman surname Patry; and a William Patry, a Robertus Patricius, and others of the family, will be found in Wiffen's Memoirs of the House of Russell, vol. i. pp. 72 et seq. The introduction of a daughter of the Earl of Salisbury into this descent is therefore utterly groundless.

Such is the erroneous fabric of the first reputed sister of Ela.

2. *The wife of Gilbert Malmaines.*

This second sister is proposed in the following passage of Clutterbuck's History of Hertfordshire:

"Parish of Great Gaddesden, manor of Southall. Amongst the lands of the Normans, which were extended in the 6th year of King John, on the conquest of Normandy by the French, we find the lands of Gatesden, of Gilbert de Malmaines in right of his wife, in the county of Hertford. (Rot. Norm. 6 Joh. m. 3.) This land, I am inclined to think, was a share of the inheritance of William D'Evreux, Earl of Salisbury; for, though William Longspé, who married Ela his daughter, has been generally considered as marrying the sole heir of the family, it seems very well ascertained that William D'Evreux had another daughter; for, in the 18th Henry III. Ela Countess of Salisbury and Nicholas Malmaines had their purparties assigned to them in the manor of Culing in Suffolk, formerly enjoyed by Alianore Countess of Salisbury, mother of Ela, and grandmother of Nicholas Malmaines, which Alianore had probably held it in dower. (Claus. 18 Hen. III. m. 26.)"

Now it is true that this record * shows the Countess Alianor to have been grandmother of Nicholas Malmaines, but it does show that the Earl of Salisbury was his grandfather; and, as it has been found that the Countess, instead of dying two years before her husband (as stated in the Book of Lacock), survived to the year 1216,† it is most probable that she took a second husband, named Gilbert de Malmaines. I have found no pedigree of Malmaines; but their son was perhaps Thomas, the wardship of whose heir was granted to the Earl of Salisbury and the Countess Ela in 1221.‡ That heir may have been Nicholas, who had his share of Culing, as described in the preceding passage, in 1234.

A BROTHER OF THE COUNTESS ELA.

In the midst of these researches respecting the Countess Ela's pretended sisters, our attention is arrested by the appearance of a brother; whose existence is proved by a charter of Earl William his father, to Bradenstoke Priory, among the witnesses to which occur the words WALTERO FILIO MEO. ‖ However, as this Walter occupies a low place in a long list of witnesses; and as we not meet with him elsewhere, it may be confidently presumed that he was illegitimate.

J. G. N.

* The foregoing agrees with an abstract in the Harleian MS. 381, f. 29; where we find the following addition:
"Salvo Henrico de Turbervill toto residuo ipsius Manerii quod remanebit ultra rationalibes partes ipsorum Comitisse & Nich'i et ultra partem Jacobi de Bovelingham et uxoris ejus."

† "Mand' est Constabulo Oxon. et Berchampsted q'd in pace tenere permittat Alienor. Comitissam Sarr. matrem Isabell' [*sic, pro* Elæ] Com. Sarr. maneria sua de Gatesden et de Eggeswerr et Wotton. T. Rege apud Bradeford, xxx die Aug. 1216." Hardy's Calendar of Close Rolls, vol. i. p. 285.

‡ Ibid. p. 468.

‖ It is printed in the Monasticon; and appears in the Cartulary in the Cotton MS. Vitellius, A. XI, f. 96.

CHAPTER V.

Marriage of Ela of Salisbury to William Longespé—His mother Fair Rosamund—Particulars of his career as Earl of Salisbury—Fate of Arthur Duke of Britany—Salisbury's campaigns in Flanders—Wars of the Barons, and Ratification of Magna Charta—Death of King John.

We have no other particulars of the marriage of Ela of Salisbury to William Longespé, beyond the information afforded by the Book of Lacock, that it was from his brother King Richard that William received the hand of the heiress. It must therefore be from this, and similar scattered circumstances, that we shall collect the date when the marriage took place, and the respective ages of the parties.

It has been seen that it was not until two years after her father's death in 1196, that Ela was discovered. This was therefore only one year before King Richard's death, which happened in 1199; and consequently the marriage, or rather affiancing, must have been concluded immediately after the heiress was placed within the power of her Sovereign Lord, and when she was only ten years of age.

William Longespé was the son of King Henry the Second, by the fair Rosamund Clifford, whose romantic name, her traditional fate, and the proximity of her bower and of her burial-place to the muses of Oxford, have all contributed to perpetuate that celebrity which her beauty acquired in her own days.

We have no direct intimation of the time of William Longespé's birth; but it may be nearly ascertained from the history of his unfortunate mother. Fair Rosamund was not known as the Royal Mistress, until after the imprisonment of Queen Alianor, on account of her siding with her sons in their rebellion.* This was in the year 1173. Then was Rosamund brought forward as the open and avowed paramour of King Henry; and it is hardly probable that a passion, which then became so prominent and conspicuous, should have been indulged in a less degree for any great extent of time before. Many historians, in fact, have supposed that it was the King's attachment to Rosamund which first urged the Queen to incite her sons to rebellion. If, therefore, we assign the intercourse of Henry with Rosamund to a period within the years 1172 and 1177, (which latter date has been ascribed to her death,) we shall probably include the true date; and the birth of William Longespé may consequently be fixed about the year 1175, which will make him thirteen years older than Ela.

* " Regina enim sua *Elianora jamdudum incarcerata*, factus est adulter manifestus, palam et impudice *puellam* retinens Rosamundam. Huic nempe *puellæ*," &c. (Chron. Joh. de Brompton, col. 1151.)

As connected with the birth of William Longespé, it is necessary to make a few remarks on another personage, himself of considerable eminence in history, whose imputed birth has tended to confuse every writer who has hitherto written on the history of FAIR ROSAMUND. Another natural son of King Henry, Geoffrey, who was first Bishop of Lincoln and afterwards Archbishop of York, has been generally called the son of Fair Rosamund, and even deemed a *junior* brother to the Earl of Salisbury.* The strict comparison of dates which has just been made, shows that William Longespé was the son of Henry's middle life; whilst Geoffrey was certainly the child of his youth, and was Bishop of Lincoln almost as early as William was born! The term *puella*, used by Brompton,† would not have been applicable to Rosamund at the time of the Queen's imprisonment in 1173, had she been the mother of the King's son Geoffrey, who was born in 1159. It therefore follows that Geoffrey was the son of another mother. His age is thus precisely recorded:

"Natus est 5º Hen. II. [1159.] Factus est miles 25º Hen. II. [1179] Elect. in Episcop. Lincoln 28º Hen. II. [1182]."
(Chron. de Kirkstall.)

This testimony of the Kirkstall Chronicle, taken by itself, tended to confuse the investigation of Ro-

---

* See Sandford's Genealogical History of England, and the Archæologia, vol. xxi.; Dugdale, however, does not mention Geoffrey with William under the title Clifford.

† See note in the preceding page.

samund's history made by Percy in his Reliques of Ancient Poetry; but the removal of Archbishop Geoffrey from the family, and the circumstance of William Longespé first appearing in history about 1198, will, on the contrary, be found to confirm the previously received accounts of Rosamund Clifford.*

The circumstance that we find nothing relative to William Longespé of a date previous to his marriage, forms a material confirmation to the view which has now been taken. We may presume that he then was a youth just rising into manhood, and that his munificent brother, King Richard, took the earliest opportunity to confer upon him a provision which would be suitable to his royal birth.

It was with such great heiresses as Ela of Salisbury, that provision was usually made for the younger offspring of royalty. Not to mention later instances of the kind, two may be noticed which belong to the same century. The heiress of Gloucester was given by King Henry the First to his natural son

* It may be added that Archbishop Geoffrey had a brother Peter, not mentioned anywhere except in the history of York Cathedral, where Geoffrey desired to make him Dean. (See Drake's York, pp. 423, 561) Peter may, doubtless, have been his brother without being the King's son; but, if he were of Royal birth, it was probably by the same mother, now unknown. Morgan, Provost of Beverley, another natural son of Henry the First, was born of the wife of Sir Ralph Bloet; and it is a remarkable coincidence which has never been noticed, that an Emma Bloet was in 1248 made Abbess of Godstow nunnery, the shrine of the body of Fair Rosamund.

Robert; and the heiress of the Warrens, Earls of Surrey, was bestowed first on an illegitimate son of King Stephen, and afterwards on a base brother of King Henry the Second.*

Such, then, was Ela's natural destiny; and it is very probable that the heiress of Salisbury was at once assigned to William Longespé, when the death of her father left her the heiress of his estates and dignity, and whilst her person was still detained from the King's possession. In such case the troubadour knight, William Talbot, was not only one whom the King could trust for his loyalty and experience, but one who was proud to be numbered among the most devoted friends of the youthful

---

* The heiress of the Warrens was an aunt of our Ela, being the daughter of her grandmother Ela of Ponthieu by her first husband William Earl Warren and Surrey. The second race of Warren were descended from the marriage of Ela's aunt and William Longespé's uncle; thus his friend and political associate the Earl of Warren (whose name will occur in subsequent pages) was the cousin-german both of himself and of his wife. The following table will show at one view the position of those connections of the Foundress of Lacock which more immediately allied her with the Royal house of Plantagenet.

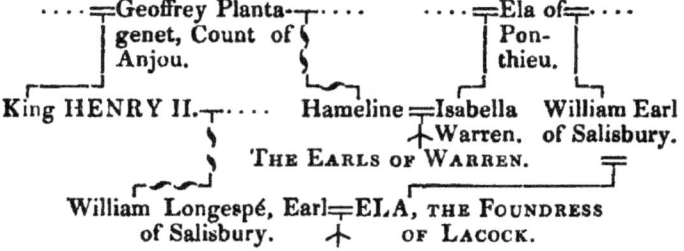

Longespé. Respecting Talbot we have this interesting fact, that his name occurs among the witnesses to several of the Earl's charters to Bradenstoke Abbey;* which shows, that, whether he had been a friend of Longespé from his early youth, or whether he had earned that friendship by his chivalric services in recovering the person of Ela, he continued in subsequent years the faithful retainer of the House of Salisbury.

Ela is now an honoured wife; and who can fail to imagine the "high heroic games" which would have taken place if this marriage had been celebrated in the reign of the chivalric Richard, when the spot selected by Ela's father for tournaments, was immediately opposite the Castle of Sarum. But we hear little of these things in the sullen and inglorious reign of the despicable John. After the marriage of Ela, we have nothing to recount of her for several years, unless it were to enumerate the names of her flourishing family of four sons and as many daugh-

---

* Also in the Close Rolls; on the 2d of May 1207, the King received by the hands of *William Talbot*, and of Geoffrey Leveel a servant of the Earl of Salisbury, forty marks from the fine of a Flemish merchant vessel which had been captured. It is probably the same William Talbot who, after the Earl's death, we find attending on the King's brother Earl Richard, in Poictou, (whither he may have accompanied the Earl of Salisbury the year before his death,) and witnessing (together with Savaric de Maloleone, mentioned elsewhere,) a truce made with King Louis in 1227. (Rymer's Fœdera.)

ters. These, however, will be found at the close of this chapter.

The Earl, as we shall find, was in very frequent attendance on the King his brother, through the vagrant life in which John's reign was spent.* That the Countess Ela would sometimes accompany the Court, may with reason be imagined; but it seems most natural to suppose that, if her own wishes were consulted, she would prefer the dignity and order of her own household, to the precarious provision of John's migratory train.

Whilst her life was passing in provincial sovereignty at Salisbury, or in the quiet retirement of some country manor, (most frequently, perhaps, in the peaceful shades of her native Amesbury,) we can only trace the current of her thoughts and anxious cares, in the active career of her princely and chivalric husband.

Of this illustrious personage it may be first remarked, that the name of William Longespé was originally derived from William Longespé, Duke of Normandy, who died in 948; and that it had also been borne by William Count of Flanders,† son of Duke Robert Curthose, and grandson of the Conqueror. His armorial coat was adopted from

---

* In the xxiid volume of the Archæologia will be found an Itinerarium of all John's movements throughout his reign, compiled by T. D. Hardy, Esq., F.S.A. He was like the wild Arab, *nescius stare loco.*

† Chron. de Mailros.

PEDIGREE III.

DESCENT OF WILLIAM LONGESPE, EARL OF SALISBURY, AND OF ELA HIS COUNTESS, FROM WILLIAM LONGESPE, DUKE OF NORMANDY.

```
                    WILLIAM LONGESPE, Duke of
                       Normandy, slain 923.
                              =
                              |
                    Richard I. Duke of Normandy.
                              =
                              |
                    Richard II. Duke of Normandy.
                              =
        _____|_____
       |                                             |
                                             Adeliza, wife of Rainald
                                               Count of Burgundy.
                                                      =
                                                      |
  Robert Duke of Nor-                          William Count of Bur-
      mandy.                                         gundy.
        |                                             =
  William the Bastard, Con-                  The wife of Odo, in her
     queror of England.                       right Duke of Burgundy.
        =                                             =
   _____|_____                                |
  |                   |                     Helen of Burgundy, wife
  Henry I. King of Eng-  Robert Duke of Nor-  of William Count of Pon-
       land.                 mandy.              thieu.
        =                      =                     =
  Matilda, the Empress,  WILLIAM LONGESPE,   Ela of Ponthieu, wife of
  wife of Geoffrey Count of  Count of Flanders  Patrick Earl of Salisbury.
     Anjou.      =          1127, ob. 1128.          =
                           Chron. de Mailros.
  Henry II. King of Eng-                       William Earl of Salis-
       land.                                         bury.
        |_____=
                         |
              WILLIAM LONGESPE, = ELA of Salisbury, Foun-
                 Earl of Salisbury.    dress of LACOCK.
```

another of his princely relations; for the six rampant lions had been first assumed, in the very infancy of heraldry, by his grandfather Geoffrey Plantagenet, Count of Anjou.* It may be added that Ela, also, through her grandmother Ela of Ponthieu, was descended from the sovereign house of Normandy, and, like her husband, could number Duke William Long-Sword among her ancestors.†

Immediately upon his marriage, or at least very shortly after, William Longespé entered upon Ela's hereditary office of the Shrievalty of Wiltshire,‡ which since the death of her father had been entrusted by the Crown to meaner hands.

On Ascension Day, being the 27th of May, 1199, King John was crowned at Westminster, in a full concourse of his nobility, among whom William Earl of Salisbury is recorded to have been present.§ On the same day, the King invested William Mar-

---

* See the engraving in Stothard's "Monumental Effigies" of the highly curious enamelled tablet, representing Count Geoffrey, with a long shield bearing the rampant lions in the same manner as on the effigy in Salisbury Cathedral.

† See the opposite Pedigree.

‡ In 1 Joh. for the fourth part of that year; for all the succeeding years till 9 Joh. inclusive. In 15 Joh. he was again constituted Sheriff of Wilts, which office he afterwards held so long as he lived. In 14 Joh. he was Sheriff for the counties of Cambridge and Huntingdon, for one half of that year; and again in 16 Joh. (Dugdale's Baronage, from the Pipe Rolls.) The Earl of Salisbury was also Sheriff of Lincolnshire for the first six years of the reign of Henry III.

§ Roger Hoveden.

shall with the sword of the earldom of Striguil (or Pembroke), and Geoffrey Fitz Peter with the sword of the earldom of Essex; "for, though," adds the chronicler, " they were called Earls, and exercised the administration of their earldoms, yet they were not till that day *girded with the sword of those earldoms, and so, that day, they served at the table with their swords girded to them.*" The same ceremonies must have taken place on the day when William Longespé was first invested with the earldom of Salisbury; but the date of that investiture has not been recorded. We may presume that it had already been celebrated in the reign of Richard.

On the 7th of June following, the Earl of Salisbury was with the King at Northampton, and there witnessed an ordinance relative to the Great Seal.*

King John was in Normandy, from April to October 1200, and again from May 1201 to December 1203. During part at least of this second and lengthened absence he was accompanied by the Earl of Salisbury, who probably attended him to his interview with King Philip at Paris in the beginning of July 1201. He was certainly with the King at Bonneville sur Toques on the 29th of October in that year; † at Bures on the 26th of December; ‡ at Angoulesme on the 4th of February 1202; § and at Vaudreuil on the 21st of April following.‖

* Rymer's Fœdera.   † Fœdera.
‡ Nichols's Hist. of Leic. i. 97.   § Fœdera.
‖ Chartæ Hibernicæ, p. 13. The document is there erroneously placed under 1201.

DEATH OF ARTHUR DUKE OF BRITANY.

It was at this time that the fatal tragedy was enacted of the youthful Arthur Duke of Britany, which has branded John in the page of history as the murderer of his nephew. The capture of Arthur took place at the castle of Mirabel, in Anjou, which was taken by the King in person on the feast of St. Peter ad vincula (Aug. 1). The young Duke was then sent as a prisoner to the castle of Falaise; and afterwards, when he had refused to adhere to King John instead of King Philip, he was removed to Rouen, where this high-spirited youth is presumed to have found his untimely death. The mode of that catastrophe is one of those mysterious transactions which must still continue in the class of "historic doubts."

The touching scenes of Shakspeare will at once arise to the mind of the reader, when these events are mentioned; and it may be recollected that the Earl of Salisbury is introduced by the poet * as one of the peers who throw off their allegiance to John,

---

* The loyalty and activity of the character which Shakspeare has named Philip Fauconbridge, would have suited the name of William Longespé; as well as the fact of being of royal, but illegitimate, birth. The materials of Philip Fauconbridge seem composed of two historical characters; of *Philip*, a natural son of King Richard, of whom little is known beyond the circumstance of his killing the Viscount de Limoges; to revenge his father's death; and of *Falcasius de Breant* (whence the name Falconbridge), a very distinguished soldier throughout the reign of John, and also a bastard, but not related to royalty.

from disgust at the horrible and unnatural crime of which they so strongly suspected him to have been guilty. Such are the combinations of times and events which are readily conceded as the privilege of the poet; but the only attention that can be paid them by the historian is to contrast them with the truth.

It is a fact that the Earl of Salisbury afterwards fell away from his allegiance to his brother (or appeared to do so); but it was at the distance of thirteen years from the death of Arthur, a distance, in fact, comprising almost the whole extent of the reign of John. During that interval, we have numberless instances of their reciprocal attachment. The rolls of King John's letters* abound in records of the King's constant bounty to his brother, not only in gifts of lands and fees, wardships and marriages, but in frequent presents of money, of timber, of wine, of venison, and of a variety of other things afforded by the royal demesnes, or which at that period contributed directly to the revenues of the crown.†

---

* By the recent publication of the Rotuli Literarum Clausarum we are made acquainted with many of the minutest occurrences in the reign of King John, a period which is thus brought forward from comparative darkness into a light almost as perfect (as far as the King is concerned) as one which is illustrated by gazettes and newspapers.

† On the 12th of May 1212, the King gave him the ship called the Countess, which had been taken by the Royal galiots. On the 18th of March 1215, the King directed the

CAREER OF EARL WILLIAM LONGESPÉ.

In the summer of 1204 we find the Earl accompanying his brother from place to place in England; being with the King at Bridgewater on the 4th of July, at his own priory of BRADENSTOKE on the 21st, at Karebroc * on the 24th, at Odiham on the 28th; at Badby in Northamptonshire on the 10th of August, at Devizes on the 29th and 30th of September, at Marlborough on the 1st of October, and at the Tower of London on the 2d of November.† On the 9th of September that year he was appointed Constable of Dover Castle, which office he held for about twenty months.‡ On the 13th of January 1205, he was with the King at a place called Sutton, probably that near Winchester, in Hampshire; § on the 18th of February at Lexinton (now Laxton) in Nottinghamshire; ‖ and on the 21st of April at Westminster.¶

In this year we first meet with the name of Wil-

---

keepers of the Bishopric of Ely to deliver 100 live pike, great and small, to be put into the pools of the Earl at Gatinton.

* Some place between Ludgershall, where the King was on 23d, and Glastonbury, where he was on the 25th. Qu. Castle Cary?

† All these dates are from the Clause Rolls. The King was at his own palace of Clarendon during the same time only on the 22d—28th of September; the 10th, 11th, 18th, 20th, and 30th of November, the 1st, 3d, and the 28th—31st of December.

‡ His successor the Earl of Essex was appointed 25th May, 8th John. Lyon's Dover, p. 202.

§ Fœdera.   ‖ Ibid.   ¶ Clause Rolls.

liam Longespé in a military command. On the 9th of June 1205, the King, being then at Portsmouth, ordered the payment of £26. 5s. 10d. for the livery of the Earl of Salisbury's ships.* John was then intending himself to embark for France, having made vast preparations to attempt the recovery of Normandy, which had been lost in the preceding year; but he was dissuaded from the present execution of his design by the Archbishop of Canterbury and the Earl of Pembroke; and, after considerable hesitation and fluctuation of purpose, he relinquished his intention. We have it recorded † however, that "his brother the EARL OF SALISBURY had already passed over, with many knights, and had landed at Rochelle, whither King John's natural son Geoffrey had preceded him shortly before." We hear nothing of their achievements; for victory continued to favour the arms of King Philip.

In less than a month the Earl was returned; for we find him with the King at Marlborough on the 3d of July; ‡ and on the 18th of August he was with him at Bere. §

The almost constant attendance of the Earl of Salisbury on his brother might thus be pursued from month to month, and from place to place; but we

* Clause Rolls, p. 38.

† In the Chronicle of Ralph Coggeshall, MS. Cotton, Vesp. D. x. f.105.

‡ Chartæ Hibernicæ, p. 14.

§ Clause Rolls.

have said, already, perhaps more than enough to show their great personal attachment. King John made another expedition to France in 1206; but with that exception he remained for some years in England, still continuing his migratory life.*

In 1209 the Earl of Salisbury was constituted Warden of the Marches of Wales.†

More stormy times were soon at hand. In the year 1211, Pope Innocent fulminated his interdict against King John. Then not a bell was heard, throughout the whole kingdom. The dead were interred without a word of " dona pacen;" no requiem was chaunted; no marriage rite celebrated; no child brought to the font for Christian baptism! At this crisis William Earl of Salisbury was still found the most faithful friend of his royal brother, through evil report as well as good. He is named first among those whom Matthew Paris calls the King's " *consiliarii iniquissimi!* "

He was of course involved in some of the scenes of humiliation which John was doomed to encounter. On the 3d of May 1213 he was present at Dover, and there witnessed the King's treaty of peace with

---

* On the 3d of June 1207, the Earl was with him at Woodstock (Clause Rolls); on the 21st of Jan. 1208, at Lambeth (Fœdera); on the 18th of March at Marlborough (ibid.); on the 19th of April at Tewkesbury (Clause Rolls); on the 11th of September, at Aston (Fœdera); and on the 18th of October at Shrewsbury (ibid.) The Clause Rolls of 9 and 10 John are unfortunately deficient.

† Dugdale. " Pat. 10 Joh. m. 3."

the Barons; on the 15th of the same month, also at Dover, in the house of the Knights Templars, he witnessed the charter by which the King resigned the kingdom and crown of England to the Pope; and on the 3d of October, at St. Paul's, London, he beheld John's mean performance of absolute homage at the feet of a legate of the Sovereign Pontiff!

In the same year, on Flanders being invaded by Philip King of France, the EARL of SALISBURY went as the General of the English forces sent in aid of Ferrand Count of that province,* supported by Wil-

* In the preceding year the Earl had been sent to Dover to meet the Count, as appears by a letter in Rymer's Fœdera dated July 20, 1212. The letter of his credentials to Count Ferrand in 1213 is also printed in the Fœdera. The King tells the Count that he had sent to his assistance William Earl of Salisbury, Reginald Count of Boulogne, Hugh de Boves, Henry Fitz-Count, and Brian de Insula. This is dated on the 25th of May. On the Close Rolls we find another letter bearing date two days later, addressed by the King to Peter de Mauley, in the following terms, the conclusion of which is remarkable, as characteristic of John's ungenerous and suspicious disposition: " We send you three hundred marks, desiring that, if our brother the Earl of Salisbury should remain in the parts of Flanders with the Count of Flanders for the convention which you know of, after the ships have returned, that then you pay them for his expenses; but if he should not remain there after the ships, then you shall return them, *and see that he knows nothing of it.* By myself at Wingham 27th May." On the 22d June the King commissioned John Fitz-Hugh and Falkes de Breant to attend to his affairs with his brother the Earl of Salisbury, whom he then sent to them, and desired them to remain with him, and consult for his advantage and honour, not acting with

liam Duke of Holland and Reginald Count of Boulogne. The expedition was unusually short; for, surprising a large French fleet at anchor in the harbour of Swine,* deserted by the soldiers who had marched to ravage the country, the English forces, having soon overcome the sailors, immediately loaded thirty† of the transports with every kind of store and provision, and sent them off to sail for England. They then proceeded to fire the despoiled vessels, amounting to a hundred or more, which were lying dry on the shore; so that, adds Matthew Paris, the French King and his nobility

him, should they consider him to be adopting improper measures. The King adds that he had deposited in the New Temple at London, 20,000 marks, which they were to draw at 1000 or more at a time as they required.

* The name in Matthew Paris. More accurate particulars of places and dates are supplied by Jacob Meir, a Flemish historian quoted by Holinshed. The place where the French fleet lay was the haven of Dam, now called Dollart Bay; the English attacked them, and landed, on the Thursday before Pentecost (May 30); were joined by the Earl of Flanders the next day; and on Whitsun even (June 1) when assaulting the town of Dam, were surprised by King Philip, who came from Ghent, and driven to their ships. The three Earls then sailed with their booty to the Isle of Walcheren.

† Erroneously " three hundred" in Holinshed! By Meir (according to Holinshed) the number of ships taken is stated as four only. The same writer, while contracting the loss of the French, probably in a still greater degree exaggerated that of the English and Flemings, which he states as two thousand men, besides those taken prisoners, amongst whom he says were twenty-two knights.

lost the most favourite treasures they had on earth.*
After a brief battle with the returning French army, the English then took to their ships; and King Philip, ruined by the great loss he had sustained, immediately relinquished his Flemish campaign.

In the latter part of the same year (1213), we find the Earl attending on King John, at Rochester October 5, at Freemantle October 28, at Gloucester December 1, and at Marlborough December 6. †

In the following January the Count of Flanders came to England, and had an interview with King John at Canterbury; after which, he returned home, taking with him the EARL OF SALISBURY, the King having agreed to assemble a more numerous army in the same country. ‡ Of that army the Earl was appointed the Marshal; his duties being to serve the campaign with the English forces, and to furnish pay from the treasury to the others engaged in the service. § On the approach of the hostile armies, the

---

* " Rex Francorum et tota fere transmarina nobilitas amiserunt quod in rebus humanis dulcimus possiderunt."

† Clause Rolls.   ‡ Matthew of Westminster.

§ This passage is so important and interesting, as describing the duties of the Marshal, that it is perhaps desirable to quote the words of the original: " Rex autem Johannes constituerat Mareschallum illius exercitus WILLIELMUM COMITEM SARESBERIENSEM, cum militia Regni Anglorum, ut cum ipsis militaret, atque aliis militantibus de fisco stipendia ministraret." Thus England then, as in modern times, paid for all! Both Matthew Paris and Matthew of Westminster notice the prodigality of this year, for John was himself with an army in Poictou; and the

English and their allies were disposed in three battalions, the commanders of the first of which were Ferrand Count of Flanders, Reginald Count of Boulogne, and William Earl of Salisbury. The battle took place on the 27th of July at Bovines, between Tournay and Lisle; and the victory was with the French.

Such are the leading facts, as related by Matthew Paris, of this ruinous campaign, in which the Earl of Salisbury occupied so prominent a station. But that historian seems not to have been aware that just a week before the battle, namely on the previous Sunday (July 20), being the feast of St. Margaret the Virgin, the English army had lost the services of its illustrious Marshal. It appears that the Earl had formed a plan to surprise the French King whilst he was attending mass, but was himself captured in the enterprise, with the rest of his party.*

It happened, however, that a cousin-german of King Philip, the eldest son of the Comte de Dreux, had been taken by the English shortly before; so that, after some negociation, the brave, but in this instance unfortunate, SALISBURY was set at liberty, it is believed early in the following year.†

former asserts that John expended in it 40,000 marks, which he had " shamefully taken from the Cistercian monks."

* Dugdale, from a " MS. Oxon. in bibl. Bodl. n. 11, f. 177 b et 178 a."

† Dugdale, from Pat. 16 Joh. p. 1, in dorso m. 13; and Ypod. Neust. in ann. 1215.

SEALING OF MAGNA CHARTA.

In the mean time, the differences between King John and his Barons were rising to a fearful height, and the month of June, in 1215, witnessed the proud triumph of the latter, and the acquisition of MAGNA CHARTA * on the field of Runnimede. At that ever memorable meeting, the whole of the Peers of England were assembled; and the great majority were in the camp of the Barons, whose army was increased to numbers the most formidable. Many, indeed, had just before transferred their support from the King to the prevailing party; and John was reduced by an imperious necessity to a reluctant and insincere concession. The higher aristocracy, however, still appeared on the Royal side; and the banner of the Earl of Salisbury † floated in the camp of his Royal brother, together with those of the Earls of Pembroke, Warren, and Arundel.

Before that same year had closed, the treacherous King, who had previously been reconciled to the Pope, and had assumed the Cross, thereby placing himself under the protection of the Church, procured from this Spiritual King of Kings upon Earth, an anathema against the Barons, and a suspension of Cardinal Langton from the see of Canterbury.

* A most beautiful copy, as regards penmanship, was deposited, and is now to be seen in the Chamber of Records at Salisbury Cathedral.

† In a letter dated the 6th of June, the King had directed Falkes de Breant to send fifty Welshmen, to be with the Earl of Salisbury, at Salisbury on the Tuesday after Easter. Clause Rolls. The Earl probably still retained his military command in Wales.

John also collected a numerous army of foreign mercenaries, with which he wrested the castle of Rochester from the confederate Barons, and then marched to St. Alban's, where he assembled his friends on the 20th of December. There, having first directed the Convent to publish throughout the country the Archbishop's suspension, he proceeded to form two armies to suppress the insurgent people; one destined for the Northern counties under his own command, and the other for the South, under the EARL OF SALISBURY and the fierce Falcasius de Breant. The proceedings of Salisbury's army were first to place garrisons in the castles of Windsor, Hertford, and Berkhampstead, to watch the city of London, where the Barons had fixed themselves, and to cut off the supply of their provisions. The Earl and Falcasius then marched through the counties of Essex, Hertford, Middlesex, Cambridge,* and Huntingdon, "laying all waste with spoliation and rapine, after the example of Holofernes, the captain of the army of the Assyrians;" placing towns under contribution, carrying off men, burning the houses of the Barons, destroying their parks and fishponds, cutting down their orchards; and at last continuing the spoliation, to a great extent, accompanied with fire, even to the

* Matthew of Paris particularly describes their havoc in the Isle of Ely, which they were enabled to enter from the dykes being frozen. They broke into the cathedral, and were only bought off from firing it by the Prior paying 209 marks of silver.

suburbs of London, and in the immediate neighbourhood of the Barons' forces. At this period the arms of the King were so successful, that the Barons had only two castles left, Mountsorrel in Leicestershire, and that of Robert de Ros in Yorkshire. At that crisis they turned for aid to Prince Louis of France, who in May 1216 landed at Sandwich.

We now encounter a remarkable change in the conduct of the Earl of Salisbury. He who had been so loyal to his Brother throughout all his difficulties, is now found suddenly to join the French Invader.* "William Earl Warren, William Earl of Arundel, William Earl of Salisbury, and William Marshall the younger," says Matthew Paris, "and many others with them, deserting King John, came to Louis, as if they accounted it now perfectly certain that Louis would obtain the Kingdom of England." In the Chronicles of Melrose, however, (in which the French Chronicles are followed,) the conduct of these Earls is attributed to craft instead of affection, and to have been adopted rather with the intention of subverting than of assisting the cause of Louis, as, it is remarked, their subsequent " treason" showed.

* On the 28th of March he was with the King at Plessey in Essex; on the 31st he had a grant of the marriage of the daughter of Ranulph de Glanville; on the 17th of August he was with the King's enemies. (Clause Rolls.) On the 17th of September, at Lambeth, he witnessed the treaty of peace with Louis. (Fœdera.)

DEATH OF KING JOHN.

John did not long survive the desertion of his best friends. On the 18th of October 1216, death terminated his turbulent and miserable reign; and during the truce made at the following Christmas, the four Earls just named, all again changed their party, and acknowledged THE YOUNG KING, HENRY the THIRD.

The circumstances of this return are more particularly related in the Chronicles of Melrose, copied doubtless from some French historian. It is there stated, that in the month of March,* whilst Louis was in the isle of Rhé, in Flanders, there unexpectedly rose against him WILLIAM LONGESPÉ, the brother of King John, the younger William Marshall, and their confederates; but by God's providence some French ships, destined for England, accidentally came at that time to the island, and Louis was delivered from their power.

Dugdale suggests, that the return of the Earl of Salisbury to the Royal side was induced by the great advantages which were held out to him by the Regent Pembroke: for he immediately did homage to the King for the county of Somerset, then granted to him; † and after the raising of the siege

---

* This date is confirmed by the Clause Rolls. On the 9th of March the King wrote to the several Sheriffs and Constables in whose jurisdictions the Earl's lands were situated, informing them that " WILLIAM EARL OF SARUM *our uncle has come to our fealty and service, and we have received him into our grace and favour,*" ordering them therefore to restore his possessions.

† " Pat. 1 H. 3, m. 4."

of Lincoln, at which he was present, he was constituted Sheriff of that county, and Governor of the Castle;* and Dugdale remarks that, in the command which was directed to Peter de Mauley to give Salisbury livery of the Castle of Sherborne and County of Somerset, he was required to do it without delay, lest the Earl should start back.†

To this it may be added that the Clause Rolls for many subsequent years teem with entries of money and lands which were conferred upon him. From some of them we gather that the King presented him with £1000 in money, the payment of which was completed in November 1219; and besides paid him yearly the sum of 300*l*. until he was provided with escheated lands of that value. Lands to the value of 500*l*. had been promised him by King John.

The guardian of the young King Henry, and his constant attendant, was the Earl of Pembroke; but the Earl of Salisbury received scarcely fewer favours from the Crown than had fallen to his share when he was the companion of the late King. Besides the weightier matters already mentioned, gifts of deer and of timber are particularly frequent; and among the latter was some for *the repair of his houses at Lacock.*

It was supposed by Dugdale that the Earl of Salisbury at this period went on the Crusade, and was present at the seige of Damietta in 1219; but this

---

* " Pat. 1 H. 3 m. 7." † " Ibid. m. 11."

statement seems to have arisen from a misinterpretation of a name in Matthew Paris.*

* The words of Matthew Paris are " de Outhlandia, de Wiche, de Saleberge, et Cestriæ Comitibus." The first three seem to be all foreigners. " Outhlandia" is Holland ; " Saleberge" is perhaps *Salzberg;* the Latin of Matthew Paris for Salisbury, in other parts of his History, is always Sarisberiensis; and the editor seems to have been aware this was another person, having in the index omitted this page among those in which the Earl of Salisbury occurs. The whole of the most illustrious Englishmen present at this siege of Damietta, are thus enumerated in the Chronicon Rofense, MS. Cotton, D. II. f. 130; " Venerunt de regno Angliæ viri nobiles et nominatissimi : illustris Comes Cestrie Ranulphus, Saero Winton. et Willielmo Harundel; et inclitis Baronibus, Roberto filio Walteri, Johanne Constabulario Cestriæ, Willielmo de Harecure, Olivero filio Regis Anglie, cum sequela sua non modica."

CHAPTER VI.

Foundation of the Cathedral of New Sarum—The Earl's Campaign in Gascony—His last perilous Voyage—Hubert de Burgh's insult to Ela, the Earl's resentment, and his Death.

ENGLAND now enjoyed some years of peace; and we may return with the Earl to his Castle of Salisbury, and to that most interesting scene, in which the pious Ela was an active party with him. This is no less than the ceremony of founding the present beautiful Cathedral of Salisbury. A particular account of this memorable occurrence has been left, as we have already mentioned, by William de Wanda, who was then Precentor and afterwards Dean of Sarum;* it is as follows:

"In the year of Grace 1220, on the feast of Saint Vitalis the Martyr, namely, the fourth of the calends of May, the foundation of the new church of Sarum was laid. The Bishop had expected that the King would have come to the ceremony, with the Legate and the Archbishop of Canterbury, and many of the nobility of England; and he had therefore in-

* The original will be found in the first volume of Wilkins's Concilia. In the translation given in Dodsworth's History of Salisbury Cathedral there are several inaccuracies.—The present Bishop of Salisbury has had a fair transcript made for ready reference of the MS. in which it is preserved, called the Register of Osmund. It contains the Annals of the Church, from Osmund to Henry III.

curred a great expense in order to prepare a solemn banquet for all comers. But the Bishop was disappointed, in consequence of a negotiation then pending with the Welsh, at Shrewsbury. He could not, however, defer the business longer, because it had been publicly announced throughout the diocese.

"On the day appointed, the Bishop came with great devotion, few Earls or Barons of the county attending, but a great multitude of the common people crowding hither from all parts. When divine service had been performed (at the old cathedral), and the grace of the Holy Spirit invoked, the Bishop, having put off his shoes, went in procession with the clergy of the church to the place of the new foundation, singing the litany. After the litany, a sermon was made to the people. The Bishop then laid the first stone for our lord Pope Honorius, who had granted the license for transplanting the church; the second for Stephen Archbishop of Canterbury, and Cardinal of the holy Roman church, who was then with the King in the Marches of Wales; and the third for himself. Then the fourth was laid by William Earl of Salisbury; and the fifth by THE COUNTESS ELA,* a woman truly praiseworthy, because she was filled with the fear of the Lord. After her, the few noblemen present added each a stone; then Adam the Dean, William the Precentor, Henry the Chancellor, Abraham the Treasurer, and the

* "Ela de Viteri" in the original, the writer confusing the Countess with her mother.

Archdeacons and Canons of the church of Sarum, who were present, did the same, amidst the acclamations of the multitude, who even wept for joy, and contributed thereto, according to their ability."*

Who can read this account of the ceremony of laying the foundation stones of Salisbury Cathedral, and "*the people weeping for joy,*" without the deepest interest, enhanced by the reflection that now the worship is so much more pure and scriptural, and six hundred years have passed over the venerable pile! †

On the 11th of August in the same year (1220), the Earl of Salisbury was at Oxford, and there witnessed the convention with Geoffrey de Marisco, Justice of Ireland; ‡ on the 7th of September 1223 he witnessed the charter of Prince Llewellin promising satisfaction to the King; ‡ on the 16th of November following he was with the King at Gloucester; § and on the 18th of August 1224 he witnessed, at Bedford, the King's acknowledgment of an aid from the Clergy. ||

During these several years of the reign of Henry III. we meet with no record of Salisbury being actively employed; but in the spring of 1224, when

---

* William de Wanda adds, that in the course of time, as the nobility returned from Wales, several of them came and laid stones, binding themselves to a certain contribution for the next seven years.

† See Letter to Lord Henley, by the author.

‡ Rymer's Fœdera.   § Clause Rolls. || Fœdera.

his nephew Richard, the King's brother, had recently received the degree of knighthood, with the Earldoms of Cornwall and Poictou, it was determined that he should flesh his maiden sword in the plains of Gascony, under the guidance of his uncle THE EARL OF SALISBURY and Philip de Albeney. They accordingly sailed with sixty knights, and all landed safely at Bourdeaux, on Palm Sunday (April 7); when they were honourably received by the Archbishop and citizens. Then, having collected an army, the Earl proceeded with his Royal nephew through Gascony, reducing to obedience those who refused homage and fealty to King Henry; particularly the castle and town of la Reole, which they took after a long siege, the town and fort of St. Macari, and the castle of Bergerac; and so in a short space they subdued the whole country, notwithstanding a hostile force sent against them, under the command of Hugh Count of the March.*

* This is the account furnished by Matthew Paris. In the Fœdera is a letter sent by the Earl of Cornwall to the King from St. Macari on the 2d of May. He tells his brother that on the Thursday (April 18) before the feast of St. Mark, they came with the army around the city of Bazas (Vasatum), and passed the night without the city, which was surrendered by the Bishop and citizens in the morning; so that all Gascony was then freed from the King's enemies except Reole, and all the nobles to the King's party except Elias Ridell; and concludes with asking for money. It is related in the Annals of Dunstable, that there was one castle which held out for nearly three months; which was probably that of Ridell; and it is also par-

It appears that the Earl remained in Gascony, with Prince Richard, during the greater part of the year, and then attempted to return to England in the stormy month of October. The voyage was very disastrous, not only from the present hardships he encountered, but in its consequences as affecting the peace of the virtuous Ela, and eventually, as was supposed, the life of the Earl himself. We shall first describe the perils of the voyage, following strictly the expressions of Matthew Paris.

The chronicler begins by relating that, " after the Earl had been many days and nights at sea, thrown about by the storms to various quarters, despairing of his life, as did the sailors themselves and all that were in the ship, he committed to the waves his precious rings and whatever he possessed in gold or silver, or valuable vestments, in order that, as he had entered naked into this temporal life, so, despoiled of all earthly honour, he might pass to his eternal country. But whilst he was driven to the utmost despair, a waxen light of large size and shining with great splendour, was seen by all in the ship, resting upon the summit of the mast, and and near it they saw standing a girl adorned with exquisite beauty, who preserved that bright waxen light, shining through the nocturnal darkness, from the violence of the wind and rain. Being encou-

ticularly stated, in the same authority, that the Earl of Salisbury left the country before the conclusion of the siege of la Reole, which lasted for nine months.

raged by this vision of heavenly brightness, both the Earl himself, and all the sailors, trusted that divine aid was vouchsafed to them; but, whilst all in the ship could not conceive what this vision portended, Earl William alone assigned the favour of the benign appearance *to the blessed Virgin Mary!* for the Earl, on the day when he had been first honoured with the belt of knighthood, had appointed *a wax light* to stand before the altar of the *most blessed Mother of God*, that it might burn during *the mass* which was *daily* wont to be devoutly chaunted, with the canonical hours, in her honour, and might exchange its *temporal* light for that which is *eternal!*

" After this occurrence, on the following dawn, the Earl was carried by the wind, with his companions, to the isle of Rhé, three miles distant from Rochelle; where, having entered their small boats,* they rowed to the shore. There was in the island a Cistercian abbey, to which the Earl sent messengers, requesting that he might therein lie concealed from his enemies, until he was favoured with a more propitious wind; to which the Abbat kindly consented, and received him and his companions with honour. The island was in the charge of Savaric de Maloleone, who at that time served the King of the French, and kept watch upon several islands on that coast with a considerable force; two of whose

---

* " Brevibus cymbis."

retainers, who well knew the Earl,* and were deputed with many others to the ward of the islands, coming in a friendly manner to him, after he had stayed there about three days, told him that, unless he left the island before the following morning, he would be captured by their comrades, who guarded the islands and straights with them. Upon this the Earl, having presented to those soldiers twenty pounds sterling, quickly flew to his ships, and trusting himself to the waves, was for almost three months constantly struggling with the raging elements, before he landed in England."

Such is the account given by Matthew Paris of this fatal voyage; and from a subsequent passage it appears that the Earl's landing was effected in Cornwall at the time of Christmas. During the interval, all his friends had despaired of his safety, except his faithful wife; who, though now a matron whose age and dignity ought to have commanded greater respect, became again an object of pursuit to the fortune-hunters of the court. The person who then had the greatest sway in the country, was the the Justiciary Hubert de Burgh; a man who was

* The soldiers of Savaric de Maloleone had good reason to know the Earl of Salisbury; for their captain had assisted him and Falcasius de Breant in their devastation of the isle of Ely, mentioned in a previous note, p. 118. (Matthew Paris.) Savaric was afterwards Seneschal of Poictou and Guienne; his name is one of very frequent occurrence in the Rotuli Literarum Clausarum. He is also one of the Troubadours commemorated in Mrs. Dobson's abridgement of St.-Palaye.

no less remarkable on account of his power and prosperity under one King, than for his trials and sufferings under another. This potent minister, with a most indecent haste, put forward a nephew of his own as a suitor to the lady of Salisbury; and the youth, entering with a kindred spirit into the interested views of his ambitious relative, at once proceeded to seek an interview with the Countess, and, it is said, to insult her with his personal addresses. Ela, however, like another Penelope, possessed a heart which could not be alienated from her absent Lord. But the story will be best continued in the narrative of the same chronicler, who has preserved so much of the interesting history of the Earl.

It is related by Matthew Paris, that, whilst King Henry was deeply affected with grief at the supposed loss of the EARL OF SALISBURY, the Justiciary Hubert came and required from him that he would bestow Earl William's wife, to whom the dignity of of that Earldom belonged, by hereditary right *, on his own nephew Reimund, that he might marry her.

* Dugdale misunderstood this clause to apply to Reimund, translating it, " who pretended an hereditary right to this Earldom of Salisbury." This is contradicted by the disdainful manner in which both the Countess and the Earl are represented to have spoken of his family. It clearly applies to Ela herself, the heiress of her paternal ancestors the former Earls of Salisbury, and in whose right Reimund, had he been successful in his suit, would have become EARL OF SALISBURY, during her life. The operation of this law of inheritance, as vested in

The King having yielded to this petition, provided the Countess could be induced to consent, the Justice forthwith sent Reimund to her in a noble knightly array, to endeavour to incline the lady's heart to his suit. But when Reimund, with flattering speeches and large promises, attempted to induce her to consent, Ela with majestic scorn replied, "that she had lately received letters and messengers, which assured her that the Earl her husband was in health and safety;" adding further, "that, if her lord the Earl had indeed been dead, she would in no case have received *him* for a husband, because their unequal rank with respect to family, forbad such a union. Wherefore," said she, "you must seek a marriage elsewhere, because you find you have come hither in vain." So Reimund de Burgh, hearing this, departed from her in confusion.*

Such was one of the most trying incidents in the life of the Countess Ela, as related by Matthew Paris. It is a remarkable circumstance, that, from the church history of William de Wanda, we find Hubert de Burgh was himself twice at Salisbury, in

Ela, will be more fully shown in the history of her son, in the ensuing Chapter.

* Whether Reimund was afterwards married does not appear; he is not noticed by Dugdale in his article on the family of de Burgh. But we learn from Matthew Paris the circumstances of Reimund's death; he was drowned at Nantes in 1230, from the horse on which he was riding by the side of the river Loire, slipping down a steep bank, into the stream.

attendance on the King, during the months in which the Earl was contending with the winds and the waves of the stormy Channel. It is therefore not surprising that the future disposal of this rich earldom should have become the subject of his ambitious speculations. Ambition seems to have had its powerful influence on his otherwise great mind. He had himself married the daughter of the King of Scotland.

The first of his visits to the new Cathedral, together with King Henry, was on Friday * next after Michaelmas, when the King offered to the church ten marks of silver, and a rich piece of silk; and the Justiciary promised to the new altar a Text—that is, a copy of the Gospels, in the original Greek,—bound in gold with precious stones, and *the relics of divers saints,* to be *devoted to the honour of the Blessed Virgin.* This precious volume was brought in the following week, by the Justiciary's clerks, Luke the Dean of St. Martin's in London, and Thomas de Kent. The second visit of the KING and the JUSTICIARY, took place on the feast of the Holy Innocents, when the latter offered in person, at the altar, with great devotion, the splendid Text, and the King at the same time offered *a ruby ring,* both the gold and stone of which he directed should be applied to the further ornament of the covering of the Justiciary's book.†

* Erroneously "Thursday" in Dodsworth's Salisbury Cathedral, p. 119.
† Wilkins's Concilia, vol. i. p. 557.

Such was the usual practice with these invaluable manuscripts;* and we should indeed be ungrateful were we to censure either the respect, however allied to superstition, with which they were regarded, or the glorious magnificence in which they were enshrined; and which alike, under Providence, contributed to hand down to posterity their precious and *solely infallible* contents, now rescued from the *human infallibility* of the unstable traditions of the Church of Rome.

To return to the transactions which took place at Salisbury during the absence of Earl William. We have seen that Hubert de Burgh was *there*, at that very time; when, we are told, he indulged the design of heaping further honours and possessions on his family, by the acquisition of the Earldom of Sarum. It could not be deemed extravagant were we to connect his liberality towards the church with his dreams of aggrandisement; under the influence of which he would naturally desire to conciliate the favour of the clergy towards that new family, which he desired to see established within the ancient castle.

When the King and Justiciary came the second

* Some specimens of these splendid volumes are still preserved, particularly in the Royal Library at Paris. Ducange has cited a variety of passages from old authors relating to the custom of adorning their exterior covers in the most sumptuous manner; and among them the following :—" Codices Evangelici *auro et argento lapidibusque pretiosis* non immerito decorantur, in quibus rutilat *aurum* cœlestis sapientiæ, nitet *argentum* fidelis eloquentiæ, fulgent miraculorum *pretiosi lapides!*" Rupertus Tuitiensis de Divinis Officiis.

time to Salisbury, the presumptuous visit of Reimund de Burgh to the Countess Ela must have already taken place; if indeed it was not made at that very time, when he might present himself supported by the immediate countenance and presence of the King and his uncle, next in authority to the King. The feast of the Holy Innocents was on the 28th of December, when Ela might possibly have heard, as she said, of the return of the Earl her husband; for it was during the days of Christmas that Longespé landed in Cornwall.

We now approach the closing scenes of the life of this brave and loyal chieftain: who, after he had landed in Cornwall, first arrived at Salisbury, on Saturday next after the Epiphany, the 4th of the ides of January (Jan. 10); and the same day, in the afternoon, on repairing to the New Cathedral, to offer his thanksgivings for his preservation and safe return, was received in procession by the clergy, with great demonstrations of joy.*

On the morrow he proceeded to the King, who who was then at Marlborough, ill in health.† His royal nephew welcomed him with great joy; and he then immediately made a heavy complaint to Henry, alleging, that whilst he had been employed in remote parts, the Justiciary had sent a certain low-bred ‡

* Chron. of W. de Wanda, Wilkins's Concilia, vol. i. p. 559.
† Ibid. What follows is from Matthew Paris.
‡ Hubert de Burgh had raised himself by his own abilities; and Reimund was probably not even a Knight.

man, who, whilst he was himself still living, would have dishonoured his wife, and have violently contracted an adulterous marriage with her. He added, moreover, that unless the King caused full reparation to be shown him from the Justiciary, he would himself seek redress for so great an outrage, to the most serious disturbance of the kingdom. Upon this the Justiciary, who was present, confessed the fault rested with him, and renewed his favour with the Earl by some valuable horses and other large presents; and so, peace being made, the Justiciary invited the Earl to his table, where, it is said, the Earl was infected with secret poison,* and, thence returning to the castle of Salisbury, took to his bed, grievously sick.

"His illness increasing, when he perceived very certain symptoms of approaching death, he caused the Bishop of the city † to come to him, that he might receive those things which befit a Christian

---

* The frequent insinuations of suspected poison which occur in old chronicles, seldom deserve any other regard than as evidences of the ignorance of the times in pathological science. It is evident that nothing could be more likely to act as poison than the royal feastings of Marlborough after the long privations of ship-board.

† Richard Poore. His effigy remains in Salisbury Cathedral; so the painter who would delineate this scene, has his portraiture and attire before him. See an engraving of the effigy, together with his seal, in Dodsworth's Salisbury Cathedral, pl. 3; and another in Britton's History of the same beautiful edifice, pl. 2 of Monuments.

in the confession and viaticum, and make a legal will of his possessions.* When the Bishop entered the bedchamber, bearing the BODY OF CHRIST, the Earl leaped from his bed towards him, entirely naked except his drawers; and *having tied a rough noose about his neck,* he prostrated himself weeping *upon the floor,* declaring that he was a traitor to the Most High! nor would he be removed until he had made his confession, and received the communion of the life-giving sacrament, that he might testify himself to be the servant of his Creator! And so, having for some days persevered in acts of the greatest penitence, he yielded up his soul to his Redeemer. And it happened, (continues the Chronicler,) while his body was being carried to its burial, for a mile between the castle and the new church, the wax candles which were borne lighted, according to custom, together with the censer, furnished a continual light in the way, amidst showers of rain and storms of wind, *openly manifesting that the Earl, who had been so deeply penitent, was then numbered with the sons of light."* So says Matthew † the Monk, which we are not hereticks enough to

---

* The will, as may be seen hereafter, was already settled.

† Dugdale has quoted Matthew of Westminster as the authority for this account of the funeral; but his narrative is merely an abridgement from that of Matthew Paris, with the additional remark that the incident of the burning lights had also occurred in the case of *Hugh the sainted Bishop of Lincoln, and Confessor.*

question; but who can read this account without lamenting the effect of superstition on such a mind as that of Longespé, however part of this interesting description may have been in unison with the purest spirit of devotion!

The exact date of the Earl's death is furnished both by our Book of Lacock and by William de Wanda; it was on Saturday the nones (the 7th) of March 1226. The latter authority gives some account of his funeral, but without mentioning the miraculous tale of the Monk Matthew. His body, we are told by De Wanda, "was brought to New Sarum, with many tears and deep sighs, on the day of his death, and at the very same hour at which, exactly eight weeks before, he had been first welcomed in triumph to this beauteous new cathedral. On the morrow, being Sunday, he was honourably buried in the new Chapel of the blessed Virgin; and there were then present, the Bishops of Sarum, of Winchester (Peter de Rupibus), and a Bishop of Ireland, Earl William Marshall (Earl of Pembroke), and Earl William de Mandeville (Earl of Essex); also the Barons, Robert de Veteripont, Hugh de Gurnay, and Ralph de Toani, with a great multitude of knights."

The interment took place in the Chapel of the Virgin, of whose patronage and favour he had esteemed himself so eminently the object.* There,

* " Among the Chapter Records are various indulgences granted to such as should visit the Church, and recite certain

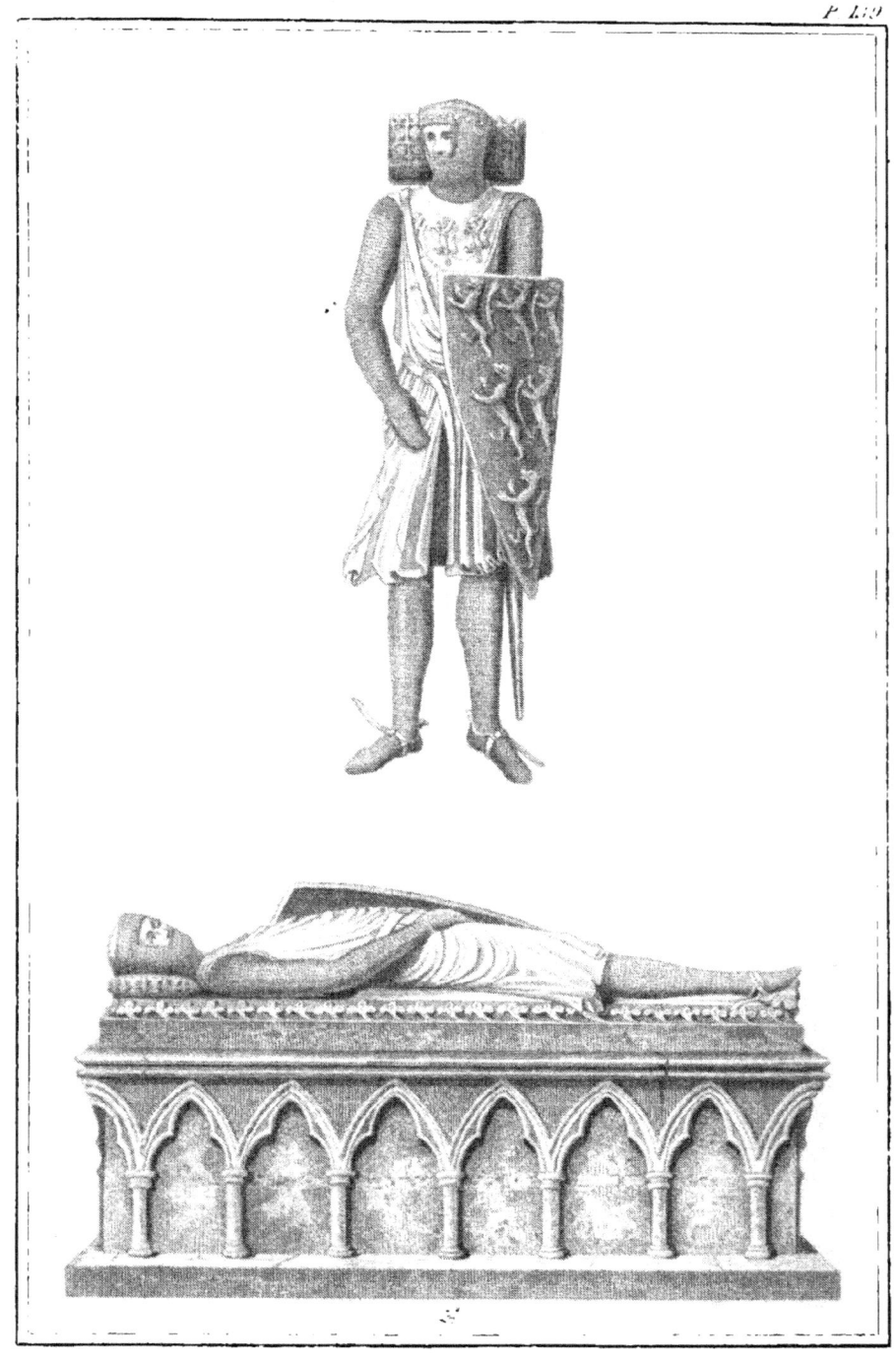

Monument of William Longespée Earl of Salisbury
in Salisbury Cathedral.

on the north, stood his monument, with his effigy, its sides ornamented with pillars and arches carved in wood, and panels richly painted, diapered, and gilt, having depicted around it, in alternate shields, the three lions passant of England, and the six rampant lioncels of Salisbury. In the year 1790, alas for Cathedral improvements! this monument was removed to its present situation in the nave; when the skeleton was found entire.*

The appearance of this " Son, Brother, and Uncle of Kings," to judge from his martial figure of grey marble, sleeping, as it were, from century to century, with his sword and shield, upon his tomb in Salisbury cathedral, must have been singularly manly and commanding.

His features are only partially exposed, through a small aperture in his hood of mail, which entirely covers his mouth and chin. His eyebrows are somewhat lofty and imperious; but the eyes seem gentle and intelligent.

His limbs are lightly cased with plaited mail,

---

prayers at his tomb. By the Archbishop of Cassel, in 1278, forty days; Robert Bishop of Wells in 1279; William Bishop of Landaff, and Walter Bishop of Sarum, in 1287; William Bishop of Sarum 1289; by John Archbishop of Dublin, 1291, for twenty days; by John Bishop of Winchester, Gilbert of Chichester, and Roger of Coventry and Lichfield, in 1295, for forty days; by Henry Bishop of Winchester in 1305; and by Roger Bishop of Sarum in 1327." Dodsworth's Salisbury Cathedral, p. 204.

* Dodsworth's Salisbury Cathedral, p. 204.

formerly gilt, which covers his hands and feet. On his body, above his mail shirt, he wears a surcoat, formerly blue painted with lioncels, and lined with crimson; this is confined by the belt of knighthood, with a golden buckle.

His long sword, reaching to his spurs, is seen by his side; but his right hand is not grasping it, as in the presumed figure of his son, in the same cathedral. It lies as it were peaceably resting at his side; as if to show he was by nature peaceable and gentle, but, when awakened, in the cause of the Cross, of his King, or of chivalry, could rise like the rampant lions on his shield; exemplifying the beautiful description of Shakspeare:

> In peace there's nothing so becomes a man
> As modest stillness and humility;
> But when the blast of war blows in our ears,
> Then imitate the action of the tiger!

In contemplating the obsequies of one of the pious and munificent Founders of Salisbury Cathedral, borne to the tomb, when the original words, in Latin, of our own affecting and sublime ritual, were solemnly chanted,—if this service, read or sung, be always impressive, how much more so must it have been, when the corpse of a nobleman so distinguished was brought, the first of the living generation, to be laid within those walls, of which he, with his pious and desolate widow, had laid one of the foundation stones! Think, reader, of the personage,—of his character—of his station—of the long line of torches from the castle to the cathedral in one straight line of a mile—of the hushed multitude, many in tears, with occasional audible laments! As the sad procession approached the cathedral, the bier was met, at the great western door, by Bishops, Noblemen, and the Cathedral Clergy, the Choristers and Precentor chanting in Latin, up the nave, the same funeral service now chanted in English, on occasion of public burials in cathedrals.* I may say this, for, among the earliest MSS. in our Cathedral is a volume containing great part of the present burial-service, in Latin (a part having been lost from the volume). This curious and beautiful MS. *secundùm usum Sarum* was written before the time of Bishop Osmund, though it is called his ritual.† How much further into antiquity the words may be traced is not decided; but it was long before anything like Popery, in its offensive shape, had its terrific dominion in these kingdoms.

The Music to which the words were sung,—the

---

* I will not insult the common understanding of every thinking being, by saying one word in defence of this holy and affecting service; when even the grammatical construction in one passage, has been *distorted*, by modern Puritanism, to suit a criticism as absurd as it is uncharitable. I allude to the words "the resurrection," in obvious answer to the words, " dust to dust."

† The ritual, printed 1555—secundum usum Sarum—is very different. I have this Breviarium Sarisburiense, and have compared it. The first hymn ends—" Melos canemus SARUM." in which there is an office for the Seven Sleepers! Die Septem dormientium!

choristers, Precentor, Bishop,* and dignitaries, chanting, in procession, before the body,—was probably no more than the *planus cantus*, with a dirge, or *Dirige*.

But who ever heard the words in English, chanted to the solemn and sublime music of Croft,† especially that exquisite verse of Purcell—

"Thou knowest, Lord, the secrets of our hearts!"

without tears.

A poet cannot advert to the circumstances that took place, as related by an eye-witness, at the funeral of the heroic chieftain of our annals of Lacock, without

A DIRGE

TO THE MEMORY OF WILLIAM LONGESPÉ,
Buried in Salisbury Cathedral, March 8, 1226.

Toll the bell—a solemn toll,
   Slow and solemn let it be,
While we pray for WILLIAM's soul,—
   MISERERE, DOMINE!

Lonely is the castled height,
   Now its scenes of glory close,—
Bear him, by the torches' light,
   To his long, his last repose.

---

* The Bishop of Salisbury, at Coronations and all national ecclesiastical convocations, whenever the King is present, is expected to attend, and, in virtue of his supposed eminence in musical science, to take the lead, as the Precentor of the Kingdom.

† Croft's service, with Purcell's most affecting verse, so lately performed over the lamented Bishop of Bristol, and over a brother Residentiary, departed from among us.

DIRGE.

Toll the bell—a solemn toll,
   Slow and solemn let it be,
While we pray for WILLIAM's soul,—
   MISERERE, DOMINE!

By torch-light from the castle hill,
   They bear him to the lighted Fane,
They bear him, mid laments and sighs,
   They bear him amid wind and rain.

Toll the bell—a solemn toll,
   Slow and solemn let it be,
While we pray for WILLIAM's soul,—
   MISERERE, DOMINE!

Nobles, Knights, and Prelate-Lords,
   Receive him at the western door,
In tears, with banner and with cross,
   And the Peace of Heav'n implore.

Toll the bell—a solemn toll,
   Slow and solemn let it be,
While we pray for WILLIAM's soul,
   MISERERE, DOMINE!

Now the Choristers in white,
   Slowly pacing up the nave,
And joining in the holy rite,
   Chant, before him, to the Grave.

WILLIAM GOOD, and WILLIAM BRAVE,
   Oh! who would not weep for thee!
Lay his body in the grave,
   DONA PACEM, DOMINE!

APPENDIX TO CHAPTER VI.

WILL OF WILLIAM LONGESPÉ, EARL OF SALISBURY.

The Earl made his Will previously to his last campaign in Gascony, and for greater security had it attested by the King's seal. It was consequently entered upon the Close Rolls, and it will be found printed, in the original Latin, from that authority, in the Excerpta Historica. As its contents touch upon several subjects noticed in this work, I shall here append a complete translation.

✠ In the name of the Father, and of the Son, and of the Holy Ghost. Amen. This is the Will of William Longespé, Earl of Sarum, made in the middle of Lent in the year from the incarnation of our Lord 1225, when it was disposed and provided that he should go into Gascony in the service of our Lord the King.

"Imprimis, I William Earl of Salisbury direct that the debt which I owe to my Lord the King since my last accompt this year before the Barons of the Exchequer at Westminster be paid to my Lord the King from the proceeds of my wardships, saving such part of it as my bailiffs can show to be overcharged.

Item, I direct that my other debts be paid from the proceeds of the land of William de Vescy,[1] which I have in my wardship, except the manor of Cathorp with its appurtenances, from which I assign 200*l.* towards the building of St. Mary of the essart of Bentlewood.[2] But when those 200*l.* have been received from that manor, it shall return to the payment of my debts until the full age of the said heir.

[1] Who became the husband of his daughter Isabella.
[2] Bentley in Middlesex? where there was a small Priory of Canons.

WILL OF EARL WILLIAM LONGESPÉ.

Item, I assign to the satisfaction of prizes unjustly taken to my use out of war by myself or my men, the moiety of all the proceeds of the wardship of the land of the heir of Earl Hugh le Bigod; and the other moiety to reward those who have served me, except the manor of Aclee,* with its appurtenances, from which I assign 200 marks to the NEW BUILDING OF THE CHURCH OF SALISBURY. But when those 200 marks have been received from that manor, it shall return to pay my debts as aforesaid, until the full age of the heir of the said Earl Hugh le Bigod.

Item, I assign to the building of the HOUSE OF GOD'S PLACE of the Carthusian order,³ all the profits of the wardship of the land of the heir of Richard de Campvill,¹ of which I am now seized, until his full age. Item, I assign to the same House a chalice of gold with beautiful emeralds and rubies; a pix of gold with pearls, and two vials of silver, of which one is gilt and the other plain; also its great chapel-furniture, namely a chasible of red satin, and a cope for the choir of red satin; a tunicle; a dalmatic of saffron silk well wrought; an alb with ornaments, an amice, a stole, a fanon, with napkins, and all its reliques. Item, I assign to the same House 1000 ewes, 300 muttons, 48 oxen, and 20 heifers.

Item, to the house of St. Mary of the essart of Bentlewood,⁵ my feast-day chapel-furniture, which I have been accustomed to carry with me,⁶ except the aforesaid two vials of silver which

---

* Oakley, in Buckinghamshire, formerly the mother church of Brill, Boarstall, and Addingrave. See the index to Kennett's Parochial Antiquities.

³ His own foundation at Hatherop in Gloucestershire; which manor he gave for that purpose on St. Magdalen's day 1222, and which the Countess Ela his widow afterwards removed to Hinton Charterhouse.

⁴ Idonea, who was married to his son.

⁵ Not known to monastic authors by that name. As the Earl favoured it next to his own foundation, and before Bradenstoke, can it have been the first germ of Lacock on another site?

⁶ In like manner, King John carried about with him a valuable

have been assigned with the great chapel furniture as aforesaid. And I bequeath to the same house my book called a porte-hois [5] Also 20 cows, 300 ewes, 100 muttons, 32 oxen, 30 goats, and 100 porkers.

Item, to the house of BRADENSTOKE 300 ewes, 10 cows, and 7 heifers.

Item, to the house of Bernecester [6] 200 ewes, 10 cows, and 8 oxen.

Item, to the house of Terrente [7] 100 ewes, 8 oxen, and 7 heifers.

Item, to the house of Kinton, [8] 100 ewes, and 6 cows.

Item, to the house of St. Helen of London, [9] 10 cows.

Item, to the house of the Ivied Monastery [10] 50 ewes and 10 cows.

Item, to the house of St. John of Wilton [11] 5 cows.

Item, to the house of Brumor [12] 50 ewes and 4 cows.

Item, to the house of Bradley [13] 100 ewes and 10 cows.

Item, to the house of Christchurch [14] 50 ewes.

Item, to the house of Farley [15] 100 ewes and 10 cows.

Item, to the house of Bruynton [16] 100 ewes and 10 cows.

Item, to the house of St. Dionis without Southampton [17] 50 ewes and 10 cows.

Item, to the lepers of the hospital of Sarum 5 cows.

Item, to the lepers of the hospital of Wilton 5 cows.

service of chapel-furniture, which, with the regalia, was lost in his last fatal journey across the Lincolnshire marshes.

[5] A portable book of prayers, or breviary.

[6] Burcester in Oxfordshire, of Augustine canons. It is remarkable that, among all the religious houses, in various counties, which follow, there is no gift to the nunnery of Godstow.

[7] Tarrent Keines, a Cistercian nunnery in Dorsetshire.

[8] Keinton, a Benedictine nunnery in Wilts, near Chippenham.

[9] A Benedictine nunnery.

[10] Ivychurch, Wilts, of Augustine canons, near Salisbury.

[11] A Benedictine nunnery.

[12] Bromere, in Hampshire, of Augustine canons.

[13] Maiden Bradley, Wilts, Augustine canons.

[14] At Twinham, Hants, Augustine canons.

[15] Monkton Farley, Wilts, a Cluniac priory, near Bath.

[16] Bruton, Somerset, Augustine canons.

[17] Augustine canons.

SEALS, Plate 1.

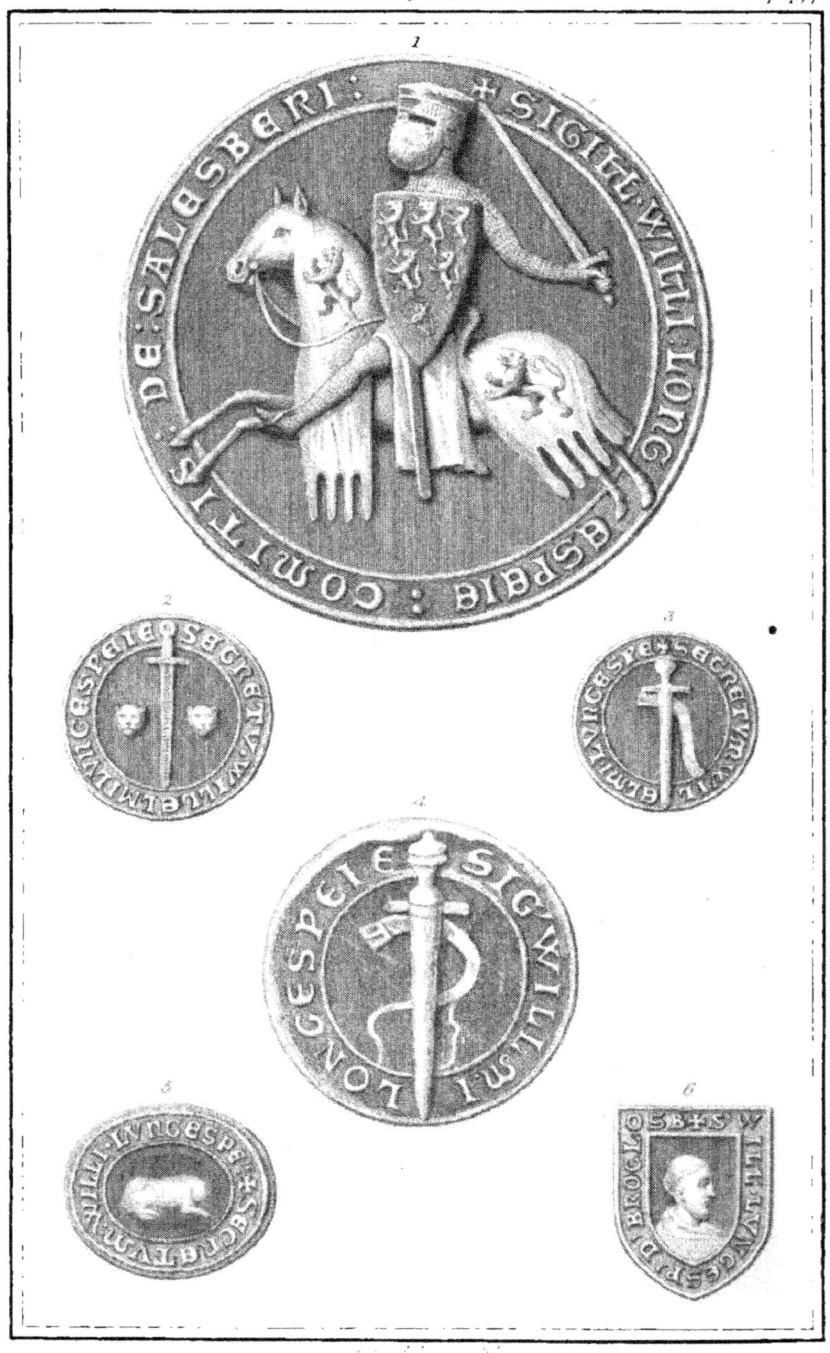

1 & 2 Great and Counter Seals of William Longespé, Earl of Salisbury.
3, 4, 5 Privy Seals of William Longespé II & III.
6 Seal of William Longespé, Rector of Brocklesby.

Item, to the house of Hundeslawe[18] 10 cows.

Item, to the hospital of St. Bartholomew of London[19] 8 oxen.

Item, to the house of St. Radegund without Dover[20] 10 oxen.

Of this my Will I appoint these executors: namely, the venerable fathers Stephan Lord Archbishop of Canterbury, the Lord Bishops of Bath, Lincoln, and Sarum, to order, confirm, and defend the same; also I appoint the venerable men and my friends, William Marshall, Earl of Pembroke, Sir William de Wanda, Dean of Sarum,[21] and Master Edmund, Treasurer of the church of Sarum,[22] to preserve and consult, and firmly assist the execution of the same; also I appoint my beloved and faithful Sir Adam de Alta Ripa, knight, and Sir J. Bonet, clerk, faithfully to execute the same by the counsel and aid of the aforesaid personages. Moreover, for the greater security and attestation of this will, my Lord the King, at my petition, has caused to be affixed to this writing his own seal, together with the seals of the aforesaid personages, and together with my seal.

The Earl's Seal is engraved in the opposite Plate. This figure differs from that on his monument in wearing a ponderous helmet, with a great front or cheek piece.

DESCENDENTS OF THE COUNTESS ELA.

The Foundress of Lacock, by her husband Earl William Longespé, had four sons and four daughters. The former were 1. William, 2. Richard, 3. Stephan, and 4. Nicholas.

1. WILLIAM LONGESPE, to whose personal history we shall

---

[18] Hounslow, Middlesex, of Trinitarian friars.

[19] Augustine Canons.

[20] Sometimes called Bradsole, a Præmonstratensian abbey.

[21] The superior clergy, those it is believed who were graduates, were styled "Sir," in Latin "Dominus," and in the latter times of the Romish church, in English "Dan."

[22] Edmund of Abingdon, afterwards Archbishop of Canterbury, and canonized (see hereafter, p. 201.)

recur whilst pursuing that of his Mother in the next and succeeding Chapters.

By his wife Idonea, daughter and heiress of Richard de Camville, he had issue four children: William Longespé the third, Richard, Ela, and Edmund.[1] Of the two younger sons nothing has hitherto been ascertained; but it is probable that the former was the same Richard Longespé who was lord of Bramley, Surrey; and, with Alice his wife, obtained a grant of free warren for that manor in 43 Hen. III. 1259.[2] He died in 1262,[3] having had no issue by Alice, who was the daughter of William de Ros, by Agatha, daughter of Roger de Clare.[4]

Ela Longespe was married to James Audley, a Baron of Staffordshire, who was killed by breaking his neck in 1272,[5] being at that time, and for two years previous, Lord Justice of Ireland; after which, his widow made a gift to the priory of Burcester, in Oxfordshire, the grant of which was ratified by her seal, representing her figure, standing, holding a shield of the arms of Longespé in one hand and another of Audley (a fret) in the other, with this inscription, SIGILLVM ELE DE AVDELEG.[6] (*Seals, Plate II.*) She died on or before 1299.[7]

It has hitherto been generally supposed that Ela Longespé was the mother of all this Lord Audley's children; but Mr. Beltz, Lancaster Herald, who has fully investigated the genealogy of the family,[8] has found reason to conclude that the four elder sons, James, Henry, William, and Nicholas, all successively Lords Audley, were the children of a former wife, now unknown; and that Ela was mother of Hugh only,[9] because the

---

[1] Book of Lacock.
[2] Rot. Cart. 43 Hen. III. m. 2.
[3] Esc. 46 Hen. III. n. 1.
[4] History of Surrey, ii. 77, 79.
[5] Chron. Tho. Wikes.
[6] Kennett's Parochial Antiquities, p. 278.
[7] Rot. Orig. 27 Edw. I. No. 21.
[8] With a view to the biography of Sir James de Audley, one of the Founders of the Garter, in his contemplated History of that illustrious Order.
[9] Hugh was certainly heir to the lands of his mother Ela, *per formam doni;* as is shown by a Writ of Certiorari, Esc. 19 Edw. II. no. 30.

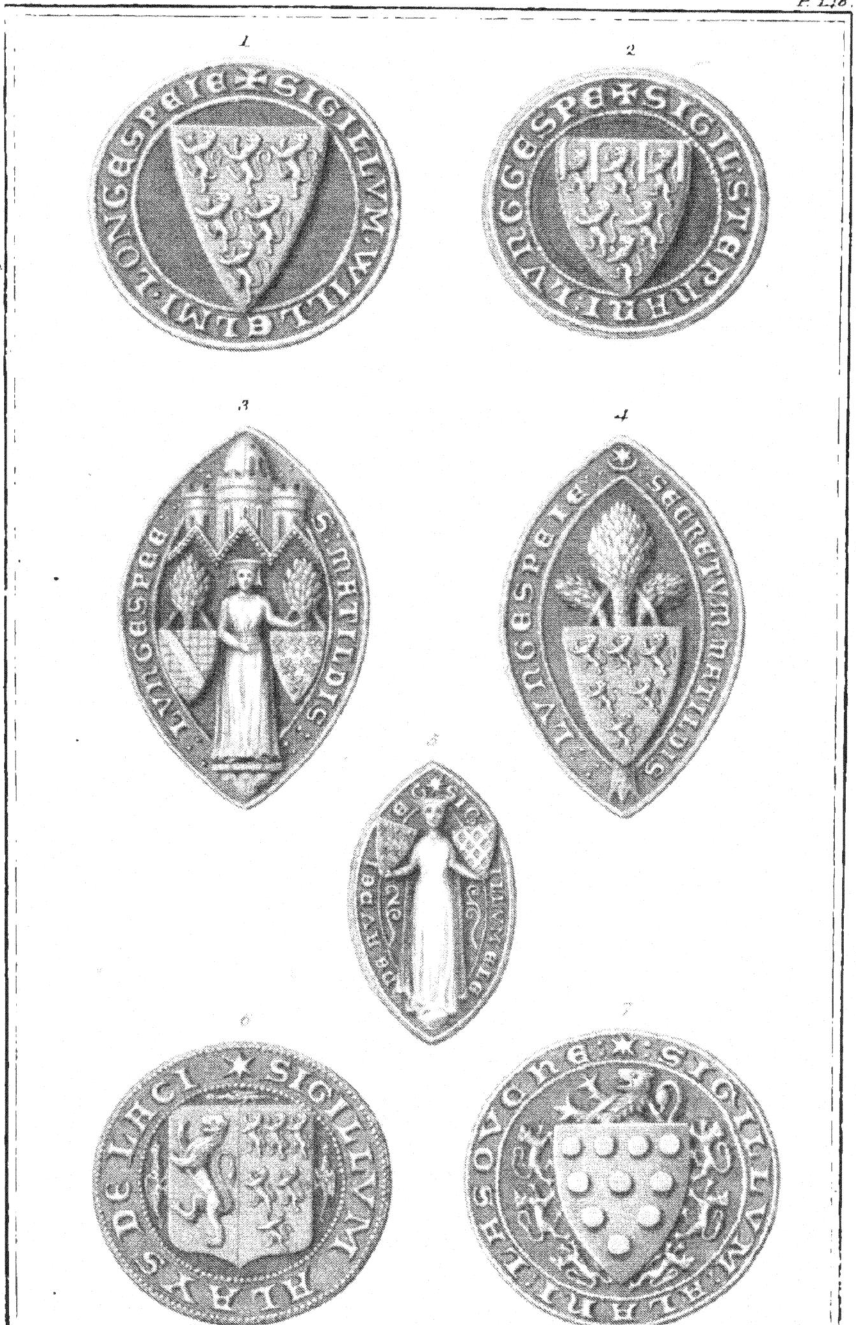

1. William Longespé II. 2. Stephen Longespé. 3, 4. Matilda Longespé.
5. Ela Audley. 6. Alice Lacy. 7. Alan la Zouche.

ountess	Nicholas =....
dau. of	Longespé,
Ride-	Bishop of
.d. 1242	Salisbury
e Laci,	1291, died
ster; d.	1297.

Zouche,	William Longe-
she was	spé, portioner of
	Brocklesby rec-
; wid. of	tory, co. Lin-
Iaurice	coln, living
l, s. p.	1324.

summoned to
321.

irl of Gloucester, ancestor
; in whom is now vested
f the HOUSE OF LONGESPE.

lands settled upon Ela in frank marriage passed by her grant to Hugh and his posterity. This Hugh appears to have been first raised into consequence through the fortunate marriage of his son with Margaret, sister and coheiress of the last Earl of Gloucester of the illustrious House of Clare, the widow of the murdered favourite, Piers de Gaveston, and a niece of the reigning monarch, Edward the Second (through his sister, Joan of Acre). After this marriage had taken place, the father and son, both named Hugh de Audley, were summoned to Parliament in 1321, with the distinctions of Senior and Junior. The latter was afterwards created Earl of Gloucester. His daughter and sole heiress, Margaret, was married to Ralph Lord Stafford; and, after the death of Alice Countess of Lancaster (hereafter mentioned), and the consequent failure of the issue of the third William Longespé, the representation of the ancient Earls of Salisbury vested in that family, and has thence descended, through the (Staffords) Dukes of Buckingham, and the families of Howard and Plowden, to George-William Stafford Jerningham, now LORD STAFFORD, and the present REPRESENTATIVE OF ELA OF SALISBURY, THE FOUNDRESS OF LACOCK ABBEY.[1]

---

[1] Though the law of female descent, as applied to Baronies by Writ, has long ceased to govern the descent of Earldoms, (in the manner it certainly did in the first centuries after the Norman Conquest,) yet our review of the ancient Earldom of Salisbury would not be complete, did we omit to notice the existence of a Pamphlet under the following title: "A Genealogical and Historical Account of the ancient Earldom of Salisbury; showing the descent of the Baron Audley, of Heleigh, from the renowned William Longespé, Earl of Salisbury, son of King Henry II. by the celebrated Fair Rosamond, and showing, also, the right of the Baron Audley to the inheritance of the same Earldom. By Sir Thomas C. Banks, Bart. N. S." 1832, 8vo. pp. 24. After what has been said above, it is unnecessary to add, that, whatever pretensions might have attached to the Lord Audley, in consequence of his presumed descent from our COUNTESS ELA, must, in the event of Hugh de Audley being proved to have been the heir of his mother Ela, be transferred to Lord Stafford.

Of WILLIAM LONGESPE THE THIRD we find no other mention in the annals of public events, except his untimely death in consequence of injuries received at a tournament held at Blyth, in the year 1257. He was a mere youth at the period of his death; but had, three years before, that is in 1254, married Matilda, only daughter and heiress of Walter Baron de Clifford, and great-niece to his own progenitor, the Fair Rosamund Clifford. Her mother was Margaret, daughter of Lewellin Prince of Wales, who had been first married to John Lord Braose, of Gower. William Longespé had with Matilda Clifford in free marriage the manor of Culminton, in Shropshire; to the grant of which his uncle (by marriage) James de Aldithley was one of the witnesses.[1]

Only two years after, when he had probably fallen into his mortal illness, it was arranged that Margaret his infant heiress should be given in marriage to Henry, son and heir of Edmund de Laci. This alliance appears to have been in the first instance negociated during the campaign in Gascony; and was finally settled on the Friday next before Christmas, when it was agreed that William Longespé should give with his daughter his manors of Burcester and Millington; and that Edmund should assign to her in dower, in the case of his son's death, the manors of Skyppys and Scales. This agreement also was witnessed by James de Audele.[2] The contract was confirmed by the King, with this further proviso, that, if Henry de Laci should die before the marriage was consummated, John his younger brother should then take his place as the husband of Margaret de Longespé. William Longespé died shortly after; as also did Edmund Laci, on St. Magdalen's day (July 21) 1257; and in consequence Henry de Laci, the husband of Margaret Longespé, succeeded to the estates of both; but, being a minor, was in ward to the King, whilst his wife was in custody

[1] Kennett's Parochial Antiquities, p. 248, from Dugd. MS. vol. l. p. 41. A seal of the third William Longespé (*Plate I.*) represents the *long sword* between two lions' or leopards' faces; these were mistaken by Kennett for Saracens' heads!

[2] Kennett, p. 251, from Dugd. MS. vol. i. p. 17.

of the Queen.¹ He became of full age in 1268, and then did homage with Margaret his wife, and had livery of all the lands whereof her father Longespé died possessed.²

The Seal of Matilda Longespé, used during her widowhood, represents her standing between two shields, the first checky, with a bend, for Clifford; the second Longespé: the reverse is occupied with a shield of Longespé, and inscribed SIGILLVM MATILDIS LVNGESPEIE. (*Seals, Plate II.*)

Her history is somewhat remarkable. In 1271, fourteen years after her husband's death, she made complaint to the King that John Lord Giffard had taken her by force from her manor-house at Canford in Dorsetshire, and carried her to his castle at Brimsfield in Gloucestershire, and there kept her in restraint. He was in consequence summoned to the King, and, being told what was informed against him, he denied the charge, saying that he took her not against her will; and tendered to the King a fine of three hundred marks for marrying her without his consent, of which the King accepted, upon condition that she made no further complaint.³ It would seem that these proceedings were a sort of friendly scheme for encountering in a favourable way the penalty incurred by the lady's having taken a second husband without the Royal permission.

In 1282 we meet with a pleasing instance of the Christian charity of Maud Longespé: On the death, in battle, of her kinsman Prince Llewellin, she wrote to Archbishop Peckham, then with the army, begging him to absolve the fallen enemy, in order that his body might receive an honourable burial: the Archbishop in his letters to King Edward, informed himself of the circumstance, but mentioned his scruples against complying with her request.⁴ She died before 1283, when John Giffard founded a cell in Oxford (afterwards called Gloucester Hall) for thirteen monks from the abbey of Gloucester, who were to pray for the souls of him and Matilda Longespé, formerly his wife. He died himself on the 28th of May, 1299; when the estates of Matilda were

¹ Ibid. p. 252. ² Dugdale's Baronage, i. 301.
³ Ibid. vol. i. p. 500. ⁴ Rymer's Fœdera.

divided between Margaret Countess of Lincoln, her daughter by William de Longespé her first husband, and Katharine, Alianor, and Matilda, her three daughters by John Giffard. Katharine, the first of these, was then already the wife of Nicholas Lord Audley, the son of James Lord Audley, of Helegh, before mentioned, (and step-son, as is now supposed, of Ela Longespé,) and was ancestress of the subsequent Lords Audley; Alianor was afterwards married to Fulke Lord le Strange, and became the ancestress of the Lords Strange of Blackmere; Matilda was not married.

To return to MARGARET, the sole heiress of Longespé, and the wife of Henry de Laci, Earl of Lincoln; who was a highly distinguished Peer in the reigns of the first and second Edwards, and sometimes in her right styled Earl of Salisbury. They had issue, Edmund and John, who both died in childhood, the former being drowned at Denbigh castle;[1] and a daughter and heiress, Alice. Dugdale has stated that Margaret Countess of Lincoln was re-married to Sir Walter Walrond; but this is an error, as she died two years before the Earl,[2] whose decease took place at his London mansion, on the site of the present *Lincoln's Inn,* in the year 1312. There was a dole, at LACOCK ABBEY, for the soul of the Countess Margaret, on the feast of St. Cecilia.[3]

ALICE LACI, the heiress of two great families, was, in 1291, at nine years of age, given in marriage to the potent nephew of Edward the First, Thomas Earl of Lancaster, Leicester, and Derby, who by this alliance added to those three Earldoms, a title to two more,—Salisbury and Lincoln. How he was subsequently overpowered as it were by his own grandeur, and, falling a victim to the jealousy of the Crown, was in

[1] He was drowned in a deep well, within a high tower called the Red Tower; which was the reason his father never finished Denbigh Castle. Powel's History of Cambria.
[2] Inq. p. mort. 4 Edw. II. no. 51. See also Hutchins's Dorsetshire, vol. iii. p. 3, and the Excerpta Historica, p. 68.
[3] See the " Yearly Alms " at the Abbey, hereafter, p. 388.

1321 beheaded at his own castle of Pontefract, is matter of national history. His marriage had previously terminated unfortunately; for in 1317 the Countess Alice, who had brought him no children, was carried off by violence from the same manor of Canford in Dorsetshire, which had been the scene of her grandmother's alleged rape before mentioned, and was carried to the Earl of Warren's castle at Reigate, when one Richard de St. Martin came forward, and claimed her for his wife on the plea of a pre-contract. This indignity, which is supposed to have originated from the political enmity of Earl Warren and the King's party, occasioned a divorce between the Earl and the Countess.

Some years after, the Countess Alice took for her second husband Eubulo le Strange, a younger son of John Baron Strange of Knockyn; he, in consequence of his marriage, was summoned to Parliament (as a Baron) from 1326 to his death in 1335, and in some documents is dignified with the title of Earl of Lincoln. He died in Scotland about Michaelmas 1335, from the fatigues of the campaign of that year; and his body was brought for interment to the abbey church of Barling, co. Linc.

Before the 8th of July in the following year, the Countess Alice had taken a third husband, one Hugh de Fresnes, a Knight of Artois; who at that date obtained livery of the castle of Buelt in Wales, which had been previously granted to Eubulo le Strange.[1] He also was summoned to Parliament on the 29th Nov. and 14th Jan. following, but died in the month of December, between those two summonses, likewise in Scotland, at St. John's town, now Perth.[2]

After these unfortunate marriages, the Countess Alice survived for thirteen years a widow. She died at length without issue Oct. 2, 1348, in the 67th year of her age, and was buried in the church of Barling, by the side of her second husband Eubulo le Strange.[3] With this lady terminated the blood of

[1] Kennett, p. 427, from MS. Dodsworth, vol. 84, f. 41.
[2] Walsingham.
[3] Inq. p. mort.; et Mon. Ang. ii. 190.

the Lacies and the elder line of the Longespés. Her estates went to Henry Earl of Lancaster, the brother and heir of her first husband, and contributed to swell that enormous rental of the Duchy of Lancaster, which afterwards encouraged John of Gaunt to aim after the Crown, and enabled his son Henry of Bolingbroke to grasp it. There is a small round seal of Alice de Laci, (but probably only her counter or privy seal,) bearing her father's and mother's arms, the single lion of Laci and the six lioncels of Longespé, impaled, inscribed s. ALAYS DE LACI. (*Seals, Plate II.*)

To return to the Children of the Countess Ela—

2. RICHARD. He was a knight when he witnessed about 1242 some charters of the Earl his brother.[1] He also witnessed one of the charters of his mother Ela to the Abbey of Lacock. He held the fourth part of a fee in Avinton, Berks, of the fee of William Longespé and the barony of Camville;[2] and it is possible he may have been the Richard who possessed the manor of Bramley, in Surrey; though perhaps there is greater probability that that person was his nephew. The Countess's son Richard died a Canon of Salisbury, and was buried at Lacock.[3]

3. Sir STEPHAN LONGESPE, Justice of Ireland. He was provided with competent estates by the bounty of his eldest brother; who in 1241 bestowed on him the manor and hundred of Sutton in Northamptonshire;[4] and in 1243 gave him the manor of Wamborough in Wiltshire.[5] In 1254 Stephan

[1] Printed in Kennett's Parochial Antiquities, p. 229, 230. See also, in p. 248, this Sir Richard de Longespé, Knt. (or his nephew of the same name) witnessing a charter of William Longespé the third, assigned to the year 1254.
[2] Testa de Nevill, pp. 111, 124, 126.
[3] Book of Lacock.
[4] See Baker's Northamptonshire, vol. i. p. 693.
[5] Cart. Harl. (Brit. Mus.) 53 B. 14; see also MS. Cotton. Julius, C. VII. f. 234. In the History of Surrey this is erroneously applied to Wamborough, in that county; but it clearly

DESCENDENTS OF THE COUNTESS ELA. 155

was appointed Seneschal of Gascony.[1] In 1255 he had a grant of the castle and town of Burgh super Mare in Cumberland.[2] In 1258, when the castle of Sherborne was surrendered to the Barons, Walter de Bruges was directed to deliver it to Stephan Longespé; in the same year he was Castellan of Corfe Castle;[3] and at the Parliament then held at Oxford, was one of the four counsellors (John de Bailol, John de Gray, Stephan Longespé, and Roger de Montalt) sent by the Barons to direct the conduct of Prince Edward.[4] In the following year he was appointed Lord Justice of Ireland, and he died in that office in 1260.[5] He is styled Earl of Ulster in the Book of Lacock; but, if he ever bore that title, it was probably only by courtesy, in consequence of his marriage with the dowager of a valiant soldier who had been made Earl of Ulster by King John. This was Hugh de Laci, who died in 1242, leaving as his widow Emeline, daughter and heir of Walter de Ridelesford; her subsequent marriage with Stephan Longespé is shown by her charter to the Canons of Ashby in Northamptonshire, in which she mentions that the Prior and Canons had agreed to place in their Martirology the names of her Lords Hugh de Lacy and Stephan de Longespé, her own name, and those of Sir Walter de Ridelesford her father, Annora her mother, and Ela and Emeline her daughters. These daughters were by Stephan de Longespé; for by her first husband she had given birth to one only daughter, Matilda, wife of Walter de Burgh, who became in right of his wife Earl of Ulster.

The daughters of Stephan Longespé were both married.

ELA was the wife of Roger la Zouche, of Ashby de la

belongs to Wamborough in Wilts, where William Longespé held a knight's fee (Testa de Nevill, p. 139), and as is confirmed by the neighbouring places mentioned in the charter, the wood of Bradene, Neweham, Stoneham, and Voxborege.

[1] Rot. Vascon. 39 Hen. III. m. 5.
[2] Cal. Rot. Cart. p. 82. [3] Annals of Burton. [4] Ibid.
[5] Archdall's Peerage of Ireland, by Lodge, vol. i. p. 63.

Zouche in Leicestershire, who died in 1285, leaving his son Alan la Zouche, afterwards a Baron in Parliament, then eighteen years of age. This Alan commemorated his descent from the house of Salisbury upon his seal, by placing around his own shield, of ten bezants, the six lions from the shield of Longespé—a practice of which some other interesting instances are found previously to the commencement of quartering arms:[1] it is inscribed SIGILLVM ALANI LA ZOUCHE. (*Plate II.*) Alan died in 1313, leaving, by Alianor, daughter of Nicholas de Segrave, three daughters his coheiresses: Ellen, wife of Nicholas de St. Maur, then aged 36, and afterwards married to Alan de Cherleton; Matilda, the wife of Robert Holand, aged 24; and Elizabeth, a nun at Brewode in Staffordshire, aged 20. Matilda became mother of Sir Thomas Holand, K.G. and the ancestress of the other great men of that illustrious house.

In 1266 the names of Emeline de Lacy (probably the mother, retaining the name of her first husband) and EMELINE DE LONGESPEYE occur together in a claim to an estate.[2] The latter was in 1292 the widow of Maurice Fitz-Maurice of Ireland;[3] yet we find her using her maiden name in 1324–5;[4] and she died without issue (as is correctly stated in the Book of Lacock) in the year 1331.[5] Her husband, Maurice Fitz-Maurice, was a cadet of the great house of Fitz-Gerald, of Ireland; being the third son of Maurice Fitz-Gerald, second Lord Offaley. He succeeded to the office of Lord Justice of Ireland in 1272 (on the death of James Lord Audley, already mentioned in

---

[1] There is one so closely resembling the present that it seems to require to be mentioned. It is the seal of William Lord Clinton, afterwards Earl of Huntingdon, who married the heiress of the baronial family of Leybourne. That family, like the Longespé's, bore six lions for their arms, and these are disposed on his seal exactly as on the seal of Alan la Zouche. This is the more remarkable, as William de Clinton was descended from the Longespé's, being the younger son of John, mentioned hereafter, p. 163.

[2] Placit. Abbr. p. 165.
[3] Ibid. p. 286.
[4] Ibid. p. 351.
[5] Esc. 5 Edw. III. n. 68.

p. 148), and held it till the following year; and died at Ross in 1286, leaving issue one son, who died the same year at Rathmore, and a daughter Juliana, married in 1276 to the Lord Thomas de Clare, brother to Gilbert Earl of Gloucester.[1]

The body of Stephan Longespé was interred at LACOCK, but his heart at Bradenstoke.[2] It does not appear that he was a greater benefactor to Lacock Abbey than by the gift of two acres of his meadow at "Nineam."[3] There are some impressions of his seal in the British Museum,[4] presenting, as his shield of arms, his brother's six lions, differenced by a label of four points,[5] inscribed SIGILL' STEPHANI LVNGGESPE. (*Seals, Plate II.*)

4. NICHOLAS LONGESPE, Bishop of Salisbury. His mother, the Countess Ela, in her widowhood and liege power, granted to him the manor of Egeswere, in the vill of Colinges, (Suffolk; see elsewhere, pp. 98, 264) at the rent of one sparrow-hawk.[6] In 1255 he was Rector of Gaddesden in Hertfordshire, and with the consent of his brother Stephan, the patron of that church, presented Simon de Hertford, chaplain, to the vicarage.[7] In 1288 he was Rector of Wickham, near Wingham, in Kent, the manor of which belonged to his kinsmen the Cliffords, and which he let in farm to the Vicar for a rent of seventy marks.[8] In

---

[1] Lodge's Peerage of Ireland, by Archdall, vol. i. p. 61; but Emeline is incorrectly given in p. 63, to Gerald Fitz-Maurice 3d Lord Offaley; and it is added that she died in 1291, which is clearly erroneous, as shown by the records relating to her quoted above.

[2] Book of Lacock.

[3] See the Cartulary in the Appendix, fo. 86 b.

[4] Harl. Cart. 53 B. 14, 15.

[5] "Estienne Longespee, d'azur a sis lioncealx d'or, ung labell de goules." Roll of Arms, temp. Hen. III. 8vo. 1829.

[6] Harleian Charter, (British Mus.) 53 B. 12.—Of the impression of Ela's seal attached to the document, the engraver availed himself in the plate given in this work.

[7] Reg. Lexington, Clutterbuck's Herts. i. 379.

[8] Hasted's History of Kent, vol. iii. p. 662, and Thorpe's Registrum Roffense, p. 687.

1290 he occurs as RECTOR OF LACOCK,[1] as well as Treasurer of the Cathedral of Salisbury; to the latter office he was appointed in 1274; and promoted from it, when advanced in age, to the Bishopric of Sarum. No fewer than nine Bishops had intervened from the episcopate of Richard Poore, who attended the deathbed of the Earl his father.[2] The temporalities of the see were rendered to him Dec. 16, 1291;[3] and he was consecrated at Canterbury on the 16th of March following. He died March 18, 1297, probably at his manor-house of Ramsbury, for there his bowels were interred; his heart was brought to LACOCK, and his body conveyed to his cathedral of Sarum, where it was interred at the entrance of the Chapel of the Virgin, under a blue slab, composed of two stones, of very extraordinary size, being 16 feet 8 inches long by 7 feet 8 inches broad;[4] they they were inlaid, as Bishop Godwin notices, with brass-plates and the insignia of his family, being one of the most early monuments of that kind known to Mr. Gough;[5] in whose time, however, the brass canopy work, &c. had been removed before the memory of man. Leland[6] has preserved an inscription, which is apparently not the original one:

"Sub hoc lapide marmoreo desuper insculpto humatum est corpus Reverendi Patris Nicolai Longespe, quondam Sarum Episcopi, qui plurima huic contulit Ecclesie, et obiit 18 mens. Maii, a°.D. 1291 [1297], ex cujus parte australi jacet Robertus Wichamton, ex parte boreali Henricus Brandesburn requiescit."

When the interments in the Lady Chapel were disturbed, during Mr. Wyatt's alterations, among several stone coffins uncovered, was one containing a chalice and patten, silver gilt, an agate ring, with the stone perforated, and a light pastoral

---

[1] See the composition he then made with the Nuns, in the Appendix, p. xxiii.
[2] Yet Mr. Cassan, in his Lives of the Bishops of Salisbury, has made him the same person!
[3] Pat. 20 Edw. I. m. 29.
[4] Gough's Sepulc. Monuments, i. p. 67.   [5] Ibid. p. cvii.
[6] Itinerary, vol. ii. f. 63.

staff of wood; the corpse they accompanied was ascribed by Mr. Gough to Bishop Longespé.[1]

It appears probable that Nicholas was married before he entered into holy orders. His mother Ela seems to speak of his actual circumstances, when, in the charter already noticed, she alludes to his heirs issuing from him " *et uxore sua sibi desponsata;* " and it may be presumed that we have a son of the Bishop in

WILLIAM LONGESPEYE, portioner of the church of Brocklesby in Lincolnshire, several of whose charters are preserved in the British Museum,[2] in which he is styled *William son of Nicholas Longespé*. These charters relate to his transactions with the abbey of Newhouse, and one of them is an indenture[3] of Ralph the Abbat and Convent, setting forth that, " they acknowledged with all their heart the laborious care and studious solicitude he had shown in conducting their business, and especially for the great sum of money which he had liberally placed to the use of this monastery, and returned him very special thanks for his vast diligence by which their affairs had proceeded favourably; and therefore considered themselves especially bound to do those things which they believed would contribute to the health of his soul, and likewise to his honour; wherefore they granted him a special participation in all their masses, prayers, abstinences, vigils, works, and other good services, and moreover granted that two secular chaplains, of good and honest conversation, found at their expense, should celebrate for twenty full years, from the feast of St. Mark 1324, in the church of Broclesby, for his soul, and the souls of his father, mother, parents, and all the faithful defunct." This mention of his ancestors without any of their names, is very tantalizing to the genealogist.

The indenture, as well as several of the other charters, has his seal appendant, which is of a small shield-shaped form, con-

[1] See the Sepulchral Monuments, vol. ii. p. ccxxxi*.
[2] Harl. Cart. 52 D. 23, 26, 53 B. 16—21.
[3] Ibid. 44 H. 20.

taining a profile head, with this circumscription: s. will' lvngesp' d' broclosb'. (*See Plate I. of Seals.*)

The Daughters of the Foundress of Lacock were:—1. Isabella; 2. Petronilla; 3. Ela; and 4. Ida.[1]

1. ISABELLA, who was married to William de Vesci, a Baron of Northumberland, and one of her father's wards (see his will, p. 144.) He was the son of Eustace de Vesci, by Margaret, daughter of William King of Scotland. She died without issue, and her husband afterwards married a daughter of the Earl of Derby, who was the mother of his family.

2. PETRONILLA. She died a virgin, and was buried at Bradenstoke, under a marble stone, at the right hand of the grave of her grandmother the Countess Alianor. (Book of Lacock.)

3. ELA. She was twice married; first to Thomas Newburgh, Earl of Warwick, who died June 26, 1242; secondly to Philip Basset, of Wycombe in Buckinghamshire, son of William Basset, Chief Justice of England. She became the second time a widow in 1271, and survived for many years after, a very wealthy lady, having had no children by either husband. In 1285 she was returned as holding the manor of Hoke-Norton in Oxfordshire, *in capite*, by the *sergeanty* of *carving before our lord the King on Christmas Day*, when she had for her fee the King's *knife* with which she cut.[2] We find several records of her piety, particularly in Oxford and its vicinity; for she seems to have lived during her widowhood at Headington, only two

---

[1] Such is the clear enumeration of their names, as stated for the second time in the Book of Lacock (see the Appendix, p. iii.); and their first enumeration, (ibid. p. ii.) when properly understood, agrees with it, excepting in omitting Petronilla, who died young. Dugdale, consulting that first passage only, enumerates, in his Baronage, five without Petronilla; namely, Isabel, Ela, Idonea (Ida), Lora, and another Ela. The two last, it will be perceived, are Lorica and Ela Fitz-Walter, the daughters of Ida, and *granddaughters* of the Countess Ela, the Foundress of Lacock.

[2] Placit. Coron. 13 Edw. I. rot. 30.

miles from that city.¹ She gave to the University 120 marks for loans to poor scholars; for which a chest was forthwith ordered to be made by the Chancellor and Proctors, to be thenceforth called the WARWICK CHEST; and several orders were made for its regulation, among which was this, that " when the mass priest and public servant of the University should circuit the schools every year according to custom, reciting the names of Benefactors, they should in their recitation *name Ela Countess of Warwick next to King Henry III. being his kinswoman.*" The Chest was existing in the reign of Edward IV.² To Merton College she gave some lands, for which the Fellows were to celebrate services on her behalf. She also founded a chantry in the nunnery of Godstow, where her grandmother Fair Rosamund lay interred; and where, until the Reformation, two chaplains received £7. 7s. yearly, for the daily celebration of masses for her soul, and 25s. were distributed in alms every year on the feast of the Lord's Supper. To Rewley abbey, in the same vicinity, she gave some lands, as Leland mentions;³ and there she also built a chapel, the foundation stone of which was discovered in 1705, bearing this inscription: D. ELA LONGESP' COMIT' WAREW' H'NC CAPELLAM FECIT, C'J' P'MIV' SIT XP'C IN GL'A. AM'. At the same place, in Dr. Stukeley's time,⁵ was a stone with this inscription: ELE DE WARWIK COMITISSE VISCERA SVNT HIC. To the neighbouring abbey of Ousney,

---

¹ The manor-house of Headington is supposed to have been a residence of the Saxon Kings. It had descended to the family of Basset. In the seventeenth century, considerable traces of foundations were noticed by Dr. Plot in a field called Court Close.

² See further particulars in Wood's Annals of Oxford, by Gutch, vol. i. p. 344.

³ Itinerary, vol. ii. fol. 20.

⁴ It is now preserved in the Bodleian Library. A fac-simile of the inscription is engraved in Leland's Itinerary, 1770, vol. ii. p. 125; and another, more accurate, in Skelton's Oxonia Restaurata, vol. ii.

⁵ Itinerarium Curiosum, i. 45.

where her body was buried, Leland says "she gave many rich jewels, but no lands." To Reading abbey she gave the manor of Southwood in the isle of Ely.¹ She was likewise a benefactress of the ABBEY OF LACOCK, by procuring for the Society the right of chiminage through the Royal Forests. In the year 1287 we find the Countess of Warwick visiting LACOCK, on which occasion she quit-claimed to the abbey her title in the manor of Hatherop.² She died on Sunday Feb. 6, 1297, and was buried at Ousney Abbey, near Oxford, where Leland saw her tomb, " a very fair flat marble, in the habit of a vowess, graven in a copper plate."

Two Seals of this lady are extant. The first closely resembles that of her Mother (p. 169), having on one side her own figure holding a hawk, and on the other side the arms of Longespé, in a shield, with a lion above and below; it is inscribed on both sides S. ELE LVNGESPEYE COMITISSE WARWIC.

In her second Seal, the coat of Basset (wavy Or and Gules) is substituted for that of Longespé; the latter is placed in her hand, on the obverse, instead of the hawk, and is balanced by the coat of Newburgh, (checky Or and Azure, a chevron Ermine,) placed over her right shoulder. The inscription on both sides is SIGILLVM ELE BASSET COMITISSE WAREWYKIE. These seals are engraved in the accompanying Plate.

4. IDA. She was married to Walter Fitz-Robert, son of the famous Robert Fitz-Walter, " the Marshal of the army of God," who headed the confederated Barons against King John. He succeeded his father in 1234, and died in 1257; leaving a son Robert, the ancestor, by Devorgoil, daughter of John de Burgh, of the long line of Barons Fitz-Walter, of Essex. Ida had also three daughters: Katharine and Lorica, *both nuns at*

¹ See the charter (Cart. Harl. 54 D. 15) printed in the new Monasticon, vol. iv. p. 45.
² See hereafter, p. 278.

SEALS, Plate III.

Seals of Ela Countess of Warwick.

Lacock; and Ela, married¹ to William de Odingsells, of Maxstoke in Warwickshire; of whom this anecdote has been preserved by Matthew Paris, that at a tournament at Brackley in 1249, after the party of foreigners headed by the King's step-brother William de Valence, had obtained the victory, with the assistance of Richard Earl of Gloucester, who had previously supported the English party and was much blamed for changing sides, they used very ill William de Odingsells, a brave knight, who sided with the bachelors (militem strenuum, qui Bachelariis annumerabatur). Sir William de Odingsells left a son Edmund, who died soon after, and four daughters, who became coheirs: 1. *Ida*, married to John Lord Clinton, of Maxstoke in her right, and lineal ancestor of the present Duke of Newcastle; 2. Alice, wife first of Maurice de Caunton, and secondly of Ralph de Perham; 3. *Ela*, married first to Peter de Bermingham, and secondly to Eustace le Poer; and 4. Margaret, married to John Lord Grey of Rotherfield. Ela de Bermingham had a daughter *Ela*, the wife of Philip Purcel.²

Ida, the daughter of the Foundress of Lacock, was in 1235 the wife of William Beauchamp, Baron of Bedford, who in that year obtained a charter to himself and Ida his wife, "*the King's cousin*," of the manor of Newport, of her dowry. It was at her instigation, according to Matthew Paris, "for he was uxorious," that, "learning to attack men of religion rather than men of war, he greatly troubled the monks of Wardon, in Bedfordshire, and oppressed in various ways the Canons of Newnham, whom he ought to have cherished and favoured." This is mentioned by Matthew Paris under the year 1252, and with respect to Newnham in the Annals of Dunstable under

¹ The Book of Lacock says "quam duxit *primo* Gulielmus de Dodingseles;" so that we may suppose Ela Fitz-Walter had a *second* husband. The sentence is imperfect (see Appendix, p. ii.) As printed in the Monasticon, these words immediately follow, " ex qua genuit Robertum;" but the name of his wife "Dernegoill" shows that the person intended is Robert Fitz-Walter, the son of Ida Longespé, not of her daughter Ela de Odingseles.

² Dugdale's Warwickshire (by Thomas), p. 941.

1254. The same annals mention her with reproach, on the death of her husband in 1260, when she received her dower at her own disposal, and, says the annalist, inflicted enormous damages on Simon de Pateshull at the manor of Cranley.

By William Beauchamp, Ida had three sons, William, Simon, and John, who all died without issue male; and three daughters, Maud, Beatrix, and Ela. Maud was the wife first of Roger de Mowbray, by whom she was ancestress of the Dukes of Norfolk, and afterwards of Roger le Strange; Beatrix was the wife of Thomas Fitz-Otes; and *Ela* was the wife of Baldwin Wake, who had three daughters, Joan, *Ida*, and Isabel. Thus we find the names of Ela of Salisbury and her daughters handed down for successive generations. The Ida (Wake) last mentioned seems to have been married to John de Steingreve. (Dugdale's Baronage, vol. i. p. 224.)

ROGER BISHOP OF COVENTRY AND LICHFIELD, A PRESUMED LONGESPÉ.

This personage, who was Bishop of Coventry and Lichfield from 1257 to 1293, bore the surname of Meuleng or Meulent, probably from having been born at Meulan in France, for it is recorded that when made a Bishop he knew very little of the English language! He was certainly related to the Royal family, being styled " nepos" to King Henry, and to Richard Earl of Cornwall, both in the account which Matthew Paris gives of his election, and in the official documents relating to it, which are preserved in the Annals of Burton. As it does not appear how he could be nephew to King Henry the Third, it has been supposed that he was a Longespé, and his name is consequently found in several authors with that *alius*. In the History of Staffordshire, indeed, (vol. i. p. 268.) he is directly stated to have been " the *third* son of William Longespé, Earl of Salisbury, and *Eva* his wife," (probably from confusion with the Bishop of Salisbury); and in a note in the same place is mentioned a conjecture of Dr. Pegge, that he was a natural son of the Earl of Salisbury, as " the Italians use the word Nepos with latitude." This latter hypothesis might be considered not improbable, had the surname Longespé been ascribed to him by any ancient authority; but that does not appear to be the case; and therefore the connection of Bishop Roger de Meulan with the house of Longespé is hitherto unsubstantiated.

We might, perhaps, with greater probability, imagine that the Earl had a natural son in one John Longespé, whom we find employed in various commissions respecting the King's horses, in the years 1214—1215.[1] He was rewarded with the land of Manasser de Hastings,[2] and with that of Roger Parlebien in Kent,[3] in the year 1215; and in 1218 with the house of Moses of Cambridge, the Jew in Canterbury, also given him by the late King John.[4] He died in 1220; for the King then granted to William le Chareter, the daily pension of twopence, which John Longespé was wont to receive of the gift of King John, from the almonry of Canterbury.[5]

In the 19th Edw. II. we meet with a Robert de Longspé, of Loddington in Northamptonshire, who was outlawed for felony in 19 Edw. II. and was then found to hold lands at Loddington, of Richard Longspé, as parcel of the manor of Rowell.[6]

There was a Thomas Longespey who was a juror of the extent of the town of Richmond in Yorkshire, made in 8 Edw. I.;[7] another, a juror at an inquest held at Northallerton, in 7 Edw. III.[8]; and a Sir Thomas Longespey, who being a rebel in 33 Edw. III. his name occurs in the Esc. pars 2, n. 59, for lands at Brumpton near Northallerton, and Neuton, near Patrick Brumpton; his lands were granted to Isolda de Pakenham.[9]

One William Lunghespee also appears in the same county, as witness to three charters without date.[10]

A William Longespé paid aid for the manor of Wickham Breaus in Kent, in 20 Edw. III. (1346).[11]

Richard Longespey was in 1318 presented to the rectory of Wermyncham, Cheshire; and in 1337, being still parson of that church, received a grant of the reversion of the manor and advowson of Willesbye from John Trussel, of Cublesdon.[12]

John Longspee, of Raggenhill, Notts. was collated to the Archdeaconry of Stow, Nov. 6, 1334, and quitted it in the following March;[13] and a John Longespy, of Dunham, close to Ragnall, with Sibel his wife, daughter of Robert Russell, of Oulcotes, Notts. occurs in a plea 2 Hen. V. concerning lands in Oulcotes and Stirop.[14]

To these we may also add a Reginald Longespy, who was instituted Rector of Abinger, Surrey, April 4, 1404, and resigned in the following year for the church of Heyghton, Sussex;[15]

---

[1] Calendar of Clause Rolls, i. 175, 176, 190.
[2] Ibid. p. 231. [3] Ibid. p. 232. [4] Ibid. [5] Ibid. p. 428.
[6] Inq. ad quod Damn. [7] Gale's Honor Richm. App. p. 48.
[8] Ibid. p. 174. [9] Rot. Pat. 33 Edw. III. m. 7.
[10] Drake's York, pp. 605, 619, 620.
[11] Hasted's Kent, vol. iii. p. 658.
[12] Cart. Cotton. xxix. 87. [13] Willis's Cathedr. ii. 127.
[14] Thoroton's Notts. p. 471. [15] History of Surrey, ii. 143.

CHAPTER VII.

The widowhood of the Countess Ela—The Earldom of Salisbury—Shrievalty of Wiltshire—Seal of the Countess Ela—Her Son's Marriage—Foundation of the Priory of Hinton Charterhouse and the Nunnery of Lacock — Descriptive notices of Hinton Priory.

HAVING followed to his grave the heroic and pious William Longespé, our thoughts are naturally fixed on his widow, the virtuous matron and affectionate mother of eight children, devoting herself to God and the care of her offspring, and the memory of her husband, for the remainder of her desolate days upon earth.

When Ela was now actually left a widow, she was either not exposed to further matrimonial suitors, or, if she was, she continued firm in her resolution to remain faithful to the memory of her first lord, and to maintain her independence in what was then termed, in legal language, "a free widowhood." Reimund de Burgh, and his uncle the potent Justiciary, could scarcely venture, after their recent repulse, again to solicit her attention, with any hope of success. If other suitors, with equal hardihood, obtruded a similar offer, it is certain she met them with as resolute a denial. Her choice, however, was singular: for ladies of large estate, at that period, were seldom permitted to remain either as virgins or widows, without a lord and protector, unless they had arrived at an advanced period of life. Her case was evidently deemed extraordinary, and so we find it mentioned in the chronicles.*

It is probable that, if Ela had accepted a second husband, he would have acquired a title to the Earldom of Salisbury, as complete, during her life, as Longespé himself had enjoyed; so closely at that period did the rights of inheritance attach themselves to the husbands of heiresses.† We are informed that her Son, when he became of age,

---

* " Post viri sui obitum, *virum omnem respuens*, vitam castitatis continuendo in domo religionis quam ipsa a fundamentis construxerat, post paucorum elapsum annorum habitum cum velo suscepit sanctimonialis." Chronicon Roffense, MS. Cotton. Nero, D. II. f. 132.

† Thus, at the same period, the heiress of Albemarle had conferred the dignity of Earl successively on her three husbands, William Mandeville, William de Fortibus, and Baldwin de Betun; it afterwards descended to her son and heir, who was born of the second husband. Isabel of Gloucester was the wife first of John (afterwards King), and secondly of Geoffrey de Mandeville, who were both Earls of Gloucester in her right. In the reign of Edward the First there was an instance of a man becoming an Earl by marrying a widow only, without her being an heiress, (as is said to have happened to Stephan de Longespé, see p. 155); but in that instance the Countess was one of the King's daughters. Her husband, Ralph de Monthermer, was Earl of Gloucester and Hertford so long as the Princess Joan lived; but on her death the dignity left him, and devolved on Gilbert de Clare the son and heir of the Princess by her first husband, whilst Ralph de Monthermer survived her for seventeen years in the rank of a Baron only.

claimed investiture of the Earldom: but that the King refused it, not in displeasure but *judicialiter*,[*] that is, by the advice of his judges, and according to the principles of feudal law. The objection probably was, that the Earldom was then vested in his Mother. Thus, Ela's entrance into the profession of a recluse, may possibly have partaken of a worldly motive, as being likely to facilitate her Son's admittance to his hereditary dignity; but, if so, it was still unsuccessful. In consequence of her protracted life, the Earldom of Salisbury continued dormant; and, as she survived both her son and grandson, was never renewed in the house of Longespé.

The office of Sheriff of Wiltshire, her right by inheritance from the Domesday Edward, and that of Castellan of Old Sarum, she was permitted to exercise in person.[†]

It was at this period of her " free widowhood," and official importance, that a Seal, of the handsome dimensions then considered appropriate to her dignity, became necessary for the ratification of the legal instruments, required in the administration of her feudal rights, her wide estates, and official

---

[*] See his interview with the Pope, hereafter.

[†] Not uninterruptedly from her husband's death; but first for three parts of the year 11 Hen. III. and likewise for the following year; but not again until the fifteenth of that reign, at which time she paid a fine of 200 marks to have the custody (i. e. the shrievalty) of the county and the castle of Sarum, during her whole life. (Dugdale, from Rot. Pip.) She exercised the office until she became a nun, in 21 Hen. III.

SEALS, Plate IV.

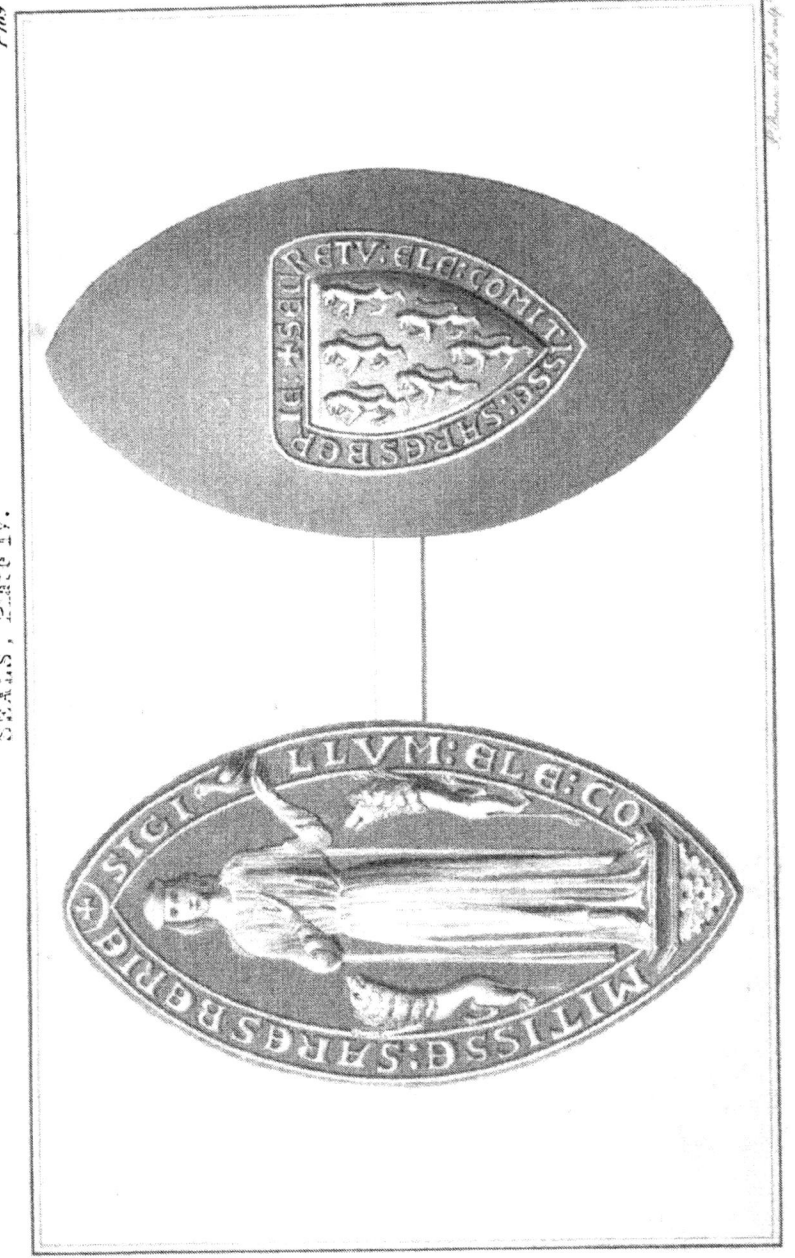

Great Seal of Ela Countess of Salisbury.

jurisdictions. Of this elegant work of ancient art a representation is placed before the reader; and, though we can scarcely regard it, like the effigy of Longespé in Salisbury Cathedral, as a *portrait* of the Countess Ela, yet we may contemplate it as the faithful resemblance of her noble and dignified deportment, and of her graceful though simple costume. Her right hand is on her breast; on her left hand stands a hawk, the usual symbol of nobility, in the figures of both sexes;* on her head is a singularly small cap, possibly the precursor of the more recent coronet; her long hair flows negligently upon her neck—on each side the royal lions of Salisbury appear to gaze upon her, like the lion in Spenser, on the desolate Una!

Such was the appearance of the august widow, when, in the midst of her pious sorrow, she devoted herself for a season to the duties of her feudal dignity and provincial sovereignty; but from the trammels of which, as we shall presently see, she soon hastened to relieve herself.

Her eldest son was a minor at the time of his father's death, and for some years after; but he had been already provided with a wife of ample domains, the heiress of the two baronies of Hay in Lincolnshire, and Camville in the county of Oxford and elsewhere.† The marriage of this lady, Idonea,

* In this and other respects the costume of the figure closely corresponds with those on the seals of her daughter Ela Countess of Warwick at p. 162.

† Madox's History of the Exchequer, p. 218.

the daughter of Richard de Camville, by Eustachia, daughter of Gilbert Basset, and granddaughter of Gerard de Camville, by Nichola, daughter of Richard de Hay, had been granted to the Earl on the 22d of April 1216, specially for the advantage of his eldest son William.* In 1226 they were already married;† but in 1231 young Longespé was still a minor, though Idonea had attained her majority.‡

* " Mandatum est Vic. Oxon. et Bercsir. quod habere fac. W. Com. Sarr. maritagium filie Ric. de Campvill genite de Eustachia que fuit filia Gileberti Basset, uxore ipsius Ricardi, ad opus Willielmi filii sui primogeniti de Ela uxore sua Comitissa Sarr. cum tota hereditate sua contingente ipsam filiam ejusdem Ricardi in baillivis suis ex parte matris suæ. T. Me ipso ap. Reygate, xxij die Aprilis 1216." Clause Rolls.

† " R. Vic. Oxon. salutem. Sciatis quod W. Longspe quondam Comes Sarum fuit nobiscum in exercitu nostro Muntgumery. Et ideo tibi præcipimus quod de Scutagio quod per summon. Scacc. exigis a Willielmo Longspe filio et hærede ipsius Comitis pro exercitu illo, de feodis militum quæ ipse Comes habuit in custodia cum filia et hærede Ricardi de Camvill, *quam prædictus Willielmus Longspe duxit in uxorem*, pacem ei habere permittas. Teste R. 21 Septemb." Kennett's Parochial Antiquities, p. 200; where also is the mandate for another favour, which seems too insignificant to have been worth asking of the King, or saving from the lawful fees of the Sheriff. " Mandat. est Vic. Oxon. quod de *bove* quem exigit a Willielmo Longspe pro seisina terræ quæ fuit Ricardi de Camvill, cujus filiam et hæredem duxit in uxorem, pacem habere facias, &c."

‡ This appears from the records of a trial in Hilary term 15 Hen. III. wherein William Longespé and Idonea were defendants, and would have stayed the process because he was under age; but, the action being laid on account of his wife, who was

We at length approach the time of the foundation of Lacock Nunnery. When, says the Book of Lacock, " Ela had now survived her husband for seven years in widowhood, and had frequently proposed to found monasteries pleasing to God, for the salvation of her soul, and of that of her husband, and those of all their ancestors, she was directed in visions *(per revelationes)* that she should build a monastery in honour of St. Mary and St. Bernard, in the meadow called Snails' Mead, near Lacock. Accordingly, on the 16th of April 1232, when she was in the 45th year of her age, she founded two monasteries, in one day; in the morning that of Lacock, in which holy canonesses might dwell, continually and most devoutly serving God; and in the afternoon the priory of Henton, of the Carthusian order."

Thus minute is the historian of Lacock in the date of this proceeding. As, however, there is proof that the foundation of both monasteries, *by charter*, had taken place some time before, it might be thought that the foundation of their *buildings* was here intended; and that the Countess Ela, on that memorable day, having witnessed in the morning the commencement of the works at Lacock, proceeded thence to Hinton, a distance of about fifteen miles, and there, in person, laid the first stone of the Carthusian monastery.

of full age, the plea was overruled; and the case is cited as a precedent by Bracton, lib. 5, f. 423.

Here, however, another difficulty presents itself; for a chronicle is extant, which, with equal minuteness in point of date, informs us that the Countess founded the church of the canons at Hinton on the 6th of November 1227.*

It will be shown in the next chapter that the first legal steps for the foundation of Lacock were certainly taken in 1229. The present chapter shall be closed with some brief notices of the sister, but evidently somewhat earlier, foundation of Hinton.

The same chronicle which has just been quoted, fixes the first foundation of this Carthusian house, by Earl William Longespé, to the feast of St. Mary Magdalen, in the year 1222. He then gave to God and the order of Chartreuse his manor of Hatherop in Gloucestershire.† The charter of this gift is not preserved; but in his will, made in Lent 1225, the establishment is mentioned under the name of LOCUS DEI. He therein gives for the building of the house, all the profits of his valuable wardship of Idonea Camville, until the full age of his heir, to whom Idonea was married; also a rich store of sacred vessels and vestments; and

* — "transtulit eos ad manerium de Hentona; et in parte ejusdem manerii *fundavit ecclesiam* eorum, anno D. 1227, 8 idus Novembris." Chronicle in the library of Lincoln college, Oxford, quoted in Leland's Collectanea, vol. ii. p. 341.

† Kennett, in his Parochial Antiquities, p. 202, mistook this for Heythrop in Oxfordshire, now the magnificent seat of the Earl of Shrewsbury near Chipping Norton; and the same mistake is repeated in Skelton's Antiquities of Oxfordshire, 4to. 1823.

MONASTERY OF HATHEROP.

the largest proportion of the cattle which he distributed among so many monasteries.*

The Carthusians, however, were not satisfied with their location in Gloucestershire. Although, says the charter of the Countess Ela, "the monks and brethren destined for that place had remained there for many years (about five as it seems), they had not been able to find in the tenements bestowed on them by the Earl,† a place suitable to their order." Therefore it was that the Countess Ela, attending to their representation, and being desirous under God's direction to perfect what her husband had so well begun, resumed the estates of Hatherop, &c., and, "in her legal power and widowhood," granted, in exchange for them, ‡ her manor of Henton in Somersetshire, with the advowson of the church, the park, and all other its appurtenances; and also the adjoining manor and advowson of Norton; to found and sustain for ever a Carthusian house, in the honour of God, the blessed Mary, St. John the Baptist, and all Saints, to be erected in the park of Henton, at the place which, like its predecessor at Hatherop, should be called the Locus Dei. This charter § was con-

* See the will before, p. 143.

† The manor of Atherop, the wood of Braden with its entirety, and the land of Cheleworth (near Chicklade) which he had of the gift of Henry Basset.

‡ Ela afterwards assigned the manor of Hatherop to her own foundation at Lacock, as will appear hereafter.

§ It will be found in the Appendix to this work, No. II.

firmed by a royal *Inspeximus*, in the 12th year of Henry III. (1227-8), a circumstance which supports the date given in the anonymous chronicle, that the church of Henton was founded on the 6th of November 1227.

Connected as Hinton Priory was, in the circumstances of its original foundation, with the Nunnery of Lacock, I have much pleasure in closing this chapter with a brief description * of its present remains, particularly as I cannot find that they have ever yet received more than very superficial attention from topographers and tourists.

On approaching the spot, the stranger is struck by the appearance of the old boundary wall of the Priory precinct, covered with ivy. It is remarkable that the attention of Leland was attracted to " a rude stone waulle by a great lenghte, as it had beene a park waulle," but it is not clear that it was exactly the same. It does not appear that the old

* Contributed by Mr. J. G. Nichols, with whom I was conducted to the spot by our hospitable friend the Rev. John Skinner, F.S.A. of Camerton, on the 15th of July 1834; who also has communicated the following remarks: "When Leland visited Farley Castle, he must have taken the lower road to Freshford, where he crossed the Frome river, and descended by the Roman vicinal way, passing out of Wiltshire in the direction of Trowbridge or Bradford, through the village of Westwood, which joined the road from Verlucio, or Warminster, to Bath, on the top of Hinton hill. By this approach Hinton abbey appeared placed on the summit of the hill, and answers well to the description he gives of it."

topographer visited the Priory itself. He seems only to have ridden past; and while he is particular in describing his journey, his information of the monastic buildings was principally derived from report :—

"From Farley (says Leland) I rid a mile off, by woody ground, to a Grange great and well builded, that belonged to Henton Priory of Carthusians. This Priory standeth not far off from this Grange on the brow of a hill, about a quarter of a mile from the further ripe (bank) of Frome; and not far from this place Frome goeth into Avon.

"I rode, by the space of a mile or more, by woods and mountain ground, to a place where I saw a rude stone wall hard on the right hand a great length, as it had been a park wall. One since told me that Henton Priory first stood there;* if it be so, it is the lordship of Hethorp that was first given to them for their first habitation. And about a mile further I came to a village, and passed over a stone bridge where ran a little brook they called Mitford Water."

The remains of Hinton Priory now consist of two distinct buildings, 105 feet distant from each other. One is a lofty structure, distinguished by several high gables. On the north side of this

* Could this be the actual site of the Priory, which Leland had previously imagined to be on another site? Thence might arise his misapprehension respecting Hatherop, which, as before noticed, is in Gloucestershire.

building the commencement of some beautifully light groining is still remaining, and is presumed to point out the situation of the church, as three stone coffins were found there in 1820.* In the southern portion of the same building is a handsome apartment, which, from its general appearance, is now commonly called the chapel; but, as there are no signs of altars or piscinæ, nor sepulchral stones, and as there is reason to suppose the church stood where it has been already mentioned, it may be fairly presumed that this was the Chapter-house, particularly as the door clearly opened upon the Cloisters. This Chapter-house (as we will venture to call it) is entered from the west by an elegant pointed door; it has a fine groined roof, and is 36 feet long by 16 feet wide. It is lighted by a triple lancet window at the east end, and single lancets at the sides, through which the dark trees, without, have a striking effect. Here literally we were saluted by the wren and the robin, as if they had come on purpose from Lacock, to meet us again, amid the ivied and solitary arches of Hinton.

From the north-west corner we proceed to a circular stone staircase, the masonry of which is very perfect. There are two floors above, in the centre of the building, and one above the Chapter-house;

* In 1827 several stone coffins were found in the burial-ground of the parish church. One of them is in the Bishop's Museum at Wells, having been presented to his Lordship by the late Rev. Benjamin Richardson, of Farley Castle.

the rooms in which present nothing very remarkable.

Proceeding hence to the other building, we find it to have been connected with that already described by a cloister, the line of which corresponds with the present walk within the garden wall. Here, in front of a garden seat, a portion of the pavement, formed of encaustic tiles, has been laid open. The weather has now nearly defaced them; but several * elegant patterns may be observed, and one presents a shield of the keys and sword in saltire, the arms of the see of Bath and Wells.

The second building contains on the ground floor two apartments. The largest of these, which we will style the Refectory, is a chamber 31 feet 6 inc. in length by 21 feet 6 inc. in breadth, with a groined roof, supported by two octagon columns 4 feet 6 inc. in circumference. A small cantle is taken out of the south-west corner to form the entrance from the exterior to another apartment, occupying the western end of this building, and which was either the Abbat's parlour or a kitchen. A very large stone fireplace may induce the ordinary visitor to assign it to the latter destination. This is indeed a great curiosity, being distinguished by small columns on each side with Norman capitals; which clearly prove that it is an antiquity equal to any part of

* In this apartment is the cast-iron back of an old grate, with the date 1552, and ornamented with a shield of the arms of King Philip, borne by an Imperial eagle, crowned.

the building. Its width is seven feet. The dimensions of this apartment are 19 feet by 11 feet 6 in.

By an exterior flight of steps, (probably in the situation, at least, of the original stairs,) we ascend to the upper floor, which is one grand chamber, measuring 46 feet by 22. There are here no original windows; but there is no reason to suppose that any alteration has been made in the dimensions of the room, or to doubt that this was the Dormitory.

The whole building shows very little innovation from the style prevailing at its first erection, and the masonry throughout is particularly fine; the few sculptured bosses and foliage which remain being perfectly sharp.

On the surrender of Henton Priory, in 1541, the community consisted of a Prior and twenty-one Monks; among the latter was one *Hugh Laycocke*, who, with one other, received the highest rate of pension, which was £8.

Just twenty years before, there was a monk of Hinton whose name has found a place in the history of England, as having contributed to the ruin of the first subject in the realm. We cannot leave these ruins without a passing remembrance of that " false hypocrite," Nicholas Hopkins, through whose " false-forged prophecies" the weak but magnificent Duke of Buckingham, the last of the great house of Stafford, was fatally betrayed in the year 1521. Hopkins had been " sometime the Duke's Confessor," and being "vainly reputed to have, by way of revelation, foreknowledge of things to come," the Duke sent several times from his princely castle of Thornbury (the Fonthill of that age), to the sequestered abbey of Hinton, in order to receive his delusive auguries; and twice, at least, he visited Hinton in person, and was told that he should come to be King. All which will be found detailed at length in the Chronicles of Hall and Holinshed.

In 37 Henry VIII. the site of Hinton Priory was granted to John Bartlet; who sold it to Matthew Coulthurst. His son sold it, in 21 Eliz. to Walter Hungerford. It continued in that family until the beginning of the last century; when Sir Edward Hungerford sold it to Walter Robinson, Esq. grandfather of Stocker Robinson, Esq. who, at his death in 1781, left two sisters his coheirs, Margaret the wife of James Humphreys, Esq. and Ellen, the wife of Joseph Frowd, Esq. The daughter of Mr. Humphreys was married to the late George Clarke Symonds, Esq. A fine old mansion, situated at a very short distance from the ruins, and apparently raised out of them, at a period subsequent to the Reformation, is now inhabited by Mrs. Symonds, to whom we are indebted for many civilities.

CHAPTER VIII.

The transactions relative to the foundation of Lacock Nunnery, and notices of the first Charters—Constantia de Legh assistant to the foundation—Alicia de Garinges the first Canoness—The Augustine Rule.

In the foundation of her Nunnery, the Countess Ela had undertaken a task which was calculated as much for a season to add to her employments, as it afterwards contributed to her repose. To the religious cares attendant on the formation of the Society, and the arrangements necessary for their pious government, was added the selection of a site for their habitation, and of adequate revenues for their support; and, more than all, the due transaction of those legal forms which the laws of the country required.

All this could not be effected at once; and hence it is that, whilst we find what is called the "foundation" of the Abbey assigned by several authorities to the year 1232, a earlier date unquestionably belongs to some of the preliminary measures.

From a chronicle formerly in the Cottonian collection of MSS.* the following entries were extracted by Dugdale :—

* Vitellius, A. VIII. (now destroyed by fire.)

FOUNDATION OF LACOCK ABBEY.

Anno MCCXXII. Hoc anno velantur primò moniales de Lakoc.

A. MCCXXIII. Isto anno primitus fundatur cœnobium de Lacok.

A. MCCXXXVIII. Hoc anno nobilis matrona, domina Ela comitissa Sarum, assumpsit habitum religionis.

A. MCCXL. Eodem anno Ela comitissa Sarum eligitur in Abbatissam.

A. MCCLVII, nonas Aprilis, deposuit se Ela Abbatissa de Lacok.

A. MCCLXI, decimo-quarto kal. Maii, obiit domina Ela comitissa Sarum, fundatrix cœnobiorum de Lacok et Hentona.

In the four latter entries these *years* agree with the narrative of the Book of Lacock; though in the two last the *months* are different. The two first entries are clearly some years too early: it may be conjectured that the date MCCXXII is a mistranscript for MCCXXXI, and MCCXXIII for MCCXXXII; in which case the first veiling of the nuns, ascribed to the former year, 1231, will coincide with the mention made in the Book of Lacock, of Alicia de Garinges, the first Canoness (more fully noticed hereafter); and the latter, 1232, will correspond with four other authorities, including the Book of Lacock[*]; which relates that it was on the 16th of April 1232 that the Countess Ela founded the

---

[*] The remaining three are: 1. the Chronicle of Matthew of Westminster; 2. that of Robert of Gloucester (edit. Hearne, p. 520); and 3. a chronicle of Malmesbury in Leland's Collectanea, vol. i. p. 379, in which place all the figures, (except those standing for the Roman M) ought to be 2, as 1220 for 1110, 1228 for 1118, and 1232 (the date in question) for 1131.

Nunnery of Lacock in the morning, and the Charter-house of Hinton in the afternoon.

We have seen, however, in the last Chapter, from the testimony of the Book of Lacock itself, that this pious design had long occupied the Countess's thoughts. It had been the subject of her dreams at night, and her visions in the day; and it will now be found that she had taken some of the necessary legal steps, at least as early as the year 1229.

We proceed to trace these preliminary arrangements for the establishment of Lacock Nunnery.

The first and most important is, of course, the Countess's own Foundation Charter; but this it was deemed necessary to fortify by others in confirmation, obtained from her Son, from the Rector of Lacock, from the Bishop of the Diocese, and from the King.

By her Foundation Charter,* the Countess Ela gave to GOD and *Saint Mary,* her whole manor of Lacock, with all its appurtenances, rights, and free customs, to found an Abbey thereon, which she willed to be named the *Locus Beatæ Mariæ,* or Place of St. Mary. This name, it will be remarked, was in correspondence with her husband's foundation of Carthusians, which he had called *Locus Dei.* The remainder of the charter simply states that the manor was to be held by the Abbess and Nuns *in free and perpetual alms,* and therefore released from

---

* See the Appendix, p. viii.

every secular exaction, due either to the King or to her heirs. This charter was solemnly witnessed by the Justiciary of the Kingdom, Hubert de Burgh;* by William Mareschal, Earl of Pembroke; by William de Warren, Earl of Surrey; by Peter fitz Hubert, Hugh de Neville, Ralph son of Nicholas the King's steward, John the Dane, Henry de Albeney, and many others.

The charter of her son William Longespeye,† was doubtless executed at the same time, as the witnesses are precisely the same. It merely recites his mother's charter, states that he ratifies it, and confirms it by the impression of his seal.

We have next to notice the Covenant made by the Countess with the Rector of Lacock.‡ This is dated; namely, on the 3d of April 1229. It shows that the Countess of Salisbury required the assent of John the Rector to build an Abbey of Nuns within his parish. In order to the peaceful commencement and progress of this undertaking, the Countess Ela, on her part, binds herself and heirs to preserve for ever every privilege of the Church of Lacock, both in great and small tithes, in mortuaries, offerings, and bequests, and in all other

---

* Whatever conclusions we might wish to have drawn from Hubert's name being attached to the foundation charter, with reference to his conduct towards the Countess Ela, there can be no doubt his name occurs merely as the first officer of the Kingdom.

† Appendix, p. x.   ‡ Ibid. p. xi.

profits accruing to the Church in its pastoral right, notwithstanding any general or special privilege, either then or thereafter to be obtained; yet so that it might be freely allowable for the household of the Abbess, whether in life or in death, to receive the church sacraments elsewhere, and to make offerings and bequests wherever they desired. It was further agreed that the Chaplains, who should celebrate the divine services in the Abbey, should *swear fidelity* to the Rector of the Church to preserve its privileges, as aforesaid; and when an Abbess should be appointed, she and her convent should by charter provide for the same indemnity; and the same should be renewed by each successive Abbess. Moreover, if it should happen to be necessary to apply to any matters there indiscreetly committed the "twig of correction!" *(limam correctionis)* for that purpose the Countess subjects the House to the jurisdiction of the Bishop and Chapter of Salisbury, and commits to them the charge of correcting such excesses, without appeal. For the preservation of this Covenant, it was written as a bipartate cirograph,* and the sides, when mutually sealed, were divided and delivered to the respective parties; at

---

* This mode of bipartite covenants, written at first on one piece of parchment, and then casually divided through the word CYROGRAPHUM (like a modern banker's check) was the most effectual preservation against forgery. The indenture of the present day has derived its *name*, and little else, from this useful practice.

THE CONFIRMATION CHARTERS. 185

Salisbury, in the presence of Robert the Bishop, Walter the Dean, Roger the Precentor, Robert the Chancellor, and Edmund the Treasurer.

On the 20th of the same month the Bishop himself,* having first inspected the charter of the Countess Ela and the cyrograph of the Rector of Lacock,† urged also by the devout requests *(pulsati devotis supplicationibus)* of William Longespeye, the son and heir of the Countess, and having received the readiest goodwill and unanimous assent of his beloved sons and brothers in Christ, the Dean and Chapter of Sarum; granted his permission that the Countess of Ela should found and construc- her Monastery, and place therein Nuns of the order of Saint Augustine; appointing that they should ever exercise and follow that Rule, and be canonically subject to the Church of Salisbury. This charter was dated at the Bishop's manor-house of of Ramsbury, where the Dean, Precentor, Chancellor, and Treasurer of Sarum were present as wit-

---

* Since the death and funeral of Earl William, Bishop Poore had been translated to Durham, and succeeded in 1228 by ROBERT BINGHAM. It is somewhat singular that these successive Bishops of Salisbury were both natives of the county of Dorset, and that the ancient and distinguished families of both are still remaining in that county.

† In the cartulary the King's confirmation is transcribed into this charter, as well as that of Ela; and in the Monasticon the Bishop's charter is accordingly headed "cartas Elæ Comitissæ, *et Regis Henrici Tertii*, confirmat;" but this is clearly an error, the King's confirmation not being yet obtained.

nesses, together with William Archdeacon of Berkshire, H. Teysson, R. de Croshal, Thomas de Ebelesborn, W. de Len, Gilbert de Stapelbrig, P. Picot, one of the chanters of Sarum, Thomas of Warwick and John of Birmingham, the Bishop's clerks, Walter and Richard his chaplains, and many others.*

Finally, on the 21st of January, a royal confirmation † of Ela's foundation charter was obtained from the hands of the Chancellor at Westminster, which was witnessed by the Justiciary Hubert de Burgh, Earl of Kent, Philip de Albiney, Ralph Fitz-Nicholas, John Fitz Philip, Richard Fitz-Hugh, Ralph de Raleghe, Henry de Capella, and others then attendant on King Henry.

Such is the first chain of legal documents illustrating the foundation of LACOCK ABBEY. The pious work was now carried forward with vigour; and the munificent Foundress had already ‡ provided, to a considerable extent, the means necessary for its permanent establishment and future support. This essential arrangement was ratified by another solemn charter; by which, "in her widowhood and liege power," the Countess Ela granted and con-

---

* Appendix, p. xiii.   † Ibid. p. xi.

‡ It is evident, indeed, that the charter now about to be noticed is rather the earlier of the two; because, whilst the other has the same set of witnesses as her Son's confirmations of *both*, this has a different set. As the other, however, received the Royal Confirmation, it obtained the more prominent place in the Cartulary, the example of which we have followed.

ELA'S SECOND CHARTER.

firmed, *to* GOD *and Saint Mary, and Saint Bernard,* and to the Nuns serving God at Lacock,

1. the manor of Lacock, with the advowson of the church of that manor, and all its appurtenances;

2. the manor of Hatherop (in Gloucestershire, which had previously belonged to the Carthusians of her husband's foundation);

3. the manor of Bissopestre (Bishopstrow, Wilts);

4. the moiety of the manor of Hedington (Edingdon in Wiltshire);

which two last belonged to her by a final agreement respecting the Honour of Trowbridge, made in the King's Court between Humphrey de Bohun and herself;

and 5. the advowson of the church of Winterborne Syreveton (now Shrewton, also in Wilts).

All these were to be held by the Nuns of Lacock in free alms, released from every secular service. due either to the King and his bailiffs, or to herself and her heirs. This charter was witnessed by Sir Walter de Godarvile, Thomas de Ebelesbourn, Nicholas Malemains, Adam the Rector of Gatesden,* Richard Longespeye (one of the Countess's sons), John de Moul, *master* Roger de Stokes, *Dan* Roger

---

* Doubtless Gaddesden in Hertfordshire, of which the Countess and Nicholas Malmaines just mentioned were the joint heirs, as before noticed in p. 98. The only Rector of Gaddesden mentioned by Mr. Clutterbuck is Nicholas de Longespé, the Countess's son, afterwards Bishop of Salisbury. The rectory was appropriated at an early period to Dartford nunnery, Kent.

de Baskervile, Peter de Salceto,* *Dan* Peter the *parson* of Trowbridge, Philip de Depeford clerk, Thomas Makerel clerk, Robert de Holte clerk, and others.

This charter was confirmed by her son, with the same witnesses as his confirmation of Ela's other charter; which circumstance shows that his ratification was given to both at the same time.

There are also in the Cartulary no less than nine other copies of confirmatory charters of William Longespé:

By the Third he promises that he will demand nothing contrary to the indenture between his mother and himself, notwithstanding a charter which the Countess had made him, concerning the concession of her manors. (fo. 7 a.)

4. Another confirmation of all his mother's grants. (fo. 8 a.)

5. A confirmation of the manors of Lacock and Hatherop, and injunction to his knights and free tenants to perform all their services to the Nuns. (fo. 9 a.)

6, 7, 8. Three charters by which he conferred, (that is confirmed) to the Nuns the manor of Bishopstrow, the estate of Hatherop, and advowson

---

* Qu? *Calceto*, the Causeway,—some ancient work, previous to that of the beneficent Maud Heath? A causeway near the town of Arundel in Sussex gave name to a Priory, called *de Calceto*. There was, however, a forest in Northamptonshire, named *Salcey*, and a person occurs, taking his name from it, Robert *de Salceto*. See Baker's Northamptonshire, i. 178.

of the parish church of Lacock. This grant was made in 20 Hen. III. (1236). (fo. 66 a.)

9. A concession that his mother should confer on the house of Lacock a moiety of the manor of Hedyngton, she having released to him an exchange of land of the Prior and canons of Bradenstoke. (fo. 76 a.)

There were also at least two benefactions of William Longespé to the Abbey, which appear to have originated with himself. These were:

1. all his land at Chittern (fo. 43 a.), confirmed by Henry III. in 1242; and 2. all the land which had belonged to Nicholas de Hamptun, in Upham (fo. 86 a.)

William Longespé the Third was also called upon to confirm the possessions of the Abbey; which he did, reciting his grandmother's charter word for word. (fo. 3 b.)

The vigilance with which the monastic societies were accustomed to solicit these confirmatory deeds, from the hands of the heirs of their original benefactors, is demonstrated by the charters throughout the Monasticon; and its necessity is shown by several cases in their earlier history, in which a fierce and graceless youth seized again upon his ancestral estates, or refused to deliver that which his father had bestowed under the influence of a deathbed remorse. An interesting account of the ceremony which attended the confirmation of gifts to monasteries, is contained in a Register of the

Abbey of Shrewsbury. One Herbert fitz-Helgot, being unwilling that any trouble should arise respecting the benefactions of his father and himself to that church, determined that, *although the King had confirmed them by a charter*, yet his *sons* also should confirm them by a grant of their own. He therefore sent them, Eutropius his son and heir, and his brothers Nicholas and Herbert, *with their pious mother*, to the church; where, when they had heard the prayers, and regranted in the Chapter-house the benefactions of their father and grandfather, they took in their head a text of the Gospel, and offered their charters upon the altar of St. Peter, before many witnesses.*

Among the benefactors enumerated in the Lacock Cartulary it is not easy to select those who were the original coadjutors of the Countess in her pious undertaking; for, as Stevens has remarked, the charters are not arranged in order of time, and for the greater part *dates* are deficient. It will therefore be most desirable to pursue our account of the contents of the Cartulary, hereafter, in the order of the several estates of which the Abbey became possessed.

There is, however, certainly one name which may be pointed out as having been amongst the earliest co-operators with the pious Ela. This is that of Constance de Legh, or Leach, of Eastleach in Gloucestershire.

* Collectanea Topographica et Genealogica, vol. i. p. 26.

Constance de Legh gave *to God and St. Mary* her whole manor of Woodmancote, *in order to found* in the town of Lacock an Abbey, which (in correspondence with the design of the Countess Ela) she desired to be called the LOCUS BEATÆ MARIÆ. (fo. 107 b.)

The first Canoness veiled at Lacock was Alicia Garinges.* There was a small nunnery at a place so named in Oxfordshire, which was also governed under the Augustine rule; it is therefore highly probable that Alicia was transplanted thence, in order to assist in the establishment of Ela's new society. In the portions we possess of the Book of Lacock, no other person is mentioned, either as Abbess or Canoness, during the eight years which elapsed after the foundation, before the religious government of the house was assumed by Ela herself. There was an Alicia who became the Abbess, some thirty years after, but that person can scarcely have been the same with Alicia Garinges.

It will be proper to close this chapter with a brief account of that Rule of St. Augustine, which, as we have seen in the charter of the Bishop of

* " Alicia Garinges apud Lacok prima Canonissa velata." (Book of Lacock.) The words which precede, " A. vero ætatis suæ xlv." were connected with this sentence in the Monasticon; but, as printed in the Appendix to the present volume, it will be perceived they belong to the Countess Ela, who was of that age at the period of the foundation.

Salisbury, it was covenanted that the Nuns of Lacock should perpetually observe.

The Rule of St. Augustine was applied, with a few necessary modifications, to monasteries of both sexes.

They were to live in a convent, not calling anything their personal property, but holding all things in common.

Food and raiment were to be distributed to them by their superior; not equally to all, but according to the necessity of each, as is written in the Acts of the Apostles, " For they had all things common, and it was distributed to them as each had need."

They were to be constant in prayer at the appointed hours; not singing except what was directed to be sung.

They were to overcome their flesh with fasting and abstinence, when their strength permitted; and when at table, they were to listen attentively to the lecture, " that so not only their mouth might receive their food, but their ears also might feed on the word of God." *

They were to be victualled from *one cellar*, and clothed from *one vestiary*; nor to murmur if the vestment they received at any time were *worse* than that they had *worn* before.

* The practice is kept up in most colleges in Oxford to this day.

No one was to perform any work for her *private advantage*, but all for the common good.

Nothing given them by their parents or relations was to be received *secretly*, but to be in the power of the superior; that, being placed in the *common stock*, it might be dealt out to the members who required it. If any one concealed any thing brought to her, the crime was to be condemned equally with theft.

Their clothes were to be washed at the pleasure of their superior, either by themselves, or by fullers. Bathing was to be allowed, if deemed necessary for health; but none were to go to the baths, or any where else, except two or three in company. And any one requiring to go anywhere, was to go with those the superior directed. In walking they were to move forward together, and to stop at the same time.

The care of the sick was to be confided to some one person, who should direct the *cellarer* to provide what was necessary for them.

All who should be appointed to the duties of the cellar, the vestments, or of the books, should serve their Sisters *without murmuring*.

Books were to be asked for at a certain hour daily, at which only they were to be obtained; but the keepers of the clothes and shoes were not to delay to deliver them, when necessary, to those that required them.

Such, with some other precepts of a more strictly

moral and religious nature, directing avoidance of anger, forgiveness of injuries, abstinence from severe words, and obedience to the superior, are the principal injunctions of the Rule of St. Augustine; which, in order that no part of it should be neglected through forgetfulness, was to be read to the brethren or sisters once in every week. Though as now preserved, and printed in the Monasticon Anglicanum, it is adapted to a monastery of men, it is supposed by Erasmus and by Bellarmin to have been originally written by the Saint for the instruction of the women, who formed a monastic society under the government of his sister.

In order to complete our view of the domestic life of the Nuns, we may here append a description of their costume, derived from a volume * which, although it was specially written for a reformed sect of the Augustins, named after St. Saviour and St. Bridget, yet in its principal features retains, no doubt, the spirit of that Order:

" The clothes of the sisters may be two chemises[1] of white flannel,[2] one for daily use, the other for washing. One gown[3] of grey cloth[4] with a cowl,[5] and sleeves extending not further than to the end of

---

* Additional MSS. (Brit. Mus.) 5208.

[1] *Camisie*.

[2] Or perhaps linen, as in the English MS. (Arundel, 146) this garment is called a *stamen*. The original word is here *burello*, a diminutive from *burrus*.

[3] *Tunica*.   [4] *Burello*.   [5] *Cuculla*.

the middle finger, the folds of which are round the hand, when they perform their manual services, shall be bound to the arms with a buckle like other sleeves. One mantle also of grey cloth, like the tunic and hood; which shall not be plaited in front, nor finely made, but tight and plain, being wholly made for *use* and not at all for *vanity:* which also ought in summer to be single, but in winter lined, not with delicate skins, but with those of lambs or sheep. Of skins of this kind a pilch[6] may also be made for the winter. The said mantle moreover shall not reach the earth by a palm's breadth, and shall be fastened by a *wooden buckle* at the breast. For the cloathing of their feet they shall have, in summer, shoes[7] reaching to their ancles, and stockings[8] to their knees; but in winter, *boots* to their knees, lined with cloth, and stockings equally high. The head-dress shall be a *fillet*, by which the forehead and chin shall be surrounded and the face be partly opened; the ends of which shall be joined by one pin at the back of the head. Over this shall be placed a veil of black linen, which, lest it should be loose, shall be fixed with three pins, one on the forehead, and two at the ears. Then over the veil shall be placed a round cap[9] of white

[6] A tippet of skins—*pellicium*, whence also the modern *pellise*. The word *pilch* occurs in Chaucer. From the *super-pellicium* is derived the modern *surplice*.

[7] *Sotulares.* [8] *Pedulos.*

[9] *Corona.* The five red drops were allusive to the five wounds of Christ. This portion of the costume was doubtless

linen, to which shall be sown five pieces of red cloth like five drops; the first piece shall be on the forehead, the second on the back of the head, the third and fourth around the ears, the fifth on the middle of the head. This cap shall be fastened by one pin in the middle of the head; and shall fit the head; and it shall be worn both by widows and virgins in token of continence and chastity."

Their usual beds were to be of straw, over which they might have two blankets,[10] of cloth or linen, and mattresses.[11] Under their heads they were to have a cushion covered with a web,[12] and a pillow[13] covered in the same manner.

An important feature of the Rule of St. Saviour, is the strict injunction of silence, during the greater part of the day; speaking being allowed only at certain intervals, except on some necessary occasions.

Conversation with secular persons was permitted only in company, and with the licence of the abbess, from noon to vespers, and this only on sundays and the great feasts of the Saints. Nor was a sister to go out of the house for this purpose, but to sit at the appointed windows; for to none was it permitted after their entrance to leave the cloisters of the monastery. If any desired to be seen by her

peculiar to the Brigetines, and should therefore be omitted in in our view of the nuns of Lacock.

[10] *Thoralia.*   [11] *Culcitris.*   [12] *Tela.*   [13] *Cervical.*

parents or honest and dear friends, she might, with the permission of the abbess, open the window, that is occasionally during the year; but if she did not open it, a more abundant reward was promised to her hereafter!

Another chapter of the same volume describes the Divine Hours to be observed by the sisters. They were daily, in worship of the Virgin, solemnly to sing her Hours, together with three lessons, as well on feasts as private days. Every day also, when notice was given for vespers, the Sisters were to assemble together, and first the right hand choir were to read one *Ave Maria*, and deeply inclining themselves to the other choir were to say, ' *Pardon us for the sake of God and his most pious mother Mary*, if we have offended you in word or deed, in *sign or nod;* for we, if there be any fault in you against us, do remit it most freely.' Then, the other choir inclining in like manner, and reading, and asking pardon, so shall they proceed to vespers. And at the end of all the Hours, they shall sing the antiphon *Ave Maria*, with the collect in this form, *Omnipotens sempiterne Deus, qui pro nobis de castissima Virgine nasti dignatus es, fac nos, quesimus, tibi casto corpore servire, et humili mente placere. Oramus et te, piissima Virgo Maria, mundi Regina et angelorum, ut eis quos purgatorius examinat ignis, impetres refrigerium, peccatoribus indulgentiam, justis in bono perseverantiam, nos quoque fragiles ab instantibus defende periculis, per eundem Christum, &c.* On all days, both feasts and private, the mass of the blessed Virgin was also to be sung by the sisters. And on every Sunday, after the mass of the blessed Virgin, the sisters were to sing, *Salve, Regina!*

Much as appears in this account at complete variance with the plain and open Word of God, who can read it without interest? The plain and scriptural Christian will remember Bishop Lavington's " Enthusiasm of Methodists and Papists compared."

THE CANONICAL HOURS.

The Church of Rome divided the twenty-four hours into seven parts, to each of which certain services were assigned. They were termed the Canonical Hours; and the time following each service, until the commencement of the next, often went under the same name. The following was their order:

Hora Matutina, Matins or Lauds, 3 A. M.
Hora Prima, Prime, 6 A. M.
Hora Tertia, Tierce, 9 A. M.*
Hora Sexta, Sext, 12 at midday.
Hora Nona, Nones, 3 P. M.
Hora Vespera, Vespers, about 4 P. M.
Completorium, Compline, about 7 P. M.,

The night was also divided into four watches; the first beginning at 6 P. M. and each lasting three hours.

* This time of the day was also called Undern.

CHAPTER IX.

Contrast of the View at Old Sarum and the Forest of Chippenham—Ela retires to the society of the Nuns at Lacock—Saint Edmund (of Abingdon) Archbishop of Canterbury—The reception of Novices, and Profession of a Nun.

WHEN Ela, yielding to the stronger impressions of her religious feelings, had resolved to retire from all connection with the cares of life, and the duties of her high station, she at length left the stately castle on the elevated ramparts of Sarisbyrig, and repaired to the religious seclusion in the Forest of Chippenham, as described in the first chapter, in which she had placed her foundation of Augustine Nuns.

There is something in the drear and treeless elevation of such a spot as that on which the Castle of Old Sarum was raised, so remote from the feelings of pensive and private sorrow, that the scene itself of a dark forest, would seem to be more conducive to piety, and humble acquiescence in the dispensations of Providence, than a Fortress, on a solitary hill, in the glare of day, commanding a wild extent of downs; where no stream was heard to murmur such as might seem almost a companion in solitude and sorrow; where no woods were heard to wave; no early woodland bird,

" Twittering from its straw-built shed,"

might call up the remembrance, and shadows, of youthful happiness; or which,

"Filling with farewell sweet the parting plain,"

might bring back, like music, " a joy, and peace, in believing," and in tears.

But all these were found in that place which Ela had fixed upon as the sacred home of her seclusion from the world, sadly, but not uninterestingly, contrasted with the City and stately Fortress she had left.

And here, without any admixture of superstitious feelings, who can be insensible to the consolation which, with all its errors, the religious belief of the period, as we before remarked, was calculated to inspire?

The souls of those separated by Death might seem to be again united, in the reveries of ardent piety, to those left to mourn their loss, for a season, upon earth; the voices of the dead might be imagined, not seldom, to mingle in the dying cadences of the vesper hymn, whispering peace and comfort to the desolate, in tones not of this world; and whilst, as such strains were heard, and the incense ascended, at the stated hours, from the altar, these feelings of abstracted devotion and affection would, day by day, gather greater strength, till the distance between earth and heaven might seem as almost lost; as if soul met soul, in a purer sphere, without the intervention of earthly corruption or the fears of earthly change!

How often might ideas like these, so beautifully expressed by the Poet of PARACLETE, have superseded all feelings of terrestrial deprivation!

> How happy is the blameless Vestal's lot,
> The world forgetting, by the world forgot!
> Labour and rest, that equal periods keep,
> Obedient slumbers that can wake or sleep,
> Desires composed, affections ever even,
> Tears that delight, and sighs that waft to Heaven!

To return—the brief particulars recorded of Ela's assumption of the habit of religion are only these: that it took place on Christmas day in the year of our Lord 1238, in the seventh year after the foundation of the house of Lacock, and in the 51st year of her age; she "having in all her actions and designs," says the Book of Lacock, "been constantly dependent on the counsel and aid of St. Edmund, the Archbishop of Canterbury, and other discreet men."

A few words may here be said respecting this Archbishop Edmund, Ela's especial spiritual counsellor. He was the same Edmund of Abingdon, who, when TREASURER OF SALISBURY, had been united with Dean William de Wanda as one of the supervisors of the Earl her husband's will;* and who had witnessed, after the Earl's death, the charter by which the Countess Ela removed his Carthusians to Hinton;† and her covenant with the

---

* See before, p. 147. † See the Appendix, p. vii.

Rector of Lacock.* His paternal name was Rich; but, like other ecclesiastics, he had relinquished it for that of his native place, the town of Abingdon in Berkshire. He first distinguished himself as a Professor at the university of Oxford, where he introduced the ethics of Aristotle. His schools were numerously frequented, and he mainly contributed to the restoration of the prosperity of that University, which had previously been deserted, in consequence of *one* of the tyrannical acts of King John. Among his pupils were many eminent men; two of whom, like himself, were subsequently elevated to the *glory of canonization,* namely, Richard de la Wich, Bishop of Chichester, and Sewall de Bovill, Archbishop of York. To these may be added Robert Grosteste, Bishop of Lincoln, Richard Fishacre, an eminent Dominican, Robert Bacon, who became his biographer; and, above all, that deep philosopher, who so far surpassed the ordinary science of his day as to acquire a supernatural character, the learned ROGER BACON. At the same time, Edmund of Abingdon was so careless of money, that, if any was forced upon him by his scholars, he would lay it in his window, and cover it with dust, saying that " Earth with earth and dust with dust should be mingled together;" and " there leaving and taking no further care about it, his scholars and companions would take it away in jest, and some that were *light-fingered* secretly!"

* See p. 185.

The historian of Oxford, Anthony à Wood, assigns the period of Abingdon's lecturing at Oxford to between the years 1219 and 1226. The scene of his exertions was known by the name of St. Edmund's Schools for many centuries after.

In 1234 Edmund of Abingdon was at once elevated from the TREASURERSHIP OF SALISBURY to the archiepiscopal SEE OF CANTERBURY. He owed this preferment to the particular nomination of the Pope (Gregory IX.); for the convent of Canterbury had previously elected another candidate. The King was present at his consecration in Canterbury Cathedral; and two years after he solemnized in the same church the marriage of King Henry with Alianor of Provence.

The Archbishop still continued a severe and rigid devotee, and was so zealously attached to the rigours of monachism, that he is said to have fallen into a consumption through too great abstinence. In consequence of the high character for devotion and austere piety which he had thus acquired, he was canonized in the 7th year after his death (which occurred in 1240, while he was dwelling in exile at Soissy in Pontiniac,) and his name was placed as a *Saint* in the calendar of the CHURCH OF ROME.*

Such was the zealous and ascetic counsellor under whose advice the Countess Ela retired into a

* The King's son Edmund, afterwards Earl of Lancaster, christened in 1245, received his name in memory of Edmund the Archbishop.

cloister. Of the ceremonial observed at Lacock, on that memorable feast of our Lord's Nativity, we have no specific account; but, as generally illustrative of the subject of this volume, we may here append some account of the ordinary proceedings attendant on the Profession of Nuns, extracted from a curious manuscript volume now in the British Museum,* written in English, and describing that modification of the Augustine discipline which was called the Rule of St. Saviour, and was adopted by the Nuns of Sion in Middlesex :—

"If any ask this religion in the way of charity, the Abbess, standing or sitting in a chair at the crates,† with the whole convent in their whole habit standing about her, each in their order religiously, the window open, shall bid her tell her desire, before all the Convent. Which heard, if the number be full, she shall say, 'We may receive none over the number limited in our Rule.' If it be void, she shall say, 'None may be professed in this religion, before an whole year of sufficient probation without; nor, after their profession, go to another religion.'‡

"If she then still desire to be admitted to the *year of proof*, the Abbess first shall examine her, how long she hath stood in her purpose towards

---

* MS. Arundel, 146.   † Grated window.

‡ Thus, in the Church of Rome, a still stronger term was in use for different monastic societies, than, in these days of modern toleration, is even applied to the *sects* into which the Christian church is now divided.

this religion, and whether she be moved thereto of herself or of any other person; secondly, if she be free of all worldly bonds, that is to say, of debt, borrowage, service, bondage, sentence of cursing, wedlock, contract, vowess,* infamy, executry, heresy, and such other; also if she desire this religion principally for God, or for any privy sickness or impotency; or else if shame, or pain of worldly adversity or any such thing, compelleth her thereto. And, after this, for the third thing, she shall tell her of the *duress* of the religion; that is to say, contempt of the world, *forgetting of father and mother*, and of all worldly friendship, except as the Rule suffereth and the Church determineth: much fasting, many *water days*, great watch, early rising, long service, daily labour, *strait silence*, lowest place, hard commandments of the Sovereign,† ready

---

* That is, an engagement to any other monastic profession.

† The " Sovereign" was the Sister into whose charge the instruction of novices and junior nuns was specially entrusted. Another nearly equivalent title is fully explained in the following passage :—" By this name, *President*, is understood any person that among the Convent gathered together in any conventual act, hath there the rule of the religion, at least for that season; for they that be so gathered, be never without a president. The *Sovereign* is president in every place; and, she absent, the Prioress is president; she absent, the eldest Search; all these three absent, the second Search; and so descending by all the Searches. Which all absent, the eldest Sister of them there present is President." Beginning of Chapter VIII. " On the President." MS. Arundel 146.

obedience, forsaking of proper will, patience in adversity, sufferance of all sharp corrections, and many such other; which may be lightly suffered for a while, but *to continue for term of life, it is hard work to some!* To the which things if she be not agreable, the Abbess shall honestly avoid her.

"If the Abbess think her disposed to this religion, she shall hear *her ability in voice, singing and reading.* Which known, she shall bid her abide upon an answer unto another convenient time, till she may have had communication with her Sisters, from whom in this case she may hide nothing for favour or dread, or for threatening of any person, of what power or dignity that ever he be.

"After this, the convent sitting in the Chapter House, the Abbess shall ask of each Sister in order by name, beginning at the eldest, whether they will have her admitted to the *year of proof* or no; and, if the *sadder* (graver) party answer "Nay," telling reasonable cause why, the Abbess, before all the convent, or a part of them, shall give her a goodly answer and let her go.

If the more holy and *sad* party grant to have her admitted to the *year of proof,* the Abbess shall use such words as these to the said person, 'Daughter, you have cause to yield praisings to God. I have communed with my Sisters, and I find them right glad of your holy purpose, and agreeable to your desire.' And then she shall say this, be there one or many of them, ' In the name of our Lord JESUS

CHRIST, and of his most holy mother, our lady *Saint Mary*, of *Saint Bridget*, *Saint Austin*, and of *all Saints*, and in the name of the whole congregation of Sisters and Brethren, and in my own name, *I admit you to the Year of Proof*,[*] after the tenour of the Rule of St. Saviour. Proceed therefore to essay yourself, how you may accord with some kind of observance of the said holy Rule, now this year; and after three months come again unto us, and in the mean time we shall take further deliberation respecting you.' She, hearing this, shall give thankings to God, and to all the congregation, and after this go with a *low head* and *forehead covered*, living under the obedience of the Abbess. And it shall be told her, 1. that she keep the times appointed for coming again; 2. how she shall demean and prove herself in the said year, with some observances according to the Rule; 3. to speak with the General Confessor for health of her soul; 4. the Abbess shall have to her words and commandments sometimes of sharpness, to prove her patience and obedience; and also the Rule and Statutes are to be read to her, in those points only that concern her person, that she may know whereto she cometh. Furthermore, the Abbess in the meanwhile may inquire, or cause to be inquired, more diligently of other persons that know her, of her life and conversation, desiring, if need be, letters of

[*] Corresponding with the Oxford Year of Probation for all scholars; in particular, for the junior Fellows of New College.

testimony thereupon, so that the day of her admitting, and month, with the year of our Lord, be put in writing by the Chantress.

" When she cometh again the second time, the Abbess shall examine her, and say to her as is expressed in the Rule; and so she shall do when she cometh again the third time."

If any one kept her *year of proof* in the outer court, and was not able to pay for her board, school, and other expences, she was to be found by the Monastery.

The ceremony of entering fully into the society, when the term of probation had expired, was called the *Renouncing the Year of Proof*. The attendance of a Bishop was necessary for its performance; and when " surety was had of his coming," the Abbess and Convent proceeded to the crates, where they that were professed knelt at a window. The Abbess then said, whether there were many or but one, ' What ask you?' The answer was, ' I ask, in the way of charity, that I may be received to live with you in this holy Congregation all the days of my life.' Then the Abbess, if she thought proper, rehearsed compendiously what had been told her from the beginning of her year of proof, concluding with telling her that she must acknowledge herself duly admitted to her year of proof, and that she was fully content therewith; promising to abide the day appointed for her profession. This was done by the novice both by word and on a written scroll; and the Abbess also, on her part, renounced the same; when either the next morning, or sometimes the same day, was appointed for the ceremony of Profession.*

Before that solemnity, the Sextoness was to arrange a *beir*, with fair new earth, *making a cross thereon with a smooth lath,* and setting it forth at the door. Each person was to be professed in her own arrayment that she had used in the world, and *not in borrowed gear:* and before any were presented to the Bishop to be consecrated, *their hair was to be clipped* by the Abbess after the manner of other monials,† with this ceremony. The Abbess repaired, with some of the nuns, to the crates, the day before the Profession, after our Lady's Mass, or after compline,‡ or any other time most convenient; and the Sextoness brought *holy water* and *a fair handkerchief,* with a clean pair of *shears* or scissors. And the window being opened, and the hair of the novice being dressed honestly § behind her head, the Abbess sprinkled holy water upon her, saying, " *Aqua benedicta sit tibi salus et vita! In nomine Patris et Filii et Spiritus Sancti.*" The convent answered *Amen.* And then, ‖ whilst the

* The earliest time was preferred, as being " most syker," that is to say *secure,* for the interests of the monastery; because, " after the renouncing, the parties might ask their *finding* in the monastery lawfully as long as they lived, though they were never professed, which, by long process, might turn to insupportable charge to the monastery."

† Nuns.   ‡ See p. 198.   § Decorously.

‖ We are obliged indignantly to suppress what follows relative to " burning love of the Almighty," to a human virgin!"

Abbess clipped her head, the Convent said, "side for side," (that is, with chant and antiphon) the hymn *Veni, Creator spiritus*. After which followed certain prayers.

On the day of PROFESSION, all the Hours * were performed before High Mass. And when the Bishop was entered into the Brethren's quire, four Sisters assigned by the Abbess brought religiously between them the *beir*, a little lifted up from the earth, two before and two behind, and set it down fair and easily before the newly professed Sister; and, inclination made toward the high altar, they turned again into the monastery, the door being shut after them. After mass it was brought in again by the same four.

When the Bishop † came to the door, he found the Novice there kneeling, and he first addressed her in these words: "*Art thou free, and unfettered by any bond of the Church, or of wedlock; of vow, or of excommunication?*" To whom she answered, "I am verily free;" when the Bishop added, "Doth not shame, or perhaps grief of worldly adversity, urge thee to a religious profession, or perchance the multitude of thy debts compels thee." She answering, (from a scroll on her hand, on which it was written) " Neither grief nor shame incites me to this, but *a fervent love of God*; and I

---

* See p. 198.

† The ensuing account of the ceremonies in the church is translated from the MS. Addit. 5208, being omitted in the Arundel MS. 146.

have already paid all my debts according to my power;" then the Bishop further added, " Seekest thou entrance into this religion in the name of Jesus Christ, and in honour of his most holy mother the Virgin Mary?" She saying, " I seek it," the Bishop brought her into the church, saying, " Lo, now she worthily enters this religion!" And when she entered the church, *a red banner* was carried before her, on one side of which was painted the image of Christ crucified, and on the other the image of the Virgin Mary; that *the new Bride,** contemplating the sign of her *new* SPOUSE suffering on the cross, might learn patience and poverty, and, looking upon the Virgin Mother, might learn chastity and humility.

When she was thus brought into the church, she was placed near the door, and the Bishop proceeded to *consecrate her ring;* after which, approaching the Novice, he said, " You ought to promise God, and me on his behalf, that you will obey thy prelates, and live according to the Rule of St. Augustine, until the end of thy life." And then the Novice answered, " I, sister [ELA], *make my profession*, and promise obedience to Almighty God, and the Blessed ever-Virgin Mary, and to Saint Augustine and Saint [Bernard], and to thee the Bishop on their behalf, and to the Abbess, and to thy successors, to live

* I trust I need make no comment on this odious representation and imagery!

without property, and in chastity, according to the Rule of St. Augustine, even unto my death."

After some further prayers and responses, the Bishop placed the ring on her right hand, and then proceeded to chant the mass of the holy Trinity; during which, after the novice had joined in the offertory, her *clothes commanded by the Rule,* (which had been prepared by the Convent,) were brought to the altar before the Bishop, who blessed them, saying a prayer. After which, she came before the Bishop, walking with bare feet, and, putting off her outer garments, stood in a single gown, ready to receive the consecrated habit, which was then put on, the Bishop saying: " Deus omnipotens det tibi veram penitenciam in tua conscientia, et perfectam contricionem in corde. In nomine Patris," &c. Then she put the conventual shoes on her feet; which act, as well as those of putting on the hood, fitting the mantle, fastening it by the wooden buckle, and covering her head with the fillet, were each accompanied by a benedictory prayer from the Bishop. Lastly, on the *imposition of the veil,* he added his final benediction.

We omit the prayers, as many of them seem as profane as disgusting; and we omit all the minute ceremonies of the solemn espousal to the visionary bridegroom, far more delicately touched by a poet, not always over delicate, in the sweet lines:

> For her the Spouse prepares the bridal ring,
> For her white virgins hymeneals sing.

Alas! how many mingled feelings of respect, interest, and abhorrence must press on the heart, from reading these accounts, strange indeed to those whose religion is the Bible. After the tedious and offensive ceremony relating to the bride and the ring, the ceremonial concludes, " And so, the Handmaid of God! having knelt down, and received the Bishop's blessing, is taken within, and THE GATE IS CLOSED!"

Let us pray that "*the gate may be closed*" for ever on such impurities and impieties relative to the "Handmaids of God!"

These details are here offered as curious illustrations of a system that has passed away, containing, amid many gross impurities and impieties, much which, till the assumption of HUMAN INFALLIBILITY, the sincerest piety might approve, and much till the establishment of the accursed Inquisition, CHARITY might forgive.

CHAPTER X.

Ela is constituted Abbess of Lacock—The ceremonies of the Election and Consecration of Abbesses.

It was on the 15th of August, 1240, the feast of the Assumption of the Virgin, that Ela, having first fullfilled the strict rules of her order, assumed the government of the monastery she had founded. The Book of Lacock states that she was then constituted the *first* Abbess; we must therefore presume that the constitution of the society was not fully completed until that year, nor, probably, were the conventual buildings; but that this important step was the crowning stone which perfected her pious work.

As we have not the means of describing the ceremonies which actually took place at the election and consecration of Ela into this religious authority, we may here extract the customary solemnities, from the Rule which has already furnished some curious particulars.

When it happened that the office of Abbess was void, the Prioress, with the counsel of eight of the oldest and most grave Sisters, and also of the Searches,* deputed a 'sad' Sister, expert in tem-

* The Searches, called in Latin *Scutatrices*, were the officers answering to the *Exploratores* or *Circatores* in the houses of

poral rule and government, to assist the Treasuresses in such things as were necessary to be done without. The Prioress and Searches continued their superintendence within. The keys of the common seals, and all other things usually kept by the Abbess, were entrusted to the Chantress* and another chosen Sister; unless in case of resignation, when the old Abbess kept them until the new one was confirmed.

On the day of Election, after the conclusion of divine service in the forenoon, the brethren immediately sung the mass of the Holy Ghost, instead of high mass, in solemn array as the occasion required. After which, the Chantress and another Sister began the hymn *Veni Creator*, which was sung to the end, by the respondent quires of the Sisters. Then the Prioress, in a low voice, said, with musical note, this versicle, *Emitte spiritum tuum*, (" Send down thy Spirit ") and these two collects, *Deus qui corda*

monks, whose duty it was to go round the whole monastery at all times of the day, except during Chapter and Collation, to discover any abuses or faults, and report them in the Chapter on the following morning. It was their especial business to see that none were absent from the Hours, or spoke when they ought not, or were *asleep during the lesson*, in which case, the Circator placed a *lantern* before the sleeping monk, who, on his awaking, was to take the lantern, and, having begged pardon kneeling, walk with it round the choir. See further in Fosbroke's British Monachism, p. 171.

* Answering to the Præcentor, or Chanter in our Cathedrals, who ought every day in the year to lead the Chant; who receives great emoluments, cannot sing holy music, and never shows his face in a stall!

and *Acciones nostras*, with *Per Jesus Christum dominum nostrum. Amen.*

After this, on the ringing of the Chapter Bell, they came to the crates of the election, in order to speak with the General Confessor, and two of his brethren confessors, who attended as witnesses only, and not to have any voice in the election. After the Pope's bull and other constitutions concerning elections had been read, some well-learned man in the law of Holy Church, attending without the crates with a notary, declared in English the three forms of election, that is to say, the way of the Holy Ghost, the way of Scrutiny, and the way of Compromise. The first was performed by the Prioress or other Sister, merely saying " What seem ye of Sister Ela? meseemeth that she is an able person to this office." And if all answered, " It pleaseth them," this way *was well sped*.

Such was probably the unanimous manner in which the first Abbess of Lacock and her successor Beatrice were elected. But the ordinary way was by Scrutiny; in which three Sisters were appointed to collect the voluntary votes of the rest: which were delivered to the General Confessor, at the crates as before; this, unless it was satisfactory, was to be repeated until the greater and more holy party of them had directed their voices upon a certain person. When the election was decided, one of the three Searches pronounced it in the following words:

" *In nomine Patris, et Filii, et Spiritus Sancti.* I, *N. N.* a Sister professed in the Monastery of Saint Mary the Virgin and Saint Bernard, of the order of Saint Austin, one of the Searches taken and made in the act of this present election, in all that I have power as in this act, and in the same power of the other two Searches, and in their name, and in the name of all our Sisters of this said monastery, have chosen in common, Sister —— of this monastery, expressly professed, being in sufficient and lawful age, born in matrimony, free, wise, and discreet, as our Abbess of this our said monastery."

When the election was thus finished, the Chantress solemnly began the Psalm *Te Deum laudamus*, which the Sisters performed with song, quire to quire, to its end.

The Abbess elect was then conducted by the elder Sisters to their quire, where she *lied prostrate* before the altar, until the end of the orison which then followed. The Sisters, kneeling in their stalls, said without musical note, *Kyrieleison, Christe eleison, Kyrieleison*, the *Pater Noster*, and *Ave Maria*. After which the Prioress said, in a soft voice, *with note,*— *Et ne nos, &c. Confirma hoc, Deus, quod operatus es in nobis. A templo tuo in Jerusalem tibi offerent reges munera. Domine, exaudi. Oremus.*

" Omnipotens sempiterne Deus, miserere huic famulæ tuæ, et dirige eam secundum clementiam tuam, in viam salutis eternæ, ut, te donante, tibi placita cupiat, et tota virtute perficiat. Per Christum dominum nostrum. Amen."

At the same time, the Confessor, with his brethren, repeated the same in their quire, all the bells ringing; and then the Confessor published the election to all the people there present.

After this, the ABBESS ELECT rose, and went with the convent to the crates of her election, where her consent was required. She was allowed no long time for consideration, but might ask respite till after meat. When it was given, the election was in goodly haste to be notified to the diocesan Bishop, or his Vicar-general, in open writing (letters patent), sealed with the common seal, his ratification of which was termed the CONFIRMATION of the Abbess.

The Bishop's attendance was then necessary, to solemnize the CONSECRATION of the new Abbess.* On the day appointed, all the "Hours" of the Sisters and Brethren were to be concluded before high mass: and when the bells were rung to that mass, the Bishop coming in his pontifical array to the grate of her election, there delivered his letters patent of confirmation; or, if that had been done already, went strait into the Monastery, being conducted by the General Confessor to the door and no further, and having with him three sad clerks, honest men, to assist him; of whom, one read the epistle, another the gospel, and the third, being in a

* A similar ceremony is enjoined in the " Pontifical," a splendid volume, in Salisbury Cathedral.

cope, attended upon the mitre. It was also necessary that one of them should be a notary.

After the door was opened, the Prioress and another Sister led the Bishop and his clerks into the Sisters' quire, the brethren then beginning, and proceeding solemnly with the *mass of the Annunciation of our Lady*. The Sisters were to be in their quire, not singing, but devoutly praying; (that is, it would appear, those that could be trusted!) " as many as may after the discretion of the Prioress and saddest Sisters, *nothing singing*, but devoutly *praying*, behaving there *honestly* as the religion asketh!" Two or three were to attend about the Abbess.

The Abbess knelt in her prayers at a form decorously arranged with tapestry and cushions; keeping such manner of observances in prostrations, kneelings, examinations, making of obedience, subscription or cross, with such other, as she was assigned by the Bishop and his clerks.

When the offertory was begun, she offered into the Bishop's hand; and after the mass she received the sacrament, on which account she was previously fasting.

The Bishop then installed her, saying *Accipe potestatem*, &c. And on his beginning *Te Deum laudamus*, the brethren proceeded with the same, all the bells ringing; during which, the Sisters proceeded, two and two together, to kneel and kiss the Abbess, she sitting in her stall.

When this and the prayers which followed were concluded, the Bishop and his clerks, conducted by the Prioress and another Sister, led the Abbess in their Chapter-house; where he caused her to sit on his right hand, the other Sisters standing in their order; and the Abbess, having the book of the Rules and Constitutions in her lap, all the Sisters made their obedience to her, if they had not done so before, laying their right hands on the book, the Prioress beginning, and each saying:

In nomine Patris, et Filii, et Spiritus Sancti.

I Sister [Beatrice of Kent] byhote* to the Abbess of this monastery, me for to keep obedience after the Rule of Saint Austin.

To whom the Abbess, then taking the Sister's hands joined together between her hands, answered thus: *And I admit thine obedience. In nomine Patris, et Filii, et Spiritus Sancti. Amen.*

When all had done the same, the Bishop and his clerks went out, as he came in, by the same door, the Sisters following him in procession to the door, and there taking his blessing.

With these rites the Countess of Salisbury was no doubt inducted into her high office of Abbess of Lacock, and the same ceremonies were repeated, on every vacancy, until the Nuns were finally expelled from their peaceful habitation.

* *Promise* or *pledge*, a word frequently used in Chaucer, where it is generally written *behighte*.

CHAPTER XI.

The Career of the Second William Longespé—His first Crusade, and Return—Claim to the Earldom of Salisbury—Interview with the Pope—His second Crusade, and quarrel with the Comte d'Artois.

THE affectionate Mother was now devoted, almost exclusively, to her stated religious services, night and day, throughout the year; but it cannot be supposed that, with the holy remembrance of her Husband, the thoughts of his children should not, at times, have been present to her, and have had a part in all her prayers. After the lapse of a few years, most of her offspring were widely separated from her; the sons on military service, the daughters conferred in marriage on distant lords. On all, and each, who can doubt she would frequently bestow some tender thoughts: and principally, amid her orisons, those thoughts would turn to her eldest born,—her favourite William,—the inheritor of the name, the name only—but with the name, the valour, and the piety, of his buried Father.

In early youth, the very next year after his father's death, this devoted Champion had enrolled himself among the SOLDIERS OF THE CROSS; and subsequently, when debarred of his hereditary dignity, with his sword his only fortune, he twice left his native country for the perilous adventures of the Holy Land,—the second time never to return! Every private prayer, breathed to Heaven at the altar by his affectionate Mother, would doubtless be for his safety in a distant land, a land of infidels, combating for that Cross of her Saviour before which she daily knelt.

But, in order to render our history of the family as complete as existing records will allow, we must resume our account of the second Longespé where we last left it, shortly after his marriage, when it appeared that in the year 1231 he had not fully attained his majority.

Yet in the next year we find him serving with the army in Wales, being present, says Matthew Paris, in the royal camp, at the time when it was grievously despoiled by a night attack of the enemy.

An old chronicle in the Bodleian Library * states expressly that in 1233 (17 Hen. III.) William Longespé was girt with the sword of Knighthood, but not made Earl of Salisbury.

As already mentioned, he had been first " signed with the Cross," in the year 1226, when Matthew Paris enumerates him with his most distinguished companions : The names are,—the Earl of Cornwall (his royal cousin), William Earl Marshal, John Earl of Chester and Lincoln, William Earl of Salisbury, G. de Lucy " his brother, ✝ " Richard Sward, and many other nobles.

* K. 84 Cart. f. 50 b. (quoted by Dugdale).

* How Geoffrey de Lucy was Longespé's " brother," though again his companion in 1247 (see p. 227) is at present unknown.

Their intentions appear to have been suspended until towards the close of the year 1239: when, on the morrow of St. Martin, an assembly of the principal Croises of England took place at Northampton, to consult respecting their journey. At this council, in order to prevent the Pope from diverting their arms against his own enemies in Italy and Germany, they bound themselves by an oath, solemnly taken in the Church of All Saints, to conduct their levies *direct to Palestine.*

It does not appear from Matthew Paris that William Longespé was present on this occasion. The oath was taken first by the Earl of Cornwall, then by Gilbert Earl Marshall, then by Richard Sward, by Henry de Trubleville, and many others. William Longespé is not here mentioned.

It seems probable that at this period, as certainly on his second voyage to Palestine, William Longespé headed another expedition, distinct from that of the Earl of Cornwall. Matthew Paris says, he left England " about the same time" as Earl Richard, but apparently it was not actually in his company.

The departure of the Royal Earl took place at Easter 1240. He previously visited the abbey of St. Alban's, in order to request the prayers of that convent, and then repaired to London, to take his solemn leave of the King; thence proceeding to Dover, and passing with many congratulations through France, he finally sailed from Marseilles, *in defiance* of the *prohibition* of Pope Gregory!

The very name of AN ENGLISH RICHARD carried terror into the hearts of the Saracens, from their remembrance of him of the LION'S HEART; but from the state of the East at that period, the Earl of Cornwall had few opportunities for signalizing his valour. On the contrary that favourable juncture appeared to have arrived at which some politic negociation alone would be sufficient to fulfil the most ardent hopes of the Christian world. A fierce dissension had arisen between the Sultan of Egypt and the Sultan of Damascus; which was balanced by the Duke of Burgundy and the Hospitallers forming a treaty with the former, and the Templars with the latter.

At this period, the Earl of Cornwall arrived in the East; and, availing himself of this posture of affairs, he became the contracting party, on behalf of the Christians, in obtaining the cession of Jerusalem and the greater part of the Holy Land. Such was the triumphal result of this expedition of the Earl of Cornwall, no less than the pacification of Palestine, and the apparent establishment of the supremacy of the Cross; although in less than two years it was succeeded by a most disastrous reverse, in consequence of the irruption of the Tartan tribes, and the murderous sacking of Jerusalem by the Carasmians.

In the mean time, the Earl of Cornwall had returned to Europe in the year 1241, and was welcomed by the congratulations of the western world.

In what degree his efforts had been assisted by the troops of Ela's son, the titular Earl of Salisbury, our information fails us in showing; but from the general aspect of history, as already noticed, we may conclude that the ardent William Longespé must have contented himself with having, in this voyage, made rather a pilgrimage than a crusade. As he seems to have departed distinctly from Earl Richard, so his return was several months after that of the Earl. He arrived in England in the beginning of March 1242.* The joy which his venerable Mother would then experience, can only have been surpassed by that which she had felt on his Father's delivery from the tempestuous ocean. Of the general rejoicings and solemnities which took place on this happy occasion, we may form some idea from those which welcomed the return of William Earl of Essex in 1194:—

" When Earl William had fulfilled the vow which he had vowed to the God of Jacob, and had worshipped in the place where *the Saviour's feet had stood*, (or, as it has been expressed by the Poet of a later age, but of all future time:

————— those holy fields
Over whose acres *walk'd those blessed feet*,
Which, fourteen hundred years ago, were nail'd
For our advantage, to the bitter Cross!)

returning with his followers, and visiting the sacred places that presented themselves on his journey, he

* Matthew Paris.

honoured them with his prayers and his offerings, and so, crossing the sea, arrived in England. Being received at home with welcome and congratulations, he transmitted to all the churches in his fee, silken cloths, to be made into chasubles, or to adorn the altars; and to us (the Abbey of Walden) he sent one of admirable work, better than the rest.

"When the Earl first honoured us with his presence after his return from his pilgrimage, we met him in procession, clothed in albs and copes, all singing, and saying with the heart as well as the mouth, *Benedictus qui venit in nomine Domini!* Thus, with universal joy, he proceeded to the greater altar, and there prostrating himself, received from the Prior benediction. After which, rising, and kneeling, he offered in an ivory box * some exceedingly precious *reliques* which he had obtained in the land of Jerusalem, and had received in gift from the Emperor of Constantinople and the Count of Flanders. On his rising, and standing before the altar, the Prior commenced in a high voice, followed by the rest, the hymn *Te Deum laudamus*. Departing thence, the Earl presently went into the Chapterhouse, that he might be there saluted by all, and receive and give to each *the kiss of peace*. Thus, when a conversation had passed of the most agreeable pleasantry and familiarity, he was conducted to the *hospitium*, where the abundance of a splendid refection was served to him and his attendants."†

* Pixis. † Monasticum Anglicanum, vol. i. p. 452.

Such we may presume to have been the reception of William Longespé, on his return from the Holy Land, at the cathedral of Salisbury, or even, with becoming changes of ceremonial, at the Nunnery of Lacock.

At a later period of the same year (1242) he was present at the battle of Xantoigne in Guienne; after which, he and the Earl of Leicester (the great Simon de Montfort) remained at Bordeaux with the King and Queen, contrary to the advice of the majority of the English Barons, and to their own great loss, in the incurring of debt.

During all this period, he continued to bear the title of Earl of Salisbury;* though his claim to the dignity was in dispute, and he had therefore never obtained possession of the revenues of the Earldom. On this account, in 1243, the King granted him an annuity of sixty marks out of the Exchequer, until he should obtain judgment upon the claim he made to the Earldom of Wiltshire, and Castle of Sarum, which judgment the King promised should be given upon his return to England.†

In the year 1247, the Bishop of Worcester (Walter de Cantilupe), and William Longespé and Geoffrey de Lucy, " in the bishoprick of Worcester," and many other nobles of the kingdom of England, in-

* Matthew Paris gives him the title of Earl in the six places already quoted, edit. 1640, pp. 389, 431, 536, 582, 590, 596.

† Dugdale's Baronage, i. 178, from " Cart. & Pat. 27 H. III. m. 3."

stigated by the example of the King of the French (the ninth Louis, afterwards sainted,) and the nobles of that kingdom, were *signed* about the season of Rogation.* But William Longespé, adds Matthew Paris, " shrewdly imagining that, like Earl Richard (of Cornwall), he might, ' reaping where he had not sown,' collect some emolument from the crusaders, went to the court of Rome, and soliciting our Lord the Pope † to further his views, said ' *My 'Lord, you see that I am signed with the cross*, and ' am prepared to proceed on the expedition with my ' Lord the King of the French, to fight for God in ' this pilgrimage. I bear a great and well-known ' name, that is, WILLIAM DE LONGESPÉ, but my for- ' tune is small ; for my Lord the King of England, ' my kinsman and natural Lord, hath taken away ' from me the title of Earl, with its estate; yet, as he ' did this judicially, and not in his anger or from an ' arbitrary impulse, I do not blame him. Thus I am ' obliged to fly to the paternal bosom of your com- ' passion ; to seek assistance from you in this neces- ' sity. For we see that the noble Earl Richard, ' although he is not signed with the cross, yet is ' gathering much money in the kingdom of England, ' from those who are signed, through the influence of ' your too bountiful favour in that behalf; and I ' therefore, who am *signed with the cross*, and in ' want, taking hope from his example, request the

---

* On the assumption of the Cross, see a note in page 235, at the close of this Chapter. † Gregory the Ninth.

'same favour for myself.' So the Pope, considering at once the *eloquence of his address*, the *force of his reasoning*, and the *gracefulness of his person*, was favourably inclined towards him; and granted him in part what he asked, that is, *a broad thong out of another's hide*.*"

By means of the Pope's Letters, as Matthew Paris afterwards mentions, the Earl of Cornwall collected an infinite sum from those desirous to *redeem their vows*; † of which the chronicler names as an instance no less than 600*l*. from one archdeaconry; and William Longespé obtained in all more than *a thousand marks*.

Longespé took his second departure for the HOLY LAND in the month of July 1249, accompanied by Robert de Vere,‡ as his Standard-bearer, and a band of two hundred Knights. "He departed," says Matthew Paris, "with the license and *blessing* of his NOBLE MOTHER the holy ABBESS OF LACOCK, being acknowledged the General of all the Crusaders of England, and joined in safety the army of the French; § when the Most Christian King received

---

* A certain share of the Earl of Lancaster's privilege.

† See page 236.

‡ Their licenses from the King were dated June 27; Longespé's to last until his return, but Vere's only for three years (Rymer's Fœdera). This document directly disproves the statement adopted by Camden and other authors, that William Longespé was *deprived of the Earldom of Salisbury* because he left the realm *without the King's permission*.

§ At Easter 1249 the fleet of Louis was shattered by a vio-

him and his followers with respect, and reckoned them among his particular friends, giving them thanks for having come to his assistance: and he beseeched all his own knights most earnestly that the customary pride and envy of the French should not excite that discord between them and the English, which had been experienced in the time of King Richard. However," adds our monkish historian, " at the instigation of the Devil, who is wont to envy the successes of men, when the French perceived *the English to excel*, and to acquire both profit and honour, they began to envy and slander them, uttering their usual sneers with jests and blasphemous oaths. As in the verse :

> Omnisque potestas impatiens consortis erit.

it might also be said,

> Omnisque superbus impatiens consortis erit."

When our patriotic chronicler reverts to the subject, he expresses himself in nearly similar terms, again quoting the Latin proverb, and giving the following as the speech of the "*most pious*" King of the French. "What madness," said he, " is this which agitates you? Why will ye persecute him, who hath come hither from remote parts to mine and your protection; who serves as the faithful

---

lent storm on the west of Syria; but the loss sustained by the tempest was amply repaired (in October) by the arrival of William of Salisbury with two hundred English knights, and other warriors from Constantinople. The sails were therefore again set, and the fleet sailed for Damietta. De Joinville.

soldier of God as you do?" Matthew then proceeds to describe the following incident as having been "the seed-bed of the Frenchmen's envy and hatred."

"A very strong tower, not far distant from Alexandria, full of ladies, the wives of certain noble Saracens, had been taken by William Longespé, not by force, but by a fortuitous and fortunate accident, the French being wholly unaware of it; whence the fame and dread of him pervaded even the remote parts of the East. And because both there and elsewhere, by the fortune of war, he had acquired much treasure, and had increased both his followers and his own honour, (which the French, though numerous and powerful, had not been able to accomplish,) so from envy they slandered and detested him, nor could they say anything in peace concerning him.

"But it happened again, that the same William, having employed some careful spies, learned by private information, that some of the wealthy Eastern merchants were going under a convoy imprudently small to a certain fair near Alexandria, where they confidently reckoned to multiply their riches. He therefore secretly, by night, hastened towards them, taking all his own soldiers with him, and rushed with a sudden attack like lightning upon the unwary merchants, who were at once slain, and their guides entirely put to flight, some also being captured; and he took possession for himself of all that convoy, commonly called a Karavan; consisting of camels, mules, and asses, laden with whole silks, pigments, spices, gold, and silver; and they also found with them some waggons with their bullocks and oxen, and some provisions both for cattle and men, of which there was then a great deficiency. And although William had slain and captured many of the enemy in the conflict, he lost himself only one knight and eight servants; he brought back, indeed, some wounded, but they were restored by medical care. So he returned to the army, *a triumphant and enriched conqueror.*

"But when this was perceived by the French, who had stayed behind in indolence, as well as deprivation, they, roused at once by the incitement of envy and avarice, met him with hostility, and, after the manner of base robbers,* took violently from him all he had obtained; laying against him as a sufficient condemnation, that by a rash audacity, contrary to the Royal ordinance and the laws of Princes respecting war, he had too proudly and foolishly disunited himself, in defiance of military discipline, from the body of the army. When William heard this, he promised himself that he should give entire satisfaction, by offering that all the victuals obtained should be distributed to the whole army as found requisite. But the French outrageously rejoined, claiming all for themselves, and despoiling him of

* For our hero's own robbery and murder, of the innocent merchants, our Monk had not a word of censure!

the whole, not without reproaches. William, therefore, being *dejected to a bitterness of spirit*, having suffered so great an injustice, laid a very heavy complaint before the King, adding that the Comte d'Artois, the King's brother, had been the leader of this aggression and violent spoliation. But the King, *as he was most pious both in mind and demeanour*, answered with a mild voice, ' WILLIAM, ' WILLIAM! the Lord, to whom nothing is concealed, ' knows that I greatly fear, lest, for the injustice and ' wrong done to you, our pride with our other sins ' should ruin us. Thou knowest how difficult it ' would be for me, in these dangers to which I am ' now placed, to interfere with my Nobles, however ' they offend.' And whilst he was saying this, the Comte d'Artois came up, excited and inflamed like a madman, and in great wrath, exalting his voice immoderately, and without saluting the King or those seated round, he exclaimed, ' What does this mean, ' my lord King? Do you presume to defend this ' *Englishman*, and to repel *your own Frenchmen?* ' This fellow, in dispute of you and the whole army, ' following his own suggestion only, has wilfully, ' against all our ordinances, taken nocturnal and ' clandestine spoils; whilst *the fame of him alone* ' *now flies over the Eastern climes*, and not that of ' the King and his Frenchmen. He hath obscured ' all our names and titles!' Which when the Most Christian King heard, turning his face and bending his look towards William, he said in a mild voice:

' Now you may hear, my friend. So quickly may
' a division arise, from which may God preserve the
' army! It is requisite in a season of such diffi-
' culty to bear with equanimity such matters, and
' even worse than these.' To whom William replied: ' So! then art thou no King, if thou canst
' not do justice upon thine own, and punish of-
' fenders; whilst I promise that I, if I should offend,
' will give satisfaction in every thing.' And being
inwardly hurt in his mind, he further added: ' *Such
' a King* I serve no longer, to *such* a lord I will not
' adhere;' and in wrath he departed from Louis,
leaving him much vexed at the occurrence. Then,
going to Acon, and continuing there for many days
with his soldiers, he published *with tears* to all there
resident, the injury he had suffered; whereby he
made them all, particularly the Prelates, to sympa-
thise with him, and to be offended with the French;
wherefore those who were skilled and experienced
in affairs of war, foretold that this was doubtless a
sad presage of what would follow, and that the displeasure of the Most High would be grievously excited by such sins. The Comte d'Artois is further
related to have said, with a loud laugh, ' Now the
army of *the magnificent French* is well cleared of *the
tail-wearers!*'* Which gave offence to the ears of

---

* There was a common story, current among the enemies of Englishmen, that their ancestors, in consequence of having treated disrespectfully St. Augustine the missionary, incurred the punishment of *wearing tails,* and that the curse was here-

many. From that time William determined to stay at Acon with the townsmen, the Templars, and the Hospitallers, and awaiting the arrival of the magnates of England that had assumed the cross, to expose to them the pride and injuries of the French; and to exhort them urgently that by themselves, and without the French, they should, by the advice of discreet and humble men, attempt to expel the enemies of Christ."

ASSUMPTION OF THE CROSS.

The devotee who had assumed the Cross, or become what the Latin chroniclers term *Crucesignatus,* was distinguished to the view of all men by a *cross* affixed to a conspicuous part of *his dress.* The custom originated with the Council of Clermont, held by Pope Urban the Second, in 1095. The crosses were received, with certain ceremonies, from the hands of Bishops or Abbats. Those worn by great men were made of silk, and worked with gold; those of the commonalty of cloth. The colour was originally crimson; but different colours were

---

ditary. The murderers of Thomas à Becket, and their abettors, were also cursed with *tails;* a punishment which was appropriately bestowed on one of them at least, Sir Robert de Broc; who, as an insult to the Archbishop, had cut off the *tail of one of his horses,* for which he was excommunicated by the Prelate, on Christmas Day, 1171, not a week before the murder. This ancient jest against the English was not forgotten in the latter part of the fifteenth century, when a French poet, Jehan Molines, wrote thus:

> Ce Cat nonne vient de Calais,
> Su mere fut Cathau la Bleue,
> C'est du lignage des Anglais,
> Car il porte *tres-longue queue!*

afterwards taken, in order to distinguish the country of the wearer. In the expedition of 1188, Philip King of France and his followers adopted a *red* cross; Henry King of England and his men *white* crosses; and Philip Count of Flanders *green*. They were usually placed on the right shoulder; but sometimes on the back, and sometimes on the breast.

The *Crucesignati* were invested with a variety of privileges and immunities. They were freed from the payment of their debts, until after their return; and exempt from interest on borrowed money; and also from some taxes (although at the same time subjected to other exactions, which were nominally for the benefit of the cause in which they embarked, but too often diverted to the personal emolument of the Pope, or of those who obtained the credit of being his commissioners.) They were also permitted to pledge their estates, without consulting their chief lords; and to have their causes tried in the ecclesiastical courts. All which, as may be supposed, led to a variety of abuses and inconveniences.

On the Crusader's departure from home, as on going a pilgrimage in later ages, he was accompanied out of his parish with a procession, and the *parish cross*, and holy water.

Multitudes assumed the Cross, who never left their native country: but their *vow* was then *redeemed* by a sum of money. There is in the Fœdera, a proclamation in the form of letters patent, of King Henry III. promising "*in good faith*" to his subjects, that no one who had been signed, or who should be signed, with the Cross in his dominions, should be compelled, on that account, to pay a greater sum of money for the *redemption of his vow*, than he had promised at the time of his assuming the cross. This is dated at Windsor, Jan. 18, 1251.*

* Pat. 35 Hen. III. m. 13. Rymer's Fœdera, i. 276. The preceding particulars have been gleaned from the Glossary of Ducange.

CHAPTER XII.

The Assault of Mansoura, and Death of William Longespé—Vision of the Abbess Ela, in her stall at Lacock.

During the absence of William Longespé from the army of the Crusaders, its Royal General received a message from the Governor of Cairo, which promised materially to facilitate the operations of the campaign. This Emir had taken offence at the Soldan's treatment of his brother, the Governor who had lost Damietta on the first landing of King Louis; and he consequently professed himself willing to deliver up Cairo to the Christians, being, as he alleged, himself in heart a convert to the faith of Jesus. At this crisis, when it was evidently desirable to concentrate all his strength, King Louis, we are told by Matthew Paris, " more than ever regretted the absence of William Longespé and his soldiers, whereby the army was so materially mutilated and scandalized; and therefore sent in haste to him, adding at the close of his message, ' *and you shall hear merry news, which shall be followed by an event long desired and a joy long looked-for, of which we wish and intreat you to become partaker.*' The rumour of this was also circulated among the inhabitants of that country, being published among the townsmen of Acon. William, therefore, at this message of so great a Prince, and chiefly on account of *its final addition*, returned with all his company to King Louis: and when he had learned from the relation of the exulting Monarch, the offer of the Emir before mentioned, he was induced, by the joy he conceived at it, to forgive all the injuries and rancour of those who had offended him."*

Under these circumstances, King Louis adopted the bold resolution of marching at once towards the capital of Egypt; and with that intention the whole army advanced in a body, towards the close of November 1249. Until their approach to the vicinity of Mansoura, they overcame both the open and insidious enmity of the Saracens; but they then found the Egyptian army encamped on the opposite side of the Achmoun canal,† resolved to contest the passage. Under the cover of two *chaschateils* the Crusaders commenced a causeway over the stream; but the Saracens ruined in a day the work of a month; and a second time, after the "cats" had been rebuilt with timber obtained with difficulty from the ships, they were immediately burnt by the destructive *Greek fire* of the enemy.

At length, at Shrove-tide (Feb. 8, 1250,) a Bedouin offered to show them a ford, and the Comte d'Artois, with his characteristic impetuosity, imme-

* Matthew Paris.
† Called by Paris and others the river Tafnis or Taniz.

diately resolved to effect the passage. At the head of fourteen hundred Knights, including the Templars and Hospitallers, with WILLIAM LONGESPÉ and his followers, he threw himself into the water; and, after a slight resistance, they succeeded in mounting the opposite bank, and the infidels were put to flight.

Thus far the Christian army was successful: and, having surmounted an important obstacle, might, under prudent guidance, have continued its march in triumph; but it was their next unhappy movement which led to the most fatal consequences, no less than the death of William Longespé and the impetuous Artois, the capture of King Louis, and the final discomfiture of this crusade.

If the Comte d'Artois had listened to the counsels of the leaders of the Military Brothers and the Redcross Knights, he would not have advanced from the river until the main body of the army had come up. By sad experience, they knew that cowardice and bravery were perpetually vacillating in the breasts of the Turks, and that their panic was generally succeeded by fury. But the fiery Comte could not regard with calmness the sight of Mansoura, deserted by many of its inhabitants; and, burning for personal distinction, he regarded their prudent counsels as the mask of pusillanimity. Matthew Paris gives at great length the sentiments expressed at the council of war; in which, after the overbearing Artois had insulted the Master of the Templars,

WILLIAM LONGESPÉ is introduced as attempting to moderate the contest, and thereupon receiving a repetition of the Comte's injurious aspersions on the English Nation.

To the Templar's advice the arrogant Comte had replied: ' Oh the old treason of the Temple! Oh 'the ancient falsity of the Hospitallers! Oh the de-'ceit so long concealed, which now so manifestly 'breaks out into view! This is that which we have 'so long conjectured, and which has been so truly 'foretold, that the whole of this Eastern land had 'now long since been conquered, had not those who 'proclaim themselves to be the Religious of the 'Temple, and the Hospital, and the rest, *impeded us* '*laymen by their deceits!* They dread that, if the 'land be subdued by the Christian forces, their own 'dominion, which is fed by such ample revenues, 'should come to a conclusion! Therefore it is that 'they destroy with various potions, and, plotting 'with the Saracens, destroy with diverse treasons, 'the faithful who come hither, girt for the business 'of the Cross! Is not Frederick,* who has expe-'rienced their snares, the best example of this?'

---

* The Emperor Frederick II. who is most conspicuous in history as the triumphant opponent of the Papal power, and against whom Gregory IX. had previously diverted the arms of the crusaders; as alluded to in the oath of the English crusaders at Northampton, noticed in a preceding page. He went to Palestine in defiance of the Pope's interdict; and, notwithstanding the triumph of his arms, was pursued by the papal

"To these satyrical and biting words, the Master of the Temple, William de Sonnac, and the Master of the Hospital, William de Castello Novo, *vexed even to a bitterness of spirit*, together replied, 'Do you 'think, noble Comte, that we have assumed the habit 'of religion only to overturn the Church of Christ, 'and, resigning ourselves to treason, to lose our own 'salvation? far, far be this from us, nay from every 'Christian!' And the Master of the Temple, being greatly irritated, then cried with a loud voice, addressing his Banner-bearer, 'UNFOLD AND RAISE OUR 'BANNER! and let us proceed to battle, that we may 'try to-day the doubtful fate of *Victory or Death!* 'We should be invincible, could we remain united. 'But if unhappily we are divided, like sand without 'lime, and deficient of the cement of charity, we shall 'become like a ruinous edifice of falling stones.'

"On hearing this, WILLIAM LONGESPÉ attempted to interpose, urging the claims to attention which the holy, and authorised, Grand Master possessed, who had long resided in the country, and knew by manifold experience the power and the craft of the Saracens. But opposition still further inflamed the passion of the Comte d'Artois; who, *taking the word out of Longespé's mouth, thundering and in-*

anathemas, and in consequence experienced the desertion of the Religious Knights, and the determined opposition of every minister of the Church Having been recalled to Europe to defend his Italian dominions, he had experienced the disastrous reverse, which closed all his triumphs, at the battle of Parma, only two years before the period of which we are now treating.

decently swearing after the French fashion,* in the hearing of many, continued his insolent exclamations, repeating those reflections on the English to which he had given utterance on a former occasion: ' Oh the cowardice,' he cried, ' of the timid *tail-* ' *wearers!* How happy would this army be if it was ' purged of *tails* and *tail-wearers!*' On hearing which, William, being shocked and provoked by his reproaches, replied: 'Oh! Count Robert, be as-' sured I will proceed undismayed to whatever perils ' of death may offer themselves. We shall be, I ' fancy, to-day, where you will not dare to touch *the* ' *tail of my horse!*' "

So Comte Robert carried all his own way; and, putting on their helmets, and expanding their banners, they proceeded towards the enemy.

Our historian Matthew proceeds to detail the fatal consequences of this fiery resolve; but we may now leave him for a contemporary author of another kind, and still greater curiosity. The fame and fate of Longespé were made known by a travelling minstrel, and his Poem *is still extant*; † af-

---

* —— " rapiens verbum ab ore ejus, more Gallico reboans et indecenter jurans."

† It is preserved in the Cottonian collection of MSS. Julius, A. v. fol. 76, b. and printed, with a translation, in the Excerpta Historica, 1831. Though the author is unknown, it is clear from the internal evidence of the Poem, that he was an Englishman, and from its existing in the same manuscript as Peter of Langtoft's chronicle, (though not on any surer authority) it has with some probability been ascribed to that author.

fording a circumstantial, though probably poetical, description of all the incidents of the battle.

The Poet opens his quaint but vivid rhymes with an address to his auditors, of which the following is a nearly literal translation : *

> List with grief and with pity who wish to be told
> Of the good WILLIAM LONGESPE the champion so bold,
> Who at Shrovetide, in Egypt, his life-blood hath spent,
> As among the great host of King Louis he went,
> At a Castle of Egypt, MANSOURA by name,
> Which shall never in Paynim relinquish its fame,
> For 'twas there that King Louis a captive was ta'en,
> With the other brave Knights who were then in his train.
> And 'twas there the Comte d'Artois, Sir Robert the fierce,
> Whose pride was the cause of so sad a reverse,
> With esquires and true knights many more, met their fate,
> So complete the disaster, the slaughter so great;
> There a host of brave men have, alas! found their grave,
> And there fell the good Knight, WILLIAM LONGESPE the brave!

---

* The following lines will furnish a specimen of the orthography of the original, as the above of its expressions.

> Ky vodra de doel & de pité oier tres graunt.
> De bon Williā Longespée ly hardy combatant
> Ke fust oscis en Babilone à la quareme pernant,
> Ke od le Roi Louys alat o son host mut graunt,
> A un chastel de Babilone Musoire est noméc,
> Ke touz jours en Peinime sera renomée
> Por ly Rois qe fust pris en cele chevachée
> Et les altres chivalers ki furent de sa meignée.
> Et ly Cunte de Artoise, sire Roberd li fers,
> (Ceo fu par son orguile : tant fu surquiders !)
> E meinz altres esquiers & pruz chivalers
> I perderunt la vie : tant urunt desturbers!
> Et meint hōme vailant i avoit dunqe oscis
> Et ly bon Willam Longespée, li chivaler hardiz.

The narrative of the Poem is commenced with a description of the successful attack of the Christians upon the Saracens, after crossing the river, their short repose, and the council of war which ensued. The sentiments of the chiefs are expressed very much to the same purpose as by Matthew Paris. The Comte d'Artois * insults the Master of the Temple by telling him, 'Ha! Dan Templar, 'you will always *wear the wolf's skin* with us.' The Templar remonstrates " courteously "; and the Count Longespé (as he is styled by the Poet) recommends attention to his experienced advice; when the Count d'Artois insolently exclaims : '*Ye 'may well be English who are such councillors.* 'We will not be arrested either by your assertions 'or your denials. We will rush forward to seek the 'Saracens, *over land and over sea!*† Then the Count Longespé, who, says the Poet, was *always quick*,‡ changed his purpose as soon as he heard that provoking speech: 'Now proceed when you

* The line of d'Artois' first speech

    Nous ne creum Sarazin de mère soit nez.

does not seem to have been properly understood by the translator in the Excerpta Historica, who has rendered it, " We do not *believe* the Saracens *to be* of mother born ! " The meaning appears to be : " We do not fear (*cre*[in]*num*) Saracen born of mother," an expression equivalent to the more modern phrase, " born of woman."

† This was probably a customary expression among the Crusaders.

‡ " Touz jours legers."

' please,' he said, ' for I will be before you. Be as
' eager as you will, I shall still be the foremost!'

So they at once assumed their lances and their swords; laced on their helmets and iron hats; the Master of the Temple commanded the horses to be harnessed, and the Count Longespé the banners to be spread; " for they were now the foremost, so valiant were they;" they entered into Mansoura, " as if it had been their own quarters."

When they had thus unadvisedly rushed into the fortress, the wily Saracens closed the gates, and the Christians suddenly found themselves entrapped as in a snare. Before them, at the further end of the fort, was the river, " deep, long, and wide ;" behind them was the well-barred portcullis; and on both hands were high stone walls. The Saracens surrounded them on all sides, " armed with Turkish bows and poisoned arrows, with long swords of well-tempered steel, and with large stones, of which they had prepared a great abundance. Then," continues the Poet, " the Saracens made a fierce attack upon us, joining in parties of five together to cast immense stones, and to crush us with heavy hammers. If God had not cared for us, not one could have escaped.

"The Count d'Artois, on his great charger, pierced with his lance the first of the enemy's ranks; but he had not heart nor courage to remain longer, so fiercely was he assailed with iron and steel. The road led strait from the gate to the river; so, immediately after overthrowing the first that he encountered, he turned towards the river, to attempt to escape by swimming. But what more the Count did cannot be told you. *His soul is in hell in great torment!"*

The pious Poet then proceeds to relate the atchievements of the Master of the Temple, who at one time would have been run through the body by the lance of an emir named Beder, had not LONGESPÉ ridden up at the moment, overthrown the emir and his great horse, and *cut off his head!* However, the Master was shortly after mortally wounded by an envenomed arrow, and " his soul was richly presented to God!" quoth the holy bard.*

The rest of the Poem relates so immediately to LONGESPÉ, and his own knights and personal followers, and is so interesting, that it must be appended without abridgement:

* The principal discrepancy between the Poet and de Joinville, the French historian of this Crusade, who was with the army, is that the latter states that the Master of the Temple lost only an eye at Mansoura; but that, on losing the other in the battle which took place on the advance of the main body under King Louis, he then expired. It will be remarked that our Poet frequently speaks as if he had himself been present on this fatal occasion: thus he gives his opinion of the number of the Saracens which met the Crusaders on landing from the river, as 3500: and in his description of the conflict he uses the first person plural.

" In that division Sir Robert de Vere was slain, a very trusty, stout, and valiant Knight. His swift horse was slain under him; and the good Knight, left on foot, stood against a wall, and fought right bravely. Seventeen Saracens surrounded him, swearing his death; and with his good and slashing sword he slew them. That day well showed them how true and valiant he was. He fought on foot until he could fight no longer. There perished his body; *his soul went rejoicing to God!*

" But we must now leave all these, and speak of the stout Knight, the best warrior, than whom a more valiant cavalier hath not fought in arms since the time of Roland.* This was the Earl Longespe, who fought most bravely, and sold his life right dearly. He, with five others, contended with rank after rank, until the evening, when he gave himself up a martyr. The first was a Templar named Sir Wymound, who was with Earl Richard† when he invested Ascalon, and therefore took that name when he was received as a Brother, and for his valour was called Sir Wymound de Ascalon. With him was the right valiant Sir Robert de Widele; and Sir Ralph de Henefeld, who by the grace of God, slew many a Saracen with his murdering sword; and Sir Alexander Giffard, the trusty knight, who was ever distinguished for his activity in arms, as was apparent one day when he turned it to advantage, by retreating from the Saracens in order to embarrass them. Sir John de Bretain, his

---

* Roland, or Orlando, the hero of a French romance.

† Richard Earl of Cornwall; his investiture of Ascalon must have taken place in 1240, and the note in the Excerpta Historica, p. 76, referring to its subsequent siege and capture by the Turks, as the origin of the Templar's name, is therefore not perfectly correct. The Poet afterwards calls him Sir *Richard* de Ascalon.

adopted Knight, who was of Bourbon and not of Normandy,* when he should have aided his lord and benefactor, cast himself into the river and was drowned.

" They advanced and fought most obstinately; and, before they fell, killed more than a hundred, such slaughter did they make of the Saracens. Each with bold heart rushed up to an amiral, and struck him dead; no defence could avail. A great cry was raised on the death of the amirals; the Saracen soldiers, the cursed race, menaced fiercely, and swore by Mahomet they would take no rest until they had amply revenged them. The Saracens were both behind and before; they made impetuous attacks on the valiant band, and struck them behind no children's blows, with their right trenchant swords of steel, for their lances were shivered in pieces. The good Knights kept firmly together, each close to the rest as well as he could: and they killed and wounded without mercy as far as they could reach. As greyhounds pursue beasts flying into the woods, so are the Christians wont to pursue the Saracens. Around these five Knights now gathered a great host of the infidels,† well provided with horses and arms; and the Knights, when they saw them, were much dismayed.‡

---

* This distinction appears to be made to show he was a Frenchman. It has been remarked, however, that the French historian Joinville is not less chargeable with national prejudice than our poet; for he does not once mention Longespé or the English.

† See the Arabic account in p. 259.

‡ Qant veint les chivalers mult sunt esmaez,

translated in the Excerpta Historica, " who, when they saw the knights, were much amazed." The word *veint* occurs three lines below, " qe nouz veint ent^r.—which *comes* against us ; " but there is here an alteration in the text,—" qant vei[e]nt,"

"Sir Alexander Giffard then said to his lord, 'Sir, for 'the love of God, what is your counsel regarding this 'host of Saracens, which now comes against us? Shall 'we remain here, or fly for fear of them?' The Earl then answered, with a stedfast heart, 'Here ought each of us 'to show his prowess. Let us rush on to encounter them 'as dogs! For the love of Christ Jesus we will die 'here; for the love of Christ Jesus came we into this 'land, to atchieve by prowess our inheritance—the bliss 'of Heaven! for no other object came we hither, to main- 'taining an army and waging war. But, Sir Alexander Gif- 'fard, if you can escape, you who have the charge of my 'property, and are my knight, distribute my goods among 'my people in this manner. First, that my soul may 'forthwith be received into bliss, give to the poor reli- 'gious to sing for me; and to the poor English who have 'fought in the army; and to the poor sick, who are in 'greatest need; and to the lepers and the orphans; that 'they may all pray for my soul! Give for my soul my 'gold and my silver; my stores and my arms give to 'my good followers; and bestow all my other goods so 'wisely, that with me you may attain to bliss with God 'Omnipotent!'

"A Knight of Normandy, who was in the retinue of the good Earl William de Longespé, and in whom Monsieur William had much confidence, cried out aloud, saying, 'Sir, for pity's sake, let us fly across this wide

---

apparently, in modern French, *quand voient*. In either case, the knights were the party struck with dismay or surprise.

* Matthew Paris attributes this cowardly speech to the Comte d'Artois himself; who, he says, when he perceived the danger in which they were placed, "shamefully and unwisely" exclaimed, "Oh, William, God fights against us! We can no

stream; so many Saracens are coming, we cannot hold out longer.' 'I will not fly,' said the Earl William Longespé; 'never shall an English knight be reproached with 'my having fled for fear of the vile Saracens. I came 'here to serve God, if it so please Him; for Him will I 'suffer death who was crucified for me! But first I 'will sell myself dearly.' Then said the Knight, 'If you 'will not go, I will go instantly; I will stay no longer.' 'Go then!' said the Earl, 'you, who have resolved to dishonour yourself, have no reason for staying here!' He fled on his good horse, which was well armed; he cast himself into the river; the stream carried him away, and, being at its mercy, he and his horse were drowned. *His soul was presently committed to the Devil!* And many another Frenchman was drowned that day, they had such fear of losing their lives; if they had fought for the love of God, their souls would have been in bliss with their Creator!

"The Earl then demanded of Brother Richard, if he wished to go; and of Sir Ralph of Flanders, who loved him very dearly; and of Sir Robert de Wideley, the stout bachelor, and of Sir Richard de Guise, who bore his banner: 'Will you now go, and leave me to remain? 'before I go, I will suffer the loss of my head!' They

---

longer resist. Fly and save yourself whilst your horse is able to bear you, and do not wait till it is too late." To which he replied, "IT PLEASETH NOT GOD, THAT THE SON OF MY FATHER SHOULD FLY BEFORE ANY SARACEN! My choice is death with glory, rather than life with shame!" There is on the whole, a remarkable correspondence between the two accounts, at the same time that they are evidently not derived the one from the other; a circumstance which is highly favourable to their general correctness.

all replied with the greatest indignation, that they would not do so for any man living. 'So God be our helper, and the valiant St. George! I commend me to God,' said each for himself. Then answered the good Earl Longespé, ' Let us keep firm together; so shall we have every advantage: so long as we can hold out, we shall sustain no loss; and, should we be slain, we shall all obtain salvation!'

"The Saracens surrounded the valiant knights, well armed, and well mounted, with trenchant swords, on foot and on horseback, before and behind; no living man could tell their number. Sir Richard de Guise, who bore the banner, as he turned round in the press, had *his left hand, which held the banner*, cut off; yet 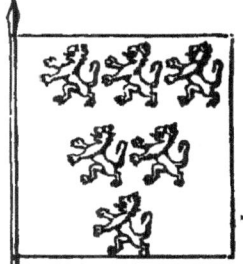 with the maimed limb he recovered the banner and retained it, like a stout and valiant and vigorous bachelor! And the bold combatant Sir Ralph de Henfield, for the sake of Christ Jesus, sold his blood very dear; as did Sir Robert de Wadeley,* the approved knight, who always went in the host to aid his lord. And Brother Richard de Ascalon, the noble warrior, right well deserved that day to attain the joy of Heaven. Their horses were slain: so they stood fast on foot, and stoutly fought for the love of God!

"Sir Alexander Giffard is well escaped, with the gold and silver which was entrusted to him. He got the horses together, and loaded them; and took the road

---

* Here and once afterwards written " Wadele," elsewhere " Widele."

towards Damietta. He leaped into the long and wide river; he wished to reach Diote, as he had promised his liege lord the good Longespé, to distribute his property according to his commands. As soon as they had entered into the river, the vile Saracens narrowly watched them, and cast on them the *Greek fire;* but they would rather have been burnt to ashes than have moved back a foot.

"The Earl was beset by the Saracens very closely: they could not kill his horse, so well was he armed, nor could they drag the valiant hero to the ground; but they *cut off his left foot from the stirrup.* Very grievous was it to see his body so mangled. When the Earl felt that he had lost his foot, he descended from his good horse, and called to Brother Richard de Ascalon, ' WHERE ART THOU, BROTHER? Assist us now, FOR WE ARE LOST!' The Brother was right valiant, and retreated not. He comforted the Earl in this pious manner, ' Be not dismayed, Sir; God will hear thy prayer, and his sweet mother who is so dear to Him!' Brother Richard de Ascalon had lost his horse; himself, though much wounded, God had preserved in the world.* But Sir Robert de Wadele, having fought until he could endure no longer, departed to God, together with his valiant companion Sir Ralph de Henfeld; who during all his life had kept the bravest company. They had inflicted great injuries on the Saracens, and cut them to pieces, and sold their lives very dearly.

---

* This is probably the sense of the line :

Meint pleie en le mond dieu avoit il rescu.

translated in the Exc. Hist. " himself God rescued from many a wound in the world."

"The Longespé supported himself on the shoulders of the Brother, his slashing sword in his hand, and with only one foot. He cut off the head of every one he could reach; and spared neither high nor low, however well armed. A Soldan said to the Earl, 'Surrender immedi-'ately; you can hold out no longer against so many; 'surrender instantly; if you will say so, I will defend 'your person, and protect you from injury.' To this the Earl answered, crying with a loud voice, 'May it please 'God, the son of the blessed Mary, that never among 'Christians it may be heard that I yielded myself to the 'Saracens so long as I had life, except it were to cut off 'their heads with my bright sword.' Then said the Soldan, whose name was Mescadel, 'If you will not do so, 'the brave Saracens shall cut you up as meat to put in 'salt. Now your Lord, in whom you confide, shall not 'save you!' The Earl replied proudly, and with a loud voice, 'Save yourself, if you can, base villain! Never to 'you or any other, will I, for threat or for pain, renounce 'Jesus Christ the omnipotent God!' Then was the Earl very closely assailed. So he again struck behind with his sharp sword, and cut down the Saracens who were around him, and all cried out loudly, 'Mercy, for God's sake!'

"Then said the Earl to his dear companion, the stout and valiant Brother Richard of Ascalon, 'Let us keep close together as long as we live, so shall we sell our lives dearly.' 'Willingly,' said the Brother; 'by Jesus the son of Mary, never will I fail you so long as I have life!' Both the heroes kept firm together, and lost no opportunity of striking their enemies with effect.

"The valiant Earl of Salisbury then became infuriate. They were both assailed by the accursed Saracens, who were all eager to cut them down with their good swords;

but they parried them like experienced combatants. The valiant Earl boldly rushed on an amiral, a son of the King of Egypt, Abrael by name, and with his trenchant blade gave him a mortal wound; it divided his head in two; and the body fell on the sand, staining it with much blood as you may be well assured. It was amply proved that his sword was of good temper. It caused the head to fly instantly aloft; the body fell at his feet, in sight of the Soldan. *His soul Ruffini carried away chanting to hell!*

"When the stout and renowned Brother Richard saw what a blow the Earl had given the amiral, he rushed forward and committed to death *five* accursed Saracens.

"Then a vile Saracen came galloping up on horseback, brandishing a trenchant sword; and, giving the valiant Earl a very heavy blow, *cut off his right hand,* in which he held his sword in front of him. Then was his noble body cruelly dismembered; the left foot and the right hand being both cut off. When he had lost his hand, he drew back, and prayed to Jesus Christ, the Almighty, that He, for his Mother's sake, might be pleased to grant him vengeance on that bitter race.

"The bold and valiant body rushed forward on one foot to a perfidious Turk, whose name was Espiraunt. In the left hand he grasped his slashing sword, and struck off the face and chin of the enemy; but the latter, in falling, gave him another blow, and caused *the left hand,* which held the sword, to fly off in front. Then the valiant Longespé fell to the ground, for he could no longer stand on one foot. The Saracens came up right joyous and glad, and with their slashing swords cut him in pieces.

"The stedfast combatant, Brother Richard de Ascalon, fell wounded and bleeding upon the Earl, nor for all the land of France would he have gone away; when he saw the Earl dead, he resigned himself also to death! Sir Richard de Guise, the good bachelor, who bore his banner, when he saw his lord die, without more delay fell upon his lord, and suffered himself to be cut to pieces!

"Thus the Earl, and his Bannerer, and his Bachelors, both Sir Ralph de Henfeld the bold and brave, and Sir Robert de Wideley, who loved him very dearly, all these five good Knights were slain, all five were thus slain together. JESUS HATH THEIR SOULS IN PARADISE!"

Such, as related in this ancient Poem, was the mortal conflict and sad end of this noble and heroic warrior of the Cross, the son of the first Longespé! Our thoughts at once revert to his aged Mother, the venerable ABBESS OF LACOCK. Nor have the pious historians, who have described these devoted atchievements of religious enthusiasm, failed to record a circumstance at once affecting, and indicative of the holy resignation, and the fervid devotion, with which ELA regarded the fall of her Son in the sacred cause of the Cross.

"In the night preceding this battle," (we again quote Matthew Paris,*) "it appeared to his mother the most noble lady Countess, and Abbess of Lacock, that A KNIGHT ARMED AT ALL POINTS was received into the opening heavens! The device upon his shield she presently recognised; yet, being overwhelmed with astonishment, she demanded who it was that, thus ascending, was received by the angels

* The vision is also mentioned by Trivet, in his Annals, and briefly in the Book of Lacock; see the Appendix, p. ii.

into such glory: and it was answered her, in an audible and distinct voice, '*William thy Son!*' Having, therefore, taken notice of that night, the vision afterwards proved to be clearly fulfilled!"

Her reception of the fatal news is described in a subsequent passage: " Mindful of the vision, she with ready spirit, clasped hands, and bended knees, broke forth into this grateful praise of God: ' O my ' Lord Jesus Christ ! I give thee thanks, who from ' the body of me, an unworthy sinner, hast willed ' such a Son to be born, whom thou hast vouchsafed ' to redeem with *the crown of so glorious a Mar-* ' *tyrdom !* I therefore trust, that by his tutelege I ' may the more quickly arrive at the roof of my ' heavenly country !' So the relators of the melancholy tidings, who had long been silent from fear, were astonished at her maternal piety ; seeing it was not resolved into words of sorrowing complaint, but rather into those of spiritual joy."

Great and extended was the celebrity atchieved by William Longespé, in his heroic and devoted sacrifice of life, to the united call of military honour and religious enthusiasm. Not only did his exploits become, as we have seen, a stirring subject for the minstrel's rhymes, but they were perpetually referred to as a signal example of martial fame, if we may credit Matthew Paris. In mentioning the differences between England and France, in 1252, that historian states, that such was the glory that William Longespé had acquired by standing his ground, when even the French King's brother, the Count d'Artois, basely fled,—that even Frenchmen could not deny that he shone, surrounded with *a crown of martyrdom,* and was to be preferred, if such a comparison was allowable, even to the blessed Edmund.* The latter, a glorious Confessor, as was manifested by the incorruption of his body and a multitude of miracles,—and the former *a Martyr openly approved, an elegant, brave, and generous Knight,*—were both alike a thorn of offence in the eyes of the French!"

Once more, under the same year, Matthew Paris mentions that, when the French messengers were sent to the Soldan of Babylon to negociate the redemption of prisoners taken in the crusade of King Louis, he said to them, " I wonder at you Christians, ' who venerate the bones of the dead, that you do ' not ask for the bones of the most illustrious Wil- ' liam Longespé? For many things, how true I ' know not, are dropped into my ears and others', ' respecting those very bones; such as, how, in the ' darkness of night, there have been appearances ' upon his tomb, and how those who have called ' upon his Lord have received many benefits from ' heaven. For, on account of his excellence and ' honourable birth, we caused his body to be reve- ' rently interred, when he was slain in battle.' In answer to whom the messengers, having consulted

* Edmund of Abingdon, the sainted Archbishop noticed in a preceding page.

among themselves, replied: 'How can we detract from this Englishman, when even these Saracens are unable to deny the celebrity of this William!' They therefore requested his bones to be given to them, which the Soldan graciously granted; and, carrying them to Acon, they reverently buried them in the church of the Holy Cross."

There is in the Cathedral of Salisbury a sepulchral effigy of a Crusader, which has been generally attributed to the second Longespé, though some writers have thrown a doubt upon that appropriation, on account of the costume. But these critics have perhaps been more scrupulous than judicious; for the armour is chain-mail, and we are not aware in what it differs from that worn at the period of his death.* And what can be more probable than that Ela should have placed a monument to her Son, in the same sacred edifice in which the bones of his brave and illustrious Father reposed?

That ELA actually did confer upon his memory this last token of her love and admiration, is rendered the more probable from the circumstance that a similar memorial (though necessarily a cenotaph) was placed to commemorate the sacred warfare of his comrade Sir Robert de Vere; respecting whom, and some others of Longespé's devoted comrades, a few notes will now be appended.

* It is engraved in Dodsworth's History of Salisbury Cathedral, pl. 2 of monuments; and in Britton's History, pl. 3.

ARABIC ACCOUNT OF THE BATTLE.

An Arabic account of the assault of Mansoura, printed in Johnes's edition of Joinville, is interesting, and remarkable for being characterised not by that flowing and poetic diction which is generally deemed characteristic of Oriental composition, but for a sedate and circumstantial detail which singularly contrasts, in the present instance, with our poetic European accounts. It appears from this Arabic historian that the first defeat, after the Christians had crossed the river, was sustained by an Emir named Fakreddin, who was slain: " The French, after the death of Fakreddin, retreated to Djédilé; but *their whole cavalry* advanced to Mansoura, and, *having forced one of the gates*, entered the town: when the Mussulmen fled to the right and left. The King of France [i. e. the Comte d'Artois] had already penetrated as far as the Sultan's palace, and victory seemed to declare for him, when the baharite slaves, led by Bihars, advanced, and snatched it from his hands; their change was so furious that the Frenchmen were obliged to retreat. The French infantry, during this time, had advanced to cross the bridge; had they been able to join their cavalry, the defeat of the Egyptian army, and the loss of the town of Mansoura, would have been inevitable.* Night separated the combatants, when the French retreated in disorder, after leaving fifteen hundred of their men on the field."

The fatal battle in which King Louis was made prisoner, took place on nearly the same spot, but not until the 5th of April, nearly two months after the assault of Mansoura, during which the crusading army had made no advance.

* This confession is remarkable, and highly honourable to the chivalry of the Crusaders.

SIR ROBERT DE VERE, THE "STANDARD-BEARER" OF WILLIAM LONGESPÉ.

It is somewhat remarkable that the Editors of the Excerpta Historica should have been at a loss for any particulars of the history of Sir Robert de Vere; as his fame is recorded in several works in alliance with that of William Longespé,* and as they were acquainted with his armorial shield, which it might be supposed would have directed them to a work of no little genealogical fame. On pursuing this clue, it would have been found that he was of the family of Vere of Drayton, whose history is included in the sumptuous work of Henry Earl of Peterborough, generally known as Halstead's Genealogies, the most magnificent volume of family history that England has produced.

Sir Robert de Vere was grandson of a knight of the same name, who was a younger brother of Aubrey the first Earl of Oxford. His father, Sir Henry, was Constable of Gisors, in France; and left by Hildeburga, daughter of Baldwin de Bosco, two sons: Sir Walter, who assumed the name of Drayton, being lord of Drayton in Northamptonshire; and Sir Robert, the hero of Mansoura. The latter became lord of Addington and Twywell, also in the county of Northampton, by gift of his uncle Sir William de Vere; and of the town of Thrapston, from the gift of Baldwin de Wake, on marrying Margaret, aunt to Baldwin. By this wife he probably had his two sons, Baldwin and John; the former of whom was the ancestor of a long line of Vere, one of the heiresses of which was

* Particularly in the account of Longespé in Dodsworth's Salisbury Cathedral, p. 195, and in Gough's Sepulchral Monuments, vol. II. p. cvi.

SIR ROBERT DE VERE.

married to the first Lord Mordaunt, in the reign of Henry the Seventh.

Sir Robert de Vere married secondly Helena, who is supposed in "Halstead" to be that Elena, the daughter of Roger de Quincy, the last Earl of Winchester of that family, who was first married to Alan la Zouche. If that was the fact, she was mother of that Roger la Zouche who married Ela, daughter of Stephan Longespé.*

About 1236 we find Robert de Vere attaching himself to Geoffrey de Lucy, who, by a charter, † granted to him, "*pro homagio et servitio suo,*" a pension of 100*s.* from his mill of Daylenton, until he could provide him with land to the same value. We have previously seen that Geoffrey de Lucy was a comrade, if not a relation, of William Longespé; ‡ though his name does not occur at Mansoura. Therefore, in attaching himself to Longespé, Sir Robert de Vere probably had the full assent of Lucy; indeed, another charter shows that the rent from the mill of Daylinton was confirmed to Helena de Vere, as part of her dower, after the death of her husband, by a charter of Geoffrey de Lucy, dated on the day of St. Sixtus the Pope (March 28) 1251. §

---

* See before, p. 155.
† Printed in Halstead's Genealogies, p. 251. In the same place is a charter, or rather letter, of Margaret de Lacy, Countess of Lincoln and Pembroke, "*a son cher amy Sire Roberd de Vere,*" requesting him to return the eating knife of jaspar, *(le cutel ad' la manche de Jaspe)* which her lord had lent him at the request of her father, as she was desirous to send it, with other things, to her lord beyond sea." On this letter the Editors partly grounded their opinion that Helena de Vere was Elena de Quincy, and therefore *sister to this Countess of Pembroke.*
‡ See before, p. 222. § Halstead, p. 253.

On going the holy voyage, Sir Robert de Vere assumed the simple ensign of St. George, *a red cross in a silver field,* and his descendants were ever after permitted to bear this emblem of his pious campaign and glorious death. It is remarkable that in " Halstead," he is described as the STANDARD-BEARER of Longespé. At Mansoura, according to the Poet, Sir Richard de Guise bore the Banner, but that was after the death of Vere; and if we admit this circumstance in the history of the latter, (which though apparently resting on no other evidence but tradition, may still be correct) it may be supposed that his *red cross* (the badge of the Crusader) was assumed as the distinguishing mark of his having filled the office of STANDARD-BEARER to the chief commander of the English crusaders. To the charter by which his widow Helena transferred the marriage of her sons to Sir Gilbert de Segrave, is attached a seal on which she is represented standing, with this *cross* depicted *on her gown,* and holding on her right hand a hawk, the symbol of her noble rank.‡

In the church of Sudborough, in Northamptonshire, she erected a monument to her lost Crusader, in which his effigy still remains, in chain armour and an ample surcoat, his legs crossed, his left arm bearing a shield, and his right hand in the act of drawing his sword, or of returning it to his scabbard. Of this monument there have been three engravings: 1. in

‡ Engraved in Halstead's Genealogies, p. 254.

Halstead's Genealogies, p. 253; 2. in Hyett's Sepulchral Monuments of Northamptonshire, pl. xi.; and 3. in an interesting little work recently published, entitled, "A Glimpse at the Monumental Architecture and Sculpture of Great Britain, by M. H. Bloxam," and to which we are indebted for the use of the cut, here inserted.

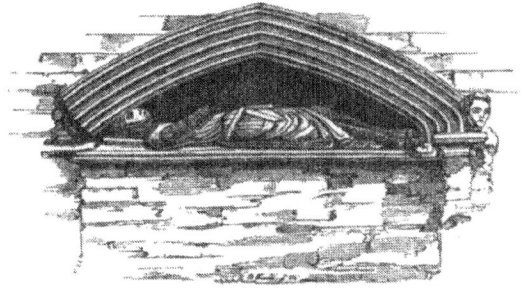

MONUMENT AT SUDBOROUGH.

SIR ALEXANDER GIFFARD.

This faithful Knight, who escaped to fulfil the dying requests of William Longespé, was, like Sir Robert de Vere, supposed by the editors of the Excerpta Historica, to be unrecorded except by the Poet. His escape, however, is also noticed by Matthew Paris, who says it was effected after he had received "*five great wounds*." The chronicler adds " he was of gentle blood, and *the son of a noble Matron, who was dwelling with the Queen of England.*"

The family of Giffard was indeed one of the most illustrious in England during the reigns of our Norman Kings. Two of them, named Walter, were Earls of Buckingham in the first century after the Conquest. Another branch, also dating from the Domesday survey, was seated at Brimsfield in Gloucestershire, the last of whom was so wealthy, that he was called *le Rych*, from his great possessions. He was the son (by another wife) of that John who married the widow of the third William Longespé.*

Sir Alexander, the hero of Mansoura, was evidently a near kinsman, and probably a cousin-german of the same John. He was the son of Hugh de Giffard, of Boyton in Wiltshire, a manor which was subinfeuded to the Giffards by the house of Salisbury, at a very early period, and which is adjacent to Sherrington, which Osbern de Giffard, the ancestor of the Giffards of Brimsfield, himself held in capite at the Domesday survey. Boyton was then held in demesne by Edward of Salisbury; but in 12 Henry II. it was held by Elias Giffard of Patrick Earl of Salisbury; and in various records it is stated to be *de veteri feoffamento*. The feudal dependence on William Longespé of his trusty knight, Sir Alexander Giffard, is thus very clearly demonstrated.

We have also the best evidence of Sir Alexander's immediate parentage. In a deed of gift to the nunnery of Tarrent in Dorsetshire, he describes himself as "the son of Hugh Giffard, of Boyton," and mentions his mother Sibilla.† This Sibilla, the "noble matron" mentioned by Matthew Paris, was the daughter and coheir of Walter de Cormeiles. His father also was equally in the royal favour; for in 1235, Henry the Third appointed Hugh Giffard to be Constable of the Tower of London; describing him as one "of our household." ‡

Two of the brothers of Sir Alexander, both originally members of the cathedral church of Wells, rose to very exalted stations. Walter became Bishop of Bath in 1264, and was Archbishop of York from 1266 to his death in 1279; Godfrey was consecrated Bishop of Worcester in 1268, and held that see for the long period of forty-three years: and both filled the office of Lord Chancellor. Their sister Mabilia was Abbess of Shaftesbury.

Godfrey, whilst Bishop of Worcester, was lord of the manor

---

* See p. 151.   † Hoare's Hundred of Heytesbury, p. 197.
‡ —"qui est de familia nostra." Some similar expression may have given rise to the misapprehension of Godwin, that Bishop Godfrey was "Regi sanguine propinquus."

of Boyton; and Sir R. C. Hoare, in his History of the Hundred of Heytesbury, has introduced his curious Will. What is more to our present purpose, a view is there given of a monumental effigy in Boyton Church, which, though the plate is inscribed with the name of Elias Giffard, was yet conjectured to be Sir Alexander by the historian himself, although unaware that Sir Alexander Giffard was a crusader,—a circumstance which confirms the identity of this *cross-legged* effigy.

Thus, at Boyton, as at Salisbury, and at Sudborough, reposes the figure of one of the champions of Mansoura. He probably did not long survive the hardships he had endured in the crusade; for the effigy " represents a person cut off in the prime of life." On his shield he bears three lions passant, the arms of the Giffards of Brimsfield, differenced by a label.

ANDRÉ DE VITRÉ.

The name of this person is here introduced, because, although it has not hitherto occurred in the narrative of the Assault of Mansoura, yet it was there he met his death, being a *cousin of William Longespé,* and of the same family as ALIANOR COUNTESS OF SALISBURY, the mother of the Countess Ela, the Foundress and Abbess of Lacock.

Since the earlier part of this volume was printed (see particularly pp. 31, 83, 97,) the genealogy of the family of the Countess Alianor (called in the Book of Lacock *de Viteri*), which had been sought in vain among the records of this country, has been discovered in those of Britany and Normandy, and proves to be of very exalted rank, worthy the alliance of an English Earl, himself descended (as shown in the pedigree at p. 107) from the Comtes de Ponthieu, the Dukes of Burgundy, and the Dukes of Normandy. The annals of this house occupy a large portion of one of those volumes of historical genealogy, in which the French are so much richer than ourselves; entitled, "Histoire de Bretagne, avec les Chroniques des maisons de Vitré et de Laval; par Pierre Le Baud," fol. 1638; and, though the name of Alianor Countess of Salisbury does not occur in that work, yet the records supplied by the kindness of Mr. Stapleton, prove her exact position in the pedigree in the most satisfactory manner.

The family of Vitré were descended in the male line from Martin de Rennes, a younger brother of Conan Duke of Britany, who died in 992; and Alianor Countess of Salisbury was through her mother first-cousin to Duke Conan le Jeune. Again, André de Vitré, brother to the Countess of Salisbury, married a cousin-german of the same Conan; and André de Vitré, his son, who was slain at Mansoura, married Catharine, granddaughter of Conan, and *half-sister* to the unfortunate PRINCE ARTHUR. These and the other links, which connected the house of Vitré with the sovereign house of Britany and the Royal families of England, will be more clearly shown by the accompanying table (PEDIGREE V.)

The circumstances of the marriage of the father and mother of the Countess Alianor, claim our notice from their connection with England. Robert de Vitré had been taken prisoner in a petty feudal war by his neighbour Roland de Dinan; who "detained him until the Comte Conan, son of the Duke Eudo* and the Duchess Bertha, and cousin-german to Roland, (see note to the Pedigree,) *returned from England*, where he was then staying *with the Queen his cousin-german*, daughter of the Comte Geoffroi his uncle.† And then, at

* M. Le Baud, throughout his History, invariably confounds Alan Niger, Earl of Richmond, the first, with Duke Eudo, the second husband of the Duchess Bertha, and makes the latter the father of her children. His mistake is obvious; for in noticing a passage in the chronicle of Robert du Mont, he translates the words, " Eudone vicecomite vitrico suo" by "le vicomte Eudon son *vainqueur!*"

† Earl Alan had a brother Geoffroi, Comte de Penthievre; and Alicia, the wife of King Henry I. is said by Le Baud and other early historians of Britany, to have been the daughter of this Geoffroi: Du Paz notices and corrects the error in his Histoire Genealogique de plusieurs Maisons de Bretagne.

PEDIGREE V.

FAMILY OF VITRE, SHOWING THE MATERNAL RELATIONS OF ELA FOUNDRESS OF LACOCK, AND THEIR CONNECTIONS WITH THE DUKES OF BRITANY AND KINGS OF ENGLAND.

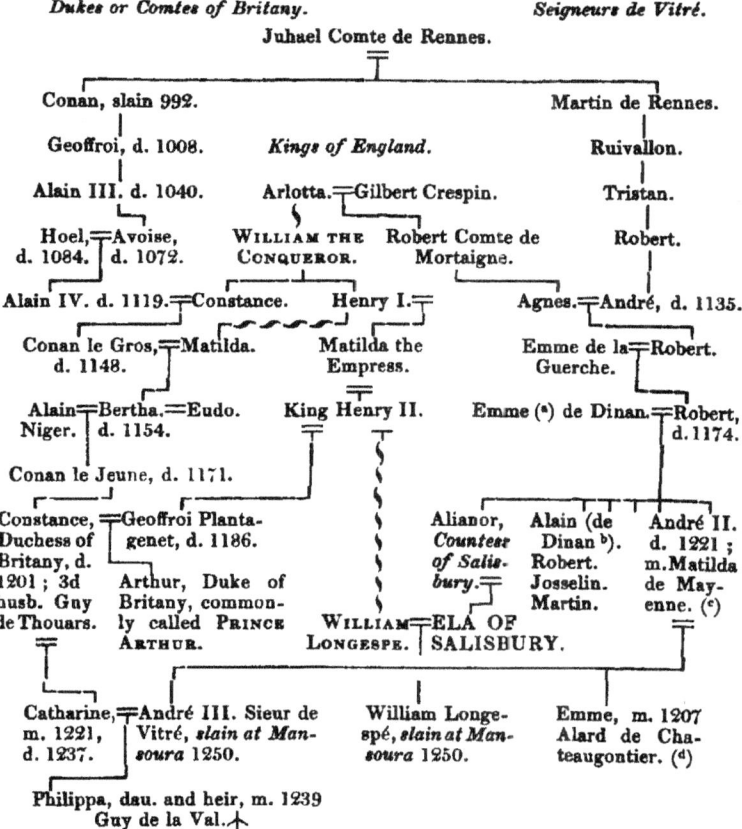

[a] Daughter of Olivier Vicomte de Dinan, by Agnorie, *sister* to Eudo Comte de Penthievre, the husband of Bertha Duchess of Britany: Eudo and Agnorie were grandchildren of Honguen, sister of Hoel, the husband of the Duchess Avoise.

[b] Made heir to his uncle Roland de Dinan *in the presence of King Henry II.*

[c] Daughter of Geoffroi de Mayenne, by Constance sister to the Duchess Bertha.

[d] Emme de Vitré was a hostage to King Richard I. for the Duchess Constance.

the desire of Conan and Roland, and for the deliverance of his body, Robert de Vitré took to wife Emme, sister to Roland, cousin-german to the said Comte Conan, and niece to the Duke Eudo, being daughter of Agnorie his sister. With which Emme he received in marriage from the Comte Conan *the land of Colinge*, with all its appurtenances, and from Roland he received Chenel*," &c. (Chroniques de Vitré, p. 27.)

Now, it is remarkable that this "land of Colinge" is the same manor of Culing or Cooling *in Suffolk*, which afterwards came to the Countess of Salisbury, and has been already mentioned in pp. 98, 157. It belonged to Earl Alan (of Richmond) at the Domesday survey; and from him had descended to his great-nephew Duke Conan, who was also Earl of Richmond in England; and he bestowed it on this Breton lord, Robert de Vitré. When Andrew the son of Robert married his sister to a husband already possessed of lordships in England, it was a natural arrangement that the English manor should be given in her dower. And this we find was the fact.

But the Earl of Salisbury was not her first husband. By the following charter copied by Mr. Stapleton from the chartulary of the abbey of Mondaye near Bayeux, now preserved in the episcopal library of that city, her brother Andrew first granted her marriage to William Paynell, lord of Hambie in Normandy and Drax in Yorkshire.

"Univ'sis s'c'e m'ris eccl' filiis &c. Andreas de Vitreio in d'no salutem. Descretionis vestre noscat intuitus et memoriter teneat, quod ego Andreas de Vitreio dedi et concessi Willelmo filio Fulconis Paganelli cum sorore mea Alienor in libero conjugio, terre mee de Normannia quam simul partiti fuimus ego Andreas et ipse Fulco Paganellus, medietatem illam quam sibi elegit in maneriis meis de Ria et Trungeio et Duxeio, et insuper xx^{ti} libras stellicorum annuatim habendas *in manerio meo de Coelinga*, etiam hoc tenendum de me et heredibus meis sibi et suis heredibus libere quiete et integre. Testibus hiis, Richardo ep'o

---

* This should be Cheuel'; it is spelt "Chefuel" in a manuscript copy of Le Baud in the Bibliotheque du Roi. It does not appear whether it was in England or in Britany.

Abrinc'. Roll' Dolens' electo. * Will'o Paganello archid. Roll' de Dignando. Alano de Rohan. &c."

The next extract, from the Cartulary of Hambie †, an abbey founded by the Paynells, shows the sister of André de Vitré actually married to the Earl of Salisbury: its date is 1206:

"Andreas de Vitreio et Robertus Cantor Parisiensis frater ejus ‡ et ALIENOR COMITISSA SALESBURI *soror eorum*, Noveritis &c. pro salute Will'i Paganelli &c. in duabus garbis decime de Ria quas Johannes persona ecclesie de Trungeio tenebat nomine canonicorum de Gastineto."

It would appear from the "Rotuli de Dominabus," p. 11, that William Paynell was dead in 1185; that his lands had been farmed for more than a year; and that the heir was three years old. There are numerous charters belonging to this family which show that William was succeeded in the Paynell lands by his brother Fulke; we may therefore conclude that the infant heir mentioned in 1185 was the nephew (not the son) of William; and the descent of Alianor's lands to the daughters of her second marriage with the Earl of Salisbury fully confirms this; for the claim of a male heir, and especially when born of a marriage on which the lands (Cooling, &c.) were first settled, could never have been passed over.

We now arrive at a fact of singular interest, after the discussion that has already taken place on the subject; and after the conflicting accounts of the circumstances in which the orphan ELA of Salisbury was placed after her father's death. This is, that not only did her mother survive the Earl for many years: but Ela had actually two sisters, of the whole blood. These ladies, however, were neither of the two parties already named in pp. 96, 98; for "the wife of Gilbert Malmaines" appears to have been the Countess Alianor herself, during a *third* marriage, which will be noticed hereafter.

* Rolland was elected Archbishop of Dole in Britany in 1177, and not consecrated for some years after.

† Excerpta among the collections of Mons. C. de Gerville.

‡ Elected Archbishop of Tours in 1208, but his election annulled by the Pope.

The names of Ela's sisters were Juliana and Joanna.

The former is proved by a charter dated 1227, in the cartulary of Mondaye, by which " Alianor quondam Comitissa Salesberiensis, pro salute animæ meæ et *Julianæ filiæ meæ*," gave ten pounds of Tours, for the observation of the anniversary of Juliana then defunct. Juliana had, in her lifetime, designated the abbey of Mondaye as the place of her interment: " Notum, &c. quod ego Juliana D'na de Tyleriis elegi sepulturum meam in abbatia S'c'i Martini de Monte Dei et ibidem dedi Deo et s'c'e conventui pro salute animæ meæ &c. xii^m libras in prefectura de Aquila, &c." Tellieres is situated between Verneuil and Nonancourt, and not far from Aigle. In the Liber Niger of the church of Bayeux is a charter of Gilbert de Tellieres, dominus de Croleio (Creully castle near that city), bearing the date 1219. This was certainly the husband of Juliana. His name occurs also in the Liber Rubeus Scaccarii.

Juliana left a daughter and heiress, Hylaria lady of Tellieres, married to James de Bovelingham, who in her right styled himself D'n's de Tyleriis (Cart. de Monte-Dei;) and whose name occurs in the close roll respecting Cooling (p. 99, antea).

JOANNA, the third daughter of Alianor Countess of Salisbury, was married to Sir Thomas Malesmains, who by her became the father of Nicholas, as rightly conjectured in p. 99. The wardship of the heir of Thomas, and Joanna his wife, was granted to the Earl and Countess of Salisbury (William Longespé and Ela) in 1221.* The following charter of Mondaye proves this portion of the pedigree most satisfactorily. " Notum &c. quod ego Nicholaus Malesmains filius d'ni Thomæ Malesmains militis pro salute a'i'e mee et a'i'ar' antecessor' et successor' meor' quietam et ratam habeo et habui elemosinam quam fecit d'na Alianora de Vitreio avia mea quondam Comitissa Saleberiensis in tempore viduitatis suæ, Deo et abbatie s'c'i Martini de Monte Dei, videlicet patronatum ecclesie s'c'i Vigoris de Trungeio, &c. Anno gratje M^o. CC^o. XXVIII."

By another charter dated in 1232, Nicholas Malesmains,

* Close Rolls, vol. i. p. 468. Johanna is also mentioned in the Fines of King John, 8vo, 1835, i. p. 142.

"pro salute a'i'e Juliane d'ne de Tyleriis," confirms her gift of twelve pounds rent in the prevôté of Aquila.

The statement in the Norman rolls, 6 Joh. respecting Gilbert de Malmaines holding Gatesden "ex parte uxoris" (before cited in pp. 98, 99) shows that Gilbert de Malmaines must have been the third husband of the Countess Alianor: he was doubtless related to the Thomas who married the Countess's daughter, perhaps even his father by a former wife; but the degree of their consanguinity has not been ascertained.

The Countess Alianor chose her burial-place, as her daughter had done, in the church of Mondaye, and in consideration thereof gave to the abbey the tithe of her land in Trungi and Rie, by charter dated 1228. The last notice of her in the cartulary is of the date of 1231, which refers to the same donation.

Such is the history of the mother and sisters of Ela the heiress of Salisbury,—hitherto unknown to our heralds and genealogists. The Earldom being regarded as an indivisible fief, and destined by King Richard for the establishment of his natural brother, the brave William Longespé, was assigned entire to the eldest daughter; whilst the younger sisters, having been married to less distinguished persons, and in their mother's country, have escaped the view of those whose researches have been confined to the records of this country.

To proceed to their cousin the Crusader. André de Vitré had joined the crusade of 1232 in the retinue of Peter Duke of Britany; and had returned safe. In 1248 he again determined to relinquish his own domains, and to accompany King Louis and the flower of the French nobility to Palestine. His son-in-law Guy Seigneur de Laval (son of Matthew de Montmorency, Constable of France), went the crusade with him. He returned and inherited the domains of Vitré; André was slain, and was the last of his family; M. de Baud says he died on *the 8th of February*; if so, it was in the same conflict in which William Longespé breathed his last.

M. le Baud states that the first Robert de Vitré accompanied William of Normandy to the conquest of England, " very fully accompanied by his knights," and received in reward " many possessions and inheritances in England, which he and his successors enjoyed for a long time after." (Chroniques, p. 12.) But this seems to be only the ordinary tale of French families, without any real authority; as the name scarcely occurs in the English records. We only find a William de Vitri, who witnessed the foundation charter of Coddenham Priory, Suffolk, by Eustace de Merch, temp. Hen. II.;* and an Alexander de Viteri, as a witness to a charter without date of St. Nicholas Priory, Exeter.† In the Liber Rubeus Scaccarii, temp. Hen. II. among the King's tenants *in Normandy*, occurs " Robertus de Vitriaco," holding " medietatem de Reia in Baiocasino, et Trungeum et Caignoles et Duxeium in Boscagio." This was either the father or grandfather of the Countess Alianor.

* Mon. Ang. 1655, i. 911.
† Collectanea Topogr. et Geneal. vol. i. p. 386.

ARMS OF VITRÉ.

Gules, a lion Argent.

CHAPTER XIII.

Affairs of Lacock Abbey during Ela's Abbacy—Early fate of William Longespé the Third—Tournament at Blyth—DEATH OF ELA—The Funeral of a Nun.

HAVING already shown, from the Rules of the Order, the most striking features of the spiritual discipline of the Nuns of Lacock, which directed the unvarying course of their domestic economy; it only remains to arrange and detail the particulars, neither numerous or copious, which are preserved in the records of the country, or in their own cartulary, relative to their temporal affairs.

The charters immediately relating to the foundation of the Abbey, have been already noticed; but there are some other records which are closely connected with its original establishment. In the year 1237, by charter dated at Windsor on the 7th of August, the King granted to the Prioress of Lacock (for there was as yet no Abbess), and " the Nuns there serving God," that they and their successors should hold for ever a *Fair* at the manor of Lacock, to last *for three days*, namely on the eve, feast, and morrow of the translation of Saint Thomas the Martyr.*

---

* See the Appendix, p. xvi. It is recorded on the Charter Rolls, 21 Hen. III. m. 2; and on m. 6 of the same year is another royal confirmation of the abbey lands.

ROYAL GRANTS TO LACOCK ABBEY.

In 1241, on the 6th of May, the Abbess Ela obtained two beneficial charters from King Henry. The first of these granted the right of holding a *weekly Market* on Tuesday.* By the second, the King gave the Abbess the privilege of having every week one cart traversing the forest of Melksham, to collect dead *wood, for fuel,* without injury to the forest, during the royal pleasure.†

It was on the very same day, being the feast of St. John ante Portam Latinam, that the Nuns concluded an agreement with the Abbat of Stanley for a part of his quarry of Haslebury, seventy-six feet wide; in exchange for one which they had previously bought of Henry Crok.‡

By these important transactions, and by the gifts of pious benefactors, the dates of which are not recorded, the virtuous Ela had the satisfaction of seeing her Abbey placed in a situation of great temporal prosperity. We must now, before noticing the closing scenes of her long career, make one more very brief digression from the annals of Lacock, in order to remark what other occurrences befel her family, besides the death of her eldest

---

* See the Appendix, p. xiv. Rot. Pat. 26 Hen. III.

† Appendix, p. xvi. The date should be "anno xxvi°," both being executed on the same day, when the King was at Portsmouth, May 6, 1241. It is enrolled on Rot. Pat. 26 Hen. III. m. 3.

‡ Appendix, p. xxii.

Son; and thus take our farewell view of the House of Longespé.

We have seen that the widowed Countess of Salisbury, though she herself had relinquished her *temporal* for a *spiritual* dignity, had yet been unable to transmit the former, before her own decease, to her eldest son and heir apparent. On the death of that valiant son, a THIRD WILLIAM became the hope of the family, and in the Book of Lacock we find him styled "*the young Earl.*" * But again the heir, an "Earl" only by anticipation, was snatched away by an untimely death; and no second member of the House of Longespé was ever confirmed in the Earldom of Salisbury.

The "mimic war" which led to this fatal event is thus briefly noticed in the chronicle of Holinshed: "In Whitsuntide (1256) was holden a great justs at Blie (Blyth in Nottinghamshire), where the lord Edward, the King's eldest son, first began to show proof of his chivalry. There were divers overthrown and hurt, and amongst others WILLIAM DE LONGESPÉ was so bruised that he could never after recover his former strength."

The field of tournament between Blyth and Tickhill had been one of the five recognised † by

---

* See the Appendix, p. v.

† " We may conclude from the terms of the writ that they were not then newly set apart for the purpose, but that the King was giving his sanction to what was before the usage. . . . The field near Salisbury is still pointed out. I have inquired

the charter of Richard the First, of which the Earl of Salisbury, the great-grandfather of this William Longespé, and father of the Abbess Ela, had been the chief commissioner.*

Matthew Paris mentions a Tournament which took place a Blyth in the beginning of Lent 1237, in which the Knights of the South of England were opposed to those of the North, and which gave rise to such animosity, that the chronicler says it was converted from a *hastiludium* into an *hostile bellum;* and the Southrons, prevailing, took several great men prisoners. The enmities which it produced continued for some time after, between Peter Bishop of Winchester, Hubert Earl of Kent, Gilbert Basset, Stephan de Segrave, Richard Sward, and others; and they were not reconciled until the Legate Otto became the mediator.

Such were some of the evils to which these ebullitions of the martial spirit of the times were found to give birth, and which called for as many efforts of the executive government to controul and check them, as have been exerted at other periods for the suppression of the more vindictive practice of duelling.

---

for the tournament-field between Tickhill and Blyth in vain." Hunter's Deanery of Doncaster, vol. i. pp. 224, 225. The scene of the tournaments near Salisbury has been described in p. 82 of the present work; that near Brackley, called *Bayard's Green*, is noticed in Baker's Northamptonshire, vol. i. p. 573.

* As noticed before in p. 81.

Another evil consequence of Tournaments was the frequent loss of life among the combatants; and some of the greatest peers in the country fell victims to these perilous games. Only fifteen years before that tournament at Blyth which now attracts our attention, Gilbert Earl of Pembroke died from a fall received at a tournament at Ware. Nor was Longespé the only sufferer at the tournament of 1257. In the ensuing passage of Matthew Paris others, who died, are mentioned; together with Roger Bigod, Earl of Norfolk, who was very severely injured; and whose name, as well as the scene of the combat, connects this "passage of arms" with that of 1237 already noticed, in which the same chivalric Earl Bigod, twenty years before, had proved the most distinguished champion.

The substance of Matthew Paris's account is as follows: " At this time died, *in the flower of their age*, Robert de Quinci, and WILLIAM DE LONGASPATHA, and Alan de Watsand, the King's clerk and justiciary, and John de Lexinton (an elegant, witty, and learned knight, the bearer of the King's seal); and Earl Roger Bigod, the Marshal, was very seriously ill, and scarcely recalled from the portals of the tomb;* who had contended so manfully and beyond their strength in the tournament of Blie, that, their sinews being relaxed, they never after recovered their health."

* He afterwards survived to the year 1270.

Thus was ELA deprived by death of both her son and grandson, her infant great-granddaughter being married to the young Earl of Lincoln. Nor were these the only trials of her maternal affections: in the year before her eldest son's death, she lost her daughter Isabella, Lady Vescy; and in the last year of her life, she was preceded to the tomb by her son Stephan, whose body was brought to LACOCK for interment; so that, of all her family, she left only two sons and two daughters surviving, one of whom, Richard, the Canon of Salisbury, died in the following year.

The five last years of her life were spent in perfect retirement, even from the peaceful rule of her monastic society. When, as the Book of Lacock has recorded, she had for eighteen years " zealously governed the flock committed to her, most devoutly serving God, and maintaining a life of close seclusion, in fastings, in watchings, in holy meditations, and *disciplines of constant strictness*, and in other good and charitable works, she at length, perceiving herself to be affected with old age, and such weakness as prevented her from benefiting *her religion* ∗ as she desired, renounced and refused to preside any longer, and during her life appointed an Abbess named BEATRICE OF KENT, on the last day of the year 1256, ‡ and in the

∗ " strenuè gubernavit." Matthew Paris also applies to her a similar expression, " *non muliebriter* gubernavit."

† Her convent, or religious order; see before, p. 204.

‡ " pridie kal. Januarii A. 1257." Book of Lacock; but in

seventieth year of her age. And thus she survived for nearly five years after, released from every care." Yet even in this closing stage of her career, we find that she " earnestly solicited "* from the King some further important benefits for the Abbey, which were conceded in the year 1260; namely, a confirmation of the Market at Lacock, and the right of *Free Warren* there and in all her other lands in England;† and a grant of land, in lieu of the right of carrying fire-wood from Melksham forest, which had been found by an inquisition not to provide sufficient dead or dry wood for a " *daily* cartload." The portion of the forest thus assigned to the Nuns consisted of forty acres, described by these boundaries: " From the hedge and " ditch of Luntesleye near Wodensdich (Wans- " dyke) up to the road called Haggestreet ‡ towards " Chittoe, and on that road as far as Little Hese- " wych, to the ditch called Aldefrithesdich, and so " to the aforesaid hedge and ditch of Luntesleye near " the Milestile on the south." The Nuns were permitted to inclose this spot of ground with a hedge

the chronology formerly in MS. Cotton. Vitell. A. viii, " A. mcclvii. nonas Aprilis." (Monasticon.)

* —— " cùm *dilecta affinis nostra* ELA, dicta *Patrona* domûs de LACOCK, nos *attentè rogasset*," &c.

† Cart. 44 Hen. III. m. 2.

‡ Hagges Street, so called at this day, is the way which leads from the Turnpike to the Fountain where Abbatia de Drogonis Fonte stood—the first Stanley Abbey, described in the author's History of Bremhill.

and ditch;* and at a subsequent period, in the reign of Richard the Second, letters patent were granted to them, to inclose the same with a pale. †

This was the last important favour granted by King Henry the Third to his "*beloved kinswoman*" the FOUNDRESS OF LACOCK.

At length, " in the seventy-fourth year of her age, on the 24th of August 1261, ‡ yielding up her soul in peace, she rested in the Lord, and was *most honourably buried* in the *choir* of the Monastery." §

What these marks of honour were, which distinguished the committal to the tomb of the mortal remains of the Foundress of Lacock, we have not any positive authority to determine. The funeral was probably attended by all, or some, of her surviving children, and perhaps by some other persons of rank. As it was a favourite practice, even with the laity, to be buried in the vestments of monachism,|| so ELA would doubtless, in that respect, be honoured with every sacred symbol and ceremony, as if she had died when actually Abbess.

* See the Appendix, p. xvii; also recorded in Rot. Cart. 44 Hen. III. m. 4, and Esc. 43 Hen. III. no. 42.

† Pat. 12 Ric. II. p. 1. m. 15.

‡ " ix kal. Sept." Book of Lacock; " decimo-quarto kal. Maii " MS. Cotton.   § Book of Lacock.

|| " In regard of burial," it is quaintly remarked by Weever, " abbeyes were most commonly preferred before other places whatsoever; and he that was buried therein *in a friar's habite*, [as were Walter de Salisbury at Bradenstoke, and Earl William de Romara at Revesby,] *if you will believe it, never came into hell!*"

We will therefore close these remarks by briefly noticing the ordinary practice observed on the death of every Nun * of Lacock:—

"When any Sister was dead, the body, having been washed, was clothed with stamen, † cowl, and mantle, wimple and veil; without the Rule coat, but *with hosen and tanned schoes*, and with a girdle; all of which were to be *of the vilest gear*, and all were buried with her except the mantle. The body was then laid on a bier, ‡ and covered with a chest, made in the manner of a lattice, that the body might be seen. It was never to be left by two Sisters, at the least, *praying for the soul*, saying their psalter, or dirige, or other prayers, until it was taken into the church."

Before the corpse was carried out to be buried, it was sprinkled with holy water, the affecting psalm, *De Profundis,* § was sung, with the prayers begin-

---

* Arundel MS. 146, ch. IX.   † See p. 194.

‡ Coffins were not used; except those of stone, and they were placed within the grave previously to the interment, ready to receive the body. An ancient painting on the walls of Winchester cathedral, represents the Funeral of a Nun; whose body, clothed in her religious habit, appears laid out on a bier, set down by the side of her grave; but there is no sign of any coffin. See an engraving of it in Carter's Antiquities, copied in Bloxam's "Monumental Architecture," 1834, p. 108. To the latter work we are indebted for the woodcut opposite, a vivid representation of a Funeral in the thirteenth century, *drawn by the hand of our old friend Matthew Paris himself*, in the MS. Cotton, Nero D. 1.

§ "Out of the Deep," &c. the 129th Psalm.

ning *Inclina,* and *Fidelium.* Whilst it was being conveyed to the church, *De Profundis* was again chanted, together with the 113th psalm, beginning *In exitu.* At the church porch, the service commenced with the anthem *In paradisam,* and then the mass of *Requiem* was performed; after which, the body was again sprinkled with holy water, and perfumed with incense, and then, with other prayers and anthems, it was consigned to that place of decay and oblivion, of which the Nun, when alive, had received a daily admonition; for a bier, strewn with a little earth, always stood before the church door; and a grave was kept constantly open in the cemetery, which was visited by the convent every day after *Tierce,* when the Abbess cast out from it with her two fingers a small portion of earth, the Sisters chanting the solemn and humiliating notes of the oft-recited *De Profundis.*

FUNERAL DRAWN BY MATTHEW PARIS.

CHAPTER XIV.

Affairs of the Abbey after the death of the Foundress ELA—Succession of Abbesses—Property of the Abbey in 1291—The hearts of Amicia Countess of Devon, and Bishop Nicholas Longespé—Ecclesiastical Survey of 1535.

THE annals of the Monastery, which were probably contained in the Book of Lacock, having been irrecoverably lost, the catalogue of Abbesses, succeeding after ELA, which can now be collected, is by no means complete. ALICIA has been placed next to Beatrix of Kent;[*] and then JULIANA, who occurs in a charter of 1288, and also in 1290.[†]

From the Ecclesiastical Taxation of Pope Nicholas, made about 1291, we may collect our first view of the yearly revenue of the Abbey. The following are the particulars, gleaned from separate entries, and it is therefore possible that some small items were overlooked. It should also be considered that, as the valuation was made for the purposes of a tax, it is perhaps below the real value:

[*] In the list formed by Stevens.

[†] Wymarca, the Prioress, whose name is mentioned by Stevens after that of Juliana, was evidently the Superior of the convent before the Foundress Ela assumed the dignity of Abbess in 1240, as she was contemporary with Hugh Abbat of Cirencester 1230—1238. (Cartulary, f. 101 b.)

		Rated value			Tenth.		
		£.	s.	d.	£.	s.	d.
Sarum	Lacock	20	0	0	2	0	0
dioc.	—— Portion of the Church	0	10	0	0	1	0
	Chittern	25	13	4	2	11	4
	Bishopstrow	11	17	0	1	3	8½
	Heddington	7	19	0	0	15	11
	Shrewton	1	0	0	0	2	0
	Aldeburne	1	10	0	0	3	0
	Wykelescote	2	10	0	0	5	0
Winton.	Shorewell in the Isle of						
dioc.	Wight	17	0	0	1	14	0
Wigorn.	Hatherop	2	2	0	0	4	2¼
dioc.	Cerney	3	11	0	0	7	1¼
		£101	12	4	£10	3	3

Among the possessions here enumerated is the manor of Shorewell in the Isle of Wight, which had been given to the Abbey, a few years before, by AMICIA COUNTESS OF DEVON, and " lady of the Isle," *together with her heart.* The date of this acquisition cannot be precisely ascertained, for Amicia was left a youthful widow so early as 1245;* but it was probably after 1262, as the donation was confirmed by her daughter Isabella, who in that year became the heiress of her brother Earl Baldwin. The tie which connected the Countess Amicia with the Abbey of Lacock, which we might otherwise have sought in vain, is shown by her foundation charter of the Abbey of Buckland in Devonshire. Among the relations whose spiritual

* She was the daughter of Gilbert de Clare, Earl of Gloucester, and widow of Baldwin Earl of Devon.

health she had then in view, was her daughter MARGARET, *a Nun at Lacock.** The maternal feelings under which she bequeathed *her heart* to rest near that daughter whom she had resigned in this world to be devoted to the services of religion, can be better conceived than described. The Countess Amicia died at an advanced age in 1296. Her body was probably interred at her own foundation of Buckland; her heart at Lacock.

The obit of the Countess of Devon was yearly celebrated in the church of Lacock Abbey on the feast of St. Andrew (Nov. 30), when four bushels of corn were distributed to the poor, and on the eve and day of that feast three poor persons were fed with bread, drink, and meat, to the value of 2*d.* each. †

The reception within the walls of our abbey, in the following year (1297), of the *heart* of the aged NICHOLAS LONGESPÉ, Bishop of Salisbury, the last surviving son of the Foundress, is another instance of pious affection. ‡

AGNES was the name of the Abbess in 1299, at the granting of a lease to Richard le Mareschal of Lacock.§ Her successor was JOHANNA DE MONTEFORT, who occurs in 1303-4. ||

It appears from a document preserved at Lacock Abbey, that on the death of an Abbess named FAITH,

* Leland's Collectanea, vol. i. p. 40.

† See the statement of the annual payments of the Abbey at the close of this Chapter.

‡ The triple division of the Bishop's mortal remains (a practice then customary), has been before noticed in p. 157.

§ Stevens. || See the Appendix.

SUCCESSION OF ABBESSES. 281

during the minority of Richard II., the Prioress of the convent, named AGNES DE WICK, was elected in her stead. The sub-prioress and nuns notify their choice to John of Gaunt, Duke of Lancaster, and King of Castile, and petition for his approval and confirmation of it. That the Dukes of Lancaster were deemed the hereditary "Founders," or patrons of Lacock, as the representatives of the house of Longespé, is shown by some pleadings which took place in the reign of Henry VIII. *

In 1408 the Abbess ELENA presented to the vicarage of Lacock; † and in 1434 a third AGNES presented to that of Cliff Pypard.‡

From the same pleadings above mentioned, it appears that an Abbess, whose name is not mentioned, died on the 6th Feb. 1483; and that MARGERY OF GLOUCESTER was immediately after elected her successor.

To Margery, as appears by the same record, succeeded the last Abbess, JOHANNA TEMYS; and though the date of her succession is not mentioned, it was probably shortly before 1516, when that trial took place. This lady continued to preside until the dissolution and dispersion of her society.

As one of the lesser Monasteries, Lacock was placed in the King's power by the Act of Parliament passed in 1536; but, in pursuance of the

---

* —" domus et ecclesia de Laycok non sunt ex fundacione Regis de jure Coronæ, set ratione Ducatus sui Lancastriæ." See p. 320, and the Appendix, p. li.

† Institutiones of Wiltshire. ‡ Ibid.

clause which empowered him to continue such as he thought proper, it was one of the thirty which he spared and reconfirmed.

But this reprieve was of scarcely three years' duration; for the Abbey of Lacock was surrendered to the King on the 21st of July 1539. The fatal document is still preserved in the Augmentation Office. It was taken before John Tregonwell and William Petre, Clerks in Chancery; and the only signature it bears is that of the former, " p me Jo. TREGONWELL:" but it is ratified by the common seal of the Abbey, from which the accompanying engraving has been made.

This seal is clearly of the same age as the foundation of the Abbey; and represents the Virgin and Child, with the Lady Abbess, placed in a niche below, kneeling in prayer.

To Johanna Temmes, the last Abbess, was assigned a pension of 40*l.*; which she still enjoyed in 1553, when a return was made of the surviving members of the monasteries, to whom pensions then continued to be paid. Her family appear to have benefited by the distribution of the monastic property.*

At the Surrender, besides the Abbess, and the Prioress, there were fifteen other Nuns, to whom the following pensions were assigned, to be paid them half-yearly during their lives: §

* See the account of the Abbey estates hereafter, under Bishopstrow, Hatherop, and Shorewell.

† The first of these lists is now printed correctly from the original in the Augmentation Office, in the volume of original

Sigillum convent beate Marie et Sancti Bernardi de Lacoo.

NUNS AT THE SURRENDER.

	Pensions assigned Jan. 21, 1540.			Remaining in 1553.		
	£.	s.	d.	£.	s.	d.
Johane Temmes, Abbess	40	0	0	40	0	0
Elenor Monmorthe, Prioress	5	0	0			
Anne Brydges	4	0	0			
Amys Patsall	4	0	0			
Elyn Benett	4	0	0			
Margarett Legetton	3	6	8			
Elsabeth Wylson	3	6	8			
Elsabeth Baynton	3	6	8			
Agnys Bygner [Bugmore]	3	6	8	3	6	8
Margarett Welshe	3	6	8			
Johane Marshall	3	0	0			
Elsabeth Wye	3	0	0	3	0	0
Elenor Basdale [Backesdale]	2	13	4	2	13	4
Anne Trace [*married* * 1553]	2	13	4	2	13	4
Scoleast† Hewes [Hures]	2	0	0	2	0	0
Elenor Maundrell	2	0	0			
Tomesyn Jerves [Jarvys]	2	0	0	2	0	0
	£.91	0	0	£.55	13	4

Signed, Jo. TREGONWELL,
WILLIAM PETRE, JOHN SMYTH.

Besides the seven pensions above mentioned, there also remained in charge, in 1553, 9*l*. 6*s*. 8*d*. in fees, and 2*l*. in annuities.

assignments of Pensions, f. 124. The list of 1553 is from Willis, and furnishes the variations in the names which are inserted in brackets.

* Of sixteen Nuns of Ambresbury, surviving in 1553, two were married; and of sixteen surviving of Wilton, the same number. Of the thirteen monks of Bradenstoke, who surrendered in 1540, only four were dead in 1553, and *four* of the survivors were married.

† Scolastica.

Having already seen an account of the property of the Abbey, made within the century of its Foundation, we shall now be enabled to compare it with another, which was formed only a short time before its Surrender. Whatever nominal increase had taken place, during the intervening period of 240 years, in the rents accruing to the convent, it is evident, from the names of the places, that but little addition had been made to the territorial extent of its possessions. If its revenue in money was nearly trebled, its chief estates were the same on which it had originally depended for support. Among the annual *payments* enumerated in the following account, occur some of the most curious facts which have descended to us respecting the history of the Abbey. We are informed of the observances in memory of the Foundress and others, in doles to the poor, and candles about their tombs; it is also there recorded that the Abbey maintained *three Priests*, for the daily celebration of divine services, and " one *discreet and learned* priest, the GENERAL CONFESSOR to the Convent, and *the teacher and preacher of the word of God.*" Some of the principal gentry of the vicinity, as well as the Abbess's own kinsmen, are also named as holding honourable offices in the service of the Abbey.

This is a portion of the general Valor Ecclesiasticus, made when King Henry the Eighth first assumed the supremacy of the Church of England, and determined to appropriate to himself those annates which had been previously rendered to the Pope. The payments to the Pope had been made upon the footing of the old taxation of Pope Nicholas; but the new payments to the Crown were to be made upon the actual value of Church property; to ascertain which this Survey was taken. It is entitled,—

"The true Value of all the Demesnes, Manors, Lands, Tenements, Rents, Tithes, Oblations, and all other profits, coming or belonging annually, or in ordinary years, to the Abbey of Lacock, whether in Wiltshire or in other counties within the kingdom of England, by the Inquisition of Sir Henry Long, Knt. Henry Pole, John Hamlyn, and John Bonham, esqrs. the King's Commissioners.*

	£.	s.	d.
Lacock	52	14	6½
Ambresbury	2	0	0
Bishopstrow	24	6	11
Upham	1	13	4
Slade	2	0	0
Hedyngton	13	19	2½
Shrewton	7	6	8
Weyclescote	6	0	0
Chittern	49	4	3½
Hannam and Bytton	1	6	4
Trowbrygge	0	8	0
Clyff Pypard	10	0	0
Uffcote	0	13	4
Bristol	0	6	8
Carried forward	171	19	9½

* Translated from the "Valor Ecclesiasticus," vol. ii. pp. 115—118. The particulars of each estate will be found more fully stated in the next Chapter.

	£	s	d
Brought forward	171	19	3½
Hatherupp	18	6	4
Woodmancote	5	6	8
Shorewell	8	0	0
£.	203	12	3¼

From this gross income were to be paid the following " Deductions and Allowances."

Remittences of Rent to Chief Lords.

	£	s	d
Chief rent to the Dean of Leicester, issuing from the land called Old Goore	0	0	6
Chief rent to the Rector of Edyngton from land in Bishopstrow	0	2	0
Chief rent to John Pagnam for land in Bishopstrow, called Hyllmede	0	0	1
Chief rent to the King from a tenement in Trowbridge, namely, the price of one lb. of pepper	0	2	0
Chief rent to John Mewes, esq. from land in Shorewell called Slocom, in compensation for one cartload of boughs and two cartloads of thorns	0	2	0
	0	6	7

Annual and perpetual Rents, and Burdens paid annually.

	£	s	d
Pension to the Vicar of Lacok, as more fully appears by a composition	1	0	0
Pension to the Vicar of Winterbourne Shrauton, in augmentation of that vicarage	1	0	0
Paid to the demesnes of Warminster for having common for cattle in that heath, throughout the year	0	2	0
To the Abbat of Cyssetur (Cirencester) for a fine for releasing the Abbess's suit to the hundred of Cirencester	0	1	0
Carried forward	2	3	0

	£.	s.	d.
Brought forward	2	3	0
To William Baleham, for disburdening the common for certain sheep within the demesne lands of the manor of Shorewell	0	6	8
Paid in default of a suit to the court held twice a year at Carisbrook, in the Isle of Wight	0	1	0
Paid for the disburdening the pasture of certain sheep on the Abbess's pasture at Slocom	0	5	0
Money paid annually to the Escheator of Wiltes	0	3	4
Paid to the Warden of the Queen's forest of Blackmore, for having common there for all the Abbess's animals, throughout the year, from time out of mind	0	4	0
For 30 lb. of wax, bought for the maintenance of four candles daily about the tomb of Sir John Blewett, Knt. generally costing 7d. a lb.	0	17	6
For 44 lb. of wax, for *twenty-five candles daily lighted throughout the year,** about the tomb of the Lady ELA LONGESPE, the Foundress, at 7d.	1	5	8
Paid on the Obit of John Goodhyne, as by his charter more fully appears	0	19	0
Paid annually, as part of the charge of the vestments of the Convent, issuing from the rectory of Clyff Pypard, of the gift of John Maydenhyth	8	0	0
For the stipend of three priests, daily celebrating divine services within the Abbey, from the time of its foundation, each taking 6l.	18	0	0
To one discreet and learned priest, the General Confessor of the convent, and the teacher and preacher of the word of God	6	0	0
Distributed on the day of the Purification of the Blessed Mary, from the gift and appointment of Jordan de Kyngston	0	13	4
	£.39	11	6

* Of course they burned only for a short time daily, during the Mass for the Dead.

Yearly Alms.

	£.	s.	d.
Paid and distributed in money to the poor on Good Friday, from the foundation of John Maydenhyth	0	6	8
To the poor in money on the feast of Saint Petronilla the Virgin, from the foundation of Sir John Blewett, Knt. on the appropriation of the rectory of Lacock	2	1	8
To the poor on the feast of St. Bartholomew the Apostle, *for the soul of Lady* ELA LONGESPE, *the Foundress*, eight bushels of corn, worth 5s. 8d. and sixteen cheeses, or dried fish *(allaces)*, worth 8s.	0	13	8
To three poor persons on the eve and day of St. Bartholomew, and on *the eve and day of the profession of the said Lady* ELA LONGESPE, to each of them daily in bread, drink, and meat, worth 2d.	0	2	0
To the poor on the feast of St. Cecilia, for the soul of Lady Margaret Lacy, Countess of Lincoln, four bushels of corn worth 2s. 8d.; and on the eve and day of that feast to three poor persons, in bread, drink, and meat, to each of them daily 2d. worth	0	3	8
In money distributed to the poor on the feast of St. Andrew the Apostle, for the soul of Amicia Countess of Devon, four bushels of corn, worth 2s. 8d; and on the eve and day of that feast to three poor persons, in bread, &c. (as above)	0	3	8
To three poor persons every day during the whole of Lent, in bread, drink, and meat, 6 loaves, 3 pottells of ale, and 6 dried fish, worth in all daily 6d.; the sum for all Lent	1	3	6
Distributed to forty-five poor on the day of the Lord's supper (Holy Thursday), in bread, &c. to each the value of 2½d.	0	9	4½
Carried forward	5	4	2½

SURVEY OF 1535.

	£.	s.	d.
Brought forward	5	4	8½
To the poor on Good Friday 22 of the convent loaves, worth in ordinary years	0	1	2
To one poor person daily throughout the year, two loaves, one pottell of ale, and in food 1*d*.-worth, in all worth 2½*d.* daily. Sum of the whole year	3	16	0½
	£9	1	6

Fees.

	£.	s.	d.
To Sir Edward Baynton, Knt.* Chief Steward of the Monastery, for his yearly fee	2	13	4
To John Bonham, Esq. Receiver-general of all manors, lands, and tenements of the Monastery	2	0	0
To Thomas Temse, Steward of the Courts of the manors	2	0	0
To the same for his fee as Auditor	2	0	0
To Edmund Thame,† esq. as Steward of the Court of the manor of Hatherupp	0	13	4
To Christopher Temse,‡ Steward of the house of the Abbess, for his yearly fee in all things appertaining to his office	6	13	4
To Thomas Mardytt, receiver or collector of the rents of the manor of Lacock	1	6	8
Carried over	£17	6	8

* Of Bromham. cousin-german to the Abbess, whose mother was Jane Baynton, his aunt (see p. 291).

† Of Fairford in Gloucestershire, near Hatherop, a family distinct from that of the Abbess. He was knighted before 1540.

‡ After the Surrender, Christopher Temse was made Receiver of all the possessions of the monastery, by letters patent dated 14 Aug. 31 Hen. VIII. and Sir Edward Baynton and Andrew his son were Chief Surveyors. Ministers' accounts, 31 Hen. VIII.

SURVEY OF 1535.

	£	s.	d.
Brought over	17	6	8
To John Junner, steward, bailiff, and collector of the rents of the manor of Chittern	1	6	8
To John Oldffyld, bailiff and collector of the rents of the manor of Hedyngton	0	13	4
To Howell Appowell, bailiff of the domain or manor of Lacock	2	0	0
	£21	6	8

Sinodals and Procurations.

	£	s.	d.
Money paid to the Bishop of Salisbury every third year, as a pension or sum for his ordinary visitation at Clyff Pypard, 4s. 6d.; at Shrewton rectory, 4s. 6d.	0	9	0
Paid to the same Bishop every third year, as a pension or sum for his ordinary visitation at the monastery of Lacock	2	13	4
To the Archdeacon of Wiltes, annually, out of the rectory of Clyff Pypard, viz. his procurations,* 7s. 5½d.; for his pension, 2s. 6d.; for the pension of the Bishop of Sarum, 3s. 4d.; for the pension of the Dean and Chapter of the church of Sarum, 3s. 4d.; in all	0	16	7½
In money paid annually to the Archdeacon of Sarum for procurations issuing out of the rectory of Shrewton	0	12	6
Total	£4	11	5½

	£	s.	d.
Total value (as before)	203	12	3½
Total of all deductions and appropriations	74	17	7½
And remains clear	£128	14	8

* The same sum as now received, 1835.

PEDIGREE OF TEMMES, THE FAMILY OF THE LAST ABBESS OF LACOCK.

From the Visitation of Wiltshire, made in 1565, by William Harvey, Clarenceux. MS. Harl. 1565, f. 48 b.

ARMS. Quarterly: 1 and 4, Party per chevron wavy Or and Az. three fleurs de lis Counterchanged, *Temmes*; 2 and 3, Argent, a pale lozengy Gules within a bordure Az. Bezanteé, *Lushill*; impaling, Ermine, three bows in pale, *Bowes*.

CREST. An antelope's head erased Or, horned and guttée Sa.

John Temmes, of Rode Ashton * in com. Wilts, marid Jane, daughter and one of the heires of Sr John Lushill, of [Lussell†] in the same com. Knight, sone and heire of Sr Symond Lushell, Knight, lord Lushill, and steward of the household to King Henry the 7, being then erle of Derbye, wch John and Jane had yssue John Temmes, sonn and heire.

John Temmes of Rode Ashton, sonn and heire of John, marid Mary, daughter of John Mychell, of Calston, in com. Wilt. and by her had yssue Will'm son and heire.

Will'm Temmes, of Rode Ashton, sonn and heire of John, marid Jane, daughter of Robert Baynard, of Lackham in the said com. and by her had yssue Robert, sonn and heire, Phillip 2 sonne, George 3 sonn, *Christopher 4 sonn, Thomas 5 sonn,*‡ *Elizabeth, marid to Robert Bath,*§ of Bisshoppstrow, in the said com. clothier.

* Now called Rowd Ashton, the seat of Richard Long, Esq. many years Knight of the Shire, and father, now living, to the present member, Walter Long, Esq.

† Visitation of 1623.

‡ There can be little doubt that the Abbess was sister to these two brothers; the former of whom (as we have seen in p. 289) was Steward of her house, and the latter Steward of the Courts of her manors, and the purchaser of the manor of Bishopstrow after the Surrender. Christopher married ——— Ringwood, and had issue Henry and William. (Visit. 1623.) This Henry was probably the same who witnessed the deed of sale of Bishopstrow, executed by John (his cousin-german) in 1578. (see p. 314.)

§ To this Robert Bathe and Elizabeth his wife, (her brother-

Robert Temmes, of Rodeashtonn, sonn and heire of Will'm, marid to his first wife Margarett, daughter of Will'm [John] Ernley, of Cannyngs in the said com. and by her had yssue Will'm, sonn and heire. After, the said Rob' marid to his 2 wiffe Jane, daughter of *(blank)* Parres, of *(blank)* and wydowe of John Ludlowe, of Hyldeverell in the said com. and by her hath no yssue.

Will'm Temmes, of London, gent. sonn and heire of Robert, marid Elizabeth, daughter of [John*] Best, of London, merchant, and by her hath yssue Elizabeth and Judyth.

Thomas Temmes, of Byshopst[r]owe in com. Wilt. 5 sonn of Will'm aforesaide, marid Elizabeth, daughter of Bowes, of London, merchant, and by her hath yssue John, sonn and heire; Ann, marid to Will'm Jordane, of Chitterne in com. Wilt. and by her hath yssue Marye. †

John Temmes, of Charewell in the Isle of Wight, in com. South. sonn and heire of Thomas, marid Katherine,‡ daughter of Lawrence Stowghton, of Stowghton in com. Surrey, gent. and by her hath yssue Lawrence, sonn and heire, Will'm 2 sonn.

A Richard Temmes was Vicar of Monkton, Wilts. in 1539. (Valor Ecclesiasticus.)

The same arms, impaling a cross patonce, are on the tomb, at Horshill in Surrey, of Susannah, wife of Matthew Teeme, who died Oct. 29, 1718, in her 31st year, " a tender *mother*."

in-law and sister) the Abbess granted a lease of the manor and conventual lands at Bishopstrow, for 99 years (see the account of that estate hereafter).

* Visitation of 1623.

† They also had issue Sir William Jordan, of Chittern, Knt. living in 1623, and Temys Jordan, his younger son. See a pedigree of Jordan in the Visitation of Wilts, taken in 1623; in which Thomas Temvs is styled of West Ashling in Sussex.

‡ Born Feb. 6, 1541-2. In the pedigree of Stoughton, Hist. of Surrey, i. 171, her husband's name is incorrectly printed *Fenys*.

CHAPTER XV.

The Estates of the Abbey.

Lacock—Notton—Hatherop—Woodmancote—Bishopstrow—Hedington—Shrewton—Chittern—Shorewell—Wiclescote—Albourn—Amesbury—Bristol—Bytton and Hanham—Calne—Chicklade—Chippenham—Cliff Pipard—Machinden—Slade—Trowbridge—Uffcote—Upham—Westbury.

In treating of the estates of the Abbey, we shall pursue, in the first instance, the order in which the places are mentioned in the charter of the Countess Ela, viz.—the manors of Lacock, (we next turn to the adjoining hamlet of Notton,) Hatherop, (here is inserted Woodmancote, the contiguous gift of Constantia de Legh,) Bishopstrow, and Hedington, and the advowson of Shrewton. We shall then proceed to Chittern, the gift of William Longespé her Son; then to Shorewell in the Isle of Wight, bestowed by Amicia Countess of Devonshire; to Wiclescote, the early gift of Katharine Luvel; and to Albourn; and, having thus noticed all the estates enumerated in the Taxation of 1291, and which always constituted their principal property, shall finally notice the other smaller estates, which were acquired from various benefactors, and at various periods.

LACOCK.

The existence of a British castle at Lacock, formed by Dunwallo, (whose æra was A.U.C. 285) and of houses belonging to the Earl of Salisbury, previously to the foundation of the Abbey, have been already alluded to.* The account of the place contained in Domesday Book, has not yet, however, been laid before the reader:

"EDWARD himself holds LACOCK. It was held by EDWIN in the time of King Edward (the Confessor), and rated as seven hides. The land is sufficient for nine ploughs. Three hides and a half of it are in demesne, in which are three carucates, seven serfs, twelve villagers, sixteen *coscez*, and three cottars. † There are two mills yielding 17s. 6d. rent; twenty acres of meadow, and half an acre of *vineyard*. The woods are in breadth and length one leuca. The manor is and was (in the Confessor's time) worth £7 (yearly)." ‡

Besides this manor, there was another small one in Lacock, distinct from the fee of Edward of Salisbury, and belonging to that of Alured of Marlborough:

"ALURED himself holds one virgate of land in LACOCK. It is enough for one plough, which is there, with one bordar; and two acres of meadow. It was worth 10s., now 5s. This land (with others before mentioned) CARLO held in the time of King Edward." §

Of this latter portion we are unable to trace the subsequent history; nor is it essential to our present purpose.

In the account of the larger manor, we have the description of a well cultivated and well peopled district. The two mills were no doubt upon the Avon. No church is mentioned; but such a population would not be left long after the Conquest without having the offices of religion brought to their own doors. The probability is that

---

* See pp. 2, 122

† The words *coscez* and *cotarii*, which have been sometimes considered synonymous, are here applied to distinct persons.

‡ Domesday Book, f. 62 b.   § Ibid. f. 70 b.

Lacock owes its church to EDWARD OF SALISBURY, or to his son WALTER, the Founder of Bradenstoke, in conjunction with the lord of the contiguous manor of Lackham, one of the early members of the family of Bloet.

On founding her Abbey, the Countess ELA transferred to the Sisterhood the whole of that manor which had belonged to her ancestor EDWARD, together with " the advowson of the Church " (of which latter more hereafter.)

The Cartulary records several minor gifts and purchases of property in Lacock; but as they are without date, it is difficult to bring them into any order or instructive point of view. In briefly noticing them, we must take them as they occur.

The first is a covenant with Roger de Bloet, then parson of Lacock, respecting a mill with a pool, and a bridge, both of which the Nuns had built; for the former he was to demand nothing from them, and the latter they were bound to keep in repair.*

In the time of the Abbess Beatrix, the successor of Ela, the Convent made an exchange of lands with Sir William Bloet; the latter giving them five acres in Short-furlong, and a spring in Lackham's-ley, from which they might convey water across his land to their conduit. The Nuns gave him in return several small parcels of land amounting to the same number of acres.† Four other documents follow respecting the watercourse.

John Sewal sold to the Abbess Juliana for four marks of silver all his messuages in Lacock; others were quitclaimed by Richard Malloc and Alditha Pilevel; by William of Chippenham, tailor, for 40s.; by Nicholas Flour; by Nicholas son of Roger of Heddington; by Edward Sweyn, Peter of Bristol, Richard of Bristol, Richard Pur-

---

* Cartulary, f. 12 a.   † See the Appendix, p. xviii—xix.

chas, Robert de le Lupegate, Matthew son of John the Carpenter, &c.*

Most of these transactions were probably anterior to the taxation of Pope Nicholas in 1291; when the property of the Abbey in Lacock was rated at £20. At the Survey of 1535 the yearly value † was estimated at £52. 14s. 6½d. of which the particulars are as follow:

	£.	s.	d.
Annual rent and value of 147 acres of arable land, in demesne	4	2	4
Rent of 133½ acres of meadow and pasture, demesne	11	2	6
Fixed rents of all customary and other tenants	31	3	0½
True value of the tithes of the rectory of the parish, in common years, in all things belonging or relating to the rectory	6	0	0
Perquisites of the courts, in ordinary years	0	3	4
Sale of wood, in ordinary years	0	3	4
	£.52	14	6½

"The site of the late Monastery of Lacock, with the parsonage and advowson of the vicarage, and all lands, tenements, rents, reversions and services, tithes, possessions, and hereditaments, in the towns, parishes, fields, and hamlets of Melksham and Calne," together with some tenements in Melksham, which were parcel of the late monastery of Ambresbury, were sold to Sir William Sherington, for the sum of £783. 12s. 1¼d., of which the first payment of £243. 13s. 1¼d. was paid to the Treasurer of the Court of Augmentations, on the 19th Nov. 1544. ‡

---

* Cartulary, ff. 17 a—25 b, 29 a, 33 b, Appx. pp. xix—xxii.

† The revenue accounted for by the King's ministers of 1539-40 will be found in p. 334.

‡ Receipts in the Augmentation Office, 35—36 Hen. VIII., f. lxxiiij.

PEDIGREE OF SHERINGTON.

From the Visitation of Wiltshire, 1565.

ARMS: 1 and 4, Gu. two crosses formées Or, each charged with a cross potent Sa. between two flaunches checky Arg. and Az. *Sherington*; 2. Az. a bend Arg.; 3. Party per pale indented Or and Azure six martlets Counterchanged; impaling, Arg. a chevron Erm. between three talbots guttee.

CREST. A scorpion in pale Or, tail in chief between two elephants' teeth, the upper part checquy Ar. and Az. the bottom Gules and charged with a cross as in the arms.

"Henry Sherington, of Sherington, in the p'ishe of Derham,* in the Com. of Norff. marid Elizabeth, daughter of [...... Felton] and by her had yssue Reignold, sonn and heire, Thomas 2 sonn, John 3 sonn, Will'm 4 sonn, Margerett, Katherin, Mary, and Ann.

Reignold Sherington in the said Com. married and dyed sanz yssue.

Thomas Sherington, in the Com. aforesaid, esqr. 2 sonn of Henry, and heire to his brother, married Elizabeth, dau. and heire of (*blank*) Framsham, in Com. Norff. esqr. and by her had yssue Thomas sonn and heire.

Thomas Sherington, of Sherington, in the Com. aforesaid, [died about 1527] marid Katherin, daughter of William Pyrton, of Littell Bentley, in Com. Essex, esqr. and by her hath yssue Sr Will'm Sherington, Knight, son and heire, Thomas 2 sonn, Henry 3 sonn, Elizabeth, Ann, Ursula, Oliva, Cescille, [married to Robert Southwell, esq. sergeant-at-law, both buried

---

* Sharington, in Norfolk, is a distinct parish some miles from East Dereham. In the reign of Henry III. occurs Gregory de Sharenton, and Peter, who conveyed lands in that place to *Oliva*, daughter of Alan, son of Jordan. But in subsequent times the family were of Cranworth, also near East Dereham Ralph Sherington, esq. great-grandson of John, of Cranworth, married the daughter and sole heir of William de la Val, of Northumberland; and was father of Henry, who married Elizabeth *Felton*, the first in the Wiltshire pedigree above. Blomefield's History of Norfolk.

at Barham, Suffolk. Blomefield's Norfolk.] and others. Elizabeth, marid to Richard Hadok,* of Ulchester; Ursula, first marid to Francis Hall, Comptroller of Calleys, after to John Banester, esq.; Oliva, marid to James Paggett, of London, esqr.

Sr Will'm Sherington, of Lacock, in the Com. of Wilts, Knight, sonn and heire of Henry, marid to his first wife Ursula, dau. naturall to Bourchoire lord Barnes, and by her had no yssue. After hee marid to his 2 wife Elyanor, daughter of [William†] Walsingham, and by her had noe yssue. He marid to his 3 wife Grace, daughter of   Farington, in Com. Devon, and widowe of Robert Paggett, of London, Alderman, and dyed sanz yssue. ‡ [had issue Margaret, wife of William Barnes, of London. *Visit.* 1623.]

Thomas, 2 sonn of Thomas, dyed sanz yssue.

Henry Sherington, of Lacock, in the Com. of Wiltes, esqr. § 3 sonn of Thomas, marid Ann, daughter of Robert Paggett, of London, Alderman, and by her hath yssue Ursula, Grace, and Oliva now liveing.

John Sherington, of Medborne, in Com. Wilts, 4 sonn of Thomas, marid Ann, dau. and heire of (*blank*) Kekwych, of Essex, and by her hath yssue Edward, sonn and heire, Olive 2 sonn, one sonn more, and 4 daughters."

Grace, the second daughter (abovementioned) of Sir Henry Sherington, was married to Sir Anthony Mildmay, of Apthorp, in Northamptonshire; but had no issue; so that the whole inheritance of Lacock came to her sister Oliva, the wife of John Talbot, Esq. of Salwarp, co. Worcester, fourth in descent from John the second Earl of Shrewsbury, from whom it has descended to the present Henry Fox Talbot, Esq.

* Hudkin. Visit. 1623.   † Ibid.
‡ The monument of Sir William Sherington remains in Lacock church. It is large, and covered with sculptured ornaments, but bears no inscription, except the name in gilt letters on the interior of its canopy.
§ Sheriff of Wiltshire 1567, Knighted 1574 (see p. 359).

RECTORY OF LACOCK.

There is in the Cartulary of Lacock a document of a date preceding the foundation of the Abbey, relating to the advowson of Lacock Church. It is a covenant between William Earl of Salisbury, and B. Bluet his neighbour, that each of them should have an alternate presentation to the Church, and that neither of them should have the power of alienating the advowson.* This shows that the Church had been erected at the joint charge of the two lords of Lacock and Lackham.

The advowson of the Church was included with the manor in the Countess ELA's foundation charter; but, before she obtained the license of the Bishop of the diocese for erecting the Abbey, she had been required to enter into a covenant with the Rector, (named JOHN,) to respect in every particular the immunities of the parish church.†

ROGER DE BLOET, the *Persona* whose name has occurred in p. 295, was probably the successor of John. In the year 1290, NICHOLAS LONGESPE, the last surviving son of the Foundress, and who in the next year became Bishop of Salisbury, was Rector of Lacock; and then made a Composition ‡ with the Abbess Juliana, respecting the third part of the tithes of her demesne lands, which he confirmed to the Nuns for the future, as they had before " received them from the time of their foundation." This document explains in what consisted the " *Porcio Abba-*

---

* Cartulary, f. 10 a. Appendix, p. xv.

† The substance of this covenant has been already recited in p. 183.

‡ Printed at length in the Appendix, p. xxiii, being recited in the Bishop's confirmation.

tisse," which was rated at 10*s.* at Pope Nicholas's Taxation in the following year; at which same time the Rectory was rated at £13. 6*s.* 8*d.*, and the vicarage at £5.

The interest of Bloet in the rectory seems to have been finally extinguished in 1311, when the whole was appropriated to the Abbey.*

In 1341, when the Ninth of corn, wool, and lambs, in every parish, was granted to the King, the following return was made from Lacock:

"The Presentation of Ralph Persones, William de Bovedoune, Richard atte Nayssche, and Andrew le Baker, parishioners of the church of Lacock, made before Sir Robert Selyman and his associates, assessors and sellors of the Ninths of corn, wool, and lambs, in the county of Wiltes, sitting at Malmesbury on Friday before the feast of St. Gregory, 15 Edw. III. (March 9, 1341,) declared—That the present Ninth of corn, wool, and lambs, granted to the King, of the church of Lacock, was in the year last past worth £9; and no more, because the Parson of the Church had there a messuage and a carucate of land worth 40*s.* a year, a pasture for oxen worth 8*s.* a year, the parsonage meadow worth 20*s.* a year, the tithe of hay worth 10*s.* a year, three mills worth 21*s.* a year, oblations, obventions, heriots, and small tithes worth 66*s.* 8*d.* a year. There was no foreigner in the parish from whom the fifteenth could be levied, nor any benefice besides the parish church."

By a supplementary return made at New Sarum, on Thursday after the feast of the Ascension, the same jury swore that "the Ninth (as before) was worth £9; and *the ninth due to the Abbess of Lacock was worth 50s.*"

---

* Pat. 4 Edw. II. p. 2, m. 22, " pro eccl. S. Cyriaci apud Lacoc perquirenda a Joanne Bloet, et approprianda." The yearly alms founded by Sir John on the same occasion, has been already mentioned in p. 288. There was afterwards, for some time, a chapel at Lackham; see the Appendix, p. xxv. and Wiltshire institutions, under 1349, and 1352.

At the Valor of 1535 Richard Burton the Vicar returned the profits of his Vicarage at £9. 1s. 4d.; from which were paid for procurations and synodals 13s. 9d. and 3s. 9d. an annual pension to the Abbess of Lacock—(who, as shown in her return, p. 286, paid him an annual pension of £1).

The first "Perpetual Vicar" on record is John de Schryvenham, the first witness to the Composition of Nicholas Longespé, the Rector, in 1290. His successors have been somewhat imperfectly collected from the Bishops' Registers.*

Vicars of Lacock.

1290 John de Schryvenham.
1318 Nicholas Skarpenham.
1342 Roger Baalon; died 1348.
1348 Thomas Bourle.
1361 Stephan de Cosham.
1376 John Gernon.
     Walter Dene, died 1400.
1400 John Smyth.
1401 Roger atte Hurne.
     Nicholas Welde.
1408 William Stephanus, *vice* Welde.
—— Thomas Bertwaye, *vice* Stevenes; resigned 1431.
1431 Thomas Goldebury, *vice* Bretewex; res. 1445.†
1445 John Harvy; deprived 1452.
1452 Thomas Appulby, *vice* Hervy; died 1453.
1453 William Aylward.
1490 Robert Wykes (Rector of Whaddon, Wilts, 1486,) resigned 1508.
1508 Walter Benett, (or Jenett,) res. 1521.
1521 Richard Burton.
     John Milner, ob. 1560.

---

* As printed by Sir Thomas Phillipps, Bart.

† In 1453 Thomas Golbury, late Vicar, had a pension of five marks yearly. Institutiones, p. 144.

VICARS OF LACOCK.

1560 Ralph Bicroft (or Rycrofte) presented by Henry Sheryngton, esq. died 1575.

1575 Robert Temple, res. 1576.

1576 Thomas Wodland.

1580 William Gibson, deprived 1582.

1582 Thomas Prest, presented by Edm. Pyrton, esq. by grant of Anne, widow of Sir H. Sherington.

15·· John Forrest, res. 1592.

1592 Richard Rocke, pres. by Edm. Cooper, by grant of the same Anne; died 1616.

1616 Robert Stapleton, pres. by Dame Oliva Sherington, widow, of Lacock.

16·· John Barnes, d. 1676.

1676 Isaac Sympson, pres. by Sherington Talbot, esq.; d. 1684.

1684 Thomas Hughes, pres. by Sir John Talbot.

168– William Wootton; res. 1689.

1689 Mathew Tate, pres. by Sir John Talbot; res. 1707.

1707 Richard Sadlington, pres by Sir John Talbot; d. 1734.

1734 John Taylor, jun. pres. by John Talbot, esq.; res. 1747.

1747 Thomas Monro, pres. by John Talbot, esq.; res. 1753.

1753 Richard Goddard, pres. by the Bishop, from lapse; res. 1758.

1758 William Atkinson, pres. by John Talbot, esq.; presented by Dean and Chapter of Sarum to the vicarage of Sutton Benger, 1744; died March 30, 1765, retaining both livings to his death.

1765 Edward Popham, D.D. pres. by John Talbot, esq.; a younger son of Edward Popham, esq. of Littlecot, M.P. for Wilts. He was also Rector of Chilton Foliot, where he resided, and died Sept. 16, 1815. He edited Selecta Poemata Anglorum Latina 1774, and Illustrium Virorum Elogia Sepulchralia, 1798. See Memoirs of him in the Gentleman's Magazine, LXXXV. ii. 377, LXXXVI. i. 190.

1814 James Paley, B.A. son of Archdeacon Paley, presented by the Marquis of Lansdowne, trustee for H. F. Talbot, then a minor. Present Vicar 1835.

The Parish Register commences in 1559.

NOTTON, co. WILTS.

Notton is a hamlet adjoining Lacock, at present the estate and mansion of my early and respected friend John Awdry, Esq.

The Nuns acquired their estate here in 1303, when Robert de Bardeneye, having first obtained the royal licence,* in order to obviate the prohibitions of the statute of mortmain, transferred to them two virgates and a half of land in Natton, for which the Abbess Johanna gave him forty marks of silver, † paying at the same time to the King a fine of 26s. 8d. for license to enter upon a lay fee.‡ A minor interest in these lands was quit-claimed to the Nuns by William son of Thomas de la Chambre, of Natton, being a rent of 5s. 7d. and a pound of cummin.§ Other interests at Notton were purchased by the Nuns of Jordan de Heydon, Isabella daughter of Robert Burel, William her son, and Hugh de Lacock, clerk. ‖ The place is not mentioned distinctly from Lacock in the Surveys.

HATHEROP, co. GLOUCESTER.

The manor of Hatherop, near Fairford, probably came to the house of Salisbury as the dower of Sibella Chaworth, the great-grandmother of Ela.¶ It was given by

---

* The charter of King Edward I. is printed in the Appendix, p. xxiv. † Ibid. p. xxv.

‡ Gross. fin. 32 Edw. I. Abbr. Rot. Orig. i. 132.

§ Cartulary, f. 42 a. Appx. p. xxvi. ‖ Ibid. pp. xiv. xxi.

¶ The name of Chaworth, not mentioned by Atkins or Fosbroke in their Histories of Gloucestershire, occurs in the account of Hatherop given in that by Bigland. Fosbroke says

Earl William Longespé to his foundation of Carthusians, and was for some years their place of habitation; but, on their removal to Hinton in Somersetshire, was resumed by the Countess Ela,* who shortly after made it part of her endowment of the Abbey of Lacock.

In the earliest day of its new appropriation, and whilst Lacock had not as yet received the pious Ela as its first Abbess,† a convention was made between the Prioress Wymerca, and Hugh Abbat of Cirencester, relative to the suits of court of the men of Hatherop. It was agreed that the bailiffs of the Abbat should come only twice a year to Hatherop to make view of frank pledge in the court of the Prioress, namely, about the feast of St. Martin, and about Hockeday; ‡ at which all the men of the liberty were to attend, and give each time to the Abbat thirty pence, whether the court were amerced or not, and the amerciaments which arose from the said view, were to remain with the Prioress. Any robber or stolen property taken were to be carried to the prison of the Abbat.

---

the manor was conveyed to Ela Countess of Salisbury by Ingeram le Waleys; but this circumstance probably belongs only to the second estate granted to the Nuns by the Countess of Warwick (and mentioned hereafter), as we know one manor belonged to the Salisbury family as early as the time of Earl William, when he endowed his Carthusians.

* See the particulars of this exchange, already stated in pp. 172—174, *antea*.

† This is clear, because Hugh Abbat of Cirencester died in 1238, and Ela was not consecrated " in primam Abbatissam " (see the Appendix, p. xxviii) until 1240.

‡ Hock-day was a fortnight after Easter: on the etymology of the name there are many opinions; but it was a usual season for courts of inquest, and the payment of money.

The covenant then proceeds to direct the appropriation of the fines in several other contingencies, the particulars of which may be seen by consulting the original document in the Appendix. *

In 1236 Hugelina, widow of Randulf de Landebroil, quit-claimed to the Nuns the third part of a hyde of land at Hetherop, for which quit-claim they gave her forty shillings.†

In the year 1246, Ela Countess of Warwick, whose dower appears to have been secured on the manor of Hatherop (probably among others), acknowledged before the King's justices at Walton that this manor was the right of the Abbess and Convent of Lacock; for which recognizance the Abbess, (her mother the Lady Ela,) granted the same to the Countess for life, to be held by the rent of 100s. paid yearly to herself and her successors. For this grant the Countess of Warwick released to the Abbess her title in £20 land which she had previously held of her brother William Longespé, at Chittern in Wiltshire. ‡

This arrangement continued for nearly forty years; when, in 1284, proceedings were commenced for the Countess's relinquishing her life interest in this estate, then described as a messuage and twelve virgates. On application to the Crown for the licence rendered necessary by the statute of mortmain, a writ for an inquisition *ad quod damnum* was issued; the jury on which returned as their verdict, that the Crown would lose jurymen, fines for murder when the hundred was amerced, and suit of

---

* See the Appendix, p. xxxvii.   † Ibid. p. xxxix.
‡ Cartulary, f. 105 b.; Appendix, p. xl.

that court.* After this, the royal licence was issued.† Finally, in 1287, the Countess quit-claimed to the Nuns her whole title in this manor; and they bound themselves to pay her, in lieu, the yearly sum of £20 sterling, under a penalty of £10 of silver in aid of the Holy Land for every term not observed.‡

By another charter the Countess gave the Nuns all the lands she had purchased of Sir Ingeram le Waleys in the vill of Hatherop, with all the villains thereon, and their *sequela*, the fields, pastures, roads, paths, &c.§

At the taxation of Pope Nicholas, in 1291, the return of the property of the Abbess of Lacock at Hatherop was made up of the following particulars:

	£.	s.	d.
One carucate of land, worth	1	0	0
Fixed rents	0	12	0
Store	0	10	0
	£.2	2	0

The sum was thus small, doubtless in consequence of the annuity of £20 being still payable to the Countess of Warwick, who we know lived until 1297.‖

At the Inquisition of the ninths, in 1341, when the ninth of corn, wool, and lambs in the whole parish of Hatherop

---

* Inq. ad q. d. 11 Edw. I. no. 92, and 12 Edw. I. no. 71, as cited in Fosbroke's Gloucestershire, ii. 451.

† See it printed from the Cartulary in the Appendix, p. xl.

‡ Ibid. p. xxxix.   § Ibid.

‖ See before, p. 162. In the same page it was stated that the Countess visited Lacock in 1287, because the charter above noticed, releasing the manor, is dated there; but, as it was probably bipartite, it was perhaps only the part executed by the Convent which bore date at Lacock.

was found to be £9. 6s. 8d., that of those of the Abbess of Lacock, part of the same, was worth 63s. 1d.*

In the reign of Edward the Third, the family of Handlo were the tenants here; and afterwards Margaret, wife of John de Appulby, daughter and heiress of Richard de Handlo, succeeded.† The Abbess had further confirmation in 1412.‡

The church of Hatherop seems to have been given to the abbey of Gloucester by Ernulphus de Hesdyng, the Domesday lord;§ there were both a rector and vicar before 1291;|| but the party by whom the patronage was exercised, does not appear, as the institutions have not been published. However, a pension of 6s. 8d. from the rectory was paid to the Abbess of Lacock, as returned by James Watson, the incumbent, at the Ecclesiastical Survey of 1535.

At the same time the following return was made of the temporal possessions of the Abbess of Lacock at Hatherop:

	£.	s.	d.
Rent of all demesne lands, meadows, and pastures, let to John Spencer senior	9	0	0
Fixed rents of all tenants, whether free or customary	9	6	4
	£.18	6	4

In the account of the King's ministers, in 1540-41, after the surrender, we find the more particular account which is subjoined:

---

* Nonarum Inquis. p. 410.
† Several records cited by Fosbroke, ii. 451.
‡ Pat. 13 Henry IV.   § Dugdale's Monasticon, i. 116.
|| Taxatio P. Nich.

	£.	s.	d.
Hatheruppe, fixed rents	0	15	0
———— rents of customary tenants	4	10	2
———— rents of tenants at will	2	4	2
———— farm of the manor	9	0	0
Oldegore, rent of lands and tenements*	1	10	0
Hatheruppe, pension from the rectory	0	6	8
———— perquisites of court	0	19	4
	£.19	5	4

This manor, with the pension from the rectory, was in 1548 sold to Sir William Sherington the purchaser of Lacock, for   and 37s. 10½d. reserved rent. He also purchased an estate in this parish which had belonged to the Priory of Bradenstoke; and afterwards sold both to John Blomer, esq.

WOODMANCOTE, co. Gloucester.

This estate was in the parish of North Cerney, about ten miles from Hatherop; and it was given by Constancia de Legh, to GOD AND ST. MARY, in co-operation of the pious design of the Countess Ela, to found in the town of Lacock an Abbey to be called the LOCUS BEATÆ MARIÆ.† She also gave the Nuns her rent of Calmundesden, another hamlet of North Cerney, being 35s. yearly paid her by the Hospitallers of Jerusalem. ‡

This lady, who in one of the charters is styled "widow,"

---

* "belonging to the late house of St. John of Jerusalem." The name of Old Gore has occurred in only one other document relative to the Abbey, namely, among the remittances of chief rent mentioned in the Valor (see p. 286).

† Cartulary, f. 107 b. Appendix, p. xli.

‡ Ibid. f. 106 b. Appendix, p. xli.

was evidently a member of the family of de Mare, who were lords of the manor of the Legh in Wiltshire,* near Malmesbury, and consequently in some instances used that surname. Calmsden had been given to the Knights Hospitallers by Mabil de Mare, wife of William de Legh.† It is remarkable that the seal of CONSTANTIA DE LEGA is among those engraved in Madox's Formulare Anglicanum, although no document respecting her has been discovered therein, or in any other place but the Cartulary of Lacock. The seal is oval, and represents her holding a species of sceptre, or fleur-de-lis slipped, in her right hand, and a hawk on her left; proving her to have been a person of rank. ‡

William de Mare, of Rendcombe, remitted to the Convent of Lacock, for seventeen marks sterling, the homage, fealty, heriot, tallages belonging to him, the aids of ploughing, sowing, harrowing, weeding, mowing, and carrying, and all escheats, and suits of all courts belonging to him and his heirs; except the suit to the view of frank pledge of the Earl of Gloucester, to be made twice a year at Rendcombe. He remitted also to them all distraints, whether to make his eldest son a knight, or to the marriage of his eldest daughter, every scutage and military service, and an annual rent of sixpence, and every other demand which by any accident could be made upon the manor of Woodmancote; and the same to the tenants of the Abbess and the villains in the said manor. §

---

* Testa de Nevill, pp. 137, 156.

† Dugdale's Monasticon, ii. 549.

‡ Henry de Mara is mentioned in the will of the second William Longespé as the principal farmer of his estates (see the Addenda): this testifies the connection between the families.

§ Cartulary, f. 107 a, Appendix, p. xli.

Nicholas de Mare, Rector of the church of Thodesthorn, remitted to the Nuns of Lacock all the title he had in two carucates of land, and 21s. rent in Woodmancote; and Walter, called the son of the chaplain of Egesworth, remitted to them all his lands there. Other smaller gifts or purchases in this place, from Ralph de Maurathin, or Mauyrdin, Agnes his widow, Gilbert de Henleie, and Henry Peverel, are recorded by their deeds in the Cartulary.*

At the taxation of Pope Nicholas, in 1291, the property of the Abbey at Cerney is thus described:

	£.	s.	d.
Fixed rents	0	17	0
One carucate of land	1	10	0
Store	1	4	0
	£.3	11	0

In 1310, Thomas de Cockleberghe and John de Menstreworth applied for licence to give to the Nuns a messuage, 36 acres, and 11s. rent in Woodmancote, previously held of the Abbess by 12d. per ann.;† and three years after the Abbess paid to the King a fine of 30s. for licence to enter this lay fee.‡

In 1454, Willelma wife of John Blount held a messuage and virgate in Woodmancote of the Abbess of Lacock, and left John her son and heir,§ who died in 1468 seised of a messuage and carucate containing 60 acres of land, and 2 of meadow, held of the Abbess, and left Simon his son and heir. ||

---

* See the Appendix, pp. xli, xlii.
† Inq. ad quod damn. 3 Edw. II. no. 75.
‡ Abbr. Rot. Orig. i. 199. § Esc. 32 Hen. VI.
|| Esc. 8 Edw. IV.

At the Survey of 1535 another name appears:

               £. s. d.
Rent of all lands and tenements, with other profits
of the same, let to farm to Edmund Thame, esq. . 5 6 8

The same amount of rent was received by the King's ministers after the surrender, and these lands were afterwards sold to Giles Poole for   and 8*s.* 4*d.* reserved rent.*

BISHOPSTROW, CO. WILTS.

Bishopstrow is in the hundred of Warminster, a mile and a half from that town, and about eighteen miles from Lacock. At the Domesday Survey it was held in demesne by EDWARD OF SALISBURY. He gave part of it, in marriage with his daughter, to Humphrey de Bohun; who, on founding his priory of Monkton Farley,† endowed it with the church of Bishopstrow; and his wife Matilda, of her own gift, bestowed a hide of land in the same place; both of which remained the property of Farley Priory until the dissolution.

The chief interest at Bishopstrow continued, however, to descend in the family of Salisbury, until the Countess Ela founded her Abbey at LACOCK; when the simple words of her charter, "*manerium de Bissopestre cum omnibus pertinenciis suis,*" ‡ were sufficient to confer the whole lordship to the Nuns.

At an early period they also acquired the mill of Bishopstrow; respecting which there are five documents in the Cartulary: 1. a grant from Adam Sweyn of his land and the moiety of the mill, for which the Abbess Beatrice gave

---

* Pat. 39 (?) Hen. VIII. Fosbroke's Glouc. ii. 510.
† See before, p. 57. ‡ See the Appendix, p. ix.

him six marks and a half; 2. the remission, in 1259, from Anastasia, widow of Helias of Bissopestre, of her part of the mill; 3. the like, in the same year, from William de Smalebrok; 4. the gift of two acres of land in Bissopestre from Edward son of Adam Serle; 5. the remission of Emma, wife of Elias Burgeys of Warminster, of her claim in the mill, and in a messuage in Bissopestre, for which remission the Nuns gave her 40s.* Agnes Waspayl also gave the convent, among other lands, an acre on the south side of the church of St. Adelm of Bissopestre.†

At the taxation of Pope Nicholas IV. about 1291, the manor of Bishopestre was rated at £11. 7s. It is thus mentioned in the Testa de Nevill: "Abbatissa de Lacock tenet de Com' Sarum villam de Biscopstre, in purâ elemosinâ, de novo feoffamento, et ipse de Rege de honore de Trobrigg." From the Hundred Rolls (3 Edw. I.) we further learn that it was estimated as half a knight's fee;‡ and the Abbess held there the assize of bread and ale. §

On the inquisition of the Ninths of corn, fleeces, and lambs, taken in 1341, the ninth of those of the Abbess of Lacock in Bishopstrow was valued at the sum of 43s. 2d.||

At the general Ecclesiastical Valuation of 1535 the following return was made of the conventual property at Bishopstrow:

---

* Cartulary, ff. 67 a.—68 b. Appendix, p. xxxi. † Ibid.

‡ "Henr. de Lacy tenet dimid. feod. milit. de R. in cap. in Bissopstre, et Abbatissa de Lakoc tenet dictum dimidium de Henrico." Rot. Hund. vol. ii. p. 276.

§ Ibid. p. 277. || Nonarum Inq. p. 169.

MANOR OF BISHOPSTROW.

	£.	s.	d.
Rent of all the demesne lands, meadows, and pastures, let to Robert Bathe, by indenture, sealed with the common seal	6	13	4
Rent of the farm of the pasture of the Abbess's sheep there, let to Robert Bathe	2	13	4
Fixed rents of all tenants, whether free or customary, of the said manor	14	19	3
Perquisites of the courts held there in ordinary years	0	1	0
	£.24	6	11

It has been already noticed, that Robert Bathe was brother-in-law to Johanna Temys, the last Abbess. The lease mentioned in this return, sealed with the conventual seal, is still existing among the title-deeds of William Temple, esq. the present owner of Bishopstrow. It is dated in the same year, 1534; and is for a term of 99 years, to Robert a'Bathe and Elizabeth his wife. It was assigned, in the 30th Elizabeth, by Clement a'Bathe to his son Richard; and in the 34th Elizabeth by Clement and Richard to Jeffrey Hawkins, of Bishopstrow, clothier.

In 32 Hen. VIII. the Ministers of the King rendered the following account of the annual revenue from the possessions of the late abbey in Bishopstrow and Trowbridge:

	£.	s.	d.
Fixed rents	2	4	1
Rents of customary tenants	5	4	6
Rents of tenants at will	2	2	0
Farm of the manor of Bishopstrow	16	13	0
Rents of tenants in Trowbridge	0	8	0
Perquisites of court at Bishopstrow	1	2	3
	£.27	13	10

In 1544, this estate (subject to the lease to Bathe) was sold to Thomas Temys, gentleman, the brother of the last

Abbess, for the sum of £505. 17s. 6d., being described as "the mannor of Busshopestrowe with the appurtenances, and cccxx sheepe-lettons within the said manor; together with the wood growing in and upon the premises." The first payment of £250 was made to the Treasurer of the Court of Augmentations, Nov. 11, 1544, and payment was made in full, Sept. 24, 1546.* In 1550 the purchase was confirmed by letters patent under the great seal, whereby a grant was made to Thomas Temys, and Elizabeth his wife, of: 1. the whole manor of Busshopstrowe; 2. the wood called Hillwood, containing seven acres, in Bishopstrow; 3. the heath and sheep-walk, and another pasture, called Whight Belles and Hencottes, a cottage called Palmers, a cottage and curtilage called Shepherd's Tenement; 4. the mills called Fullinge Mill, Gygge Mill, and Griste Mill, and five acres of land in Bishopstrow marsh; and 5. the stock of 320 sheep called "whethers." The clear annual value of the whole was then estimated at £26. 10s. 3d. before deducting the tithe; and it was held by the service of the fortieth part of a knight's fee, and the yearly rent of 53s. 0¼d. to the Court of Augmentations, payable by the name of the tenth part thereof.†

In 1578 the manor of Bishopstrow was sold by John Temys to John Middlecot, and Henry Temys was a witness to the deed of sale. Its subsequent descent will be found in Sir R. C. Hoare's History of Wiltshire.

---

* Receipts in the Augmentation Office, 36—37 Hen. VIII. f. lxiiij b, and 38 Hen. VIII. f. lxx.

† Letters Patent, May 1, 4 Edw. IV. printed at length in Hoare's Hundred of Warminster, pp. 70—72.

HEDDINGTON, co. WILTS.

Heddington is in the hundred of Calne, about five miles from Lacock. It is surveyed in Domesday Book among the lands of Edward of Salisbury.

It was a mediety of this manor that was conferred on the Abbey by the original endowment of the Countess Ela; to which gift her son William Longespé gave his consent by a special charter, she releasing to him at the same time an exchange of land in Hatherop, to be made to the Prior and canons of Bradenstoke (who had probably before some interest at Heddington), and also a rent of £10, from Seperige and Heanton.*

John de Ripariis, by his charter, made known to his men of Hedinton, whether free tenants or those in vilenage, that he had given to the Nuns of Lacock, all his land and rent in Hedyngton, for the support of *two chaplains singing for the faithful defunct to the end of time.* †

Michael de Cheldrinton gave them a virgate of land in Hedyngton, for which the Abbess Ela gave him twenty-four marks of silver. John Pie gave them for 10s. a marl-pit; and Ralph Angens gave them all the land he had in this manor. ‡

At the taxation of Pope Nicholas, in 1291, the Convent's estate at Hedyngton was rated at £13. 19s. 2¼d.; and the revenue remained the same at the Valor of 1535, being then described under the following items:

---

* Cartulary, f. 76 a. Appendix, p. xxxii.
† Ibid.   ‡ Ibid. p. xxxiii.

	£.	s.	d.
Annual rent of all demesne lands, meadows, and pastures, let to John Oldffyld, under the Convent seal	5	6	8
Fixed rent of all tenants, whether free or customary	8	11	0½
Perquisites of courts in ordinary years	0	1	6
	£.13	19	2½

The Ministers' return of 31 Hen. VIII. furnishes a different account, the name of Amesbury being connected with Heddington, as follows:

	£.	s.	d.
Hedington, fixed rents	0	6	0
———— rents of customary tenants	9	15	3½
Amesbury, fixed rent	2	0	0
Hedington, farm of the manor	8	6	8
———— perquisites of court	0	0	7¼
	£.20	8	7

SHREWTON, CO. WILTS.

At the time when this place was first connected with the Abbey of Lacock, it went by the name of Winterbourn Syreveton; but after a time the first word was dropped, and the latter was abbreviated to Shrewton, by which the place is now known. It is situated in the hundred of Branch and Dole; and the adjoining parish was called Winterbourn Maddington, though now Maddington only. At a very short distance are Winterbourn Stoke, and Winterbourn Parva, or Asserton; and, indeed, among the downs of Wiltshire and Dorsetshire, this name, derived from the occasional streams which appear only in the winter season, occurs as frequently as that of Roding, or Roothing, in Essex.

MANOR OF SHREWTON.

Among the Wiltshire manors of Edward of Salisbury, surveyed in Domesday Book, are four Winterbourns, beside Winterbourn Stoke. It would therefore be difficult to say which of them is the present Shrewton; though there can be little doubt that the latter name was derived from the place having belonged to Edward and his descendents, the hereditary Sheriffs of Wiltshire, and therefore called the Sheriff's, or Syreve-ton. There is also a Shreveton in Dorsetshire, now called Shrowton, alias Ewern Courtenay.

In her original endowment of the Abbey of Lacock, the Countess Ela included the advowson of Winterbourn Syreveton. The ordination of the church was settled in 1241 by Bishop Bingham; who, after very long and ample compliments to Ela, who had then assumed the office of Abbess, ordained that, on the death or cession of Hosbert, then Rector, the tithe of corn of the whole parish, the demesne fields and chief manse of the church (which, however, was to be held by the Vicar until another was provided for him,) should be appropriated to the uses of the abbey; the rest of the fruits being reserved to the Vicar; and the patronage of the vicarage reserved to the Bishopric (in which it has ever since continued). During the life of the Rector Osbert, he was to pay the Abbey the sum of two marks, under the name of pension of his church; which Hosbert confirmed by a charter of his own. †

By two other charters the Nuns received a tenement at Winterbourn Syreveton from Ivo the merchant; and a rent of 20s. from Hugh Burgonensis. ‡

---

* See the charter in the Appendix, p. xxviii.
† Appendix, p. xxx.   ‡ Ibid.

At the taxation of Pope Nicholas, made about 1291, the Abbess of Lacock was returned to have temporal property at Shrewton to the value of £1; and the church (the appropriation of which is not mentioned) was rated at £8. At the Survey of 1535 the following return was made:

	£	s.	d.
Rent of all lands, meadows, and pastures, let to James Wheler	0	13	4
Rent of the farm of the rectory,* let to James Downe	6	13	4
	£7	6	8

In the Ministers' accounts of 1539-40 the former rent is the same; but the farm of the rectory is advanced to £8. 6s. 8d.

SHOREWELL, ISLE OF WIGHT.

Amicia Countess of Devon, and lady of the Isle of Wight, in her widowhood, gave, with her heart,† to the Nuns of Lacock, her whole manor of Shorewell, with all its appurtenance, and *all the men* dwelling thereon, with their *sequela*. She also granted it as disafforested land, therefore free from any claim as for forest or warren.‡ The gift was confirmed by her daughter, Isabella de Fortibus, Countess of Albemarle and Devon; who also remitted to the Nuns the suit of court, ward, and relief, which was due to her from Shorewell; and by another charter granted that the Nuns should have all the fines of

---

* At the same time the clear value of the vicarage of Shrewton was £7. 0s. 2d.

† See before, p. 279.   ‡ Cartulary, f. 128 b.

the men of the manor, whenever it had happened they were fined in her court of Newport; only they were to attend the hundred-court of West Medina, at Carisbrook, twice in the year.*

At the compilation of Testa de Nevill, early in the reign of Edward I. it was returned that the Abbess of Lacock held in chief of the Countess Isabella one fee, of which she kept in demesne the manor of Shorwell, and one virgate of land in Walpan was then held by the chaplains of Burton.

That portion of the Abbess's privileges at Shorewell, which consisted in suit of court, appears to have been involved in frequent litigation. In the rolls of Parliament of 1347 is a petition of the Abbess, praying the restoration of the amerciaments of the men of the manor in the court of Newport, which had been taken by the King's officers: it was referred to the Chancellor.† The perquisites were probably thereupon restored; but in the reign of Henry the Seventh they were again abstracted, in consequence of an inquisition held Nov. 3, 1508, pursuant to a royal commission, the verdict of which declared that the Abbess, who died in 1483, had held the manor of King Edward IV. *by military service*, but that Margery of Gloucester, her successor, had taken possession of the manor, and had held it until the taking of the inquisition, without having received the legal restitution out of the King's hands, requisite for lands held by that tenure.

In consequence it appears to have been taken into the hands of the Crown, and withheld from the Abbey for

---

* Cartulary, f. 129 b.; see the stipulations more at length in the Appendix, p. xlv.

† Rotuli Parl. vol. ii. p. 182.

more than seven years; when Joanna Temys, the last Abbess, brought forward her plea in Chancery, stating that *the House and Church of* LACOCK *were of the foundation of our Lord the King, by reason of his Duchy of Lancaster*,* and that her predecessor, who died in 22 Edw. IV. was seised of the manor in her own demesne, as of fee, in right of her House and Church, and held it of the heirs of Amicia Countess of Devon, and lady of the Isle of Wight, *in free, pure, and perpetual alms*. The King's counsel claimed the patronage of the Abbey for the King, as in right of the Crown, and not as of the Duchy of Lancaster, and defended the verdict of the inquisition of 1508: but at length the cause was finally settled in the court of Chancery at Westminster, on the 2d of June 1516, and the claims of the Abbess fully confirmed.

At the taxation of Pope Nicholas, about 1291, the Abbess's manor of Shorewell was rated as of £17 yearly value; the inquisition of 1508 stated it was then worth £16 yearly beyond reprisals; and by the Ministers' accounts, after the dissolution, it is shown to be then let for the same sum to Thomas Temys and his assigns for a term of 80 years, by a lease from the Abbess his sister, dated 3 Sept. 21 Hen. VIII.

The cartulary contains several quit-claims to the Nuns from their tenants at Shorewell, to which a general reference is sufficient in this place. †

In a Survey of the Isle of Wight, taken in the 2d Eliz.

---

* The representation of the Foundress of Lacock was considered to have descended through the Lacies to the Earls and Dukes of Lancaster (see the Pedigree at p. 149), and so to the Crown, which thus became the hereditary Founder, or Patron.

† Cartulary, ff. 128 a, 128 b, 131 a, 132 a. App. p. xliv, xlvi.

Shorewell was found to be in the possession of Thomas Temes, esq. At the latter end of the same reign it was purchased by Sir John Legh. *

CHITTERN, co. Wilts.

At the period of the Domesday Survey there were two manors at " Chetre," which had belonged to distinct Saxon proprietors, but were then held in demesne by Edward of Salisbury. They are situated in the hundred of Heytesbury, adjoining to Shrewton already noticed, and have since become the parishes of Chittern All Saints, or Upper Chittern, and Chittern St. Mary. Though now two distinct parishes, they form (says Sir R. C. Hoare) but one manor or lordship, which belongs to Paul Methuen, Esq. of Corsham.

The monks of Bradenstoke had possessions in Chittern All Saints, of the gift of several members of the house of Salisbury; but the Nuns of Lacock had the largest manor there, and it was, indeed, their principal estate, being of greater value than that at Lacock itself.

Their first acquisition in this place appears to have been by the arrangement which the Foundress made with her daughter, Ela Countess of Warwick, in the year 1246; when, in return for a life-interest in the manor of Hatherop (as already noticed under that head), that lady released to the Abbey of Lacock, land of £20 yearly value in Chittern, which her mother, or brother, had previously given her in dower on her marriage.

Two years after, William Longespé was induced to confer on his mother's foundation " the whole land of

---

* Worsley's History of the Isle of Wight.

Cettre," excepting only the knight's fees, with their services, one virgate of land, and half an acre of meadow, and the whole land of Ela Countess of Warwick, (which, under the preceding arrangement, was already in their possession).

This grant of William Longespé received a confirmation from King Henry the Third in 1247;* and nine years after another royal charter gave the Nuns a market, a fair, and free warren at Chittern. †

The virgate of land mentioned in William Longespé's charter seems to have been shortly after relinquished to the Nuns by Alicia de Cettre; and perhaps it was the same Alicia (then called de Cornailes) who also released to them a rent of *cheese* which was due to her in the manor of Chittern. In the same manner Walter the Falconer released to them an annual cart-load of boughs, which were due to him from their wood of Chicklade, in right of the tenement he held of them in Chittern. By another charter, the Abbess Ela, and her Convent, released to John Falconer the service he owed them for three virgates of land in Chittern, namely, *one sparrow-hawk and one falcon;* instead of which he was to pay them yearly half a mark of silver. By another covenant he resigned to them his title to five acres in the east field of Chittern, for which they gave him four marks and a half of silver, four quarters of wheat, and five quarters of barley.

Three other charters in the cartulary, relating to Chittern, (and one of which furnishes the name of the Abbess Juliana,) belong to the year 1289, and record the purchase

---

* Cartulary, f. 43 b. Rot. Cart. 32 Hen. III. m. 3.

† Rot. Cart. 41 Hen. III. m. 9.

from William de Horton, Margaret widow of Edmund le Rous of Beremham, and Matilda widow of John de Merweden, of their titles to one messuage and two carucates of land in Chittern, for which they each received 20s.*

At the Taxation of Pope Nicholas, in 1291, the estate of Lacock Abbey at Chittern was rated at 25l. 13s. which exceeded by one fifth the value of the lay property of the monastery at Lacock.

At the inquisition of the ninths, in 1341, the ninth of corn, fleeces, and lambs, in the parish of Chittern, was valued at 56s. 8d. within which sum the portion belonging to the Abbess of Lacock was valued at 21s. 3d.†

In 1447 the belfry of the Abbess of Lacock, and the bell in the same, and all her other houses in the manor of Chittern, were suddenly burnt by lightning.‡

In the ecclesiastical survey of 1535 we find the following particulars relating to Chittern:

	£.	s.	d.
Rent of all demesne lands, meadows, and pastures, let to John Morgan and William Merkett	10	10	0
Fixed rent of all tenants, whether free or customary	24	11	7½
Rent of the farm of the sheep-walk	13	6	1
Rent and profits of courts	0	16	0
	£.49	4	3½

But the actual receipts five years after, when the estates were under the management of the King's " ministers," show a considerably larger sum, partly arising, however, from the sale of timber:

---

* Cartulary, f. 58 b. Appendix, p. xxvii, xxviii.

† Inq. Non. p. 156.

‡ Pat. 25 Hen. VI. m. 1. The Pat. 4 Edw. IV. p. 1, m. 1, also relates to this manor.

		£.	s.	d.
Fixed rents	. . . .	1	7	0
Rents of customary tenants	.	19	0	3½
Rents of tenants at will	. .	2	14	0
Diverse farms . . .	.	39	18	8
Sale of wood	. . .	21	13	0
Perquisites of courts	. .	0	16	7
		£.84	19	6½

The John Morgan mentioned in the Valor was not the first of his family who was farmer of the manor of Chittern. A few years before, Edward Morgan, of Chittern, esq. (apparently his brother) died seised of the manor, as held under the Abbess.* In his will, quoted by Sir R. C. Hoare, he mentions his uncle, John Morgan senior, John Morgan his brother, and his children Peter, Edward, Philip, John, Isabel, Elizabeth, Jane, and Joan.†

Anne Temys, neice to the last Abbess of Lacock, was married to William Jordan, of Chittern;‡ but no connection of that family with the abbey lands, has been traced. The names of Milbourne and John Flower occur as the principal landholders after the dissolution, and they were succeeded by the family of Michell.

WICLESCOTE, CO. WILTS.

This place is surveyed in Domesday Book under the land of Hugh Lasne. Its name does not appear in modern lists of the villages of Wiltshire: but it was a hamlet of the parish of Wroughton, and it seems to be identical with Coate, seen on the map between Swindon

---

* Inq. post mort. 20 Hen. VIII.
† Hoare's Hundred of Heytesbury, p. 171.
‡ See before, p. 292.

and Wamborough. The donor was Katharine Luvel, who was sister to Philip Basset, the second husband of our Foundress's daughter, Ela Countess of Warwick.* Philip

---

* See before, p. 160; where, however, Philip is incorrectly stated to have been son of William Basset. By a comprehensive pedigree of this wide-spreading house, formed by Erdeswick and Dugdale, and printed in the History of Leicestershire, vol. iv. p. 904, it is shown that William Basset, of Sapcote, was cousin-german to Philip. The latter was the son of Alan Basset of Wycombe, by Aliva, daughter of Stephen Gay (not Gray, as there printed), which Alan was a grandson of Ralph, Chief Justice of England in the time of Henry I. Philip himself was Chief Justice of England, appointed in 1261, as was his son-in-law Hugh le Despenser. We may add that Philip Basset and his sister Katharine were also cousins once removed to the daughter-in-law of the Foundress ELA, the wife of William Longespé the Crusader; as shown in the following brief table:

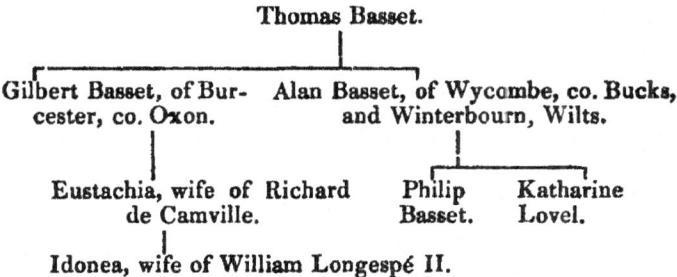

Katharine was the wife of John Lovel, the direct ancestor of the Barons Lovel, of Tichmarsh. In the pedigrees of Lovel she is incorrectly called Aliva. That was the name of her mother, as above mentioned; as also of her neice, the heiress of Philip Basset, married first to Hugh le Despenser, and afterwards to Roger Bigod, Earl of Norfolk.

Basset confirmed his sister's gift, by charter, and by a second remitted to the Nuns the suit of court due from the land to his manor of Wootton. Another charter states that Katharine had bought the land of Roger Lof,—that is, probably, his interest as mesne tenant; who, again, remitted to the Nuns, by charter, his title to the estate, on the receipt of five marks; and John Lof his son confirmed the same.* At the taxation of Pope Nicholas, about 1291, this estate was rated at 2*l*. 10*s*. In 1530 (4 June, 22 Henry VIII.) it was let, for sixty years or term of life, to John Goddarde, sen., John, Thomas, Thomas *(ita)*, and John his sons, at the annual rent of 6*l*.; and it was granted by the King to the same party about 1540. †

ALBOURN, CO. WILTS.

This is a small town six miles and a half north-east of Marlborough. The name does not occur in Stevens's extracts from the Cartulary; but the estate of the Abbey here was an early acquisition; for we find it in the Taxation of Pope Nicholas in 1291, rated at 1*l*. 10*s*. It is also mentioned in the Hundred Rolls of 1285 (13 Edw. I.)

"The Abbess of Lacock holds a certain tenement in the manor of Audeburne, which used to follow this hundred (Selkeley), as the other free tenants of that manor; and that suit has been subtracted for sixteen years, the jurors know not by what warrant." ‡

After this, the name of this estate does not occur.

---

* These several charters are contained in the Cartulary, fol. 82 a—83 b; see the Appendix, pp. xxxiii—xxxiv.

† Ministers' Accounts, 31 and 32 Hen. VIII. in the Augmentation Office.

‡ Rot. Hundred. ii. 270.

We have now reviewed, in the order of their importance and period of acquisition, all the possessions of the Abbey, the names of which occur in the Taxation of Pope Nicholas, made in 1291. Scarcely any property of importance was acquired after that time: but the remaining estates will now be briefly noticed in alphabetical order.

AMESBURY, co. WILTS.

Matilda Eborardi gave all her land in the manor of Ambresbury; for which Philip de Depeford, her widower, acknowledged himself to be bound to pay the annual sum of 40s. for ever.* The same was described in the Valor of 1535, as a "chief rent from the land of the Lady Prioress of Ambresbury, lying in West Ambresbury." In the Ministers' accounts, Ambresbury is connected with Hedington.†

BRISTOL.

Agnes, widow of Athelm Germund, gave the Nuns two stalls, or shops, in the town of Bristol, charged with an annual rent to the King of 12d., for every service; and Matilda, his daughter, gave them 2s. annual rent from her house which was situate between that of Gerard le Franceis and the church of St. Lawrence, free of every secular service. John Tyke, of Bristol, gave a house which he held near Monkbridge, with the vacant land thereto belonging. ‡

---

* Cartulary, f. 63 b. App. p. xxx.
† See before, p. 316.   ‡ Cart. f. 123. App. p. xliv.

At the Survey of 1535 the rent of these tenements in ordinary years was stated to be 6*s.* 8*d.*; in the Ministers' accounts of 1539-40, 13*s.* 4*d.*

BYTTON AND HANHAM, CO. GLOUCESTER.

Petronilla, daughter of Robert de Damenville, gave the Nuns twenty-two acres of arable land of her demesne in Bytton, (five miles from Bristol) viz. in Northfelde, &c. *

Robert Marmiun remitted to them all the title he had in the lands and tenements which Robert Perpunt held at Hanum (in the parish of Bytton); for which release the Nuns gave him 40*s.* †

At the Surrender, both these estates were let to John Taylor; Hanham, by lease dated 11 Feb. 24 Hen. VIII. to him, Juliana his wife, and John his son, at the rent of 13*s.* 4*d.*; and Bytton, by lease dated 4 March, 21 Hen. VIII. to him, and John and Philip his sons, at the rent of 13*s.* ‡

CALNE.

Galiena of Calne, the widow of Herbert fitz-Peter, gave to the Nuns a messuage in that town, of the King's fee, and a messuage in Church-street, an acre of land in Rix-furlong, another at Bernsted, six acres which she had bought of Nicholas Cynnoc, two purchased of Walter son of Matthew le Bret, and all the land lying between Hernewie-street, and the lands held by Gille the Baker and Humfrey Bere; paying thence annually 6*d.* to the King, 12¼*d.* to the Rector of Calne, 6*d.* to the heirs of Nicholas Cynnoc, and for service to the King whatever was due; and to the heirs of Walter son of Matthew le Bret 3*d.* and to the heirs of Alexander de Stodele 8*d.* §

---

* Cart. f. 119 b, 120 a. App. p. xliii.   † Ibid.
‡ Ministers' Accounts.   § Cart. f. 94 b. App. p. xxxv.

This last rent of 8*d.* was afterwards remitted to the Nuns by Roger de Stodlegh.*

No property of the Abbey at Calne is noticed in the Valor of 1535; but in the Ministers' accounts of 1539-40, occurs merely:

   Calne—a vacant plot of land . 6*d.*

CHICKLADE.

The Abbey had a close in the wood of Chicklade, connected with their estate at Chittern. In 1267, Walter Giffard, the Priors of Brumere and Farley, William le Droys, Simon de Brokeburg, and Benedict Silvester, consented that the Nuns should hold for ever their close at Chicklade whether old or new.†

The title in this tenement, and in the custody of the wood of Chicklade, was quit-claimed to them by Joan daughter of William Larcher.‡ The cartload of boughs, which one of their tenants, Walter the Falconer, claimed in right of his tenement in Chittern, has been already mentioned under that place.§

CHIPPENHAM.

Agnes de Roudon gave all the land which Roger Soper once held, with the buildings and all appurtenances, in the town of Chippenham, and one plot of land; ‖ and Henry of Bechampton gave all his land and tenement in the same town.¶

---

* Cart. f. 94 a. App. p. xxxv. † Cart. f. 52 b. App. p. xxvi.
‡ Cart. f. 53 b. App. ibid.   § See p. 322.
‖ Cart. f. 96 b. App. p. xxxvi. ¶ Cart. f. 97 a. App. ibid.

CLIFF PYPARD, co. WILTS.

The name of this place does not occur in Stevens's extracts from the Cartulary. The advowson of the church became the property of the Abbey about the year 1398; being the gift of John Maydenhithe.* The greater part of its revenue, namely 8*l.*, was expended in the vestments of the convent, and 6*s.* 8*d.* was distributed in alms to the poor on Good Friday. †

In 1535, this rectory was let to John Hoper at 10*l.* rent; but in the Ministers' accounts of 1539-40, the fee-farm of the rectory is set down as 1*l.* 16*s.*

The following Vicars were presented by the Abbesses of Lacock:

1421 Nicholas Frankelyn, vice John Smyth; res. same year.
1422 John Cook, vice John King.
    John Derneford, res. 1434.
1434 William Towe.
1436 John Derneford, pres. by the Abbess Agnes,‡ res. 1439.
1439 Nicholas Kempston, res. 1441.
1441 John Cleydon, d. 1468.
1468 William Hegges, exchanged for vicarage of Rowde 1489.
1489 Richard Foster (Vicar of Rowde 1485), died 1513.
1513 John Gerrard, d. 1544.
1544 William Hodgekinson, presented by Thomas Temyse, on the grant of Joan Temyse, late Abbess.

---

* Pat. 22 Ric. II. p. 2, m. 14, 15. "Joh'es Maydenhithe, et alii, pro Abb' de Lacock, Clyve Pipard dimid. acr' terr' et advoc' eccl'ie approprianda." The manor and advowson had been named in the inquis. p. mort. of John de Cobham of Chissebury, Wilts., in the preceding year, 21 Richard II.

† See before, pp. 287, 288.

‡ In the Wiltshire Institutions, p. 126, the two lines, "Agnes Abbatissa de Lacok," and "Johannes Heryng, armiger," patron of Foxlegh, are transposed.

MACKINGDON, co. WILTS.

This is the name of a manor in which the Abbess of Lacock acquired an interest, about the year 1297, from the gift of Isabel de Pipard;* but how long it belonged to the Convent does not appear.

SLADE, co. WILTS.

Joan de Oseville, widow of William de Rugdon, gave the Nuns 40s. yearly rent of a tenement which Walter of the Slade held in the parish of Box, together with the same Walter (being a serf, attached to the land), and all the service due from him and his heirs. The estate was free of all secular service. † This gift was confirmed by Walter de Pavely. ‡

Walter de Godarvile § released to them the suit which Walter de la Slade was wont to make to him in his hundred of Chippenham, from three weeks to three weeks. ||

---

* " Maghinden maner' extent. Isabel Pipard pro Abb'issa de Lacock." Esc. 25 Edw. I. no. 54. Calendar, vol. i. p. 143. In the Testa de Nevill, Richard Pipard appears as holding half a knight's fee in " Mekindon."

† Cart. f. 97 a. App. p. xxxvi.   ‡ Ibid.

§ Walter de Godarville, the lord of Chippenham, was in 1216 a Knight of the household of the famous Falkes de Breant (often mentioned in connection with the Earl of Salisbury in the early part of this volume); and in that year gallantly defended Hertford Castle against Louis of France. In 1231, being Warden of the castle of Montgomery, he there fell into a stratagem contrived by a monk, who induced him to ford a river at an unsafe place. (Matthew Paris.)

|| Cart. f. 100 a. App. xxxvii.

In the Valor of 1535 this is described as a chief rent of 40*s.* arising from the land and tenements of Henry Nowell, and again as a "fixed rent" from Richard Nowell in the Ministers' accounts.

TROWBRIDGE.

Ralph le Franceis gave to the Convent a burgage and land which he had of the gift of Adam the Goldsmith in the town of Trowbridge, paying every year to Adam 1*d.* and to the chief lord 1 lb. of pepper, for the whole service. *

In the Valor of 1535, and again in the Ministers' accounts, the rent of this tenement is mentioned as being 8*s.*; in the latter the name of Trowbridge is also mentioned as being connected with some rents at Bishopstrow. †

UFFCOTE, co. WILTS.

This place is situated between Cliff Pypard and Draycot Foliot, in the hundred of Kingsbridge.

Humphrey de Bohun, Earl of Hereford and Essex, Constable of England, gave the Nuns various rents in Offcote, amounting to 19*s.* 4*d.* ‡ remitting them at the same time 12*d.* due to him from a tenement in Heddington. § He also directed the several tenants, Walter Mauduit of the Frithe, Walter de Okeburn, Peter Bonhome of Ofcote, and the Prior or Master of the hospital of St. John at Calne, to render the services due for the same

---

* Cart. f. 98 a. App. xxxvi.   † See before, p. 313.
‡ See the particulars in App. p. xxxiv.   § Cart. f. 87 a.

tenements in future to the Abbess.* In 1280 the Master of Calne Hospital engaged, by charter, to pay the rent of 12*d.* as before, but the Abbess remitted his suit of court every three weeks, for suit twice a year, with 12*d.* for scutage. †

In the Valor of 1535, and in the Ministers' accounts, we find this only particular at Uffcote:

Chief rent issuing from the land of John Savage   13*s.* 4*d.*

UPHAM, CO. WILTS.

William Longespé gave the convent all the land which had once belonged to Nicholas de Hamptun in Upham, ‡ near Albourn. The estate was let by the Abbess 14 Jan. 19 Hen. VIII. to John Godderd, and to John, Richard, and Thomas his sons, at the annual rent of 1*l.* 13*s.* 4*d.*; and was granted to him by the King, with the estates at Wiclescote and Wamborough.

WESTBURY.

Anastasia de Pavely gave 20*s.* annual rent in the manor of Westbury, which was confirmed by her father Walter de Pavely.§ This was either the Walter who died in 1297, or his grandfather of the same name, who died in 1255;|| in which latter case his daughter may have been the same Anastasia, who, as the widow of Elias of Bishopstrow, has been before mentioned under that place.

---

* Cart. f. 88 a. App. p. xxxv.
† Ibid. f. 89 b. App. ibid.   ‡ Cart. f. 86 a. App. p. xxxiv.
§ Cart. f. 65. App. p. xxx.
|| See the pedigree of Pavely, in Hoare's Hundred of Westbury, p. 3.

Account of Receipts at Lacock, by the King's Ministers, in 31 Hen. VIII. (1539-40).

(Abstracted from the original Roll in the Augmentation Office.*)

	£	s.	d.
Fixed rents	1	18	3
Rents of customary tenants	18	7	10
Rents of tenants at will	10	14	4½
Various Farms	19	5	6
Farm of the Rectory	6	13	4
Movable rents of 6 cocks and 18 hens from customary tenants	0	4	0
Annuity from the Vicarage	0	3	9
Tolls and profits of the yearly fair on St. Thomas's Day	0	2	4
Perquisites of the two courts held this year, with 30s. fines of lands	2	11	5
	£60	0	9½

Under the fourth head of "Farms" occur:

	£	s.	d.
The farm of the Mansion called the Abbat's lodginge, with two houses called the Parsonage and the Gatehouse, with the bakehouse, brewery, barns, stables, dovecotes, gardens, orchards, pools, &c.	2	0	0
Farm of fishing on Avon, from the foot-bridge between Lacock and Beauley, to the end of the meadow called Rydingmeade	0	1	0
Farm of 307 acres of arable land	5	2	4
Farm of sheepwalk and three acres belonging, called the Barton	0	3	0

---

* In the roll for the next year, abstracted in the New Monasticon, no account is rendered from Lacock, because it had been then granted to Sir William Sherington.

CHAPTER XVI.

Dissolution of Religious Houses in England—Dispersion of the Nuns of Lacock—VALEDICTION, and Last View from Old Sarum—Concluding Reflections.

WE have now traced the annals of Lacock Abbey, to the time when that royal exemplar of all that was most ruthless in tyranny—all that was most inexorable in revenge—all that was most odious and loathsome in lust—all that was most sordid and insatiate in avarice—HENRY THE EIGHTH, with the abused title of DEFENDER OF THE FAITH, smote, through the Kingdom, the unnumbered beautiful edifices, which had served, in their earlier day, the cause of peace, learning, hospitality, and charity; and which, in lieu of devastating Poor-laws, might, under proper regulations, have continued to serve the same holy purposes, reformed, like the Church of England, after the BIBLE HAD BEEN OPENED, and human traditions had vanished, like the dreams of the Seven Sleepers!* But *venit summa dies!* The word was pronounced—" Down with them, even unto the ground!" In the majesty of silent desolation, they yet seem to hallow the scenes, through the Land, where their august and scattered fragments are strewn.

* Latimer, with his honest earnestness, entreated two or three in every shire might be continued, *not in Monkery*, but as establishments for learned men, &c. and for the sake of hospitality. Southey's History of the Church.

Among these desolated houses, Lacock has preserved, from that day to this, its most perfect ancient form, the cloisters, the cells of the Nuns, its ancient walls and ivied chimnies, almost entire.

The hypocritical formality with which this imperial robbery was accompanied, would excite every feeling of virtuous indignation, if the humble and uncomplaining submission of the helpless daughters of piety and charity did not demand our tears. Let us contemplate the scene which in all these houses of religion, peace, seclusion, and charity, was generally exhibited, at the time when the stern visitation, by interested Commissioners, took place. The Abbess and Nuns, or Prior and Monks, are summoned before the visitors in the Chapter House.

In the instance of this Nunnery, the Abbess and her Nuns are called before these same Commissioners, having offered up their supplications for the last time together, and we may conceive them standing in silent submission before the army of cold and acute Inquisitors, in the Chapter House of their Convent. The instrument has been already prepared, signifying that the Abbess and her Nuns, " of their own *will* and free *consent*, without *compulsion*," did, out of " pure conscience," resign for ever FOR THE KING'S USE, their *whole property and possessions!!* and this instrument they were *compelled* to confirm even for the morsel of bread granted in their destitution!

All remonstrance, complaint, or refusal, were equally interdicted; the crimes alleged were such as the Wolf could easily find when the Lamb was accused; though many of the charges, without proof, are too enormous not to excite instant indignation at the falsehood. See, in Speed, the disgusting catalogue of monastic monsters, so set down, in cold blood, with not the slightest proof adduced, and with no reply, but indignant silence!

Undoubtedly, abuses and relaxation of moral discipline, in many instances, were found.

But there is one calm dispassionate appeal, so touching and so natural, of one Abbess, that I shall lay it before the reader. The writer is the Abbess of that very convent, GODSTOW,* in Oxfordshire, where the beautiful, but unfortunate, mother of the first noble Longespé, Fair Rosamund, had her tomb.

---

* The following exquisite Latin lines, on the ruins of God-stow Nunnery, were written by Archbishop Markham, when at Oxford:

>Qua nudo Rosamonda humilis sub culmine tecti
>   Marmoris obscuri servat inane decus;
>Rara intermissæ circùm vestigia molis,
>   Et sola in vacuo tramite porta labat.
>Sacræ olim sedes riguæ convallis in umbrâ,
>   Et veteri pavidum religione nemus.
>Pallentes nocturna ciens campana sorores
>   Hinc matutinam sæpe monebat avem;
>Hinc procul, in mediâ tardæ caliginis horâ,
>   Prodidit arcanas arcta fenestra faces.
>Nunc muscosa extant sparsim de cespite saxa,
>   Nunc muro avellunt germen agreste boves.
>Fors et tempus erit, cùm tu, RHEDYCINA, sub astris
>   Edita, cum centum turribus ipsa rues.

Letter of the Abbess of Godstow to Cromwell, the Visitor, complaining of Dr. London.

"Pleasith hit your Honour, with my moste humble dowtye, to be advertised, that where it hath pleasyd your Lordship to be the verie meane to the King's Majestie for my preferment, most unworthie to be Abbes of this the King's Monasterie of Godystowe; in the which offyce I truste I have done the best *in my power to the mayntenance of God's trewe honour*, with all truth and obedience to the King's Majestie; and was never moved nor desired by any creature in the King's behalfe, or in your Lordship's name, to *surrender and give up* the House; nor was ever mynded, nor intended so to do, otherwise than at the King's Gracious Commandment, or yours. To the which I do, and have ever done, and will submit myself most humblie and obedientlie. And I TRUST TO GOD, that I have *never offendyd God's Laws*, neither THE KING'S, wherebie that this poore Monasterie ought to be suppressed. And this notwithstanding, my good Lorde, so it is, that Dr. London, whiche (as your Lordship doth well know) was agaynst my promotion, and hath ever sence borne me great malys and grudge, like my mortal enemye, is sodenlie cummyd unto me, with a greate rowte with him, and here doth *threten me and my Sisters*, sayeng that he hath the King's Commission to suppress this House, spyte of my teeth. And when he saw that I was contente that he shoulde do all things according to his Commission, and shewyd him playne that I wolde never surrender to his hande, being my awncyent enemye; now he begins to entreat me, and to *invegle* my Sisters, one by one, otherwise than ever I herde tell that the King's subjects hathe been handelyd, and here tarieth and contynueth, to my greate coste and charges, and will not take my answere that I will not surrender till I know the King's Gracious Commandment, or your good Lordship's. Therefore I do moste humblie beseche you to contynue my good Lorde, as you ever have bene; and to directe your honorable letters to remove him hens. And whensoever the King's gracious commandment, or yours, shall come unto me, you shall find me most reddie and obeyant to folloe the same. And notwithstanding that Dr. *London*, like an untrew man, hath informed your Lordship, that I am a spoiler and a waster, your good Lordship shall know that the contrary is trewe; for I have *not alienatyd one halporthe* of goods of this Monasterie, movable or unmovable, but have rather increas'd the same, nor never made lease of any farme or peece of grownde belongyng to this House, or then hath beene in times paste, alwaies set under Convent Seal for the wealthe of the House. And therefore my very truste is, that I shall find the Kynge as gracious Lord unto me, as he is to *all other* his subjects, seyng I have not offendyd; and am and will be moste obedyent to his most gracious commandment at all tymes with the Grace of Allmighty Jesus, who ever preserve you in honour longe to endure to his pleasure.

Amen. Godistow, the Vth daie of November.
Your moste bownden Beds Woman,
KATHERINE BULKELEY, *Abbes there*.

This simple and affecting letter, from the very House where the Mother of Longespé was buried, is a proof of this poor woman's blameless integrity, and, that of the Sisters of her mournful society. It is also a proof of her pious resignation; and, moreover, a proof to what hard measures, and to wh worldly craftiness, she, with so many others, was exposed.

Notwithstanding all the enormities, the account of which the Visitors published, I should be much more inclined to think that most of the Superiors and Sisters of these Houses were guilty of no more than this poor Abbess; that is, guilty of having possessions, to which they were legally entitled, and for which insatiate avarice, and tyranny, panted.

Of what description of persons many of the Commissioners were, is proved by the conduct of this very Dr. London, who could insult a virtuous woman in her sorrows, and who himself afterwards, convicted of Perjury, was justly exposed to public degradation and scorn.

The measures of the Commissioners were imperative, and sometimes they proceeded, as at Glastonbury, to the extreme penalty of death, on a charge of HIGH TREASON! On the other hand, if they recommended the religious to the King's favour, it was on account *of their readiness to yield* to the imperial mandate!

The following Letter of the Prior of Hinton, the sister-foundation of Lacock, addressed to his brother in London, contains some remarkable passages, presenting the picture of a mind hesitating between a sense of duty and the terrors of arbitrary power:[*]

[*] From Ellis's Original Letters, Second Series.

Jhus.

In Owr Lord Jhesu shall be yowr Salutation. And where ye marvelle that I and my brotherne *do nott frelye and voluntarilie geve and surrendure* upe owr Howse at the mocyone off the Kyngs Commissinars, but stonde styfflye (and as ye thynke) obstenatlye in owr opynion, trulye Brothere I marvelle gretlye that ye thynke soo; but, rather that ye wolde have thowght us lyghte and hastye in gevyn upe that thynge whyche ys *not owrs to geve, but dedicate to Allmyghtye Gode for service to be done to hys honoure contynuallye*, with other many *goode dedds off charite* whiche daylye be done in thys Howse to owr Christen neybors. And consideryng that ther ys no cause gevyn by us why the Howse shull be putt downe, but that the service off Gode, religious conversacion off the bretherne, hospitalite, almes deddis, with all other owr duties be *as well observyde in this poore Howse as in eny relygious Howse in thys Realme or in Fraunce;* whiche we have trustyde that the Kynges Grace wolde considere. But, by cause that ye wrytte off the Kyngs hye displeasure and my Lorde Prevy Sealis, who ever hath byn my especialle good Lorde, and I truste yette wyll be, *I wyll endevere* my selffe, as muche as I maye, *to perswade my brotherne* to a comfformyte in thys matere; soo that the Kyngs Hynes nor my sayd good Lorde shall have eny cause to be displeside with us: trustyng that my poor brothern (whiche knowe not where to have theme lyvynge) shall be charitable looke uppon. Thus our Lord Jhesu preserve yow in grace. Hent'. x. die Februarii.

E. Hord.

To hys brother Alen Horde in
Medylle Tempulle, dd.

The pensions assigned to the superiors were generally sufficient, and they frequently obtained the opportunity of benefiting their relations by a favourable lease, or an incipient title to some of the conventual estates, as appears to have been the case with the Abbess of Lacock.

The prize was thus held out to those who, in uncomplaining acquiescence to irresistible power, resigned their ancient homes, so long devoted to seclusion and prayer. But what was held out to those less complying? not the prize, but punishment. Crimes the most revolting and incredible were brought forward, as we have said, on the gratuitous depositions of *interested* men, without trial or witnesses, or judge or jury!

Burnet, bred among the Iconoclasts of the school of John Knox, seems, though an English bishop, quite convinced of the justice of the infliction, presuming that " these Houses were *built solely on fraudulent pretences* of praying the souls of the Founders out of purgatory!" No! These beautiful buildings were raised *pro salute animarum*—for the souls' health of the Founders and benefactors; but were they built for this only? No! they were raised for those *Deum servientes*, through all ages; for those who, living apart from the world, had dedicated their lives to the service of God, in pious retirement, and for the sake of charity. But if they had been raised *exclusively*

MOTIVES OF THE DISSOLUTION. 343

for those who, with mistaken views, prayed or "*sung*" for the dead, is that a reason for their universal destruction? It must ever be remembered, they were not raised for this purpose *alone :* it was that peaceful piety might find an asylum, that charities might be dispensed to the poor, hospitality to the rich ; and if the DEAD were remembered and recommended in the prayers of surviving friends, BEFORE THE BIBLE WAS OPEN—would this be a crime so to be visited on all those houses of peace and charity, in which, at least, it might be said, that—

"Pitye is not dead!"

and if abuses, in the long course of prosperity, were inseparable from such institutions ; what comparison can there be between the most dissolute of their inmates, and the loathsome tyrant, at whose feet their riches were rolled? and whose tyranny could only be equalled by his avarice—his lust— and his revenge?

The imagination may faintly conceive, but what language can adequately express, the feelings of forlorn destitution which must have weighed down the hearts of these poor women of suppressed Nunneries,* some of them perhaps having been secluded

---

* " That the Nunneries were more universally entitled to compassion than the houses of the Monks, and Canons, and Friars, cannot be denied. Hume has very justly observed, that, at that period, a woman of family who failed of a settlement in the marriage state, an accident to which such persons

from social life through the best and fairest portion of their lives, and who were now turned adrift, to find, where they might, a sojourn till the earth received their ashes, and the prayers of their Sisters in sorrow, for their souls' repose, were offered to the God whom they had served so long.

> Some natural tears they dropt, but wip'd them soon;
> The world was all before them, where to seek
> Their place of rest, and Providence their guide.

There were then no Poor Laws; and though some of the Abbesses were sufficiently, not to say amply, pensioned, the Nuns received the humblest means of subsistence. There were no poor-houses, wherein they might receive some portion of that charity which it had been their care to dispense to others. They were dismissed into a world, of which they had so little experience; and happy was that Sister who could return in peace to a parental hearth, not yet deprived for ever of the humble circle which had gladdened her youthful years.

Although the domestic portions of the Abbey of Lacock, and its splendid cloisters, yet remain in remarkable perfection, its church was wholly destroyed,

---

were more liable than women of lower station, had really no rank which she properly filled; and a Convent was a retreat both honourable and agreeable, from the inutility and often want which attended her situation." Ellis's Original Letters, First Series, vol. ii. p. 72.

and not a vestige can be traced of its ancient altars; the bones of the honoured Foundress and her family were alike disregarded. She had peacefully sunk to her last repose within the walls of her own edifice, having established its prosperity in temporal matters, and its discipline in all the religious objects of its foundation; and no thought at any time had entered her imagination, that, in years to come, her charters would be set at nought, their royal confirmations given to the winds, and her pious bounty itself annihilated, by the arbitrary will of a King or Parliament.

One single mark of respectful remembrance has been paid to the Countess Ela. Her epitaph is still preserved on a stone * within those Cloisters, which once echoed to the foot-steps, and resounded the Ave-Marias, of the Nuns. The carved roof, overhead, still entire, preserves a grotesque assembly of men in ludicrous attitudes, and monsters, which seem to mock the impotent devastation of the

* If this stone be the same which formerly covered Ela's grave in the church, and not that of a more recent Abbess, to which the inscription has been transferred (and the correct formation of the characters appears to negative its being a modern copy), it was clearly a sepulchral memorial renewed at a period considerably subsequent to her decease. The gravestone in Salisbury cathedral of her son the Bishop, who survived her for half a century, is one of the earliest examples of brass plates: and, besides, the style of these (as far as their outline can show it) marks a subsequent age. (See a further description in p. 351.) The renewal of the monuments of Founders was a practice of which there are many instances.

destroyers of so many kindred Establishments! These uncouth figures, as if in defiance of the malice and tyranny of man, present to the pensive and contemplative visitor, a vivacious and startling aspect, strangely contrasting with the surrounding silence, or the plaintive notes, at times, of the disconsolate and wintry wren.

And now, having endeavoured faithfully to tell the story of the fortunes of Ela Countess of Salisbury, and the noble Family of Longespé, and relate the Annals of the Abbey of Lacock, to the period of its dissolution, we bid farewell to the cloisters and tomb of Ela, and to the ivied chimnies of this ancient and interesting historical scene. We bid them farewell with parting prayers for the stability of the structure, and the prosperity, under happier auspices, of the present possessors; with parting prayers, that the smile of peace may be witnessed, and the song of harmony heard under its roof for centuries to come, as when this history was first meditated, on hearing accidentally the music to the ancient hymn, "Gloria in excelsis," sung by four female voices, in the very spot where it had been heard nearly six centuries ago.

MODERN STATE OF LACOCK ABBEY.

Lacock Abbey was visited in 1801 by Mr. John Carter, F.S.A. the well-known architectural antiquary, who shortly after transmitted to Sir Richard Colt Hoare, the following brief remarks, accompanied by a collection of drawings, which are preserved in the library at Stourhead, and some of the most important of which have been furnished by that zealous patron of Wiltshire topography for the illustration of the present volume.

" The remains of this grand female seclusion are more extensive, and in better preservation, than any thing of the kind within our kingdom. Though few vestiges of the church are to be met with, yet the site of the domestic parts is complete. Great praise is due to those who have preserved the ancient particulars, and for the very great care evinced to keep each part of the arrangement in the best repair; not as garden ruins, or picturesque embellishments, but as specimens of fine architecture, and as a spot sacred to the memory of female virtue and religious vows.

" A south-east view of the building* (as engraved in the accompanying Plate) presents a mixture of the ancient

---

* The aspect of Lacock Abbey at various periods may be observed from the following views published previously to those in the present volume: 1. by S. and N. Buck, 1732, folio, copied in a reduced size, shortly after, in the Universal Museum; 2. in Britton's Beauties of Wiltshire, dated 1815; 3. and 4. in Neale's Gentlemen's Seats, 1826.

and modern architecture, and is the most picturesque point from which it is viewed. On the left of the tall turret is seen a wall with traces of arches, from which it is inferred that the north aisle of the body of the church stood here.

" The gallery on the top of the wall of the octangular turret, appears to have been the work of James or Charles the First's time; and not according to the received story, on foot here, that this gallery in particular was a part of the original building, and that one of the Nuns jumped from it into the arms of her lover. On the right of the turret the exterior arches (once windows) to the vestry, chapter-house, and bathing-chamber are seen."

A ground-plan of the Nunnery, by Mr. Carter, is given in the opposite Plate, the references in which are as follow:

A. Approach to Nunnery.—B. Offices erected about the 16th century.—C. Court-yard.—D. Modern gateway.—E. Modern flight of steps.—F. Site of the great hall.—G. Crypt under the Refectory, now a modern hall.—I. Cloisters.—J. Gravestone of ELA.—K. Supposed bathing-chamber.—L. Stone lavatory.—M. Avenue.—N. Chapter house.—O. Gravestone.—P. Tomb of Ilbert de Chaz.—A. Vestry.—R. Supposed north wall of the Church.—S. Terrace.

" It is believed that a very small portion of the original walls of the domestic part of this edifice are destroyed; and, however injudicious may have been the modern decorations which have been introduced, yet when we compare the remnants still left of this monastic building, little regret should be left on the present occasion. The church is wholly gone; yet its situation may be determined by certain arches stopped up on the south side of the cloisters.

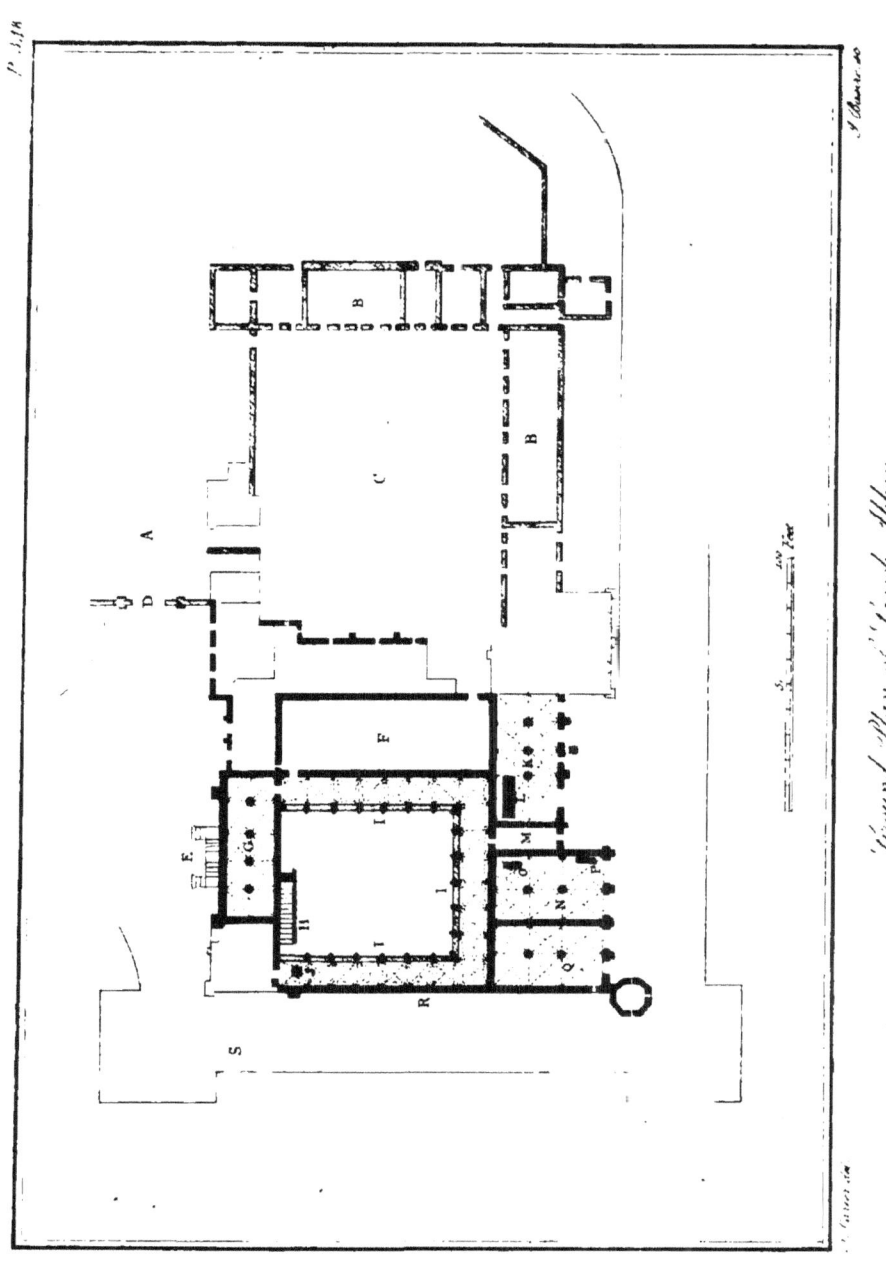

Ground Plan of Laurents Abbey.

Chapiteaux d'Colonnes in Grand Alles

"The elegant capitals in the vestry-room and cloisters merit our attention; they represent female heads, in compliment probably to Ela, the Foundress of the Abbey. There are also some other curious devices in sculpture.

"In the bathing-chamber, chapter-house, and vestry, the architecture appears to be of the early kind; and that of the cloisters about the time of Henry IV. The chimneys are curious, and highly ornamented."

In the year 1806, the Rev. George Witham, residing at Lacock, as Chaplain to the dowager Countess of Shrewsbury, compiled and printed with his own hands a short History of Lacock Abbey, from which the following extracts are made :*

"The valley in which this Abbey is situated, on the river Avon, is very rich and pleasant, about 13 miles east of Bath, having to the east the beautifully wooded Bowden-hill, at the distance of about a mile; between which and the Abbey (according to the tradition of the country, there was formerly a religious house called Bewly Court) a priory or cell in all probability to some monastery, but of which I find no mention in ecclesiastical writers; it is now a farm-house, and some of its walls have an air of antiquity.

"The remains of the Abbey are extensive, containing almost two squares.

"The CLOISTERS are some of the most perfect of religious houses that have fallen into private hands in the

---

* " THE HISTORY OF LACOCK, or Locus Beatæ Mariæ, from Dugdale, Stevens, &c. With additions on the Present State of the Abbey. LACOCK, by the Rev. G. Witham, 1806." small quarto, pp. viii. 44, a literary curiosity of great rarity.

kingdom, if we except those of our cathedrals, where care has been taken to preserve antiquity in all its beauteous forms. Within these cloisters most of the Nuns were buried, as is customary in all female monasteries."

An excellent view of the Cloisters was published in Britton's Architectural Antiquities of Great Britain, 4to. 1808. The grotesque carvings of the roof are occasionally varied by coats of arms; of which the following is an account, the names of the owners being partly suggested:

Bendy of six, Or and Azure. *Sysung*.
Argent, a lion rampant and bordure engrailed Or.
Gules, a lion rampant Argent, *Mowbray*.
Argent, a cross flory Azure. *Sutton*.
Gules, a fess between two chevrons Argent.
Or, three Torteaux and a label of three points Azure. *Courtenay*.
Azure, a fret Or. *Amundevill*.
Gules, a pair of wings conjoined Or. *Seymour*.
Or, three piles Azure. *Bryan*.

Gules, a lion rampant Or. *Albini*.
Vert, a golden E, for ELA.
Or, three Torteaux and a bordure Gules. *Courtenay*.
Argent, a chevron between three chaplets Gules. *Ashton*.
Per pale indented Gu. and Vert, a chevron Or. *Heytesbury*.
Gules, three fishes naiant Argent. *Roche?*
Azure, on a dancette Or four escallops Gules.
Argent, on a cross Vert four fleurs-de-lis of the First.
Gules, a fess between six martlets Or, a bordure Azure. *Sir William Beauchamp, of Sussex*.
Gules, a dancette Argent. *Papworth*.
Or, a chevron Gules. *Stafford*.
Sable, a fess between two chevrons Or. *Baynard*.

The gravestone now inscribed with the epitaph of the Countess Ela, (already recited in p. 5,) is 5 feet 6 in. long by 4 feet wide; and bears the indentations for brass plates, which represent a tabernacle or canopy, with two shields of arms at each side. It is clearly of a date long subsequent to the death of the Abbess Ela, and was probably substituted for her first less splendid coffin-lid. There is a second gravestone, once inlaid with brass, answering to nearly the same description; and which may be attributed to one of the latter Abbesses.

Among some curious fragments of sculptured stone, which are preserved in the cloisters, are two portions of a coffin-lid, of far greater antiquity. It is ornamented in a singular manner, with three croziers engraved in outline as represented in the annexed cut; and may justly be considered the sepulchral memorial of one of the earliest Abbesses; or, with great probability, as that which once covered the spot where the heart of Nicholas Longespé, the aged Bishop of Salisbury, was deposited. Its size, which is only 16 inches long, by 10 inches wide in the upper part, is favourable to the latter conjecture.

To resume Mr. Witham's remarks:—" From the cloisters there was a communication by a door into the room that is now called the Nuns' Kitchen. In general there was no direct communication in monasteries from the cloisters to the kitchen, therefore I take it to have been the Refectory; and the more so as there was also another communication to this room, which I suppose was the buttery; there are also three pillars along the middle of it, which is not uncommon in religious houses. There is now in this place a very large stone trough, hewn out of a single stone, in length 11 feet 3 inches, in breadth 4 feet 11 inches, and in depth 2 feet; but for what use I can form no adequate conjecture: it may have been placed here since the dissolution of the monastery, and have been taken out of the farm-yard, where it might have served cattle.

" From the cloisters there was a door into the chapter-house, in which there are two tombstones; one, by tradition, was that of a Nun who was found entire in her habit, but soon, on opening the coffin, mouldered into dust. The other was brought from Monkton Farley."

The form of the inscription on this last-mentioned stone is so extraordinary, that it has been thought sufficiently curious to be represented in fac-simile *(see the Plate)*. When read at length, the words are

    Hic jacet Ilbertus   de Chaz bonitate refertus,
    Qui cum Brotona   dedit hic perplurima dona.'

A practice which was prevalent in the decline of the Roman empire, and which was imitated by our earliest monastic scholars,* is here exhibited in excess. Within

---

* Other instances of this species of writing are the epitaphs on William Deincourt, in Lincoln Cathedral, about 1100, (en-

HIC IACET ILBERTUS DE CARRO. BONA DEDIT PLURA
DE DHAT BONITA TE: RERTO.QUI: BROTONA: DEDIT HIC: PER: PLURI MA:DONA: +

Gravestone of Ilbert de Chaz,
formerly at Farley Priory, and now at Lacock Abbey, Wilts.

such letters as afford cavities practicable for the purpose, those letters which immediately follow are placed (in small); the extent of the whole being thus compressed in a surprising degree, at the same time that the height of the inscription remains very considerable,* and is therefore more visible at a distance, however difficult a task it may prove, on closer inspection, to decypher it.

In the present instance, the monks of Farley appear themselves to have felt that this puzzling involution of the letters was carried to too great an extreme; and in consequence they had the inscription repeated, at length, though in a much smaller size, round the margin of the stone. With respect to this smaller inscription, it is worthy of observation that its antiquity is probably but

---

graved in Dugdale's Baronage, Hall's Trivetus, Gough's Monuments, vol. ii. pl. xiv. Pegge's Sylloge of Inscriptions, pl. iv.) that of Bishop Roger, at Salisbury Cathedral, 1139, (engraved in Archæologia, vol. ii. pl. 13, Gough's Monuments, vol. i. pl. iv. Gough's Camden, vol. i. pl. xi.) and that on Archbishop Theobald, at Canterbury, 1161, (in Archæologia, vol. xiv. pl. 10.); the dedication stones of Tewkesbury and Postling (in Pegge's Sylloge of Inscriptions, plates i and iii); but none of these are so compressed as the epitaph of Ilbertus de Chaz; and the only inscription which in this respect approaches it, is that on the dedication stone of St. George's, Southwark, engraved in Archæologia, vol. ii. pl. xiii., Gough's Monuments, vol. i. pl. iv. and Pegge's Sylloge, p. 56. The epitaph at Magdeburg, in Germany, of Edith, an Anglo-Saxon Princess (though supposed to be not quite so ancient as her time), is also engraved in this style; see the Gentleman's Magazine, vol. c. i. 195.

* The length of this inscription is 4 feet 9 inches, the height of the first stroke of the letter H is six inches, that of the last D $3\frac{1}{2}$ inches.

little removed from that of the larger one: from fifty to a hundred years is perhaps all the difference. The letters are all squarer; and the E and C are closed, the former taking a round back, as is usual in what are termed Lombardic characters; but it is very remarkable that, in one part (near the centre of the inscription, when the carver may have been doubtful of his space,) the contractions of the original are retained much as before,—in the words REFERTUS, QUI CUM— The name of the party is in the smaller inscription spelt CHAT, though in the larger the final letter is clearly different, and may be safely read as z, which orthography, is supported by the charters of Monkton Farley, printed in Dugdale's Monasticon. The following extracts from the Confirmation charter to Farley of Humfrey and Margaret de Bohun, to which Ilbertus de Chaz is himself the first witness, set forth his " plurima dona," and prove the justice with which that phrase was employed in the epitaph:

" Præterea concedimus eis et confirmamus *Broctonam*, quam ILBERTUS DE CHAZ eis dedit, solutam et quietam ab omni servitio ad nos pertinente. . . . . . . Et decimam de Cluttona cum uno homine sex solidos reddente in eadem villa, ex dono Ilberti de Chaz, et ecclesiam de Fcrenberga post mortem Haraldi presbyteri, et ecclesiam de Cluttona, ex donatione prædicti Ilberti, et ex dono ipsius decem solidatas terra de Hethesingtona (*vel* Hethelhamtune)."

This charter not only fully illustrates the " many gifts " of Ilbert de Chaz; but it fixes his æra as a contemporary of Humfrey de Bohun the Sewer of King Henry the First, who died in 1185, thus showing the date of this very ancient and curious monument.

The " Brotona " mentioned in the epitaph is Broughton in Wiltshire, near Melksham, and the manor there given by Ilbert de Chaz received the same name of Monkton which was applied to Farley itself. In 1526, as appears from a roll in the Augmentation Office, the priory received from the manor of Monketon in Broughton a yearly income of 13*l.* 10*s.* 8*d.*, from Clutton 4*s.*, from Farneburgh 12*s.* 8*d.*, and from Hichilhamton 8*s.*; so that they had good reason to preserve the memory of this liberal benefactor.

The curious gravestone which has given rise to these remarks, was brought to light in the year 1744, after having been buried for two centuries; for a rabbit-warren had been formed over the site of the priory church of Monkton Farley! On the ground being levelled, in the year mentioned, the pavement of the chancel appeared nearly complete, and several gravestones and skeletons were disclosed. Two of the former were adorned with sculpture, one of them representing a prior named Lawrence, and the other a man's bust and a lion, which from its situation near the altar, was attributed to the founder. These, it is feared, were destroyed; for when Mr. Gough made inquiry respecting this inscription of Ilbert de Chaz in the year 1772, he was told "it had lately been broken to pieces* to mend the roads!" Such was probably the fate

---

* Mr. Gough in consequence copied in the Archæologia, vol. ii. (in illustration of an essay on Bishop Roger's tomb at Salisbury, mentioned in the last note,) a very imperfect copy of this inscription, which had been engraved in the Gentleman's Magazine for March 1744, shortly after its first discovery. See the account of the remains in vol. xiv. of that miscellany, p. 139, copied in vol. i. of Camden's Britannia, by Gough; Mr. Britton, (to whom Topography and Cathedral history and illustrations are so much indebted,) when quoting the same account, in the third volume of his "Beauties of Wiltshire," seems to have confused the parish church of Farley with that of the priory. The plate from the Archæologia is also printed in Gough's Camden, vol. i. pl. xi. and in his

of the other sepulchral memorials; but the unique monument before us had fortunately been removed from the power of the destroyers, having been transferred by Lord Webb Seymour, the owner of Farley, to the congenial shades of Lacock Abbey, where it is now carefully preserved, but little injured by time or its long interment.

We now resume the extracts from Mr. Witham: —

"Near to the chapter-house is the vestry, or sacristy, with doors of communication to the church and cloisters; there remain in it places for vesting, for chalices, and for the priests to wash their hands before and after mass, &c.

"There is now a spacious terrace-walk on the ground where the church once stood.

"The altar appears to have been placed to the east. The church has no aisles, and was very long, which leads me to suppose that the Nuns' choir was behind the altar, as we find in several monasteries of women, to keep themselves more sequestered from the public. Next to the choir was the altar; then the body of the church, which was in general for the use and accommodation of the Lay Sisters, and others who might occasionally visit the church for the convenience of hearing prayers. Adjoining to the church was the treasury, in the lower part of the tower, where there are several recesses for the convenience of laying up their best and most precious church furniture, &c.

"The north wall of the church is still standing, with marks of arches and windows, filled up with stone and mortar. On the top of this wall two persons may walk abreast, between two strong stone rails, and command very picturesque views of Bowden Park, Lackham House, and a fine fertile country, terminated by the downs.

Sepulchral Monuments, vol. i. pl. iv. Though Mr. Gough afterwards heard of the original being at Lacock, he appears never to have seen it, nor to have obtained a correct copy.

" The middle chamber of the tower is reserved by the family as a repository for their writings, and other valuables, amongst which is the Magna Charta of King Henry III. of inestimable value, being the only perfect one in the kingdom, owing to the accident which happened to that of Durham,—it is in breadth twelve inches and three quarters, and in length (including the fold) twenty inches and a half; the seal is of green wax pendant by a skein of green silk, rather broken off in two edges. It has the following endorsement upon it, in a contemporary hand:

" *Ex deposito militum Wilteshir Henrici Regis filii Johannis Regis, de libertatibus et quibusdam consuetudinebus per Angliam constitutis.*

" This charter seem to have been designed for the use of the knights and military tenants in Wiltshire, and to have been deposited for that purpose in the monastery of Lacock by the Foundress ELA, Countess of Sarum, whose husband William Longespé was Sheriff of Wiltshire from 15th of John till his death, 10 Henry III. (during which period this charter was granted), and ELA herself executed the same office in the two succeeding years.*

* " The Magna Carta of 9 Henry III. under seal, from which Blackstone printed a copy in his edition of the Charters, and which he suggested was the Charter designed for the use of the Knights, or Military Tenants of Wiltshire, is still preserved by the family of the Talbots of Lacock Abbey, in that county." First General Report of the Commissioners on Public Records, p. 97. There is a copy of the Magna Carta of King John among the records of the Dean and Chapter at Salisbury (though it was overlooked when search was made by order of the Commissioners),—" apparently written by the same hand as that which has been engraved." Dodsworth's Salisbury Cathedral, p. 202.

"The hall is a noble structure, in length 48 feet, in breadth 30 feet, and in height 32 feet. Its lofty ceiling is of stucco, adorned with the arms of many noble families. Several niches are occupied by images of figures in composition work, executed by a foreign artist, emblematical of the foundation of the Abbey, and the family of the noble Foundress."

These we do not admire so much as Mr. Witham; but he should here have noticed that the windows are "richly dight" with stained glass, principally consisting of old armorial coats of the family of Hungerford.

"The visitor is next conducted into the dining-parlour, which from its size and proportion is esteemed inferior to no room in the county; its dimensions being 32 feet by 28, and 18½ in height. In this room are several well executed paintings; and amongst them one of King Charles the First, by Vandyck; and another of Henry VIII. by Holbein. There is also a large sideboard of *verde antique*, 7 feet 3 inches in length, and 3 feet 5 inches in breadth.

"The picture-gallery contains the family portraits.

"The library is over the vestry, and contains many valuable and scarce books, both ancient and modern.

"What is at present called the stone gallery seems to have been the Dormitory, or perhaps the common working-room, for the Nuns. It is now divided the whole length on the west side into bed-chambers; the east side is a long and convenient gallery with painted glass in the windows.

"There are some ancient chairs, said to have been part of the camp furniture of King Charles the Second. Also a prodigiously large pair of elk or moose-deer horns, much admired by the curious for their magnificent appearance."

One of the bed-chambers at Lacock is still remembered as that which was fitted up for the reception of Queen Elizabeth. This was in the year 1574: when the Virgin Queen was also at Longleat and Wilton;* and it is most probable that it was on this occasion that she knighted her host, Sir Henry Sherington, who is recorded to have obtained that honour in the same year.

During the Civil War, Lacock House was garrisoned for the King, and was taken by the opposite party shortly after Cromwell had won Devizes, in Sept. 1645. The following announcement of the event is from a contemporary newspaper called The True Informer, Numb. 23, for Sept. 27, 1645:

"Lacock House in Wiltshire is surrendered to Colonel Devereux, Governour of Malmsbury, his forces, and other forces before it: and the Governour and Souldiers therein are marched forth, and our forces in possession of it, with all the armes and ammunition therein. The conditions of the surrender were to this effect:
1. That the Governour, Officers, and Souldiers shall march forth with their armes, to a garrison of the enemies'.
2. That the House, with all the armes, ammunition, and provisions in it be surrendered to the Parliament's forces."

On the receipt of the news, the House of Commons made an "Order on Sept. 26, for the Ministers the next Lord's day, to give thanks to God for the good success of the Parliament's forces in Pembrokeshire, at the Devizes, and Lacock House."†

The lord of Lacock had been himself taken prisoner in the previous March: "Mr. Sherington Talbot and Mr. Dowdeswell, Commissioners of Array in Worcestershire, were taken and sent up to London."‡

---

* See Nichols's Progresses of Queen Elizabeth, i. 408, and Preface, p. xviii.
† Whitelocke's Memorials. ‡ Ibid. p. 130.

Near the house is a square piece of water, which is evidently the successor of the capacious monastic fishponds. At one end of this water is now stationed, upon a pedestal, the large metal pot called the Nuns' Boiler, which, when seen by Stevens, remained in the kitchen. On the exterior of this massive vessel is the following inscription:

" A PETRO WAGHUENS IN MECHLINIA EFFUSUS FACTUSVE FUERAM, ANNO MILLESSIMO QUINGENTESSIMO. DEO LAUS ET GLORIA CHRISTO.

" I was molten or made by Peter Waghuens, of Mechlin, in the year 1500. Praise be to God and glory to Christ."

This vessel, thus placed, remains the last relic and memento of the charities of the former inmates of Lacock Abbey; and on the pedestal of this hallowed but somewhat grotesque monument of ancient beneficence, I now deposit my historical and recording Pen.

LAST VISIT TO OLD SARUM, WITH CONCLUDING REFLECTIONS.

It was on the 16th day of February,—having completed the last sheets of this long story of other days, I stood on the summit of the silent mound of Old Sarum, the eventful scene of much of this history. I stood on the site, as it is conceived, of EDWARD THE SHERIFF's Castle, recalling the names, and characters, and events, of a distant age, when, on this spot, a City shone, with its Cathedral, and its Norman Castle, lifting their pinnacles and turrets above the clouds; and here, on this majestic and solitary eminence, the Regal form of the stern Conqueror, his mailed Barons, the the grey-haired and mitred Osmund, who had exchanged his sword for a crozier — and young Edward, ancestor of the Foundress of Lacock, seemed as shadows, to pass before me, followed by the crowned Troubadour—Richard of the " Lion's Heart"—his heroic Brother, William of the " LONG SWORD ;" and ELA his bereaved and pious Widow, pale, placid, and tearful, the Foundress of that Abbey whose Annals we have been the first, thus distinctly, to relate.

I turned my eyes, and beheld the vast and solitary plains below, stretching on every side, like Ocean— To the north-west, hid only by an intervening elevation of the Downs, STONEHENGE, " wonder of ages," was still sitting in her sad glory, to which most ancient Temple of the Sun it might be conceived the Bards, descending in procession, whilst it was yet dark, on solemn festivals, from the sacred hill of Salisbury,* and joining in the open space, between the vast forests,† struck their harps in acclaim, as the mighty object of their adoration slowly ascended above the eastern hills.

To the west, south-west—east, and north-east—strode on, in a direct line, over hill and vale, with traces, after fifteen centuries, distinct as yesterday—the FOUR MIGHTY ROMAN ROADS, here meeting as in a centre. Immediately on our right, a little below the mound on which the Norman banner floated from the aerial keep of the Citadel, we‡ marked the site of the ancient and vanished Cathedral,§ the foundations of whose walls, owing to the dryness of last summer, were discovered, of which

* Solis-bury. See Davies's Celtic Antiquities, " hill of bards."

† Namely, of Clarendon, united with the New Forest, and extending to the sea—the vast woody track of Cranbourne Chace—Great Ridge—Groveley, &c.

‡ The Rev. Mr. Skinner, Rector of Camerton, Somerset, (who has proved, we think beyond all doubt, that the district surrounding that parish was the site of the ancient Camalodunum,) Archdeacon Macdonald, and Mr. Hatcher, author of a late History of these scenes, " Old and New Sarum."

§ Built between 1078 and 1091, consecrated 1092, demolished 1332.

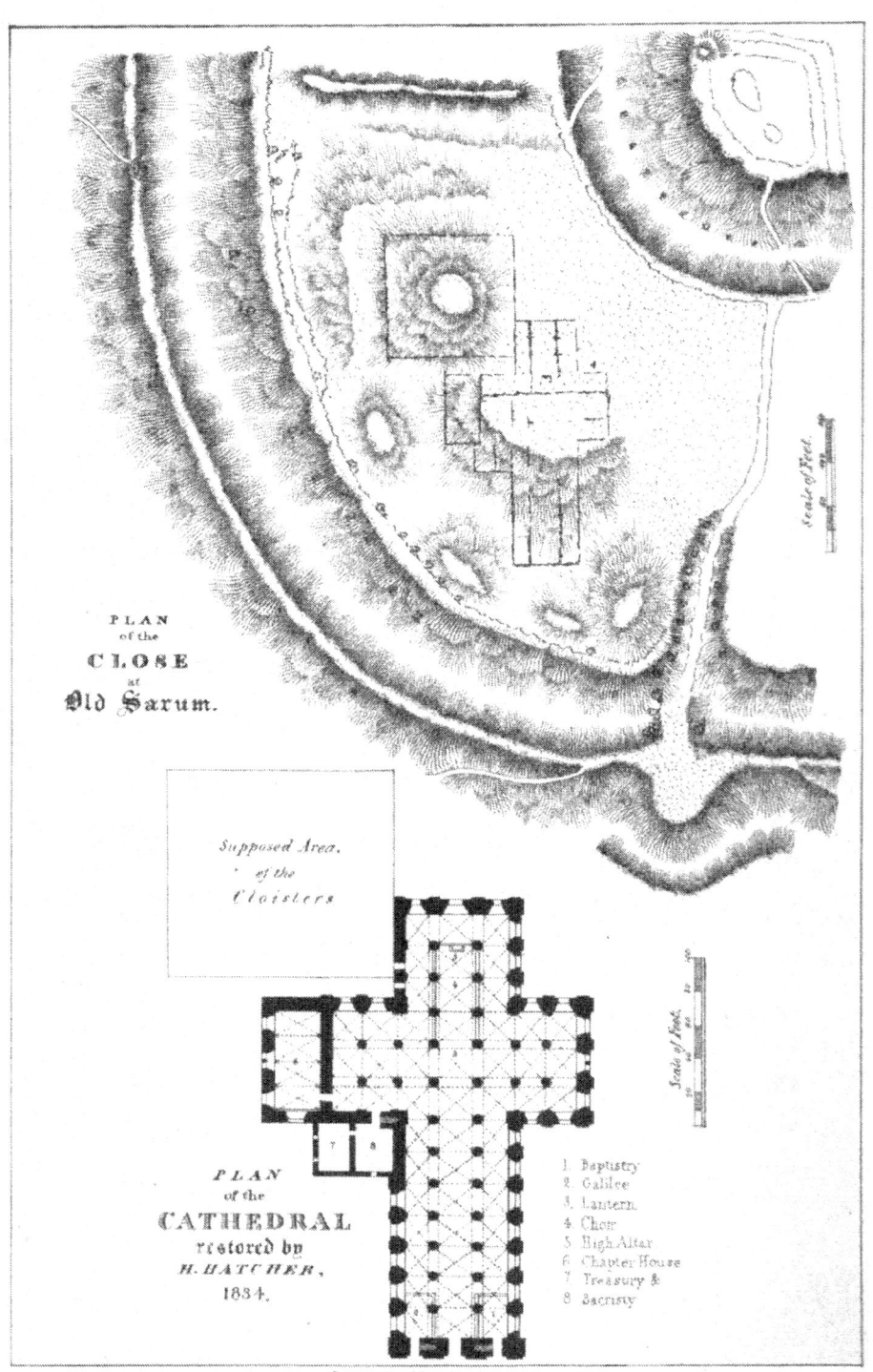

the outlines, exactly as they appeared, are here given, from a sketch taken on the spot in Sept. 1834.*

Towards the east, anciently appeared the battlements of Clarendon Palace; to the south-west, is the field of tournament, of which the chivalrous Cœur de-Lion appointed five in England; to the east and south-east, crowning the further heights, the camps, occupied by the Belgic invaders, in their progress to the Severn, still seem'd to awe the surrounding country; whilst a series of barrows terminated the view, until their forms were lost in the distance.

But the most interesting sight remained. On the left, surmounting the towers and lesser spires, the houses, and smoke, of the City of the Living, shone the aerial spire of the Cathedral of New Sarum, with the morning sun on its elfin shaft; and could we be insensible to the thought, that

* By Miss Ryland.

within those walls the sacred rites of Christian worship, with a purer and more scriptural service, had been uninterruptedly kept up — save in the short intervening space of the fanatical republick — for SIX HUNDRED years, as duly and solemnly as when the youthful Henry, and his Justiciary, Hubert de Burgh, offered their gifts on the Altar?* with this difference, indeed, that the plain sacramental bread had succeeded the Elevation of the Host, an emblem derived from the ancient Druidical worship of the sun, on its first elevation above the horizon?† And could we forget that the PLAIN OPEN WORD OF GOD, the white amice, the decent forms, had succeeded the pompous ceremonial and pageantry of Popish rites; whilst the children of the choir, instead of tossing to and fro their censers, with the words in Latin, repeated by rote, " meá culpâ, meâ maximâ culpâ," now,

* When this subject was before noticed (p. 133) it was omitted to be mentioned, that Hubert de Burgh's offering remained with the Church of Salisbury, as one of its greatest treasures, until 1536, when, in an inventory of the jewels, &c. belonging to the church, occurs: " A TEXT after John, gilt with gold, and having precious stones and the relicks of dyvers seynts. *Ex dono Huberti de Burgh, Justiciarii Domini Regis Henrici III.*" Antiq. Sarisb. p. 201.

† The emblem is therefore round, surrounded with a blaze of jewellery, as rays of the luminary which it represented. This might be called, indeed, the " ancient faith!!" as the early corruptions of the Christian creed have been absurdly called.

after the chant, are seen, bending their heads over their Bibles, as the lesson for the day is read, presenting one of the most interesting sights of the PROTESTANT, or rather *purer* Catholic Church.

To return to the desolate hill. No human creature was in sight, save some poor women gathering sticks among the thorns of the ramparts. A few sheep were bleating in the foss. The rivers Nadder and Avon were seen tranquilly meandering in the nether vale; whilst the solitary tree, in an adjoining meadow, under which, for centuries, the burgesses for this antient City had been elected,—now with its bare trunk seemed to resemble its fortune.

I descended, musing on the events which a new Parliament, under new auspices, might bring forth, either FOR GOOD OR FOR EVIL; perhaps in the end destined to leave the PRESENT CATHEDRAL AS DESOLATE AS THE FORMER !—These events are in the hand of God; be ours submission and prayers.

Salisbury, Feb. 19, 1835.

STONEHENGE.

I make no apology for taking this opportunity of publishing my final sentiments * on this mysterious structure. That it is Druidical, a vast Temple raised to the Sun, the second Deity† of the Celtic mythology, seems now to be the universal opinion.

I have already stated my conviction that the inner circle of sienite is the original temple, the greater sarsen circle being the addition of the Belgæ, who also worshipped the Sun.

But the circumstance I am about to mention seems still more decisive as to the designation of this mysterious erection. A *black* stone was, of old, held *sacred* to the Sun; see Gibbon, in the Chapter relating to the Emperor Heliogabalus. It was lately suggested by Mr. J. Stoughton Money, (a very young man, but devoted to antiquarian pursuits, in the morn of ingenuous youth,) that the stone called the Altar Stone at Stonehenge, is *black*, different from the granite, and from those of the inner circle also.

A small piece of one of the stones of the inner circle, when polished, has been ascertained, from competent authority, to be a variety of sienite rock which now bears the name of diorite, being a mixture of fine particles of hornblende and compact feldspar; the former of various shades of green, from lighter than the specimen in question to greenish black, or even *quite black*, as in the gigantic Scarabæus in the British Museum; the latter white, or more or less tinged by the colouring matters of the green hornblende. There are some Egyptian statues of exactly the same substance." This is a singular fact, when the monkish tradition is that these stones were brought from Africa!

As Avebury and Stonehenge were raised to Mercury and the Sun, and as their two great Promontories—Mercurii et Apollinis, are marked in ancient maps of Africa, so to these two Deities the ancient cities of Baal-bech, and Tadmor, in the Desert, were raised. The authors of the Ancient History conceived that Tadmor meant the same as the Latin Palmyra. I contend that Tadmor was the city so called from the Ægyptian Thoth,—Tad; in opposition to Baal-bech, the city of the Sun; Tadmor having been built by Solomon when an idolator of the Gods of Ægypt, being married to Pharoah's daughter.

* See the "History of Bremhill," and "Hermes Britannicus," by the Author.

† As the larger and more ancient Temple, at Avebury, in my opinion, was raised to the *first* and greater deity of the Celts—Thoth, or Mercury.

ADDENDA AND CORRIGENDA.

PAGE 12, line 2, for " the " *read* these.

P. 21, line 14, for " now " *read* afterwards.

P. 30, line 11, for "youngest " *read* eldest ; and erase the note for the reasons stated in p. 102.

P. 31, line 14, erase the words "daughter of Tirrel de Mainers" (see p. 97).

P. 53, for "Newmarch" *read* Neufmarché ; and for "Brenneville" *read* Brenmule. In the early MSS. of Ordericus Vitalis, in the library at Alençon, the reading is Brenmula; the termination of ville would not be apposite to the locality, as described by the historian: "Prope montem qui Guercliva nuncupatur, liber campus est, et latissima planities, quæ ab incolis Brennimula vocitatur."

P. 55. A reconsideration of the record relating to the widow of Edward of Salisbury, combined with some further evidence that has been more recently discovered, has led to the conclusion that there must have been a *second* person of that name. It is at least certain that Walter de Salisbury was the son of the Domesday Edward by another marriage, or *his* descendants would have inherited the fief of Raimes, instead of its devolving on Stuteville. But when we find the widow given to a second husband—Pagan de Hocton—so late as 1131, it appears improbable that she should have been the wife of a person who was Sheriff of Wiltshire at the Domesday survey, forty-five years before.

A connection, however, is perceptible between the Edward of Salisbury who married the heiress of Raimes, and the Norman stock of Roumare; as he occurs as a benefactor to the Abbey of St. George of Bocherville, the foundation of Ralph de Tancarville, the presumed brother, as noticed in p. 69, of Robert Fitz Girold of Domesday Book, and Edward of Salisbury the Sheriff.

From the cartulary of Bocherville, in the Public Library at Rouen, Mr. Stapleton transcribed two charters, by the former of which "Edwardus de Salesberiis" gave the monks certain serfs and their rents; which, by a second charter of Robert de Estotevill, made at the request of Leonia his wife, are recognized as 50s. rent, " in hospitibus de RAMIS." It appears from the " Description de la Haute Normandie," vol. i. p. 492, that the fief in the Pays de Caux, including the parishes of St. Vigor de Vimerville, Guillerville, &c., the manor-house of which was in the parish of Gomerville, went by the name of Ramis;* and in 1343 a descendant of Estoteville, or Stuteville, founded a chapel in honour of the Virgin "au manoir de Rames." The Roger de Ramis of Domesday Book, the possessor of the fief, had evidently transferred his surname, taken from his *caput baroniæ in Essex*, to his Norman manor-house and its demesne.

The name of Edward of Salisbury attests the foundation charters of the Cistercian abbey of Savigny in Normandy in the year 1112.

The precise relationship of Leonia de Stuteville, and the other parties mentioned in pp. 55-6, to Edward of Salisbury, the Domesday Sheriff, it is not easy to determine; but in its future consideration it will be well to bear in mind the descent of the barony of Rayne or Ramis.

Alicia de Tany was the daughter of William fitz Jocelin, or Gozeline, who was living in 1165 (Liber Niger), and was married, not to Graelent de Tany, but to Picot de Tany, who died about 1180, leaving five sons, of whom the eldest was aged 20 in 1185, and two daughters (Rot. de Dom. pp. 39, 46).

Of Leonia de Stuteville nothing more has been found than is already noticed in p. 56.

With respect to the widow of Edward of Salisbury (the younger?) who was married secondly to Pagan de Hocton, it may be remarked, that among the charters of Ouston Abbey, is one of Matilda the daughter of Pagan de Hocton, and so probably her daughter; and another by which Robert Grimbald

* In the feodary of Philip Augustus, compiled in 1220 (Bibl. Reg. Paris, 8408), is this entry: " Item, p'd'c'us Henricus (de Estotevill) tenet Wimmonville et Gillarvill in Audebertot de feodo de Raimes."

granted the land which William de Hocton had in Duninton, co. Lincoln, Matilda his widow giving her consent. This seems to be the same Matilda, daughter of Pagan; she had probably married a person who assumed the name of herself and her land; but there is no proof that she was the wife of Robert Grimbald, as assumed in the title given to her charter in the Monasticon.

The proper arrangement of these several parties must be left to the discovery of further evidence.

P. 60, line 4, for " 1071" *read* 1093.

P. 89, line 19, for " and leaving" *read* I leave.

P. 95, last line, for " 1197 " *read* 1196.

P. 132. In this page it is stated to be unknown whether Reimund de Burgh found another lady to accept him after his rejection by the lady Ela Countess of Salisbury. His wife has since been discovered; and it is very remarkable that she proves to be another dowager Countess; obtained, doubtless, through the persevering provision of his uncle, the potent Justiciary. This was Christiana, widow of William Mandeville Earl of Essex, who died in 1227, only two years after the Earl of Salisbury.* She was the daughter of Robert Lord Fitz-Walter, and sister to that Walter Fitz-Robert who married Ida Longespé, the youngest daughter of the Countess Ela.

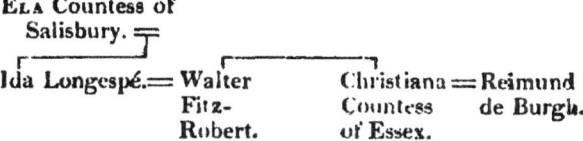

Morant, in his History of Essex (quoting Plac. 11 Hen. III. rot. 16), states that the manor of Alfethestun, in the parish of

* Dugdale (Baronage, vol. i. p. 205) has made Christiana the second Countess of a former Earl William de Mandeville, two generations higher, who died in 1190, thirty-seven years before; and in p. 706 says that the Earl who died in 1227 had no wife; but, independently of Reimund de Burgh, this is improbable; for her grandfather died in 1198; her father in 1234; and her brother lived until 1257, after marrying, as shown above, a daughter of Ela Countess of Salisbury.

Great Dunmow, was granted to Reimund de Burgh about the year 1226. On the 10th of April, 1231, King Henry the Third confirmed to the Maison Dieu at Dover, which was *a foundation of Hubert de Burgh*, (inter alia) 100s. rent from the manor of Dersyngham, which that hospital had of the gift of Christiana de Mandeville, Countess of Essex.

The projected marriage of Reimund de Burgh with the Countess Ela of Salisbury, might have proved a parallel with that which King John forced on Margaret the mother of Baldwin Earl of Devon. That dowager lady was given to John's successful general and cruel dispenser of the fire and the sword, Falkes de Breant, whom Matthew Paris terms " that impious, ignoble, and base-conditioned man ;"—a marriage, adds the monkish chronicler, on which these lines were written :

> Lex connectit eos, amor, et concordia lecti,
> Sed lex qualis ? amor qualis ? concordia qualis ?
> Lex exlex ; amor exosus ; concordia discors !

P. 136. Though a difference of nine years will scarcely affect the spirit of the remark made in this page, alluding to the episcopal effigy in Salisbury cathedral, which has been generally attributed to Bishop Poore ; it may be worth while to put forth the suggestion, that the monument in question in all probability does not belong to that prelate, but to his successor, Bishop Bingham, who died in 1246, and was buried at *the north side of the altar*, which was the situation of this monument. Bishop Poore did not die Bishop of Salisbury, but was translated to Durham ; expiring at the monastery he had founded at his native village of Tarrent, in Dorsetshire, his heart was buried there, but his body was carried (as was then customary with those of Bishops) to his own cathedral of Durham, where it was interred in the Chapter-house.

P. 148. Richard, the younger son of William Longespé II, by Idonea, daughter of Richard de Camville, appears to have had a part of his mother's inheritance in Somersetshire. Collinson, in his History of that county, vol. ii. p. 358, quotes from Rawlinson's MSS. : " Iste Will'us Longespee habuit exitum Ricardun Longespee D'num de Charlton-Camville."

P. 160. Erase the words "son of William Basset, Chief Justice of England," and refer to p. 325.

P. 181. In the Annals of Nicholas Trivet, the translation of the Carthusians to Hinton is placed under 1227, and the foundation of Lacock under 1232. This is another testimony to the accounts which have been preferred in the text. The same annals also record the profession of the Foundress under 1236, instead of 1238, as in the Book of Lacock. "ELA Saresburiensis Comitissa, *spreto sæculo*, habitum Canonissarum apud Lakok accepit; inter quas effecta est postea Abbatissa."

P. 182. The names of LOCUS DEI, and LOCUS BEATE MARIE, given by the Earl and Countess of Salisbury to their monastic foundations, may be illustrated by some parallel instances. Foremost may be mentioned GODSTOW, which has the same signification in Anglo-Saxon. There was another Locus Dei in the diocese of Rouen; as also an Insula Dei on the river Andelle; a Mons Dei in the diocese of Lisieux; a Vallis Dei in the diocese of Seez, and a Vallis Dei at Bitham in Lincolnshire. The last was corrupted into Vaudey, as the French Mons Dei was into Mondaye. Rewley Abbey, near Oxford, was an abbreviation of de Regali Loco. In 1316, when Thomas Earl of Lancaster granted the monks of Whalley a new site, it was to be called the Locus Benedictus of Whalley. There was a monastic house named Vale St. Mary, in Cornwall; one de Valle Crucis in Denbighshire; and one de Valle Salutis, in Ireland. In Yorkshire was Mountgrace, and the same name of Gratiæ Montis occurs in Bavaria.

P. 186, line 7, *read* 31st of January, 1230.

P. 187, line 10, for "Edingdon" *read* Heddington.

P. 190, last line, for " or Leach of Eastleach in Gloucestershire" *read* of Legh in Wiltshire. (see p. 309.)

P. 191. The superior of the convent of Lacock before the lady Ela became the first Abbess, was the Prioress Wymarca. (see p. 278.)

P. 222. In 1233, " Rex cinxit Thomam de Warewic cingulo Comitatus Warewic." Claus. Hen. III. m. 9. Dugdale (Baronage, i. 72.) states that this took place at the same time that " WILLIELMUS LONGESPE accingitur gladio militari, sed non fit

Comes Sarum." (MS. in Bodl. Lib. Cant. K. 84, f. 50 a). It was on occasion of the Whitsuntide feast, when the King held his court, or Parliament, at Gloucester; and he also knighted, at the same time, Roger Bigot, Earl of Norfolk, and Hugh de Vere, Earl of Oxford.

P. 230. I am informed by M. Michel, a literary gentleman who has been investigating the treasures of the libraries in England, under the patronage of the French government, and who corrected the orthography of the extract from the ancient poem given in p. 243, that Guillaume de Machault, in le dit de l'Alerion, King's MSS. Paris, no. 7609, p. 109, col. 2, relates an history of Louis IX. who gave to William Longuespée a white horse, with which he was much pleased.

P. 255. After the news of William Longespé's death had arrived in England, his executors proceeded to the performance of his will, which had doubtless been prepared, as was customary, previous to his departure on the Holy voyage. On the 27th Sept. 1250, the King directed his letters to Henry de Wengham, that he should permit the executors to have free administration of all the goods and chattels of the deceased, because Stephen Longespé and Henry de Mare had given security for such debts as he might have owed to the King. And that Wengham should take into the King's hands the lands which were of the inheritance of Idonea the wife of the said William, that she might thenceforth take nothing from the issues of the said lands until she had come to the King, and done what of right she ought to do. And because the King had granted by his letters patent to the said William, that he might deliver to farm to whom he pleased, his manors of Albourn, Amesbury, Trowbridge, and Canford, from the feast of St. Michael in the King's 32d year, for the next four years complete, it was commanded to the said Henry that he should permit Henry de Mare, and the other farmers, to hold the said manors in peace, and in no respect to interfere with those manors during that term. (Rot. Claus. 34 Hen. III. m. 4.) Idonea, the widow, had seisin of the lands of her inheritance on the 14th Oct. following (Ibid. m. 3).

P. 258. The effigy of William Longespé the Crusader is also engraved in Stothard's "Monumental Effigies."

P. 355. Ilbert de Chaz held lands of the Bohuns in Normandy as well as in England. Cats, the place from which he derived his name, is a parish in the arrondissement of St. Lo, and canton of Carentan. St. Georges and St. André de Bohon are parishes in the same canton. The following charter, from the cartulary of the neighbouring Abbey of Montbourg, has been communicated by Mr. Stapleton:

"Notum sit omnibus presentibus et futuris quod ego Ilbertus de Caz do et concedo in perpetuam elemosinam abbatie s'c'e Marie Montisburgi, ecclesiam de Caz, cum omnibus ad eam pertinentibus, libere et quiete, pro salute anime mee et omnium antecessorum meorum, concedentibus domino meo Unfrido de Bohun, et nepotibus meis Willelmo de Greinvill et Bartholomeo le Bigot, et ut firma sit imperpetuum hæc donatio signo dominice crucis hanc chartam confirmo et munio coram subscriptis testibus, Ilberto + Unfrido de Bohun, Bartholomeo le Bigot, et multis aliis. (fol. 104.)

The families of Greinville and Bigot succeeded to the inheritance of Ilbert at Cats. In the Cartulary, p. 105, follow charters from Adam de Greinvill, confirming to the Abbey of Montbourg the church of St. Gregory of Caz, "sicut eam prefate abbatie dedit Ilbertus de Caz antecessor meus;" and from William le Bigot, exchanging two pieces of land with the abbey in the parish of St. Gregory of Caz. The family of Magnevill had also a share or moiety in the advowson of the church of Caz, of the fee of Reviers.

MARKET CROSS AT LACOCK.

These pages must not be finally closed without recording the fate of a beautiful Cross, which stood in the market-place at Lacock from the days of the Abbey until a recent period. Its light and elegant shaft was destroyed about ten years ago, in order to furnish stone for erecting the village school-room! A view of it is preserved in the Antiquarian and Topographical Cabinet, published in 1800.

THE BOOK OF LACOCK.

In the MS. Harl. 5019, f. 231, et seq. is a transcript of the historical narrative of the Book of Lacock, somewhat fuller than that printed in the Appendix. It is said to have been taken "Ex libro antiquo manuscripto membran' in custodia Johannis Stowe, 1598;" consequently before the volume became the property of Sir Robert Cotton. Though the additional passages are not very important, yet, as it was our intention to print all that remained, they shall now be given. It appears to have commenced with this notice of the Conquest:

Anno ab incarnatione Domini milessimo sexagessimo sexto, Will'mus Bastardus cognomento Nothus, filius Roberti Ducis Normaniæ, fratris Emme matris S^{ti} Edwardi regis et Confessoris, qui per adoptionem S^{ti} Edwardi erat hæres regni Angliæ, sed Haroldus filius Comitis Godwini Cantie contra fidelitatem quam juraverat Will'o predicto ut duceret filiam ipsius, et ut reservaret regnum sibi Anglie post mortem S^{ti} Edwardi, coronavit seipsum. Will'o hoc audito, cum manu valida, stipat' militibus pluribus regnum Anglie invasit et subjugavit, ac Haroldus devicitur. Erat quidam, &c. (as in the first page of the Appendix.)

In p. ii. line 8, for "et" this copy reads "id est"; line 15, for "fertur" occurs "fortis"; in last line but two, "Normann. novem annis nutrita."

After p. v:

Hic Edmondus frater regis Ed'i filii Henrici duxit in uxorem reginam Navarre, genuit ex ipsa prefatum Dom. Thomam heredem suum, et alium filium Dom. Henricum de Lancastre; isti duo fratres, de stirpe regia progeniti, avunculi fuerunt regis Francie tunc temporis regnantis, et Regine Anglie Isabelle viventis.

This last passage shows, that this portion at least of the narrative was compiled in the time of Queen Isabella, who died in 1357.

APPENDIX OF DOCUMENTS.

No. I.

THE BOOK OF LACOCK.

The following is the whole that is now known to be extant of what was called the BOOK OF LACOCK, the fate of which at the Cottonian fire is noticed in the Preface. These extracts have been preserved in Vincent's MSS. at the College of Arms.

Comites Sarisburiæ.

Erat quidam miles strenuus Normannus, Walterus le Ewrus, Comes de Rosmar, cui propter probitatem suam Rex Guil. Conq. dedit totum dominium de Saresburia et Ambresburia. Antequam iste Walterus le Ewrus in Angliam venit, genuit Geroldum, Comitem de Rosmar, * Mantelec, qui genuit Guillelmum de Rosmar * le Gros, qui genuit Guil. de Rosmar le Meschyn, secundum, qui genuit Guillelmum, tertium de Rosmar, qui obiit sine liberis.

Postquam Walterus le Ewrus genuit Edwardum, natione Anglicum natum, postea Vicecomitem Wiltes, qui habuit uxorem de qua genuit quandam filiam nomine Matildam, quam postea Humphridus de Bohun duxit in uxorem, et quendam filium nomine Walterum de Saresburia. Iste Walterus de Saresburia duxit uxorem nomine Sibillam de Cadurcis, de qua genuit Patricium primum Comitem Sarum.

[*f.* 18 *b.*] Idem Walterus vero fundavit Prioratum de Bradenstok, et constituit in eodem Deo perpetuo deservientes Canonicos regulares; qui post mortem uxoris induit tonsuram et habitum Canonicorum, et ibidem corpora eorum in uno tumulo

---

* The important words between * * have been omitted in the Monasticon. In a brief extract in Brooke's "Second Discovery," we read "Rosmar *et* Mantelec."

collocantur juxta presbyterium. [quorum animæ requiescunt in cœlo.*] Patricius vero, ejus filius, genuit ex uxore sua Ela, Guillelmum Comitem Sarum.

Guillelmus vero duxit Alianoram de Viteri, de qua genuit filiam unicam nomine Elam aº D'ni M.C.LXXX.VIII. quæ data est D'no Guillelmo Longespe, filio Regis Henrici secundi, cui D'nus Rex Ric'us reddidit Comitatum de Rosmar, sicut hæreditatem et jus hæreditarium suum et ipsius Elæ, quod sibi accessit et accidit de jure hæreditario Edwardi de Sarisburia, filii Walteri de Ewrus.

Guillelmus Longespe, ex prædicta Ela, liberos genuit quorum nomina sunt hæc: (1) Guillelmus Longespe secundus, qui viriliter contra hostes Xp'i in Terra Sancta dimicans, ibidem pro nomine Jesu contumeliam patiens, vitam temporalem finiens, in Xp'o sine fine victurus, ut fertur, athleta Dei ad cœli palatium aº D'ni M.CC.XL.IX. ascendit. [cujus animam domina Ela mater ipsius, tunc existens abbatissa de Lacock, vidit cœlos penetrans in stallo suo, et horam cœteris sororibus denuncians.*] Genuit etiam (2) Ricardum, qui fuit Canonicus Sarum, cujus corpus apud Lacock tumulatur; (3) Stephanum Com' Ulton, cujus corpus apud Lacock humatum est, cor vero ejus apud Bradenestok optinet sepulturam; et (4) Nicholaum, qui fuit Ep'us Sarum, cujus corpus apud Sarum tumulatur, cor itaque ejus apud Lacock, viscera vero apud Ramisberiam; (5) Isabellam de Vescy; (6) Elam, quam duxit Comes Warwik, et postea Philippus Basset, quæ remansit sterilis; (7) Idam de Camyle,† quam duxit in uxorem Walterus filius Roberti, de qua genuit: Catarinam et Loricam, quæ velatæ erant apud Lacock; Elam, quam duxit primo Guillelmus de Dodingseles, de qua genuit ....; Robertum, qui Dernegoill ...

Ela ergo uxor Guillelmi Longespee primi nata fuit apud Ambresbiriam, patre et matre Normannorum. Pater itaque ejus defectus senio migravit ad Xp'm aº D'ni M.C.XC.VI. Mater ejus ante per biennium obiit; quorum corpora apud

---

* These passages are supplied from the Monasticon.
† The words "de Camyle" are inexplicable, and perhaps interpolated.

Bradenestok sunt tumulata juxta vestibulum ibidem sub lapide marmoreo. Interea D'na charissima Ela, patre et matre orbata,* per cognatos et notos adducta fuit in Normanniam, et ibidem sub tuta et arcta custodia nutrita. Eodem tempore in Anglia fuit quidam miles nomine Guillelmus Talbot, qui induit se habitum peregrini, in Normanniam transfretavit, et ibi moratus per ii annos, huc atque illuc vagans ad explorandam Dominam Elam Sarum. Et illa inventa exuit habitum peregrini, et induit se quasi Cytharisator, et curiam ubi morabatur intravit, et, ut erat homo jocosus in gestis antiquorum valde peritus, ibidem gratanter fuit acceptus quasi familiaris. Et quando tempus aptum invenit, in Angliam repatriavit, habens secum istam venerabilem Dominam Elam, et hæredem Comitatus Sarum, et eam Regi Ricardo præsentavit. At ille lætissimè eam suscepit, et fratri suo Guillelmo Longespe maritavit, per quam liberos subscriptos habuit, videlicet, Guillelmum Longespe secundum, Stephanum, Ricardum, Nicholaum, Isabellam Veisy, Petronillam quæ obiit in virginitate et apud Bradenestok juxta latus aviæ suæ dextrum ibidem sepulta sub lapide marmoreo, Elam, et Idam.

Aº D'ni M.CC.XX.VI. D'nus Guillelmus Longespe primus nonas Martii obiit, cujus corpus apud Sarum est humatum. Ela vero uxor ejus vii annis supervixit in viduitate, et proposuit autem sepius ut fundaret monasteria Deo placentia, pro salute animæ suæ et mariti sui, et omnium antecessorum suorum: quæ per revelationes habuit ut in prato testudinum, Anglicè *Snaylesmede*, prope Lacock monasterium ædificaret in honorem Sanctæ Mariæ Sanctique Bernardi, et usque ad finem complevit sumptibus suis propriis, id est de Comitatu Sarum quod fuit hæreditas sua. Fundavit etiam Prioratum de Henton ordinum Cartusiæ; una die duo Monasteria fundavit, primo mane xvi kal. Maij aº M CC.XXX.II. apud Lacock, in quo sanctæ degent Canonissæ continuo Deo famulantes et devotissimè; et Henton, post nonam; aº vero ætatis suæ xlv. [Alicia Garinges apud Lacok prima Canonissa velata.†] Aº vii post fundationem domus

* After this, in the Monasticon, a blank, and the word .... Dani. † Monasticon.

de Lacock, hoc est aº D'ni M.CC.XXX.VIII., Domina Ela Lungespee, nobilis matrona, assumpsit habitum religionis apud Lacock, aº ætatis suæ li. [viii. kal. Januarii, in suis et actibus et præpositis, omnibus perpetratis secundùm consilium et auxilium S. Edmundi Cantuar. Archiepiscopi, et aliorum virorum discretorum semper seipsam indulgens *] Aº D'ni M.CC.XL. xviii kal. Septemb. confecta est D'na Ela Lungespe fundatrix in Abbatissam primam de Lacock, aº vero ætatis suæ liii. Ubi monasterium suum et gregem sibi commissum multis annis strenue gubernavit et Deo devotissime servivit, arctam vitam ducens, in jejuniis, in vigiliis, sanctis meditationibus, et disciplinis assidue rigidis, ac aliis operibus bonis caritativis, decem et octo annis. Demum vero, cernens se senio et nimia debilitate affectam, cum non potuit ut voluit religioni suæ prodesse, renunciavit et recusavit præesse, et dum vixit Abbatissam præfecit nomine Beatricem de Cantia, pridie kal. Januarii aº M.CC.L.VII., aº ætatis suæ lxx. Sicque fere quinque annis post vixit sine omni cura libera; aº ætatis suæ lxxiv, ix kal. Septemb. animam suam in pace optinens, requievit in D'no aº M.CC.LX.I. et in choro dicti monasterii decentissime tumulata.

Sequitur de Guill⁰ Longespee secundo, primogenito filio Guillelmi Lungespee primi.

Guill: Lungespee secundus, genuit de Idonea Candoill (*esset* Camvile) uxore sua, Guill. Lungespee tertium, Ric'um, Elam, et Edmundum; quam Elam duxit Jacobus de Audele, de qua genuit Guillelmum de Audele, qui submersus fuit apud Snowdoun in guerra Walliæ, Nich'um de Audele, qui duxit Catharinam filiam Johannis Giffard, qui genuit Hugonem de Audele.† *Lib. Lacock, fol.* 19 *b.*

* Supplied from the Monasticon.
† The two eldest of the *five* sons of James Lord Audley are here omitted; and Hugh, who is here made his grandson, was the youngest of the five; and it has been already stated in p. 148. is supposed to have been his only son by Ela Longespé. Perhaps we should read " qui genuit . . . . . ; Hugonem," &c.

De Stephano, 2 filio, et ejus sequela.

Stephanus Lungespee sub rege H. iii. Justiciarius in Hybernia et Dominus capitalis erat ordinatus. Duxit in uxorem Emelinam Comitissam de Ulton, per quam erat Comes de Ulton; genuit ex ea (1) Elam de la Souch, quam duxit Rogerus de la Souch, de qua Alanus de la Souch, qui duxit in uxorem Alianoram filiam Nicholai de Segrave, de qua genuit Elam, Matildam, Elizabetham; Rogerum de la Souche,*(2) Emelinam, quæ nupsit Mauritio filio Mauritii. *Lib. Lacock, f.* 19 *b.*

De Guill. Lungespee tertio, filio Guillelmi secundi Lungespee primogenito.

Guill: Lungespee tertius, filius Guill: Lungespee secundi, duxit in uxorem Matildam filiam D'ni Walteri de Clifford, ex qua genuit unicam nobilissimam filiam Margaretam nuncupatam, et postea juvenis Comes obiit. Dicta vero Margareta nupsit illustrissimo viro D'no Henrico de Lacy, Comiti Lincolniæ, qui genuit ex ea Edmundum et Johannem de Lacy, qui viventibus patre et matre mortui sunt; genuit etiam ex ea unam nobilissimam filiam Alesiam nuncupatam, quæ hæres eorum nupsit egregio Comiti de Lancaster, Leicester, et de Ferrers, Thomæ nuncupato, filio D'ni Edmundi fratris Regis Edwardi, filii Regis Henrici iii, et de hæreditate sua et uxoris suæ quinque comitatus optinuit, viz. Com. Sarum et Lincoln et tres prænominatos. A°M.CCC.XX.I., undecem kal. Aprilis D'nus Thomas illustrissimus Comes Lanc. proditus et captus a propria gente sua, et apud Pontem-fractum ductus, regnante tunc filio patrui sui scilicet Edwardo nobili rege Angliæ filio illustris regis Edwardi, et in castro suo proprio apud Pontem-fractum pro justitia et jure regni justus et innocens morti adjudicatus est, et cum eo quamplures nobiles Angliæ. *Ex Lib. Lacock, foliis* 19 *et* 20.

* The words " Rogerum de la Souche " seem superfluous, or misplaced.

No. II.

CHARTER OF THE COUNTESS ELA FOUNDING THE PRIORY OF HINTON CHARTERHOUSE

(See page 173)

[Cart. 12 Hen. III. m. 4, per Inspeximus.]

Universis sanctæ Matris Ecclesiæ filiis ad quos præsens scriptum pervenerit, ELA COMITISSA SARR. æternam in Domino salutem.

Noverit universitas vestra quod dominus meus et quondam maritus Willielmus Longespee Comes Sarr. volens construere domum ordinis Chartusiæ, per assensum meum et bonam voluntatem, donavit ordini Chartusiæ manerium de Atherop in .... et boscum suum de Bradene cum integritate sua, et terram de Cheleworth quam habuit ex dono Henrici Basset, ut ibi manerent tam monachi quam fratres ad serviendum Deo imperpetuum secundùm consuetudinem et ordinem Chartus. Set quia monachi et fratres ad locum ipsum destinati, licet stetissent ibi per plures annos, non potuerunt invenire in prædictis tenementis locum ordini suo competentem, ego volens intuitu Dei perficere quod prædictus maritus meus bene inceperat, in ligia potestate et viduitate mea, post mortem ipsius, et pro anima ipsius, et pro anima Comitis Willielmi patris mei, et pro salute mea et puerorum meorum, et pro animabus omnium antecessorum et hæredum meorum, donavi et concessi et hac carta mea confirmavi ordini Chartusiæ, in escambium prædictorum tenementorum, *totum manerium meum de Henton cum advocatione ecclesiæ et parco* et omnibus aliis pertinenciis suis sine ullo retinemento inde michi et hæredibus meis. Et similiter *totum manerium meum de Norton cum advocatione ecclesiæ* et omnibus aliis pertinentiis suis, sine ullo retinemento michi et hæredibus meis: reservatis tamen michi et hæredibus meis serviciis militaribus omnium illorum qui de me tenent in prædictis maneriis per servicium militare; Excepto servicio Ricardi parcarii et hæredum suorum de j. virgata terra quam tenet in Henton, quod servicium pertinebit in perpetuum ad prædictos monachos et fratres, sive prædictus Ricardus defendat prædictam virgatam terræ per custodiam parci, vel per servicium militare; et etiam salvis michi et hæredibus meis kachiis forincesis, quæ sunt extra terminos prædictorum maneriorum; *Ad fundandam, construendam, et in perpetuum sustentandam quandam Domum ordinis Chartusiæ,* in honore Dei et beatæ Mariæ et sancti Johannis Baptiste, et omnium Sanctorum, *in parco de Henton,* in loco qui vocatur LOCUS DEI. Habendum et tenendum in puram et perpetuam elemosinam monachis et fratribus ibidem Deo servientibus secundum consuetudinem et ordinem ecclesie Chartusiæ. Et ego et hæredes mei warantizabimus prædictis monachis et fratribus prædicta tenementa cum pertinentiis, contra omnes gentes, et defendemus eos de omnibus serviciis et consuetudinibus et secularibus demandis. Et ut hec donatio, concessio, et confirmatio mea rata et stabilis inperpetuum permaneat, eam presentis scripti testimonio, et sigilli mei impressione corroboravi. Hiis Testibus: Domino Joscelino Bathonensi episcopo, domino R. Sarr. episcopo, magistro Edmundo de Abendon thesaurario Sarr., magistro Elia de Derham canonico Sarr., Reginaldo de ...... tunc vic· Wiltesir., Barth. de Turbervill, Willielmo Gereberd, Waltero de Pavily, Johanne Gereberd, Baldewino filio Willielmi tunc senescallo comitis Sarr., Michaele de Cheldrinton, Willielmo de Burneford, Nicholas de Hedinton clerico, Rogero Lond....

No. III.

ABSTRACT OF THE CARTULARY OF LACOCK ABBEY,

Now in the possession of Henry Fox Talbot, Esq. in the Record Turret at Lacock.

(*From Stevens's Monasticon, Appendix, pp.* 355-366.)

Carta Fundationis Abbatiæ de Lacock per Elam Comitissam.

Sciant presentes et futuri quod ego ELA COMITISSA SARUM, pro Deo et pro anima Comitis Willielmi Longespe mariti mei, et omnium antecessorum suorum et meorum, et pro salute mea et Willielmi Longespeie filii mei primogeniti, et omnium aliorum liberorum meorum et heredum meorum, in viduitate et ligia potestate mea, dedi et concessi et presenti carta mea confirmavi Deo et beate Marie et sancto Bernardo, *Manerium meum de Lacock cum advocatione Ecclesie* ejusdem manerii et cum omnibus pertinentiis suis et libertatibus et liberis consuetudinibus in omnibus locis et in omnibus rebus sine aliquo retinemento, *ad faciendam ibidem Abbathiam monialium* quam volo nominari LOCUM BEATE MARIE. Quare volo ut Abbatisse et moniales ibidem Deo imperpetuum serviture habeant et teneant totum predictum Manerium cum pertinentiis suis in liberam, puram, et perpetuam elemosinam, solutum penitus et quietum ab omni seculari servicio pertinente ad dominum Regem et Ballivos suos et ad me et ad heredes meos, et ab omni modo servicii et exactionis quocumque casu possit exigi de terra illa. Et ego ELA et heredes mei warantizabimus, defendemus, et acquietabimus prefatis monialibus totum prefatum manerium cum advocacatione Ecclesie et omnibus aliis pertinenciis suis ita liberum et quietum sicut aliqua elemosina liberius dari potest versus omnes homines et feminas imperpetuum. Hiis testibus: Huberto de Burgo, comite Cancie, Justiciario Anglie, Willielmo Marescallo comite Pembroke, Willielmo de

Warrene comite Surreye, Petro filio Herberti, Hugone de Nevile, Radulfo filio Nicholai senescallo Domini Regis, Johanne Daco, Henrico de Albenaco, et multis aliis.

Hæc charta habetur in Monast. Vol. 2do. p. 342; hic autem inseritur eo quod hic fit mentio de Sancto Bernardo, qui in illo exemplari non nominatur. [STEVENS.]

Alia Carta ejusdem Elæ Comitissæ.

[Fol. 1, b.]

Sciant presentes et futuri quod ego ELA COMITISSA SARUM, pro Deo et pro anima Comitis Willelmi Longespeie mariti mei et omnium antecessorum suorum et meorum, et pro salute mea et Willelmi Longespeie filii mei primogeniti et omnium aliorum liberorum meorum et heredum meorum, inviduitate et ligia potestate mea, dedi et concessi et presenti carta mea confirmavi Deo et beate Marie et sancto Bernardo et sanctimonialibus apud Lacock Deo servientibus *manerium meum de Lacock cum advocatione ecclesie* ejusdem manerii et cum omnibus pertinenciis suis, et *manerium de Hatherop* cum omnibus pertinentiis suis, et *manerium de Bissopestre* cum omnibus pertinenciis suis, et *medietatem manerii de Hedrington* cum omnibus pertinenciis suis, que me contingunt per finalem concordiam inter Humfridum de Boun et me in curia Domini Regis factam de honore de Treubrigge; et *advocacionem ecclesie de Winterbourn Syreveton;* cum omnibus libertatibus et liberis consuetudinibus in omnibus locis et in omnibus rebus sine aliquo retinemento. Quare volo quod moniales apud Lacok Deo imperpetuum servituræ habeant et teneant tota predicta maneria in liberam, puram, et perpetuam elemosinam, soluta penitus et quieta ab omni seculari servicio pertinente ad dominum Regem et Ballivos suos, et ad me et ad heredes meos, et ab omni modo servicii et exactionis quocunque casu possit exigi de dictis terris. Et ego ELA et heredes mei warrantizabimus, defendemus, et acquietabimus prefatis monialibus tota prefata Maneria cum dictis advocationibus Ecclesiarum, de Winterbourn Shreueton scilicet et Lacok, et cum omnibus aliis pertinentiis suis, ita libera et quieta sicut aliqua elemosina liberius dari potest, contra omnes homines et feminas imperpetuum. Hiis Testibus: Domino Waltero de Godarvile, Thoma de Ebelesbourn, Nicholao Malemains, Ada rectore de Gatesden, Ricardo Longespeye, Johanne de Moul, magistro Rogero de Stokes, domino Rogero de Baskervile, Petro de Salceto, domino Petro persona de Treubrigge, Philippo de Depeford clerico, Thoma Makerel clerico, Roberto de Holte clerico, et aliis.

Willielmus Longespeye confirmat Donationem Ele matris suæ.

[Fol. 2, a.]

Universis sancte Matris Ecclesie filiis ad quos presens scriptum pervenerit, Willielmus Longespeye salutem in Domino. Noverit universitas vestra nos cartam venerabilis matris nostre Ele Comitisse Sarum in hiis verbis inspexisse. *(Hic repetit primam Cartam dictæ Comitissæ de verbo ad verbum, sicut superius, et deinde procedit in hæc verba.)* Hanc igitur donationem et concessionem ratam et gratam habentes, eam, sicut carta dicte Ele matris nostre testatur, presenti pagina sigilli nostri impressione munita, confirmavimus. Hiis Testibus: Huberto de Burgo comite Cancie, Justiciario Anglie, Willelmo comite Pembroke, Willelmo de Warenne comite Surreye, Petro filio Herberti, Hugone de Nevile, Radulfo filio Nicholai senescallo Domini Regis, Johanne Daco, Henrico de Albeneto, et multis aliis.

[Fol. 2, b.]

Idem Willielmus Longespeye per aliam cartam suam recitat et confirmat secundam cartam matris suæ sicut superius, iisdem testibus.

[Fol. 3, b.]

Willielmus Longespeye filius supradicti Willielmi per cartam suam confirmat eandem donationem, aviæ suæ cartam recitans de verbo ad verbum.

Henricus tertius, Rex Angliæ, confirmat Donationem Elæ Comitissæ.

[Fol. 4, b.]

Henricus Dei gratia Rex Anglie, &c. Archiepiscopis, Episcopis, Abbatibus, Prioribus, Comitibus, Baronibus, Justiciariis, Vicecomitibus, Prepositis, Ministris, et omnibus Baillivis et Fidelibus suis, salutem. Inspeximus Cartam Ele Comitisse Sarum in hec verba. *(Hic recitat de verbo ad verbum primam Cartam dictæ Comitissæ, et deinde procedit in hunc modum.)* Nos igitur hanc donationem et concessionem ratam et gratam habentes, eam pro nobis et heredibus nostris concedimus et sigillo nostro confirmavimus. Hiis Testibus: predicto Hugone de Burgo comite Cancie Justiciario Anglie, Stephano de Segrave, Philippo de Albeneto, Radulfo filio Nicholai, Johanne filio Philippi, Ricardo filio Hugonis, Radulfo de Ralege, Henrico de Capella, et aliis. Dat. per manum venerabilis patris R. Cicestrensis Episcopi cancellarii nostri apud Westm. xxxi die Januarii, anno Regni xiiii*.

Conventio inter Elam Comitissam et Rectorem Ecclesiæ de Lacock, circa immunitatem dictæ Ecclesiæ parochialis.

[Fol. 5, a.]

Convenit inter dominam Comitissam Sarum, requirentem assensum Johannis Rectoris Ecclesie de Lacock ad edificandam Abbathiam monialium in parochia sua de Lacok, ex una parte; et eundem Johannem Rectorem ex altera: videlicet, quod dicta Ela Comitissa, ut predictum ipsius propositum ingressum pacificum penitus et progressum perpetuo sortiretur, obligavit se et heredes suos per presens scriptum de omnimoda indemnitate dicte Ecclesie de Lacok imperpetuum conservanda tam in decimis majoribus et minoribus quarumcunque rerum, secundum quod debentur a laicis decimari, quàm in sepulturis mortuorum, et in obventionibus et legatis et in aliis quibuscumque proventibus jure pastorali ad Ecclesiam pertinentibus memoratam, non obstante aliquo privilegio generali vel speciali impetrato vel in posterum impetrando; Ita tamen quod liceat liberè familie Abbatisse predicte quocumque voluerint alibi sive in vita sive in morte ecclesiastica percipere sacramenta et oblationes facere et legata. Capellani vero qui in Abbathia jam dicta divina pro tempore celebrabunt, Rectori prefate Ecclesie Parochialis fidelitatem jurabunt de indempnitate ejusdem Ecclesie conservanda; et cum fuerit ibi Abbatissa disponente Domino constituta, ipsa et ejus conventus per cartam suam cavebunt de indempnitate omnimoda dicte matricis Ecclesie conservanda sicut predictum est. Et hoc faciet queque Abbatissa post aliam. Quod si forte actis ibi aliquibus indiscrete limam correctionis apponere sit necesse, dicta Comitissa dictam domum jurisdictioni Episcopi et Capituli Sarum subjecit, ac ejusdem excessus commisit eisdem appellatione postposita corrigendos. Ut autem ista conventio robur optineat perpetue firmitatis, confectum est inter prefatos Comitissam et Rectorem presens Cyrographum bipartitum, cujus partes hinc inde acceptate et sigillis eorum signate remaneant penes ipsos in istius conventionis perpetuum argumentum. Actum apud Saresburiam in presentia domini Roberti Sarisburiensis Episcopi, Domini Walteri Decani, Rogeri Precentoris, Roberti Cancellarii, Edmundi Thesaurarii, tertio nonas Aprilis, anno gratie Mº. CCº. XXº. Nono.

Robertus Episcopus Sarisburiensis cartam Elæ Comitissæ de fundatione confirmat.

[Fol. 5, b.]

Universis sancte Matris Ecclesie filiis ad quos presens scriptum pervenerit, Robertus miseratione divina Sarisburiensis Ecclesie minister humilis, salutem eternam in Domino. Cartam dilecte in Christo filie nobilis Ele Comitisse Sarum inspeximus in hæc verba. *(Hic recitat de verbo ad verbum Cartam dictæ Comitissæ sicut superius, et post eam Cartam confirmationis Regis Henrici tertii* sicut supra, et deinde procedit in hæc verba.)* Quamobrem, ex commissa nobis cura pastoralis officii, eorum vota divinitus inspirata, quorum per cotidianam instantiam solicitudinem gerimus, tenemur ex justitie debito et ex gratie beneficio paterna diligentia promovere, quod dicta nobilis in hac parte tam salubri consilio providit, affectione sincera prosequendum duximus et favore. Nolentes quod tam pii tam sancti propositi consummatio retardetur, per quod et cultus Dei crescere et ecclesie decor per Spiritus Sancti gratiam magnifice poterit dilatari. Habito igitur cum dilectis filiis Capituli super hiis cum debita deliberatione tractatu, inspecto etiam cyrographo inter Comitissam predictam et Johannem ecclesie de Lacok Rectorem de indempnitate Ecclesie memorate confecto, pulsati insuper devotis supplicationibus W. Longespeye ejusdem Comitisse filii et heredis, de voluntate gratissima et assensu unanimi dilectorum in Christo filiorum ac fratrum nostrorum dictorum W. Decani et Capituli Sarum ob honorem et reverentiam Dei et gloriose genetricis sue semperque virginis Marie, et ad cultum ampliandum divinum; auctoritate pontificali *concedimus quod predicta Ela Comitissa abbathiam fundet et construat in manerio supradicto de Lacok, ac moniales de ordine Sancti Augustini ibidem constituat;* statuentes ut quecumque fuerint ibi pro tempore constitute ejusdem Sancti regulam similiter et ordinem exerceant et in perpetuum imi-

---

* See the remark in p. 185.

tentur, et Ecclesie Sarum et nobis nostrisque successoribus per omnia et in omnibus canonice perpetuis temporibus sint subjecte; Salva etiam indempnitate per omnia sancte Matris ecclesie, sicut in memorato cyrographo continetur quod quidem in suo robore in perpetuum statuimus duraturum. Quod ut robur optineat perpetue firmitatis presens scriptum sigillo nostro et sigillo capituli nostri fecimus communiri. Dat. apud Remmesberiam per manum W. de Purl clerici nostri, xii kal. Maii, pontificatus nostri anno primo. Hiis Testibus: Domino W. Decano, R. Precentore, R. Cancellario, et E. Thesaurario Sarum, Magistris W. Archidiacono Berkesire, H. Teysson, R. de Croshal, Thoma de Ebelesborn, et W. de Len, Gilberto de Stapelbrig, et P. Picot cantore Sarum, magistris Thoma de Warwick et Johanne de Bermingham clericis nostris, Waltero et Ricardo capellanis nostris, et multis aliis.

[Fol. 7, a.]

W. Longespeye per cartam suam promittit quod nihil exiget contra cyrographum inter ipsam et se confectum, ratione cartæ quam mater sua Ela Comitissa ei fecit de concessione maneriorum suorum, &c.

[Fol 7, b.]

Jordanus de Heydon dedit Abbatissæ de Lacock et Conventui ejusdem loci duas acras terræ arabilis in campis de *Hatton*, pro qua concessione dicta Abbatissa dedit ei tres marcas et dimidiam in gersuma.

[Fol. 8, a.]

W. Longespeye iterum confirmat omnes Donationes matris suæ.

Carta Henrici tertii Regis Angliæ de Mercato Monialibus concesso apud Lacock.

Henricus Dei gratia Rex Anglie, Dominus Hibernie, Dux Normannie et Aquitanie, Comes Andegavie, Archiepiscopis,

Episcopis, Abbatibus, Prioribus, Comitibus, Baronibus, Justiciariis, Vicecomitibus, Prepositis, Ministris, et omnibus Ballivis et fidelibus suis salutem. Sciatis nos concessisse et hac carta nostra confirmasse, pro nobis et heredibus nostris, dilectis nobis in Christo Ele Abbatissæ de Lacock et Monialibus ibidem Deo servientibus quod ipse et successores earum in perpetuum habeant quoddam *Mercatum ad manerium suum de Lacok* singulis septimanis *per diem Martis*, nisi mercatum illud sit ad nocumentum vicinorum mercatorum. Quare volumus et firmiter precipimus pro nobis et heredibus nostris quod predicte Ela Abbatissa et Moniales ibidem Deo servientes et successores earum in perpetuum habeant et teneant predictum Mercatum apud manerium predictum de Lacok, bene et in pace et libere et quiete cum omnibus libertatibus et liberis consuetudinibus ad hujusmodi Mercatum pertinentibus, sicut predictum est. Hiis Testibus: venerabilibus patribus W. Eboracensi Archiepiscopo, W. Karleolensi, W. Wigorniensi, et W. Exoniensi Episcopis, B. comite le Bigot, W. de Cantulo, Johanne filio Galfridi, Galfrido Dispensario, Waltero de Lintona, et aliis. Dat. per manum nostram apud Portesmouth sexto die Maii, anno regni nostri vicesimo sexto.

[Fol. 9, a.]

Sequuntur in Registro istæ Cartæ, viz. Conventio inter W. Comitem Sarum, et B. Bluet vicinum suum, super Advocatione Ecclesiæ de Lacock, quod unus eorum habeat Donationem dictæ Ecclesiæ una vice et alter altera vice, et quod neuter eorum possit alienare dictam Advocationem.

Carta W. Longespeye confirmans Monialibus de Lacock Manerium de Lacock et Manerium de Hatherop, et injungens militibus et libere tenentibus ut faciant omnia servitia sua predictis Monialibus.

[Fol. 9, b.]

Repetuntur Cartæ W. Longespeye duæ, et Henrici Regis, quæ supra habentur ex foliis 2, 4.

Carta Henrici tertii, Regis Angliæ, de Feria Monialibus de Lacock concessa.

[Fol. 10, b.]

Henricus Dei gratia Rex Angliæ, &c. Archiepiscopis, Episcopis, Abbatibus, Prioribus, Comitibus, Baronibus, Justiciariis, Vicecomitibus, Prepositis, Ministris, et omnibus fidelibus et Ballivis suis salutem. Sciatis nos concessisse et hac carta nostra confirmasse pro nobis et heredibus nostris Priorissæ de Lacock et monialibus ibidem Deo servientibus quod ipse et successores sui habeant in perpetuum quandam *Feriam apud manerium de Lacok duraturam per tres dies*, scilicet, in vigilia et in die et in crastino translationis Sancti Thome Martyris, nisi feria illa sit ad nocumentum vicinarum Feriarum. Quare volumus et firmiter precipimus pro nobis et heredibus nostris quod predicte Priorissa et Moniales et successores sui habeant et teneant in perpetuum Feriam predictam bene et in pace libere et quiete et integre cum omnibus libertatibus et liberis consuetudinibus ad hujusmodi Ferias pertinentibus, nisi Feria illa sit ad nocumentum Feriarum vicinarum, sicut predictum est. Hiis testibus, W. de Raleg thesaurario Exon, Aumarico de Sancto Amando, Johanne filio Galfridi, Johanne filio Philippi, Bartholomeo Pecch, Johanne de Plesseis, Hamone filio Philippi, et aliis. Dat. per manum venerabilis patris Radulphi Cicestrensis Episcopi et Cancellarii nostri, apud Wyndeshour, septimo die Augusti, anno regni nostri vicesimo primo.

Carta Regis Henrici tertii de Bosco mortuo Monialibus de Lacock concesso.

[Fol. 11, a.]

Henricus Dei gratia Rex Anglie, &c. omnibus Ballivis et fidelibus suis ad quos presentes littere pervenerint salutem. Sciatis nos concessisse dilecte nobis in Christo Abbatisse de

Lacock quod singulis septimanis habeat unam carrectam semel itinerantem in foresta nostra de Melkesham ad mortuum boscum, ad focum suum sine dampno eidem foreste quandiu nobis placuerit. In cujus rei testimonium literas nostras eidem Abbatisse fieri fecimus patentes. Teste meipso apud Portesmouth sexto die Maii, anno regni nostri xxvi°.

Carta ejusdem Regis Henrici de Placea in Foresta de Melkesham Monialibus de Lacock concessa.

Henricus Dei gratia Rex Anglie, Dominus Hibernie, et Dux Aquitanie, Archiepiscopis, Episcopis, Abbatibus, Prioribus, Comitibus, Baronibus, Justiciariis, Vicecomitibus, Ministris, et omnibus Baillivis et fidelibus suis salutem. Noverit universitas vestra quòd, cùm dilecta affinis nostra Ela dicta Patrona Domus de Lacock nos attente rogasset ut eidem Domui sue ad sustentationem suam de gratia nostra subveniremus de una carectata buste diurna de mortuo vel sicco bosco vel de viridi in foresta nostra de Melkesham, et per inquisitionem captam inde per dilectum et fidelem nostrum Robertum Waleraunz tunc Justiciarium foreste nostre citra Trentam fieri fecimus, accepissemus quod mortuus vel siccus boscus non sufficeret ad unam carectatam diurnam, et quod utilius esset nobis assignare Abbatisse et Monialibus dicte domus quandam placeam in quadam parte foreste, nos pro salute anime nostre et animarum antecessorum nostrorum et heredum nostrorum dedimus, concessimus, et hac carta nostra confirmavimus, pro nobis et heredibus nostris, predictis Abbatisse et Monialibus *quadraginta acras bosci in predicta foresta nostra*, per perticam nostram de foresta, infra metas subscriptas, viz. de haya et fossato de Luntesleye ascendendo juxta Wodenesdik usque desuper viam que vocatur Haggestrete versus Chetowe, et desuper ipsam viam usque parvam Hesewych ad fossatum quod vocatur Aldefrithesdich, et de dicto fossato de Aldefrithesdich, usque ad predictum fossatum et haiam de Luntesleye juxta Milestile ex parte australi; habendas et tenendas eisdem Abbatisse, et Monialibus et successoribus suis, ad sustentationem Domus sue, de nobis et heredibus nostris, in liberam puram et perpetuam elemosynam, quietas de vasto et regardo, et de visu forestariorum viridariorum, et de omnibus aliis ad forestam et forestarios viridarios et eorum ministros pertinentibus. Ita tamen quod liceat eisdem Monialibus placeam illam fossato et haya pro voluntate sua includere, ita quod fere nostre eam ingredi non possint, et eam sic inclusam sibi et successoribus suis tenere in perpetuum. Et si contingat quod fere nostre per defectum clausure sue placeam illam ingrediantur, fere ille nobis remaneant capiende ad voluntatem nostram. Ita quòd, cum voluerint dicte Moniales, placeam illam reincludant quòd fere nostre eam ingredi non possint, sicut predictum est. Hiis testibus, Ricardo de Clare Comite Gloucestrie et Herefordie, Rogero le Bigot Comite Norfolcie et Marescallo Anglie, Hugone le Bigot Justiciario Anglie, Philippo Basset, Johanne Merunsell Thesaurario Eborum, Johanne de Burgo, Henrico de Bathonia, Rogero de Thurkelby, Gilberto de Preston, Nicholao de Hanslo, et aliis. Datum per manum nostram apud Westmonasterium tertio die Junii, anno regni nostri quadragesimo quarto.

[Fol. 12, a.]

Conventio inter Moniales de Lacock, et Rogerum de Bloet personam de Lacock, super quodam Molendino cum stagno, et quodam Ponte, a predictis Monialibus erectis, viz. quod predictus persona nihil possit exigere de Monialibus nomine molendini, et quod eædem Moniales teneantur predictum pontem erigere si ceciderit, et satisfaciant dicto personæ, pro omnibus damnis si dictus pons non fuerit erectus.

[Fol. 12, b.]

Beatrix Abbatissa de Lacock et Willielmus Bluet miles fecerunt inter se excambium terrarum. Dictus Miles dedit Abbatisse totam terram suam in la Scorteforlange continentem quinque acras jure hereditario in perpetuum, et quod Moniales possint includere predictam terram et totam terram suam in

Buriforlange, et etiam concessit unum fontem super terram suam in Lackhamesleie, ita quod possent eum includere, et ultra quod possent Moniales conducere aquam dicti fontis super terras ejusdem Willielmi ad aqueductum suum. Pro hac concessione Moniales dederunt prædicto Willelmo Bluet croftam quam tenuit Thomas de Ponte, et terram quam tenuit Alditha de la Hele, et terram quam Petrus Pulche tenuit, et unam acram terræ in Wiveleshange, et dimidiam acram terræ in la Nihoke, que omnes particulæ continent quinque acras.

[Fol. 13, b.]

Sequitur alia Carta de Aquæductu supradicto.

[Fol. 14, a.]

Conventio inter supradictum Willelmum Bluet et Moniales de Lacock de cursu aquæ ad Molendinum juxta Claustrum.

[Fol. 15, a.]

Roberti de Holta licentia concessa monialibus de Lacock ducendi aquam per terram suam.

Licentia Willelmi Bluet de eodem conductu.

[Fol. 17, a.]

Johannes Sewal per cartam suam confirmavit Julianæ de Lacock Abbatissæ et ejusdem loci Conventui, pro quatuor marcis argenti quas ei præ manibus dederunt, omnia messuagia sua in villa de Lacock. Cartæ præcedentes exhibent jus quod idem Johannes habuit in dictis messuagiis.

[Fol. 18, a.]

Ricardus Malloc quietum clamavit eidem Abbatissæ et Conventui totum jus quod habuit vel habere potuit in uno Messuagio in villa de Lacock.

Alditha Pilevel quietum clamavit Aliciæ Abbatissæ et Conventui de Lacock, totum jus quod habuit in quodam Burgagio in villa de Lacock.

[Fol. 19, a.]

Willielmus de Chippenham scissor dedit Beatrici Abbatissæ et Conventui de Lacock, messuagium cum domibus, curtilagiis et omnibus pertinentiis suis in villa de Lacock, pro qua donatione dicta Abbatissa et Conventus dederunt ei quadraginta solidos sterlingorum.

[Fol. 23, a.]

Nicholaus Flour, consensu Mariæ uxoris suæ, confirmavit donationem quam Johannes filius Rogeri de Hedyngton fecit per cartam suam Abbatissæ de Lacock, et ejusdem loci Conventui, de omnibus Burgagiis seu tenementis quæ aliquando contingebant et contigisse poterant prædictam Mariam uxorem suam nomine dotis per mortem Rogeri de Hedyngton, quondam viri sui.

[Fol. 23, b.]

Nicholaus filius Rogeri de Hedyngton reddidit et concessit Abbatissæ et Conventui de Lacock, omnia tenementa quæ de eis tenuit in Lacock.

[Fol. 24, a.]

Edwardus Sweyn, de Lacock, dedit et concessit Monialibus de Lacock, totam terram et tenementum, &c. quæ aliquando habuit vel habere potuit in Lacock; pro qua donatione dictæ Moniales concesserunt ei et Isabellæ uxori suæ, ad totam vitam utriusque, unam liberationem secundum quod continebatur in quodam scripto inde inter eos confecto.

[Fol. 25, a.]

Edwardus Sweyn dedit eisdem Monialibus totam terram et tenementum quod Ricardus pater suus habuit de dono Ricardi de Wyck in Lacock et Lacham, et terram quam pater suus habuit de Willelmo Clovegiffre, et duas acras terræ in Stretforlanga, et unam croftam quæ vocabatur Wodecroft in Lacock et Lacham, reddendo inde annuatim duodecim denarios heredibus Ricardi de Wycke, et unum obolum heredibus Willelmi Clovegilofre, et dimidiam libram cumini hæredibus Ricardi Albi, et unum obolum heredibus Sewell, et unum denarium Capellæ de Lacham ad lumen Beatæ Mariæ, et unum obolum hæredibus Johannis filii Jordani, pro omni servitio seculari.

[Fol. 25, b.]

Petrus de Bristoll dedit Monialibus de Lacock duo messuagia cum pertinentiis in villa de Lacock, reddendo inde tres obolos annuatim Rogero de Hedyngton, et Hugoni clerico unum denarium, pro omni servitio.

[Fol. 26, b.]

Isabella filia Roberti Burel, pro decem marcis argenti sibi præ manibus solutis, relaxavit et quietum clamavit Monialibus de Lacock totum jus et clamium quod habuit in duabus virgatis terræ cum pertinentiis in villa de Lacock et Natton.

[Fol. 27, a.]

Willelmus Burel, filius Isabellæ supradictæ, confirmavit donationem matris suæ.

[Fol. 28, b.]

Hugo de Lacock clericus dimisit Monialibus de Lacock terram et tenementum quod habuit in villa de Natton, de dono Thomæ de la Ford clerici, pro qua dimissione dictæ Moniales dederunt dicto Hugoni viginti et duas marcas sterlingorum in gersuma.

[Fol. 29, a.]

Ricardus Purchas quietum clamavit Beatrici Abbatissæ et Monialibus de Lacock, totum jus et clamium quod habuit in toto tenemento quod Willielmus de Donelis et Isabella uxor ejus tenuerunt in Lacock apud Wycke, cum ædificiis, pratis, &c.

pro qua quieta clamatione dictæ Moniales dederunt prædicto Ricardo Purchas, et Ricardo filio suo, ad valenciam tertiæ partis prædictæ terræ excepto mesuagio, ad totam vitam suam, reddendo inde annuatim unum denarium, pro omni servitio.

[Fol. 30, a.]

Robertus de la Lupegate dedit Monialibus de Lacock, duas acras et dimidiam terræ arabilis cum pertinentiis in cultura quæ vocatur Kechelcroft juxta novum clausum dictæ Domus de Lacock.

[Fol. 30, b.]

Henricus Crok dedit eisdem Quarreram inter terram domini Sampsonis de la Bore et Walteri Campedene, cum libero ingressu et egressu, quamdiu ipsa durare poterit.

Robertus Abbas de Stanlega in Wiltesire, et Conventus ejusdem loci, dederunt eisdem Monialibus unam partem quarrariæ suæ de Haselbyria, habentem in latitudine sexaginta et sexdecim pedes, et in latitudine quicquid eorum fuit, ad capiendam petram quantam inde capere poterant, in escambium illius quarrariæ quam Moniales emerunt de Henrico Crok. Dat. anno gratiæ M^o. CC^o. quadragesimo primo, die Sancti Johannis ante portam Latinam.

[Fol. 33, b.]

Matheus filius Johannis Carpentarii dedit dictis Monialibus unum mesuagium in villa de Lacock, pro qua donatione dictæ Moniales dederunt ei unam marcam Esterlingorum.

[Fol. 34, b.]

Robertus de Holta concessit quod eædem Moniales liberam habeant potestatem fodiendi et aquam suam ducendi per terram suam, et conductum suum reparandi.

Carta Willelmi Episcopi Sarum, Compositionem initam inter Nicholaum Longespee Rectorem Ecclesiæ de Lacock, et Moniales de Lacock, recitans et confirmans.

[Fol. 35, b.]

Pateat universis quod nos Willelmus, Dei permissione Episcopus Sarum, inspeximus quandam compositionem initam inter discretum virum dominum Nicholaum Longespee, Thesaurarium Ecclesie nostre Sarum, Rectorem Ecclesie de Lacock, vero sigillo dicti Domini Nicholai signatum, ex parte una, et religiosas dominas dominam Julianam Dei gratia Abbatissam Monasterii de Lacock et ejus Conventum ex altera, sub eo qui sequitur tenore. Universis sancte Matris Ecclesie filiis, presentes literas inspecturis, Nicholaus Longespee, Rector Ecclesie de Lacock, Sarum Dyocesis, salutem in Domino. Ad universitatis vestre notitiam tenore presentium volo pervenire quod cum suscitata esset querela inter me et religiosas dominas dominam Julianam Dei gratia Abbatissam Monasterii de Lacock et ejus Conventum, super tertia parte decimarum garbarum de dominico suo provenientium, videlicet de terris hiis que jacent in le Hinhoc, in Weteleye, in le Langeley, Suthbiria in Asseleye, in le Inlonde super Cockeleye, et in Monlesham, quas infra limites Parochie mee de Lacock percipiunt, et se percipere debere dicunt Abbatissa et Conventus supradicte, de dono venerabilis domine, domine Ele Longespee, Comitisse Sarum, matris mee, predicti Monasterii Fundatricis. Hec tandem ad perpetue pacis fundamentum compositio inter nos amicabilis intercessit, viz. quòd ego, quàm tenuis et exilis sit earum porcio decimarum predictarum quas sine gravi detrimento predicte Ecclesie de Lacock percipere possunt et habere, quamque jugis et intenta sit earum devocio apud Deum devote perpendens, de voluntate et assensu expresso Reverendi Patris domini Willelmi Dei gratia Sarum Episcopi ac venerabilium dominorum Symonis Decani et Capituli Sarum, pro me et successoribus meis, sponte pure et absolute concedo ut dictum Monasterium de Lacock, et Sanctimoniales ibidem Deo servientes et futuris temporibus servituræ, habeant percipiant et in perpetuum possideant integre pacifice et inconcusse tertiam partem decimarum predictarum de supradicto dominico suo proveniencium, sicut a tempore fundacionis suæ perceperunt et percipiunt in presenti. Renuncians simpliciter pro me et successoribus meis omni exactioni prosecutioni et juri quod michi et eisdem competunt in hac parte vel in futurum competere possunt quoquo modo. In cujus rei testimonium presens scriptum sigilli mei impressione munivi. Hujus rei sunt testes Dominus Johannes de Schryvenham vicarius perpetuus de Lacock, Willelmus de Wollesleye vicarius de Kalne, Johannes vicarius de Canyngg, Benedictus de Lincoln clericus, Willielmus scriptor, Johannes de Herterigg, Lambertus de Roscumbe, Nicholaus de Rudham, et plures alii. Datum apud Kalne, tertio nonas Septembris, anno Domini M°. CC°. nonagesimo. Quam compositionem ratam habentes et acceptam, ipsam auctoritate pontificali ad peticionem dictarum parcium de consensu Decani et Capituli Ecclesie nostre Sarum duximus confirmandam. In cujus rei testimonium presentes litteras tam sigilli nostri quam Decani et Capituli nostri Sarum impressione fecimus communiri. Datum apud Sunnyngg tercio decimo kal. Aprilis, anno Domini millesimo ducentesimo nonagesimo, et consecrationis nostre secundo.

Carta Edwardi primi Regis Angliæ, licentiam concedens Roberto de Bardenye quod ipse possit dare Monialibus de Lacock quædam tenementa et terras.

[Fol. 40, b.]

Edwardus Dei gratia Rex Anglie, Dominus Hibernie, et Dux Aquitanie, omnibus ad quos presentes littere pervenerint salutem. Licet de communi concilio regni nostri statuerimus quod non liceat viris religiosis seu aliis ingredi feodum alicujus ita quod ad manum mortuam deveniat, sine licentia nostra et capitalis domini de quo res illa immediate tenetur; per finem tamen quem dilecta nobis in Christo Abbatissa de Lacock fecit nobiscum in Cancellaria nostra, concessimus, et licenciam dedimus, pro nobis et heredibus nostris, quantum in nobis est, Roberto de Bardeneye, quod ipse duo mesuagia et duas virgatas terre et dimidiam cum pertinentiis in Natton juxta Lacock, dare possit et assignare prefate Abbatisse et Monialibus ejusdem loci, Habenda et tenenda eisdem Abbatisse et Monialibus, et earum successoribus in perpetuum. Et eisdem Abbatisse et Monialibus quod ipsæ predicta mesuagia et terram cum pertinentiis a prefato Roberto recipere possint, et tenere sicut predictum est, tenore presentium similiter licentiam dedimus specialem. Nolentes quod predictus Robertus aut heredes sui, prefatæ Abbatissa et Moniales, vel eorum successores, ratione statuti predicti per nos vel heredes nostros inde occasionentur, molestentur in aliquo vel graventur. In cujus rei testimonium has litteras nostras sibi fieri fecimus patentes. Teste meipso apud Dunfermelin vicesimo quinto die Novembris, anno regni nostri tricesimo secundo.

[Fol. 41, b.]

Finalis concordia facta in Curia Regis Edwardi primi, apud Eboracum, anno tricesimo secundo dicti Regis, inter Johannam Abbatissam et Conventum de Lacock ex una parte, et Robertum de Bardenye ex altera, de duobus mesuagiis duabus virgatis terræ et dimidia cum pertinentiis in Natton juxta Lacock. Dictus Robertus recognovit predicta cum pertinentiis esse jus ipsius Abbatissæ et Ecclesiæ suæ, et pro hac recognitione Abbatissa dedit ei quadraginta marcas argenti.

Idem Robertus de Bardeneye per cartam suam dedit dictis Monialibus duo mesuagia et unam virgatam terræ et dimidiam in Natton et Lacock.

[Fol. 41, b.]

Idem per aliam cartam dedit eisdem omnes terras et omnia tenementa sua in Natton.

[Fol. 42, a.]

Willielmus filius Thomæ de la Chambre, de Natton, quietum

clamavit dictis Monialibus totum jus quod habuit in quinque solidatis septem denariatis et una libra cymini annui redditus provenientis de terris et tenementis in Natton, et totum clamium quod habuit in dictis terris.

[Fol. 43, a.]

Willelmus Longespeye dedit eisdem totam terram de Cettre, exceptis feodis militum cum eorum serviciis et una virgata terræ, et una dimidia acra prati, et tota terra Elæ Comitissæ de Warwick.

[Fol. 43, b.]

Henricus tertius, Rex Angliæ, confirmavit prædictam donationem per cartam suam, de anno regni sui tricesimo secundo.

[Fol. 49, a.]

Alicia de Cettre quietum clamavit dictis Monialibus totum jus quod habuit in una virgata terræ in villa de Cettra, et in una domo et placea in Lacock, ante portam cymiterii Abbathiæ.

[Fol. 52, a.]

Anno regni Regis Henrici tertii tricesimo tertio, Nicholaus de Hedyngton, coram justiciariis Regis, recognovit tres carucatas terræ cum pertinentiis in Cettra esse jus Monialium de Lacock.

[Fol. 52, b.]

Anno ejusdem Regis quinquagesimo secundo, Walterus Giffard, Priores et Conventus de Bromore et Ferleg, Willielmus le Droys, Simon de Brokebyria, et Benedictus Silvester concesserunt quod prædictæ Moniales imperpetuum tenerent clausum suum apud Ciclet tam vetus quam novum.

[Fol. 53, b.]

Johanna filia Willelmi Larcher quietum clamavit dictis Monialibus totum jus et clamium quod habuit in aliqua terra et tenemento et custodia nemoris de Chicled.

[Fol. 54, b.]

Walterus le Fauconer remisit Monialibus unam annuam carectatam virgarum de Bosco ipsarum de Chicklad quam debebant ei ratione tenementi quod de eis tenebat in Cettra.

[Fol. 56, b.]

Ela Abbatissa de Lacock, et Conventus ejusdem loci, remiserunt Johanni Falconario servitium quod eis debebat pro tribus virgatis terræ in villa de Cettra, viz. mutationem unius espervarii et unius falconis, et pro hac remissione dictus Johannes obligavit se et heredes suos singulis annis reddere dictæ Abbatissæ et Conventui dimidiam marcam argenti.

[Fol. 57, a.]

Johannes Falconarius remisit Monialibus de Lacock totum jus suum in quinque acris terræ quas habebat in campo de Cettra orientali; pro qua remissione dictæ Moniales dederunt ei quatuor marcas et dimidiam argenti, quatuor quarteria frumenti, et quinque quarteria ordei.

[Fol. 57, b.]

Johannes Parcarius recognovit se debere eisdem Monialibus octo solidos redditus annuos.

Alicia de Cormailes remisit eisdem redditum casei quod ei debebatur de manerio de Cettra.

[Fol. 58, a.]

Willelmus de Horton remisit eisdem, pro viginti solidis quos ei dictæ Moniales dederunt, totum jus quod habebat in uno mesuagio et duabus carucatis terræ in Chitterne. Dat. anno regis Edwardi primi decimo septimo.

[Fol. 58, b.]

Margareta vidua Edmundi le Rous, de Beremham, remisit

Julianæ Abbatissæ et Conventui de Lacock, totum jus suum in uno mesuagio et duabus carucatis terræ in Chytterne, pro qua remissione dictæ Moniales dederunt ei viginti solidos argenti.

[Fol. 59, a.]

Matildis vidua Johannis de Merweden remisit eisdem Monialibus totum jus quod habuit in uno mesuagio et duabus carucatis terræ in Chiterne, anno regni regis Edwardi primi decimo septimo, et pro hac remissione dictæ Moniales dederunt ei viginti solidos.

Carta Roberti Episcopi Sarum, de Ordinatione Ecclesiæ de Wynterborn Sireveton.

[Fol. 60, a.]

Robertus Dei gratia Episcopus Sarum, dilectis in Christo filiabus Ele eadem gratia Abbatisse et Conventui Monialium de Lacock salutem, gratiam, et benedictionem. Cum juxta merita deceat premia dispensare, non est gerendum graviter aut indigne si clarioribus virtutum radiis coruscantes, suis hoc meritis quasi ex debito vendicantibus in optinendis graciis ceteris preferantur, ut dum bene meritos congruis premiis alii conspiciunt muneratos, ad bene merendum emulacione laudabili forcius animentur. Cum igitur tu, filia Abbatissa, dum olim inter secli nobiles dignitate seculari fulgeres, eo tibi qui ubi vult spiritu spirat desuper inspirante, patrimonium tuum Domino dedicans, illud quibusdam monasteriis que in eodem ut cultum divinum ampliares de novo fundasti, de salute propria cogitans provide duxeris applicandum; ac postmodum tua teque salubriter obnegans habitu religionis suscepto, ea que prius te gracia prosequente adeo virtutum profeceris incrementis, quod meritis tuis exigentibus auctoritate et assensu quorum interfuit in hac parte disponente Domino, in primam predicti Monasterii Abbatissam assumpta, gregis tui numerum ac hospitalitatis graciam tui regiminis tempore laudabiliter duxeris ampliandos; quare possessiones predicti monasterii que nunc sunt expensarum eidem incumbentium honera nequeunt sustinere; nos ob vite mundiciam et religionis fervorem que in novella monasterii vestri plantacione florere cognovimus, ac meritorum tuorum optentu quo magis in vobis unitatis interioris federa sinceriori caritate solidentur ac hospitalitatis munera liberalius et libentius exhibeantur, capituli nostri Sarum accedente assensu, de Ecclesia de Wynterborn Sirreveton vestri patronatus taliter duximus ordinandum; videlicet quod, Hosberto nunc Rectore ejusdem cedente vel decedente, decima garbarum tocius parrochie ejusdem, pratum dominicum, et mansus capitalis Ecclesie predicte, quem tamen Vicarius ejusdem precario tenebit donec in alio manso competenti eidem provideritis, in usus vestros proprios et perpetuos cedere debeant in futurum. Residuo fructuum Ecclesie memorate ad perpetuum ipsius Vicarium pro tempore futurum qui extraordinariis oneribus inter vos et ipsum pro rata porcionum vestrarum parciendis, onera ordinaria eidem incumbentia sustinebit nomine perpetue vicarie spectaturo; in qua nobis et successoribus nostris de assensu vestro jus patronatus reservamus. Interim vero duas marcas annuas a prefato Rectore in beati Michaelis et resurrectionis Dominice festis pro equalibus porcionibus percipiendas de ejusdem Rectoris assensu, Ecclesie ipsius pensionis nomine, vobis duximus constituendas. Ut autem hec donacio nostra perpetue firmitatis robur optineat, presens scriptum tam sigillo capituli nostri Sarum quam nostro fecimus consignari. Hiis testibus, Domino Roberto decano Sarum, magistro Rogero precentore, magistro Radulfo cancellario, domino Henrico thesaurario Sarum, magistris Egidio archidiacono Berksire et Stephano archidiacono Sarum, magistris Raddulfo de Eboraco, Thoma de la Wile, Waltero de la Wile, Petro de Cumbe, Galfrido de Bedeford, canonicis Sarum, magistro Ricardo de Bienham, Petro de Wynborn capellano, magistro Rogero de la Grene, Roberto de Wychampton, et aliis. Dat. 1 kal. Januarii, pontificatus nostri anno tertio-decimo (1241).

[Fol. 60, b.]

Hosbertus Rector Ecclesiæ de Wynterborn Sireveton supranominatus per cartam suam confirmavit eisdem Monialibus supradictas duas marcas annui redditus sicut in carta Episcopi.

[Fol. 61, a.]

Ivo Mercator dedit eisdem Monialibus tenementum suum in manerio de Wynterborn Syreveton.

[Fol. 61, b.]

Hugo Burgonensis dedit viginti solidos per annum in manerio de Wynterborn Syreveton, qui reddebantur ei pro duabus virgatis terræ, et totum jus suum in dictis duabus virgatis.

[Fol. 63, b.]

Matildis Eborardi dedit eisdem totam terram suam in manerio de Ambresburia, reddendo inde debitum dominis feodi.

Philippus de Depeford recognovit se teneri solvere dicto Conventui quadraginta solidos annuatim imperpetuum in villa de West Amberesbury pro terra que fuit Matildis uxoris dicti Philippi.

[Fol. 65, a.]

Anastatia de Pavely dedit viginti solidos annui redditus in manerio de Westbyria percipiendos.

[Fol. 65, b]

Walterus de Pavely confirmavit prædictam donationem filiæ suæ Anastasiæ.

[Fol. 66, a.]

Willielmus Longespeye, per tres cartas suas, contulit dictis Monialibus totum manerium de Bissopestre, terram de Hathrop, et advocacionem Ecclesiæ parochialis de Lacock. Hæc concessio facta fuit anno regni Henrici tertii vicesimo.

[Fol. 67, a.]

Adam Sweyn concessit eisdem totam terram et medietatem molendini cum pertinentiis quæ habuit in manerio Abbatissæ de Lacock, apud Bissopestriam, pro qua donatione Beatrix Abbatissa dedit dicto Adæ sex marcas et dimidiam argenti.

[Fol. 67, b.]

Anno 1259, Anastasia relicta Helyæ de Byssopestre remisit eisdem Monialibus totam partem suam Molendini de Bissopestre cum pertinentiis.

[Fol. 68, a.]

Anno 1259, Willielmus de Smalebrok remisit eisdem totam partem suam Molendini de Bissopestre, et prati.

[Fol. 68, b.]

Edwardus filius Adæ Serle dedit eisdem duas acras terræ cum pertinentiis in villa de Bissopestre.

Emma quæ fuit uxor Eliæ Burgeys de Weremenistre, remisit eisdem totum clamium quod habuit in Molendino in villa de Bissopestre, et in uno mesuagio in eadem villa, pro qua remissione dictæ Moniales dederunt dictæ Emmæ quadraginta solidos sterlingorum in gersumam.

[Fol. 69, b.]

Rogerus Capellanus renunciavit totum jus quod habuit in terræ quæ fuit patris sui in Lacock.

[Fol. 71, a.]

Agnes Waspayl concessit eidem Conventui mesuagium suum, cum gardinis, croftis, et pratis, et tota terra sua in Horspol, et septem acras terræ super croftam Jordani de Smalebroke, et duas acras terræ supra Mothull, et unam acram terræ ex australi parte ecclesiæ Sancti Aldelmi de Bissopestre, et duas acras terræ apud Rubge, et unam acram terræ in Kenescumbe, et unam acram terræ super caput de la Langeforburdesende, et quatuor averia et unum affrum in mora de Smalebrok, quieta de pannagio et herbagio, reddendo inde annuatim unam rosam dictæ Agneti, et unum denarium domino feodi pro omni servicio, &c. salvo regali servitio.

[Fol. 71, b.]

Anno Regis Henrici tertii quadragesimo quinto, dicta Agnes finem fecit cum prædictis Monialibus coram Justiciariis Regis de supradicta donatione.

[Fol. 73, a.]

Anno ejusdem Regis tricesimo tertio, Willielmus Maudut concessit prædictis Monialibus communam pasturæ ad ducentas oves in bruera sua apud Wermenistre per totam brueram et per totum annum pascendis, excepto clauso suo, reddendo inde duos solidos sterlingorum pro omni servitio.

[Fol. 73, b.]

Robertus Swotyng quietum clamavit eisdem totum jus suum in una crofta apud Mamborn, cum sepibus et fossatis ad dictam croftam spectantibus desuper Hullewode, pro qua quieta clamatione dictæ Moniales dederunt ei unam acram terræ arabilis cum pertinentiis in villa de Bissopestre.

[Fol. 76, a.]

Willelmus Longespey concessit quod mater sua Ela conferret Domui de Lacock medietatem manerii de Hedyngton, et ipsa relaxavit prædicto Willelmo excambium terræ Prioris et Canonicorum de Bradenestok, in Hatherop, dicto Priori et Canonicis faciendum, et decem libratas redditus Esterlingorum de villa de Seperige, et de Heanton, die Sancti Martini annuatim percipiendas.

- Johannes de Ripariis per cartam suam notum facit hominibus suis de Hedinton, tam liberis quam tenentibus in vilenagio, se dedisse Monialibus de Lacock totam terram suam et redditum de Hedyngton pro sustentatione duorum Capellanorum cantantium pro fidelibus defunctis usque ad finem sæculi.

[Fol. 76, b.]

Idem significat per aliam cartam.

Michael de Cheldrinton dedit eisdem Monialibus unam virgatam terræ cum pertinentiis in villa de Hedyngton, pro qua concessione Ela Abbatissa dedit ei viginti quatuor marcas argenti.

[Fol. 78, b.]

Johannes Pie dedit eisdem Monialibus unam marleram pro decem solidis argenti.

[Fol. 79, a.]

Radulphus Angens concessit eisdem totam terram quam habuit in manerio de Hedyngton.

[Fol. 82, a.]

Katherina Luvel concessit eisdem totam terram suam de Wyclescote, absque omni servitio, &c.

Alia carta ejusdem Katherinæ eandem concessionem recitat, sed addit quod Moniales redderent inde Rogero Lof a quo terram illam emerat unam libram cimini ad festum sancti Michaelis, et facerent nihilominus capitalibus dominis feodi illius servitium inde debitum.

[Fol. 82, b.]

Philippus Basset, frater prædictæ Katherinæ, cartam ejus superius memoratam recitat et confirmat.

[Fol. 83, a.]

Idem Philippus remisit dictis Monialibus sectam curiæ quam ei debebant in manerio suo de Worton pro prædicta terra de Wekelescote.

[Fol. 83, b.]

Rogerus Lof remisit dictis Monialibus totum jus quod habuit in predicta terra de Wyclescote, pro qua remissione dictæ Moniales dederunt ei quinque marcas argenti.

Johannes Lof, filius Rogeri, idem confirmavit.

[Fol. 86, a.]

Willelmus Longespeye dedit eidem Conventui totam terram cum pertinentiis quæ quondam fuit Nicholai de Hamptun in Upeham.

[Fol. 86, b.]

Stephanus Longespeye dedit eisdem duas acras prati sui in Nimeam.

[Fol. 87, a.]

Humfridus de Boun, Comes Herfordiæ et Essexiæ, Constabularius Angliæ, dedit eisdem viginti solidos et quatuor denarios annui redditus, viz. de Waltero de la Frithe, pro tenemento suo et medietate unius dimidiæ hidæ terræ in campis ibidem 5s. annuatim; de Waltero de Okeborn pro tenemento suo et una virgata terræ apud Hofchote sex solidos et octo denarios; de Petro Bonhome de Hofchote, pro tenemento suo et una virgata terræ in campis de Hofchote 6s. 8d. et de Priore Hospitalis Sancti Johannis de Calne, pro tenemento suo et una virgata terræ in campis de Hofchote 12d. cum homagiis, &c. libere et quiete ab omnibus sectis, &c. Præterea remisit eis 12d. de annuo redditu quos ei reddere consueverunt pro tenemento quod de eo tenuerunt in villa de Hedyngton.

Idem Comes mandavit Waltero Maudut, de la Frithe, quod in omnibus servitiis quæ ei facere solebat pro tenemento in la Frithe, intendens esset in futurum Abbatissæ et Conventui de Lacock. Datum apud Horsefend, die Purificationis Beatæ Mariæ virginis, anno regni Regis Edwardi 2do.

[Fol. 88, a.]

Eodem modo mandavit Waltero de Okeborn, pro una virgata terræ apud Hofcote, et Petro Bonhome de Ofchote pro tenemento et una virgata terræ in campis de Ofchote; et Priori Hospitalis Sancti Johannis de Calne, pro tenemento et una virgata terræ in campis de Ofchote.

[Fol. 88, b.]

Hunfridus de Boun, &c. nepos prædicti Hunfridi Comitis, in carta sua recitat et confirmat superiorem donationem avi sui.

[Fol. 89, b.]

Magister Hospitalis Sancti Johannis de Calne, recognovit, anno octavo Regis Edwardi primi, se teneri Abbatissæ et Conventui de Lacock in 12*d*. annui redditus pro quodam tenemento in Ofcote, quod de eis tenebat in capite, et pro eodem tenemento sectam ad curiam de Lacock, de tribus septimanis in tres septimanas cum scutagio. Abbatissa vero et Conventus divinæ charitatis intuitu duxerunt dictam sectam bis per annum, cum solutione 12*d*. pro scutagio.

[Fol. 94, a.]

Rogerus de Stodlegh dedit eisdem Monialibus 8*d*. redditus annuos quos Galiana relicta Herberti filii Petri ei reddere consuevit de tenemento quod de eo tenuit in villa de Caln.

[Fol. 94, b.]

Galiena de Caln dedit dictis Monialibus unum mesuagium in villa de Caln, de feodo domini Regis, et unum mesuagium in Churchestrete, et unam acram terræ in Rixforlonge, et aliam acram ad Bernestede cum quodam mesuagio, et sex acras terræ quas emit de Nicholao Cynnoc, et duas acras terræ quas emit de Waltero filio Mathei le Bret; et totam terram quæ jacet inter Herewiestrete et terras quas habuerunt Gille Pistor et Hunfridus Bere; reddendo inde annuatim domino Regi sex denarios, et Rectori Ecclesiæ de Caln 12*d*. et quadrantem, et heredibus Nicholai Cynnoc 6*d*. et regale servitium quantum ad illos pertinet; et hæredibus Walteri filii Mathei le Bret 3*d*. et hæredibus Alexandri de Stodele 8*d*. pro omni servitio.

[Fol. 95, a.]

Eadem Galiena per aliam cartam dedit eisdem Monialibus totum mesuagium suum in villa de Caln.

[Fol. 96, b]

Agnes de Roudon dedit totam terram quam Rogerus Soper aliquando tenuit, cum ædificiis ei omnibus pertinentiis, in villa de Chippenham, et unam placeam terræ.

[Fol. 97, a.]

Henricus de Bechampton dedit totam terram suam et tenementum in villa de Chipeham (nunc Chippenham).

[Fol. 98, a.]

Radulfus le Franceis dedit eidem Conventui burgagium et totam terram quam habuit de dono Adæ aurifabri in villa de Treubrige, reddendo inde annuatim dicto Adæ unum denarium et capitali domino unam libram piperis, pro omni servitio.

[Fol. 99, a.]

Johanna de Osevilla, relicta Willelmi de Rugdon, dedit eisdem redditum quadraginta solidorum annuatim percipiendum de tenemento quod Walterus de la Slad tenuit in parochia de Boxa, cum eodem Waltero, cum omni servitio debito ab eodem Waltero et hæredibus suis; hæc omnia libera ab omni servitio seculari.

[Fol. 99, b.]

Walterus de Pavely dictæ Johannæ cartam recitat et donationem confirmat.

[Fol. 100, a.]

Walterus de Godarvilla relaxavit eisdem Monialibus sectam quam supradictus Walterus de la Slade facere ei solebat in Hundredo suo de Chippeham de tribus septimanis in tres septimanas.

[Fol. 101, a.]

Ela Comitissa Sarum dedit totum manerium suum de Hatherop cum pertinentiis.

Willelmus Longespeye, dictæ Elæ filius, confirmavit donationem matris suæ.

Conventio inter Hugonem Abbatem Cyrencestriæ et ejusdem loci Conventum ex una parte, et Wimarcam Priorissam et Conventum de Lacock ex altera.

[Fol. 101, b.]

Hæc est Conventio facta inter Hugonem Abbatem Cyrencestrie et ejusdem loci Conventum, videlicet quod predicti Abbas et Conventus Cyrencestrie concesserunt pro se et successoribus suis imperpetuum quod eorum Baillivi tantummodo bis in anno venient apud Hetherop ad visum franchi plegii faciendum in Curia predicte Priorisse et Conventus de Lacock, scilicet de loquelis ad coronam domini Regis spectantibus, et omnibus aliis ad visum franchi plegii pertinentibus, videlicet, circiter festum Sancti Martini, et circiter Hockeday, quando Baillivi predictorum Abbatis et Conventus curiam predictam facient summoniri; ita quod omnes homines infra libertatem predictæ Priorisse et Conventus de Lacock manentes, nisi qui rationabilem causam habeant quare venire non possint, ad predictos duos dies venient, ubi omnes loquelas ad visum franchi plegii Baillivis prædictorum Abbatis et Conventus monstrabunt, que ad dictos duos dies per visum Baillivorum Abbatis et Conventus terminabuntur; et homines infra libertatem predicte Priorisse et Conventus de Lacock manentes ad singulos

duorum dierum dabunt predictis Abbati et Conventui triginta denarios, sive curia amerciata fuerit sive non, pro omnibus occasionibus et amerciamentis ad predictum visum pertinentibus; et amerciamenta si que ibi evenerint, predicte Priorisse et ejus Conventui remaneant; ita quod si latro et latrocinium capta fuerint in libertate predicte Priorisse et Conventus de Lacock, ducentur sine dilatione ad prisonam Abbatis et Conventus Cyrencestrie et ibidem recipientur et judicabuntur. Similiter si clamor levatus fuerit in libertate predicte Priorisse et Conventus de Lacock, et per stultitiam conquerentis vel per fortiam Vicecomitis, vel per Baillivos suos, trahatur illa predicta loquela ad Comitatum Gloucestrie, et per Abbatem et Conventum vel per eorum Baillivos extrahatur eadem loquela, vel si aliquis alius clamor in libertate prædicte Priorisse et Conventus de Lacock levatus fuerit, et per Baillivos earum vel per Baillivos Abbatis et Conventus Cyrencestri attachiatus, Abbas et Conventus Cyrencestrie de omnibus extraneis extra libertatem predicte Priorisse et Conventus de Lacock manentibus, occasione predictorum clamorum attachiatis, amerciamenta habebunt. Similiter predicta Priorissa et ejus Conventus de omnibus hominibus in libertate sua manentibus et occasione predictorum clamorum attachiatis habebunt amerciamenta. Similiter si aliqua querimonia facta fuerit per aliquem de averiis captis et retentis contra vadium et plegium de predicta Priorissa et Conventu de Lacok, vel aliquo alio in eorum libertate manente, Abbas et Conventus Cyrencestrie loquelas illas et amerciamenta inde provenientia habebunt. Similiter si quis inventus fuerit in libertate predicte Priorisse et Conventus sui de Lacock, qui sit extra assisam domini Regis et ibidem ultra unum annum et unum diem moratus fuerit sine licentia Baillivorum Abbatis et Conventus, Abbas et Conventus Cyrencestrie amerciamenta si que inde inciderint, habebunt. Et omnis quicumque fuerint qui in tethyngam intrare debebunt, coram Baillivis Abbatis et Conventus Cyrencestrie in tethingham intrabunt, salvo denario de ingressu tethynge tethingmanno predicte Priorisse et Conventus de Lacok. Et omnes alie loquele et querele predicte Priorisse et ejus Conventui remanebunt. Et ut hæc conventio rata et stabilis imperpetuum permaneat, presens scriptum inter predictum Abbatem et Conventum Cyrencestrie et Priorissam sepe dictam et Conventum suum de Lacock, est ad modum Cyrographi confectum, et parti predictorum Abbatis et Conventus sigillum dicte Priorisse et Conventus de Lacock est appensum; et similiter parti Priorisse et sui Conventus sigillum predictorum Abbatis et Conventus est appositum.

[Fol. 103, a.]

Hugelina relicta Randulfi de Landebroil quietum clamavit eisdem Monialibus tertiam partem unius hyde terre in villa de Hetherop, anno regni Regis Henrici filii Regis Johannis xx^{mo}, pro qua quieta clamatione dicte Moniales ei dederunt quinquaginta solidos.

[Fol. 103, b.]

Ela Longespeye Comitissa Warriwici quietum clamavit eisdem totum jus quod habuit in manerio de Hatherop, pro qua quieta clamatione dicte Moniales obligaverunt se reddere dicte Comitisse £20 sterlingorum annuatim ad vitam suam; sub pena £10. argenti in subsidium Terre Sancte solvendarum pro singulis terminis et loco non observatis, una cum dampnis et expensis, &c. Dat. apud Lacock, die sabbati proximo post festum Sancti Edmundi Regis et Martyris, anno regni Regis Edwardi filii Regis Henrici sextodecimo.

[Fol. 104, b.]

Eadem Ela Comitissa per aliam cartam dedit eisdem totam terram quam emit de domino Ingeramo le Waleys in villa de Hatherop, cum omnibus villanis et sequelis eorum, pratis, pascuis, pasturis, viis, semitis, &c.

Licentia Regis Edwardi primi Elæ Comitissæ de Warwick concessa de ponendo terras in Hatherop ad manum mortuam.

[Fol. 105, a.]

Edwardus Dei gratia Rex Anglie, Dominus Hibernie, et Dux Aquitanie, omnibus ad quos presentes littere pervenerint salutem. Licet de communi consilio regni nostri providerimus quod non liceat viris religiosis seu aliis ingredi feodum alicujus ita quod ad mortuam manum deveniat sine licentia nostra et capitalis domini de quo res illa immediate tenetur, volentes tamen dilecte nobis Ele Comitisse Warwyk gratiam facere specialem, dedimus ei licentiam quantum in nobis est, quod unum mesuagium et duodecim virgatas terre cum pertinentiis in Etherop dare possit et assignare dilectis nobis in Christo Abbatisse et Monialibus de Lacock, tenenda et habenda sibi et successoribus suis imperpetuum; et eisdem Abbatisse et Monialibus quod mesuagium illud et terram ab eadem Comitissa recipere possint, tenore presentium similiter licenciam concedimus specialem. Nolentes quod prefata Comitissa, seu predictæ Abbatissa et Moniales, ratione predicti statuti per nos vel heredes nostros inde occasionentur in aliquo vel graventur. Salvis tamen capitalibus dominis feodi illius serviciis inde debitis et consuetis. In cujus rei testimonium has litteras nostras fieri fecimus patentes. Teste meipso apud Karnarvan iv^{to} die Maii, anno regni nostri duodecimo.

[Fol. 105, b.]

Ela Comitissa Warwick coram Justiciariis Domini Regis apud Walton, anno tricesimo Regis Henrici filii Regis Johannis, recognovit manerium de Heythrop cum pertinentiis esse jus Abbatisse et Conventus de Lacock; et pro hac recognitione predicta Abbatissa concessit predicte Comitisse predictum manerium tenendum tota vita sua de predicta Abbatissa et successoribus suis reddendo inde per annum centum solidos sterlingorum. Et post mortem ipsius Comitisse predictum manerium redire debebat ad dictas Abbatissas. Pro hac concessione et remissione ipsa Comitissa remisit et quietum clamavit de se et heredibus suis predicte Abbatisse, &c. totum jus et clamium quod habuit in viginti libris terre quas predicta Comitissa prius tenuit de Willelmo Longespeye in Cettre imperpetuum.

[Fol. 106, b.]

Constancia de Lega, vidua, dedit eisdem Monialibus redditum suum de Calemundesdem, scilicet 35s. per annum quos ei solebant reddere Hospitalarii Jerosolemitani.

[Fol. 107, a.]

Willelmus de Marre de Ryndecumbe remisit eidem Conventui pro septemdecim marcis sterlingorum, homagium, fidelitatem, relevium, herietum, tallagia ad eum pertinentia, auxilia arandi, seminandi, herciandi, serculandi, metendi, et cariandi, et omnimodas escaetas et sectas omnium curiarum ad se et ad heredes suos spectancium. Excepta secta ad visum franci plegii domini Comitis Gloucestrie bis per annum apud Rindecumbe facienda. Remisit etiam eisdem omnes districtiones factas et faciendas, auxilium ad faciendum militem filium suum primogenitum, et ad filiam suam primogenitam maritandam, omne scutagium et servicium militare, et redditum annuum sex denariorum, et omnimodas demandas que aliquo casu fieri possent de manerio de Wodemancote; et idem tenentibus Abbatisse et villanis in dicto manerio.

[Fol. 107, b.]

Constancia de Lega dedit Deo et Beate Marie totum manerium de Wudemanecote, ad faciendam in villa de Lacock Abbathiam Monialium, quam voluit nominari Locum Beate Marie.

Nicholaus de Mara, Rector ecclesie de Thodesthorn, remisit Monialibus de Lacock totum jus quod habuit de duabus carucatis terre et 21 solidis redditus in Woudemanecote.

[Fol. 111, a.]

Walterus dictus filius Capellani de Egesworth, remisit eisdem Monialibus totam terram suam quam habuit in Wudemanecote.

[Fol. 111, b.]

Radulphus de Maurathin dedit eisdem Monialibus pratum quod habuit manerio de Wodemancote juxta pontem de Beroford, quod vocabatur Malewardesham.

[Fol. 112, a.]

Agnes relicta Radulfi de Mauerdin, dedit eisdem tertiam partem cujusdam prati quod vocatur Malewardesham.

Gilbertus de Henleie dedit duas acras terræ arabiles in campis de Wodemancote, pro qua donatione Moniales dederunt ei undecim solidos et decem denarios in garsuma.

[Fol. 112, b.]

Idem Gilbertus per aliam cartam dedit quatuor acras terræ et dimidiam in eisdem campis de Wodemancote, pro viginti solidis argenti.

[Fol. 113, a.]

Alia carta ejusdem remittit eisdem Monialibus easdem quatuor acras et dimidiam.

[Fol. 113, b.]

Idem Gilbertus per aliam cartam concessit eisdem decem acras terræ in Wodemancote, pro qua concessione dictæ Moniales dederunt ei quadraginta et tres solidos et sex denarios sterlingorum.

[Fol. 114, a.]

Idem concessit alias duas acras terræ arabilis in eadem villa, pro qua donatione recepit a Monialibus octo solidos sterlingorum.

[Fol. 114, b.]

Duas alias acras concessit, pro quibus dederunt ei Moniales decem solidos.

[Fol. 115, b.]

Gilbertus de Henlega concessit Conventui de Lacock, quod ipse non venderet ad terminum nec in perpetuum aliquam terram vel aliquid de tenemento suo sine licentia conventus; et si faceret quòd liberum possent habere ingressum dictæ Moniales in omnibus tenementis suis et ea habere in perpetuum.

[Fol. 117, a]

Henricus Peverel, de Wodemancote, concessit eisdem Monialibus duodecim acras terræ arabilis in Wodemancote, jacentes in campo qui vocatur Morecumbe, reddendo inde ad Pascha Johanni Gerard, unum par cyrothecarum de pretio unius oboli, cum eas querat ad domum suam in Wodemancote pro omni servitio, salvo Regali servicio.

[Fol. 118, a.]

Henricus Peverel de Wodemancote remisit eisdem totum tenementum cum pertinentiis quod de eis tenebat in Wodemancote, reddendo inde annuatim Galfrido Peverel et hæredibus suis sex denarios annuatim pro omnibus serviciis.

Anno regni Regis Henrici filii Regis Johannis, Constantia de Lega, coram Justiciariis Domini Regis, recognovit duas carucatas terræ cum pertinentiis in Wodemancote unde placitum warantiæ fuerat inter eas, esse jus Conventus de Lacock.

[Fol. 119, b.]

Petronilla filia Roberti de Damenevilla concessit eisdem Monialibus viginti duas acras terræ arabilis de dominica terra sua in manerio de Button, videlicet in Northfelde, &c.

[Fol. 120, a.]

Robertus Marmiun remisit eisdem totum jus quod habuit in

terris et tenementis quæ Robertus Perpunt tenuit apud Hanum, pro qua remissione dictæ Moniales dederunt ei 40s.

Petronilla de Damenvilla dedit eisdem totam terram quam habuit in manerio de Button, faciendo inde Regi debitum servitium.

[Fol. 123, a.]

Agnes relicta Athelmi Germund dedit eisdem duo stalla in villa de Bristoll, reddendo inde annuatim domino Regi duodecim denarios annuatim pro omni servitio.

Matildis filia Athelmi Germund dedit eisdem duos solidos annui redditus de domo sua quæ erat sita inter domum Gerardi le Franceis et ecclesiam Sancti Laurentii, solutos ab omni seculari servitio.

[Fol. 123, b.]

Johannes Tyke de Bristoll dedit domum quam tenuit versus Monkebrige, cum terra vacua ad eandem domum pertinente, solutam ab omni seculari servitio.

[Fol. 128, a.]

Walterus filius et heres Radulfi Godwyne de Rubrigge dedit et quietum clamavit eisdem Monialibus unum mesuagium et totam terram et tenementum cum communi pastura et omnibus aisiamentis et pertinentiis suis quæ habuit de hereditate sua in Ruthrugge, tenendum ab eisdem tanquam jus earum pertinens ad liberum manerium earum de North Schorewell, libere, quiete, &c. ab omni exactione. Pro hac concessione dictæ Moniales dederunt ei centum solidos argenti in gersumam.

[Fol. 128, b.]

Beatrix relicta Egidii de Sancto Stephano reddidit et quietum clamavit totum jus et clamium quod habuit in terra quæ vocatur Sydewynesfurlang in Northscorewell.

Amicia Comitissa Devoniæ et Domina Insulæ, in viduitate sua, pro animabus mariti sui et omnium parentum suorum, dedit Monialibus de Lacock cum corde suo totum manerium suum de Schorewell cum omnibus pertinentiis suis, et cum omnibus hominibus in predicta terra degentibus et eorum sequelis, et omnibus aliis pertinentiis. Preterea concessit eisdem prædictum manerium cum omnibus pertinentiis suis desaforestatum, ita quod nihil occasione forestæ vel warennæ ab eis aliquo tempore exigatur.

[Fol. 129, b.]

Isabella de Fortibus Comitissa Albemarlæ et Devoniæ, et Domina Insulæ, filia Amiciæ Comitissæ prædictæ, confirmavit donationem matris suæ.

Eadem Isabella remisit eisdem Monialibus sectam curiarum, wardam, et relevium, quæ ei debebant de manerio de Schorewell supradicto.

Eadem Isabella per aliam cartam suam concessit quod dictæ Moniales habeant omnia amerciamenta hominum suorum manerii de Schorwell supradicti in Insula de Wycht quotiescumque dictos homines in curia sua de Neuport amerciari contigerit; salvis tamen eidem Isabellæ Comitissæ et heredibus suis amerciamentis de transgressionibus sibi, heredibus, Ballivis et ministris suis, per predictam Abbatissam seu homines suos qualitercumque illatis. Ita etiam quod omnes homines dictæ Abbatissæ dicti manerii sui de Schorewell veniant ad visum franchi plegii, vel Lagheday, sive Hundredum de Westmedeine apud Caresbrok bis per annum coram Baillivis predictæ Isabellæ Comitissæ et heredum suorum ad pacem domini Regis attingendam, et ibidem faciant presentationes et responsiones sicut alii de predicto Hundredo ibidem faciunt de omnibus articulis qui ad visum franchi plegii sive Lagheday spectant secundum consuetudinem in partibus illis usitatam. Et si aliquis vel aliqui hominum seu tenentium dictarum Abbatissæ et Conventus dicti manerii sui de Schorewell, pro assisa panis et cervisie fracta, vel pro aliquo alio delicto pro quo judicium meruerint corporale, puniri debeant per Ballivos et considerationem curie predicte Isabelle et heredum suorum, fiat de eis judicium secundum legem et consuetudinem regni. Et predicta Abbatissa et Conventus concedunt pro se et successoribus suis quod si aliquod scriptum in manibus suis vel successorum suorum de cetero inveniatur per quod homines et tenentes sui quieti esse debeant vel esse consueverunt de veniendo ad Hundredum predicte Isabelle Comitisse vel heredum suorum quod appellatur Lagheday sive visus franci plegii, vel per quod dicta Abbatissa et Conventus vel earum successores visum franci plegii sive Lagheday de hominibus et tenentibus suis tenere poterant vel consueverant, quòd idem scriptum quoad articulum illum, scilicet franchi plegii sive Lagheday Hundredi, pro nullo habeatur, quia quicquid juris vel clamii habuerunt in predicto visu habendo seu tenendo tenore presentis scripti remiserunt predictæ Comitissæ.

[Fol. 131, a.]

Willelmus de Poldon remisit Monialibus de Lacock, totum jus quod habuit in manerio de Northschorewell in Insula de Wyght, anno Regis Edwardi (*primi*) tertiodecimo, pro qua remissione Moniales ei dederunt triginta marcas argenti.

[Fol. 131, b.]

Willelmus Huse de Poledon, anno quartodecimo Regis Edwardi filii regis Henrici, coram Justiciariis dicti regis, recognovit unum mesuagium et duas carucatas terræ cum pertinentiis in North Schorewell, esse jus Monialium de Lacock, et pro hac recognitione dictæ Moniales dederunt ei triginta marcas argenti.

[Fol. 132, a.]

Jordanus de Kynggeston quietum clamavit eisdem unam virgatam terræ cum pertinentiis in Schorewell, exceptis duabus carectatis spinarum et una carectata virgarum quas annuatim recipiebat in boscis dictarum Monialium; ita tamen quod predictus Conventus haberet annuatim de predicta virgata terræ unam marcam argenti in die Purificationis Beatæ Mariæ ad pitanciam.

[Fol. 136, b.]

Placita coram domino Rege apud Westmonasterium de termino Sanctæ Trinitatis, anno regni Regis Henrici VIII^{vi} viiivo. Rot. xiii. inter placita Regis. Memorandum quod Reverendissimus in Christo pater Thomas permissione divina Cardinalis Archiepiscopus Eboracensis, Domini Regis Cancellarius, die Veneris proxima post Octabas Sancti Johannis Baptistæ, isto eodem termino coram domino Rege apud Westmonasterium, per manus suas proprias deliberavit hic in Curia quoddam Recordum coram domino Rege in Cancellaria sua apud Westmonasterium secundo die Junii, anno regni Regis Henrici VIII^{vi} post Conquestum Anglie viiivo. Suth.

Compertum est per quandam Inquisitionem captam apud Castrum de Carsbroke in Insula Vecta in Comitatu Suthampton tertio die Novembris anno regni Regis Henrici septimi vicesimo quarto coram Abbate de Quarre, Amicio Paulet milite, Nicholao Wadham milite, Thoma Wadshawe, et Thoma Thomas armigeris, necnon Johanne Grenge, Jurisperitis Commissionariis dicti domini Regis in Insula prædicta virtute commissionis dicti domini Regis eisdem commissionariis directæ et huic Inquisitioni consignatis, per sacramentum xii^{cim}. &c. Qui inter alia dicunt super sacramentum suum quod Abbatissa domus et ecclesiæ de Lacock, in Comitatu Wiltes, ex fundacione dicti domini Regis, fuit seisita de manerio de Schorewell cum pertinentiis in Insula prædicta in dominico suo ut de feodo, et tenuit manerium prædictum cum pertinentiis de Edwardo quarto nuper Rege Angliæ in capite per servitium militare, et quod manerium predictum cum pertinentiis valet per annum in omnibus exitibus ultra reprisas sexdecim libras, et quod prædicta Abbatissa obiit sexto die Februarii, anno regni Edwardi quarti nuper Regis Angliæ vicesimo secundo; et quod Margeria Gloucestriæ Abbatissa immediate post mortem prædictæ Abbatissæ intravit et intrusit in manerium prædictum cum pertinentiis, et manerium prædictum cum pertinentiis a tempore mortis prædictæ Abbatissæ prædecessoris suæ tenuit et occupavit, et omnia exitus et proficua inde per totum idem tempus et deinceps usque tempus captionis Inquisitionis prædictæ habuit et percepit absque aliqua restitutione inde habita extra manus regias, prout per Inquisitionem illam in Cancellariam domini Regis retornatam et in filaciis ejusdem Cancellariæ remanentem plenius apparet. Et modo hic terminus Sanctæ Trinitatis, videlicet secundo die mensis Junii anno regni Regis Henrici octavi viii^{vo}, venit hic in curiam Cancellariæ ejusdem domini Regis, coram eodem domino Rege, Johanna Temys, Abbatissa de Laycock, per Ricardum Wellys attornatum suum, et queritur predictam Margeriam nuper Abbatissam de Lacock predicta in dicta Inquisitione nominatam, predecessorem ipsius Johanne nunc Abbatisse, a possessione manerii predicti colore Inquisitionis predicte ammotam fore et expulsam. Et hoc minus juste quia protestando quod predicta Inquisitio minus sufficiens est in lege, ad quam ipsa nunc Abbatissa necesse non habet nec per legem terre tenetur respondere pro placito, die quod predicte Domus et Ecclesia de Laycoke, in Inquisitione predicta specificate, sunt ac toto tempore dictorum nuper regis Henrici VIII^{mi}, et Edwardi IV^{ti}, et diu antea fuerunt ex fundatione domini Regis ratione ducatus sui Lancastrie, ac quod predicta nuper Abbatissa in dicta Inquisitione primo nominata predecessor ipsius nunc Abbatisse fuit seisita in dicto manerio de Shorewell cum pertinentiis in dominico suo ut de feodo in jure Domus et Ecclesie suarum predictarum, et illud tenuit de heredibus Amicie quondam Comitisse Devonie et Domine de Insula predicta, in liberam puram et perpetuam elemosinam, et obiit de tali statu inde seisita; post cujus mortem predicta Margeria nuper Abbatissa in Abbatissam Domus et Ecclesie predictarum debite electa et prefecta fuit, per quod eadem Margeria nuper Abbatissa, &c. in manerium predictum cum pertinentiis intravit et inde fuit seisita in dominico suo ut de feodo, in jure Domus et Ecclesie suarum predictarum, ac exitus et proficua inde per tempus predictum habuit et percepit prout ei bene licuit, quousque ipsa a possessione manerii predicti colore Inquisitionis predicte minus juste ammota fuit et expulsa; dictaque Margeria nuper Abbatissa postea obiit, post cujus mortem eadem Johanna nunc Abbatissa in Abbatissam domus et ecclesie predicte debitè electa et prefecta fuit, absque hoc quod predicte domus et ecclesia sunt aut unquam fuere ex fundatione dicti nuper Regis Henrici septimi aut aliquorum progenitorum suorum Regum Anglie ut de jure corone sue Anglie prout per inquisitionem predictam compertum existit. Et absque hoc quod predicta nuper Abbatissa in dicta Inquisitione primo nominata tenuit predictum manerium cum pertinentiis seu aliquam inde parcellam de dicto nuper Rege E. quarto in capite per servitium militare aut aliter vel aliquo alio modo quam per eandem transactionem allegatur aut quod habeat seu unquam habeatur aliquod recordum preter recordum inquisitionis predictæ per quod liquere potest quod predictum manerium seu aliqua inde parcella unquam tenebatur de predicto nuper Rege Edwardo quarto aut aliquo alio Rege Anglie in capite aut per servitium militare prout per Inquisitionem predictam similiter compertum existit. Que omnia et singula eadem nunc Abbatissa parata est verificare prout Curie constabit, &c. unde petit judicium et quod manus domini Regis inde amoveatur, &c.

Et Johannes Erneley qui pro domino Rege sequitur in hac parte inde allocutus dicit protestando quod predicte domus et ecclesia sunt et a tempore quo non extat memoria fuerunt ex fundatione predicti nuper Regis Henrici vii^{mi} et progenitorum suorum Regum Anglie, prout per Inquisitionem predictam superius compertum existit. Pro placito dicit quod predicta nuper Abbatissa in inquisitione predicta primo nominata tenuit predictum manerium cum pertinentiis de predicto nuper Rege E. quarto in capite per servitium militare prout per inquisitionem predictam superius similiter compertum existit. Et hoc pro eodem domino Rege petit quod inquiratur per prieram. Et predicta nunc Abbatissa similiter. Igitur dies data est eidem nunc Abbatisse coram domino rege in octava Sancti Johannis Baptiste ubicumque tunc fuerit in Anglia, ad faciendum et recipiendum quod justum fuerit in premissis. Et preceptum est Vicecomiti Suthampton quod venire faciat coram eodem domino Rege ad diem illum xxiv^{or}. tam milites quam alios probos et legales homines de visneto manerii de Shorwell qui prefatam nunc Abbatissam nulla affinitate attingant, ad recognoscendum per eorum sacramentum super premissis plenius veritatem. Ad quas quidem octavas Sancti Johannis Baptiste isto eodem Termino coram domino Rege apud Westmonasterium venit predicta Johanna Temys nunc Abbatissa de Lacock per Willelmum Inssard attornatum suum. Et Vicecomes retornavit xxiv^{or} Juratores quorum nullus, &c. Igitur preceptum est Vicecomiti quod non omittat, &c. quin discretos per omnio terre, &c. Et quod de Exit. Et quod habeat corpora eorum coram Rege in octavis Sancti Michaelis ubicunque, &c. vel coram Justiciariis domini Regis ad Assisas in Comitatu predicto capiendas assignatis die Lune proximo ante festum Sancte Marie Magdalene apud Wynton per formam statuti, &c. Venerunt ad faciendum jure predicto, &c. Idem dies datus est tam prefato Johanni Erneley qui sequitur, &c. quam prefate nunc Abbatisse, &c. ad quas quidem octavas Sancti Michaelis coram domino Rege apud Westmonasterium venit dicta Abbatissa per Attornatum suum predictum et prefatos Justiciarios domini Regis ad assisas, coram quibus, &c. missum hic recordum suum coram eis habitum in hec verba. Postea die et loco infra contento coram Ricardo Elyot et Lodowico Pollard Justiciariis domini Regis ad assisas in Comitatu Suthampton capiendas assignatos per formam statuti, &c. venit infra nominata Johanna Temys Abbatissa domus et ecclesie de Laycock per Ricardum Mathewe attornatum suum. Et Jurati Juramentis unde fit mensio exactis similiter venerunt et super hoc proclamacio pro domino Rege solempniter facta si quis pro ipso domino Rege Justiciariis predictis, servientes et attornatos ipsius domini Regis et juratos predictos informare vellet veniret et audiretur. Et Thomas Ellyot pro domino Rege ad faciendum se optulit per quod procedatur ad captionem Inquisitionis predicte Jurati predicti ad hoc electi, triati et jurati dicunt super sacramentum suum quod infra-scripte domus et ecclesia de Lacock non sunt nec unquam fuere ex fundacione infra nominati nuper Regis Henrici viimi aut aliquorum progenitorum suorum Regum Anglie ut de jure corone sue Anglie. Set dicunt super sacramentum suum quod predicte domus et ecclesia de Lacock, infra scripte in Inquisitione specificate, sunt et unquam fuerunt ex fundatione domini Regis ratione Ducatus sui Lancastrie. Et ulterius dicunt super sacramentum suum quod infra nominata Abbatissa in infra scripta inquisitione prius nominata nunquam tenuit manerium infra scriptum de Shorewell seu aliquam inde parcellam de infra nominato Rege E. quarto per servitium militare, vel immediate aliquo alio modo. Set iidem Jurati dicunt quod predicta Abbatissa in Inquisitione predicta primo nominata tenuit manerium predictum cum pertinentiis de heredibus infra nominate Amicie quondam Comitisse Devonie, et Domine de Insula Vecte, in liberam puram et perpetuam elemosinam modo et forma prout predicta Johanna Temys inferius allegavit. Super quo visis premissis et per Curiam hic intellectis omnibus et singulis premissis servientes domini Regis ad Leges ac ipsius Regis Attornatus ad hoc convocatus et presentibus concessum est quod manus domini Regis a possessione ipsius Regis predicti manerii de Shorewell cum pertinentiis in Insula predicta amoveatur &c. Et quod predicta Abbatissa domus et ecclesie de Lacock, in Comitatu Wiltes, ad possessionem ejusdem manerii de Shorewell cum pertinentiis in Insula predicta, una cum exitibus et proficuis inde a tempore captionis Inquisicionis predicte hucusque perceptis restituatur. Salvo semper jure Regis si quod, &c.

Sequitur in hoc registro de Lacock Petitio Willelmi Sands Militis, Vicecomitis Suthamptoniæ, petens exonerari de £16. de exitu manerii de Shorewell supradicti, de qua summa Barones Scaccarii eum exoneraverunt.

Notandum quod Chartæ in hoc registro non sunt dispositæ secundum ordinem temporis, et quod maxima ex parte deest data, sicut videre est in his excerptis.

DEED RELATING TO LACOCK FAIR.

(From the original at Lacock Abbey.)

Feut a remenbrer q̃ le Jeody apres la Translacion de Seynt Thomas le martyr Lan de reugne le Roy Edward trentisme q̃rt. furñt baillez cynk deniers e maille a mon Sire Johñ de Holt Chivaler atenyr en owelyne* mayn tantq: ala feste de Seynt Bartholomeu. queu deniers Labbesse de Lacok prist en noun de toun a sa fayre de Lacok des genz ...... de Keyneshm̃ de sa vile de Marsvelde e est aconvenuz entre la diste Abbesse e Sire ...... de ...... chaumberer de la meson de Keynesham̃ · q̃ le dist Johñ vendra a Leglise de Lacok le jour de Seynt Bartholomeu e monstra ses munemenz queus eus unt de lour feoffour par queus eus deyvent estre quietez de toun deuer en tote fayres · ausi come il mettent lor chalang· Escrist a Marsfelde le jour e lan auant nome (1306).

Translation.

Done to remember that on the Thursday after the Translation of Saint Thomas the Martyr, in the 34th year of King Edward, there were delivered five pence and a farthing to Monsire John de Holt, Knight, to hold in ...... hand until the feast of St. Bartholomew. Which pence the Abbess of Lacock took under the name of a toll or duty at her fair of Lacock, from the people of ...... de Keynsham, of his town of Marsfield. And it is agreed between the said Abbess and Sir ——, Chamberlain of the house of Keynsham, that the said John shall come to the church of Lacock the day of Saint Bartholomew, and shall show their title-deeds, which they have from their original grantor, by which they claim to be exempt from paying toll at all fairs. And also how they put their challenge. Written at Marsfield the day and year above-named.

NOTE.

This short document, which is in good preservation, bears a precise date. The feast of the Translation of St. Thomas was July 7. The old French words " maille," a farthing, and " toun," a toll or duty, are worthy of remark.

* This word is illegible.

THE GREGORIAN LITURGY, AND ANCIENT HYMN,

GLORIA IN EXCELSIS.

The following account of the MS. entitled the Gregorian Liturgy, preserved in the Library of the Dean and Chapter of Salisbury, has been kindly furnished to me by Mr. Hatcher.

This manuscript is justly regarded as a curious piece of antiquity, though the title given to it is perhaps scarcely appropriate. It was probably written before the time of Bishop Osmund. The decorations of the capital letters are drawn with a pen, and exhibit considerable skill in design, and great fertility in invention, for no two are exactly alike. It was lent to the celebrated Elizabeth Elstob,* by the Dean and Chapter of the time, and by her partly transcribed. Her copy is in the possession of Sir R. C. Hoare, Bart.

According to the Table prefixed to the Calendar, we may deem the manuscript of at least as early a date as the year 959. This Calendar ends in 1006.

The contents are :—Tables and Rules for forming a Calen-

---

* Elizabeth Elstob, sister of William Elstob, the divine and antiquary, was born at Newcastle in 1683. She acquired a considerable knowledge of the Saxon language, and thus attracted the notice of the learned Dr. Hickes. In 1709 she published, by his recommendation, the English Saxon Homily, on the birthday of St. Gregory, with an introduction, the purpose of which was to show the conformity of the Church of England with the Anglo-Saxon Church. In 1713 she offered to the public " Some Testimonies of Learned Men in favour of an intended Edition of the Saxon Homilies." This enterprise she unfortunately was not encouraged to prosecute. She published a Saxon Grammar in 1715, and afterwards kept a school at Evesham. She received a pension from Queen Caroline, but it ceased on the death of her Royal patroness. She died in 1756, in humble circumstances.

dar, and a Calendar, regularly computed, for the whole year. In each month is drawn the corresponding sign of the Zodiac.

Next is the Psalter, in Latin, with an interlineary interpretation, in Anglo-Saxon. The Latin copy was evidently made by a person not acquainted with that language, from the errors which frequently occur, particularly in the division of words The Anglo-Saxon interpretation is by a different hand, and apparently at a different time. It is not, however, as has been supposed, a literal translation, but merely the Anglo-Saxon word, answering to the Latin word, without any regard to the sense, or to the structure of the Saxon language. The object of this interlineary interpretation seems to have been, to enable the priest, to comprehend the general purport of what he was reading or chaunting in Latin. To many words and phrases, however, no interpretation is given; and in some instances, the Anglo-Saxon does not quite correspond with the Latin. This part of the Manuscript is defective. The omissions are the first Psalm, part of the 2nd, the 52d, 53rd and 54th, the 101st and 102nd, the 110th, 130th, 131st, and 132nd.

After the Psalms follow the Canticles, the Lord's Prayer, the Apostles' Creed, and the Athanasian Canticle, or Creed. These are also accompanied by an Anglo-Saxon interpretation. With respect to the last, however, the version is in a different hand, probably later, and approaching nearer to a literal translation.

Next is the Litany, and afterwards a series of Collects, the last of a later period, and both without any interpretation. The volume terminates with some fragments, which may possibly have been part of the Burial Service, but of a still later date than the rest, and without any apparent connection with it.

There seems to be a sort of frontispiece very curiously drawn for the Penitential Psalms.

 Psalm 88.

 D'ne D's salutis meæ: in die clamavi et nocte coram te.
  God hælo minre on daeg ic clypede 7 nihtes beforan the

THE "GLORIA IN EXCELSIS." lv

Intret in conspectu tuo oratio mea: inclina aurem tuam ad
Ingaeth on ansyne thinre gebed min onhyld earan thine to
precem meam. Quia repleta est malis anima mea: et vita
bene minre Fortham gefullaed is yvel sawel min 7 lif
mea inferno appropinquavit.
min on helle neahlæhte.

Psalm 148.

Laudate D'n'm de celis: laudate eum in excelsis: Laudate
Heriath of heofenan hine on heahnesse Heriath
eum om's angeli eius: Laudate eum omnes virtutes eius.
hine ealle englas his Heriath hine ealle maena his
Laudate eum sol et luna: Laudate eum omnes stelle et
sune 7 mona storran 7
lumen:
leoht.

The omission of the words repeated, shows that a translation was not intended.

I cannot refrain from quoting one of these Canticles, the "Gloria in excelsis," here styled *Oratio pura cum laudatione*, as the source from which the beautiful forms of supplication and thanksgiving, in our Communion Service, are derived.*

GLORIA IN EXCELSIS D'NO.   Et in terra pax, hominibus
Wuldur on heahnesse Gode   7 on eorthan sibbe   mannū
bonæ voluntatis Laudamus te Benedicimus te Adoramus te Glo-
godes willan We heriat the We bletsiat the We gebiddat the We
rificamus te Gratias agimus tibi propter magnam gloriam
wuldiat the We thancas wedath the fore myclum wuldre
tuam: D'ne D's rex cœlestis D'n's pater omnipotens D'ne
thinū drihten God cininge heovenlic god fæder Ælmihti Drihte
fili unigenite Jh'u X'te D'ne D's Agnus D'i Filius
sunu ancenned haelend Crist drihten God lamb Godes sunu
Patris qui tollis peccata mundi miserere nobis, qui
Fæder thu the ascyndest synna midanærdes milsa us thu
tollis peccata mundi Suscipe deprecationem n'ram. Qui
the name synna midanærdes onfoh halsunga ure thu
sedes ad dextera' Patris miserere nobis. Q'm tu solus
the sitst on tha swythran thæs Fæder milsa us forthā thu ana

s'c's Tu solus d'n's Tu solus altissim' Jh'u Xp'e cum s'c'o
hali thu ana drihten thu ana schyhsta   mid haligo
Sp'u. In gloria Dei Patris. Amen.
Gaste   on wuldre Godes faeder thæt si.

See the remarks on this ancient Hymn in an early part of this volume, p. 18.

INDEX.

ABBESSES, election of, 214, consecration, 218; of Lacock, 273, 278, 280.
Abingdon, St. Edmund, Archbishop of Canterbury, 147, 201-3, 257.
Albemarle, the daughters of Stephen Earl of, 76, 79*.
Albourn, abbey estate at, 326.
Alms at Lacock, 288.
Amesbury nunnery and bower, 81, 106; estate of Lacock abbey at, 327.
Arms in the cloisters at Lacock, 350.
d'Artois, Robert Comte, 233, 238, et seq.
Ascalon, Sir Richard, or Wymound, 247, 251-4.
Audley, Ela Lady, 148
Augustinian rule, 191.
Basset, Philip, 160, 325.
a'Bathe, family of, 313.
Baynton, Sir Edward, 289.
Beatrice of Kent, the Abbess, 273.
Beauchamp, Ida and William, 163.
Bentlewood monastery, 145.
Bertrand, Adelicia and Robert, 79*.
Bewly court, 349.
Bingham, Bp. Robert, 185, 370.
Bishopstrow, 58 note, abbey of Lacock's manor at, 311.
Birds, on the notes of, 15.
Bloet, B. 299; Sir Ralph, Emma, 103; Sir Roger, 295, 299; Sir John, 287, 288, 300; Sir William, 295.
Blyth, tournaments at, 270.
Bohun, Humphrey cum Barba, 24; Humphrey the Great, 55, 56; Matilda, 55, 57; Engelger, 79*.
Bovelingham, James, 99, 265.
Bradenstoke abbey, 20, 27, 31—37, 146; King John at, 111,
Breant, Falkes de, 109, 114 note, 118 note, 119, 370.
Brenmule (misprinted Brennevill), battle of, 53, 367.
Breteville, Robert de, 56.
Bristol, Lacock abbey estate at, 327.
Britany, Arthur Duke of, 109; pedigree of Dukes, 265*.
Brus, Peter de, 76.
Burgh, Hubert de, 130; visit to Salisbury, 133; supposed to poison the Earl of Salisbury, 136.
———— Reimund de, 131, 135, 369.
Bytton, abbey estate at, 328.
Calne, abbey estate at, 328.
Camville, Idonea de, 145, 148, 159; barony of, 170.
Castle at Lacock, 2, 293.
Chapel, moveable, 145.
Chateau Galliard, 92.
Chaz, Ilbertus de, inscription to, 352.
Chester, Ranulph I. Earl of, 71, Ranulph II. 74.
Chicklade, abbey estate at, 329.

Chippenham, abbey estate at, 329.
Chittern, manor of, 321.
Cirencester abbey, convention with Lacock abbey, 304.
'Cleeve abbey, 78*.
Cliff Pypard, abbey estate at, 330; vicars of, *ib*.
Clifford, Rosamund, 101, 161.
Clinton, John, 163, William, 156.
Confessor at Lacock, 287.
Cooling, manor of, 98, 99, 157, 265*.
Corfe castle, 73.
Cormeiles, Sibella, 264; Alicia, 322.
Cornwall, Richard Earl of, campaign in Gascony, 127; crusade, 223, 247; his revenue from the crusaders, 228, 229.
Coronation of Richard I. 81; of King John, 107.
Crusades, oath at Northampton in 1239, 223; expedition of Richard Earl of Cornwall, *ib.*; return of a crusader, 225; crusade of St. Lewis, 229, *et seq.*; custom of assuming the cross, and its attendant privileges, 225.
Devereux, family of, 41, 85.
Devon, Amicia Countess of, 279, 288.
Earldoms, investiture of, 108; succession of, 167. *See* Salisbury and Lincoln.
Edward of Salisbury. *See* Salisbury.
ELA, Countess of Salisbury, the foundress and first abbess of Lacock, her birth, 80; secretion in Normandy, 83; discovery, 88; marriage, 103; assists at the foundation of Salisbury cathedral, 125; insulted by Reimund de Burgh, 132; her widowhood, 166; founds the abbey of Lacock, 171; assumes the habit of religion, 201; anniversary of her profession, 288, 371; vision of her son, 255; resigns the abbacy, 273; death, 275; her epitaph, 5; seal, 168; gravestone, 345, 351; charters, to Hinton priory, Appx. vi.; to Lacock abbey, viii. ix.
Essex, William Earl of, 138, 369; Christiana Countess of, 369.
Fair at Lacock, 268; deed relating to the tolls of, Appx. lii.
Farley priory, 57, 146; sepulchral antiquities found at, 355.
Fauconbridge, Shakspeare's character, 109.
Fitzmaurice, Maurice, 156.
Fitzwalter, Ela, 163; Ida, Katharine, Lorica, Robert, 162.
Frederick II. the Emperor, 240.
Fresnes, Hugh, 153.
Funeral service, 141; of William Earl of Salisbury, 138; of a nun, 276.
Gaddesden, Herts, 157, 187.
Gant. *See* Lincoln.
Garinges, Alicia, 191,
Geoffrey, Abp. of York, 30, 102.
Giffard, Sir Alexander, 247, 249, 251; biographical notice of, 263.
——— John Lord, 151; his children, 152.
Gloria in Excelsis, hymn of, 18, Appx. lv.
Godarville, Walter de, 187, 331.
Godderd, family of, 326, 333.
Gregorian Liturgy in the cathedral library at Salisbury, Appx. liii.

INDEX.

Guise, Sir Richard, 250, 251, 255.
Gurney, Hugh de, 138.
Hannam, abbey estate at, 328.
Haslebury quarry, 269.
Hatherop priory, 145, 172; manor of, 303.
Heart, interment of the, 279, 280.
Heddington, manor of, 315.
Henefeld, Sir Ralph, 247, 250, 251, 252.
Hinton priory, foundation of, 171; description of its remains, 174; foundation charter of, Appx. vi.
Hocton, Pagan de, 55, 367.
Hopkins, Nicholas, 178.
Hours observed by the nuns, 197; the canonical, 198.
Interdict, in 1211, 113.
Jewel, Bishop, 37.
John, Earl (afterwards King), anecdote of, 77; coronation, 107; migratory life, 106, 113; death, 121.
Jordan, family of, 292.
Kiss of peace, 226.
Keynsham, deed relating to the exemption of its inhabitants from tolls at Lacock fair, Appx. lii.
Laci, Alice, 152; *See* Lincoln.
Lackham, chapel of, 300.
Lacock, castle at, 2, 293; Domesday survey, 294; houses of Earl of Salisbury at, 122; market, 268, 274; fair, 269, Appx. lii.; foundation of the church, 295; estates of the abbey at, *ib.* rectors of, 299; vicars, 301. market cross, 373.
LACOCK ABBEY, situation, 2; foundation of, 171; early history and charters, 180—189; Ela appointed first abbess, 214; charters of privileges, 268, 274; succession of abbesses, 273, 278, 280; taxation in 1291, 279; surrender and seal, 282; pensions, 283; survey of, 1535, 284; officers, 289; estates, 293; hereditary founders, 320: rents, &c. in 1540, 334; present remains, 347; interior of the mansion, 358; visit of Queen Elizabeth, 359; the surrender in 1645, *ib.* nuns' boiler, 360.
────── Book of, history of, Pref. v. extracts from, 374, Appx. i.—v.
Laycocke, Hugh, 178.
Lancaster, Alice Countess of, 152.
Legh, Constancia de, 190.
Leybourn, armorial coat of, 156.
Lincoln, Earldom of, 47, 68, 75.
────── William de Romara, Earl of, 72.
────── Gilbert de Gant, Earl of, 79; Gilbert II. 80.
────── Henry Laci, Earl of, 150, 152; Margaret Countess of, 152, 288.
Longespe, pedigree of, 149; arms, 107; seals, 147, 148.
────── Alice, 148.
────── Ela, 148, 155, 160.
────── Emeline, 156.
────── Idonea, 170.
────── Isabella, 160.
────── Margaret, 152.
────── Matilda, 151.
────── Nicholas, 157; presumed gravestone at Lacock, 351.
────── Petronilla, 160.
────── Richard, 148, 154, 370.
────── Sir Stephen, 154.

INDEX.

Longespe, William, Duke of Normandy, 106.
——— William, Earl of Salisbury. See Salisbury.
——— William II. marriage, 169; knighted, 222, 371; first crusade, 223; subsequent career, 227; interview with the Pope, 228; his second crusade, 229; his quarrels with the Comte d'Artois, 233, 241, 244; death, 254; posthumous fame, 256; bones buried at Acon, 258; monumental effigy at Salisbury, 258; children, 148; will, 372.
——— William III., his history, 150; death, 250, 272.
——— William, Rector of Brocklesby, 159.
——— miscellaneous records of the name, 165.
Louis IX. 229, 233, 237, 372.
Lucia, Countess of Chester, 70, 73.
Lucy, Geoffrey de, 222, 227, 261.
Luvel, Katharine, 325.
Machinden, abbey estate at, 331.
Magna Charta, sealing of, 118; copy at Lacock, 357.
Malmaines, family, 98, 265.
Maloleone, Savaric de, 105, 129, 130.
Maniers, Tirel de, 96.
Mansoura, assault of, 238; poem thereon, 242; Arabic account of, 259.
de Mare, family of, 309, 373.
Market at Lacock, 269, 274.
Marlborough, royal court at, 135.
Maydenhyth, John, 288, 330.
Melksham forest, 269, 274.
Monasteries, their usual situations, 6, 200; reflections on, 200; confirmation charters, 189; reflections on their dissolution, 335; names conferred on, 371.
Morgan, family of, 324.
Mowbray, Mabella wife of Nigel, 96.
Newhouse, abbey of, 159.
Norfolk, Roger Earl of, 272.
Notton, abbey estates at, 303.
Nuns, rule of St. Augustine, 191; costume, 194; religious observances, 196; reception of novices, 204; profession, 210; election of abbesses, 214; consecration, 218; funeral 276; names of those of Lacock, 191, 279, 283.
Obits at Lacock, 287.
Odingsells, Ela and William, 163.
Officers of Lacock abbey, 289.
Old Sarum, 24, 61, 199; sonnet to, 63; plan of the cathedral, 363.
Patry, William, 98.
Pavely, Anastasia, Walter, 334.
Pembroke, William Earl of, 121, 122; the younger, 138, 147.
Perche, Hawise Countess of, ped. 39.
Pipard, Isabel, 331.
Poetry:—Lines to Lady Valletort, 12; sonnet to Old Sarum, 63; lines on children gathering flowers in the cathedral church-yard of New Sarum, 64; Lay of Talbot the Troubadour, 89*; Dirge of Earl William Longespe, 142.
Poore, Bp. Richard, 136, 370.
Presbiterium, 27.
"President" of a convent, 205.

Priests in Lacock abbey, 287.
Profession of nuns, 210.
"Religion," monastic signification of the word, 204, 273.
Raimes, or Rayne, feif and family of, 367, 368.
Reliques, 226.
Revesby abbey, 69.
Rewley abbey, 161.
Richard I. coronation of, 81; death, 100.
Romara, family of, 44, 51, 65—79; William de, 53, 54
Rosamond, Fair, see Clifford.
Rupibus, Bp. Peter de, 138.
Salseto, Peter de, 188.
Salisbury cathedral, foundation of, 124—126; visited by Henry III. 133; text presented by Hubert de Burgh, ib.; reception of Earl William Longespe on his return home, 135; his funeral, 138, monument, 4, 139; his bequest to the building, 145; lines to children gathering flowers in the church-yard, 64; monument of William Longespe II. 253; of Bishop Longespe, 158; of Bp. Bingham ascribed to Bp. Poore, 370. See Old Sarum.
———— Earldom, 108, 131, 149, 169, 227, 266, 272.
———— Edward de, 22, 37, 49—51, 53 bis; Walter de, 27, 28.
———— Patrick first Earl of, 28, 30; William Earl of, 80.
———— Ela Countess of, see ELA.
———— William Longespe, Earl of, birth, 101; attendance on King John, 106—113; introduction by Shakspeare, 109; his campaign in Flanders, 114; marshal of the King's army, 116; taken prisoner, 117; joins Prince Louis, 120; acknowledges Henry III. 121; not at the siege of Damietta, 122; campaign in Gascony, 127; last voyage and shipwreck, 129—130; returns home, 135; supposed to be poisoned by Hubert de Burgh, 136; death-bed, 137; funeral, 138; monument, 4, 14, 139; will, 144; seal, 147.
Seals: of Bradenstoke priory, 31; of William Earl of Salisbury and the house of Longespe, 147, 148; Ela Countess of Warwick, 162; Ela Countess of Salisbury, 168; of the abbey of Lacock, 282.
"Search" of a convent, 214.
Selby abbey, 49, 59.
Sherington, pedigree of, 297.
Shorewell, manor of, 318.
Shrewton, manor of, 316.
Shrievalty of Wiltshire, 22, 107, 168; rents of, 37.
Slade, abbey estate at, 331.
"Sovereign" of a convent, 205.
Stanley abbey, 9.
Stonehenge, 61, 366.
le Strange, Eubulo, 153.
Stuteville, Leonia, 55, 368.
Tailboys, Yvo, 51, 70.
Tails, ascribed to the English, 234, 242.
Talbot, William, 86, 105.
Tany, Graelent de, 56; Picot, 368.
Temmes, or Temys, Johanna, the last abbess, 281; her pension, 282; pedigree of her family, 291.
Text presented to Salisbury

cathedral by Hubert de Burgh, 133, 354.
Thame, Edmund, 289, 311.
Toani, Ralph de, 138.
Tournaments licensed by Richard I. 81; field near Salisbury, 82, 105, 270; at Blyth, 270; evil consequences of, 271; at Brackley, 271.
Troubadours, 87.
Trowbridge, abbey estate at, 332.
Tynemouth abbey, 59-60.
Uffcote, abbey estate at, 332.
Ulster, Earldom of, 155.
Upham, abbey estate at, 333.
Vere, Sir Robert de, 227, 247; biographical notice of, 260.
Vesci, Isabella de, 160; William de, 144, 160.
Veteripont, Robert de, 138.
Vitré, notices of the family, 264*.
Virgins, the Eleven Thousand, 18.
Walter le Eurous, 21, 39, 44; Cellarius, 59.
Wamborough, 154.
Wanda, William de, 124.
Warren, Earl, cousin to Ela of Salisbury, 104.
Warwick, Ela Countess of, 160.
Westbury, abbey estate at, 333.
Wiclescote, abbey estate at, 324.
Wideley, Sir Robert, 247, 250, 251, 252.
Will of William Earl of Salisbury, 144; of William Longespe II. 372.
William the Conqueror, his visit to Salisbury, 23—27.
Woodmancote, manor of, 308.
Wymarca the prioress, 378.
la Zouche, Alan, 156, 261.

LIST OF PLATES.

	Page
View of Lacock Abbey, drawn in 1834 . *Frontispeice*.	
Seal of the Priory of Bradenstoke . . .	31
Monument of William Longespé, Earl of Salisbury	139
SEALS, Plate I. of the House of Longespé . .	147
———, —— II. of the House of Longespé . .	148
———, —— III. of Ela Countess of Warwick .	162
———, —— IV. of Ela Countess of Salisbury .	169
———, —— V. of the Convent of Lacock . .	282
View of Lacock Abbey in 1801, by John Carter, F.S.A.	347
Ground Plan of Lacock Abbey	348
Capitals of columns	349
Sepulchral Inscription of Ilbertus de Chaz .	352
The Nuns' Boiler	360
Plan of the Cathedral Close of Old Sarum . .	363

The Binder will insert the five Pedigrees at the pages marked on each, and mentioned in the Contents. Pp. 23—24 and pp. 35—36 are cancelled; the quarter-sheet pp. 77*—80* is to follow p. 80; the quarter-sheet pp. 87*—90 is to follow p. 88; and the half-sheet pp. 263—266 is introduced instead of pp. 263—266, which are cancelled.

JOHN BOWYER NICHOLS AND SON,
25, PARLIAMENT STREET, WESTMINSTER.